To My Brother-in
Law John Zamon

Thanks for
Believing in this
Book —

Shane Collins

(Keith Scott)

Men of Steel

Shane Collins

authorHOUSE®

AuthorHouse™
1663 Liberty Drive, Suite 200
Bloomington, IN 47403
www.authorhouse.com
Phone: 1-800-839-8640

This book is a work of non-fiction. Unless otherwise noted, the author
and the publisher make no explicit guarantees as to the accuracy of
the information contained in this book and in some cases, names of
people and places have been altered to protect their privacy.

First published by AuthorHouse 10/18/2007

ISBN: 978-1-4343-3155-7 (sc)

Library of Congress Control Number: 2007906430

Printed in the United States of America
Bloomington, Indiana

This book is printed on acid-free paper.

Reno, Nevada 1978:

Sixteen-year-old Shane Collins walked through the island of the Texaco gas station. Already six feet tall, he'd added nine pounds of muscle to his lean frame since the spring, bringing his weight to 190. He'd accomplished this by eating like a pig, taking protein supplements and working out with weights five times a week. He was looking forward to playing football in the fall, which was why he was working out like he was training for the Mr. Olympia contest. He'd played his freshman year in San Francisco in 1976, but his family moved to Reno the following year and he didn't play his sophomore year. His father, Jack Collins, had bought the station with his nephew the previous October.

Highway 395 South ended just a block north of the station making Kietzke Lane, the road the station was on, "Business 395," while the highway was being constructed.

Business was booming in Reno in the late 1970's. The MGM Grand Hotel-Casino was being built, as was the Sahara Reno and the Money Tree. The Peppermill was expanding, as were the Eldorado and John Ascquaga's Nugget. The building boom had brought hordes of construction workers from California, Arizona, Oregon, Utah, Idaho and every other state in the union. These people needed houses, which furthered the building boom.

The workers made big money, and they spent it, buying new cars and pickups in record numbers, and partying hard in the casinos they built. Harrah's, owned by legendary gaming pioneer Bill Harrah, set the standard, and the standard was high. One could see Frank Sinatra in an intimate showroom and have a steak and lobster dinner while doing so. Elvis Presley

1

appeared regularly at Sahara Tahoe until his untimely death in 1977. Waylon Jennings, Willie Nelson, and Jessie Colter appeared at Harrah's. The Oak Ridge Boys, who had the number one country album in the land, appeared at the Nugget.

Besides the gambling and entertainment, Nevada, of course, had legalized prostitution in rural counties (i.e. outside Reno or Las Vegas). The famous Mustang Ranch Brothel was only eight miles outside of town. Joe Conforte, who owned the Ranch was something of a pop-culture folk hero. Some people viewed him as a criminal, and others viewed him as a charming rogue. In Nevada, his long running feud with Senator Bill Raggio was legendary. He'd been running whorehouses since 1955. He used trailers and used to move them back and forth across county lines to evade the authorities.

Finally, in 1967, the Nevada legislature made clear the guidelines on legalized prostitution. In 1971, although the original "Ranch," which was a few connected mobile homes, still stood and did business, he opened "Mustang II" which was a lavish place with a lush bar, Jacuzzis, swimming pool, bondage dungeon and an in-house beauty parlor for the girls.

A former cab driver, Conforte promised cab drivers a percentage of the girl's take if they brought people to the Ranch. The cabbies were motivated. One Mexican fellow who picked men up at the airport supplemented his income handsomely by immediately asking, "Girls, *Senor*?" The madam would alert the girl, and she'd just raise the price to cover the cabby's commission.

The house minimum for a quickie was $20.00, but your fantasies were limited only by your wallet and imagination. Besides Mustang there was the Moonlight Ranch, the Starlite Ranch, and the Kit Kat Ranch outside of Carson City, which was only thirty miles from Reno.

The Winter Olympics was at Squaw Valley in 1960, and they are still open as well as Mount Rose and Boreal Ridge ski resorts. Lake Tahoe is one of the most beautiful lakes in the nation. The Ponderosa Ranch, where the hit televison series "Bonanza" was filmed from 1959-1973, was open to the public like an amusement park. The motto on the sign that said, "Welcome to Nevada" was "recreation unlimited."

This was why hundreds of organizations had their yearly conventions in Nevada. Why should a group of executives go to a boring place like Topeka,

Kansas when one could go to Reno or Vegas, and drink, gamble and get laid, all on the company expense account? The Teamsters Union was holding their annual convention in town right now.

Shane's father had been an expert mechanic at the largest Ford dealership in northern California, in charge of used car reconditioning, prior to moving to Reno. Jack Collins had moved his family for two reasons. One, the schools in San Francisco were getting bad. Although they'd lived in a "good" neighborhood, the police were called to Shane's school almost weekly. Jack figured Shane could have toughed out a couple more years. He was a smart kid, who didn't do drugs and only got in trouble for fistfights.

However, he and his wife had two younger kids, and they didn't want them to have to go to rough schools. Secondly, Jack's older sister and older brother lived in Reno, and he and his wife had always liked visiting.

Nevada was adopting California's smog standards, and Jack had gotten one of the first smog licenses in Nevada. Thus they had every car dealer on "Auto Row" beating down their door to get cars ready for sale. Shane walked over to the smog machine where one of the mechanics, Ben, a guy of about twenty-one or twenty-two, was working on a 1970 Corvette. It said "LT-1" on the hood -- the option code for the fire-breathing 370 horsepower 350 V-8 engine.

"What do you think of this, baby?" Ben asked as he saw Shane look under the hood.

"It's a butchered piece of shit," Shane replied.

"Why do you say that?" Ben asked.

Shane rolled his eyes in disgust. "A *real* LT-1 has an aluminum intake manifold and a 780 Holley carb. This one has an iron manifold and a quadrajet carb. It doesn't have the camel-hump heads, and they didn't get HEI distributors until 1975. Some fool stole the LT-1 and put an Impala or pickup engine in this thing," Shane finished.

"Jesus Christ," Ben muttered. "You should write for car magazines."

"I have," Shane said. "I've been published in *Car Craft* and *Popular Hot Rodding*."

"Hey, that's you," Ben said.

Shane turned around as his cousin Dan, his father's partner, had just pulled up in a gorgeous 1973 Hurst/Olds 442. It was white with gold stripes with the Hurst Dual/Gate shifter, swivel captain's chairs, a digital tach, and power everything.

"See if it'll do a burnout, Shane," Dan said sarcastically as he got out of the car.

Shane was well known, and much scolded, for smoking the tires on any muscle car that came in. Shane slid behind the wheel and punched it. The 455 cubic inches responded, and the big Olds lit up the right rear tire, creating a smoke cloud that would rival the Chicago fire. Shane did two complete "brodies" in the lot before parking it.

"Definitely your best work yet," Ben said, smiling.

"Thank you. Thank you very much," Shane replied, in his best Elvis impersonation.

Shane's mother, Kate, a beautiful woman of thirty-five, came out of the office with fire in her eyes. "Very cute. How are you planning on paying for the transmission or the rearend if it blew out?"

"Sorry," Shane replied, trying unsuccessfully to look repentant.

"That still can't top the one Jack did yesterday in his Trans-Am," Ben said.

"Jack needs to grow up too," Kate growled. "And you need to go back to work."

"Yes, ma'am," Ben said and retreated under the hood of the Corvette, rather than face the "wrath of mom."

"And you!" she said, turning on Dan, "I heard you tell him to do a burnout. He was a nice kid before he came to work here. Stop encouraging him to be a delinquent."

"Kate, I was just...."

"Shut up!" Kate said, cutting off his feeble defense. "I knew you when you were a teenager. Save it."

At that moment a brand new Cadillac pulled into the full-service island.

It wasn't a limousine, but it was a Fleetwood Brougham D'Elegance with the chrome package and expensive wire wheels. A tough-looking guy in a suit wearing mirrored sunglasses was driving. It appeared that a man and a woman were in the back seat.

"What can I do for you?" Shane asked pleasantly as he went up to the driver's window.

"Fill it up with unleaded."

"Want me to check the oil?"

"No, it's okay. But wash the bugs off the windshield, will you?"

"Sure."

Shane washed the windshield and went to the back of the car. He put the pump nozzle in the tank and set it on automatic. It would shut off when the tank was full, and he could top it to the nearest penny. He stood absentmindedly by the right rear fender when the right-rear door opened. A gruff male voice said something, and there was laughter from inside the car. A woman in a cocktail dress got out. Shane could see her flawlessly pedicured bare feet sticking out the door. The toenails were a fiery red and her skin was exquisite olive.

"I have to put my shoes on," she giggled.

She put on a pair of five-inch heeled backless mules, and stood up. She could have been his mother's age, maybe a little younger, maybe a little older, it was hard to tell, but she still took Shane's breath away. In the heels, she was a little taller than he was, which meant barefoot, she was about 5'8" or 5'9". The black dress clung to her curves like she was poured into it and her firm breasts were practically bursting out of the low-cut gown. It was backless, and her back was firm and flawless like the rest of her. Shane was sure she was naked under it. Her face was all ovals, almond-shaped eyes with too much mascara and a mouth with pouty lips. Her skin looked Mediterranean, but her eyes looked slightly Oriental. She was an exotic beauty to say the least. From her frosted hair to her painted toes, she shouted "expensive, but worth it."

Shane turned his head, not wanting to leer like a fool, like his friends did whenever they saw an attractive woman. He was glad that he did when the tough-looking driver and a tall guy in his sixties wearing an expensive suit got out of the car. Shane felt the woman's left hand run up his back, and his muscles tensed a little involuntarily. She ran her right hand up his right forearm. Her hand was soft and warm. She ran her left hand through his hair, and let her long nails tickle his ear.

"What do we have here?" she purred in a whiskey voice that one heard from women in James Cagney gangster movies. "Tarzan, Superman, or King Kong?"

"He's a good lookin' boy isn't he?" the older guy said.

"I'll say," the woman replied, still rubbing his arm. "I'll bet you have to beat the girls off with a stick."

"Not really," Shane replied, blushing a little.

"You're not hanging out with the right type of girls then."

"I see that now," Shane said, and everyone burst out laughing.

The woman kissed him on the cheek. "You are so cute," she said.

"Go to the bathroom, Yvonne. We're already running late," the older guy said, still laughing.

"Where is the ladies' room?"

"Around the corner to the left. It should be unlocked."

She sauntered off, her heels clicking on the concrete of the island. Shane tried to watch her ass without being obvious.

"I'll bet that made your day," the driver said.

"My morning anyway," Shane replied, drawing a laugh from the driver and the older guy.

"Do you believe this kid?" the driver said.

"I like him," the older guy replied. "What's your name, son?"

"Shane."

"My favorite movie."

"My mom says that too. That's why she named me Shane, because she liked that movie."

"Your mom sounds like a smart lady. Tell me, Shane, are you a Sullivan?"

"My mom is."

"What's your mother's name?"

"Kate."

"Katy Sullivan!" The guy said incredulously, going into a coughing fit. "Her father's name was Red Sullivan," he said, still coughing.

6

"Red Sullivan was my grandfather," Shane said.

"I knew it!" the older guy said, banging an open palm on the Caddy's trunk hard enough to make his driver flinch. "I thought I was seein' a ghost when you washed the window. You look just like he did when he was young."

"He ran the unions in San Francisco," Shane said proudly.

"He ran more than that," the old guy replied. "If you did business on the docks or in construction in the Bay Area in the thirties and forties, you did it with Red Sullivan. My God, was he a fightin' son-of-a-bitch. Ruthless bastard when he had to be, but only in matters of business with some kind of reasonable compliant." It seemed that the guy was speaking as much for his driver's benefit as for Shane's. "Nobody fucked with Red. Not twice."

"Would you like to meet my mom?" Shane asked. "She's right over there," he said, pointing to the front of the station, where his mother was talking to Dan and his father.

"That's Katy?" the older guy said. "Christ, I should have known she'd grow up to be a goddess."

"She looks like Marilyn Monroe. I'd like to...," the driver said, but the old guy stopped him cold.

"Jimmy," he said in a conversational tone, and the guy stopped. "It's his mother, for Christ's sake. Show a little respect."

"Sorry, kid. I didn't mean any disrespect. I'm sure your mother's a fine lady."

"It's okay," Shane replied, a little confused and unnerved. *This big tough guy apologizing to me.*

Shane was a big kid, and had kicked his share of asses on the football field and in fights with other teenagers.

He remembered what his friend Tommy had told him after Tommy had got his ass kicked over a parking space one night. "Us football players think we're invincible and we scoff at guys our dad's or our uncle's ages. I can speak from experience. Some of those thirty-five or forty-year-old guys are pretty tough. It ain't easy to beat up a man."

Shane figured it out. The tough-looking driver, who was about six feet tall and 200 pounds, and carried himself with supreme confidence, wasn't worried about Shane. He was worried about the older guy. Respect. Respect for a past reputation. Respect for the fact that he'd be willing to go all the way. Respect for the fact that if he couldn't physically do it himself, he had the power to order it.

"Katy won't remember my face, I haven't seen her in probably twenty-five years. I used to let her play with my brass knuckles when I had meetings with her father. Little shit was cuter than Shirley Temple, wearing these frilly dresses, and playing with brass knuckles. God she was cute," the older guy said, coughing and lighting a cigarette.

"Your doctor said you should quit," the driver put in.

"When my mother dies you get the job," the older guy sneered.

The driver didn't say anything, but shook his head in disgust. Yvonne walked up, blew Shane a kiss and got back in the car.

"How much do I owe you?" The older guy asked.

"Fifteen dollars."

He pulled a huge wad of cash out of his pocket and peeled a twenty off. "Keep the change. Tell your mother 'Blackie' said hello. And that she raised a fine boy."

"You sure you don't want to talk to her?" Shane asked.

"Kid, the last time she saw me she thought I was Superman. Let's leave it at that. Don't tell her what that Kryptonite has done to me, okay?" Blackie said, crushing out his cigarette.

"I won't," Shane replied.

"Thanks, kid, you remind me of your granddad. See ya."

Shane ran into the office where his mother was going over paperwork. "That guy in the Cadillac gave me a five dollar tip."

"Good for you," Kate replied, not looking up from her work.

"He said he knew your father. He said you used to play with his brass knuckles when you were a little kid."

"Blackie," Kate said as she jumped out the chair. She ran outside, but the Cadillac was already driving away.

"How come Nana never talks about my grandfather?"

Shane asked. "This guy made out like he was Don Corleone or something. I could write a *Roots*-type book with a gangster twist."

Kate smiled. "I don't know about that, but I'll tell you about your grandfather after dinner tonight."

Shane was working on his car. It was a 1970 Camaro.

It was beat up, which was why his dad was able to buy it so cheap. Jack knew Shane would enjoy building it to his own exact specifications. Shane had helped his dad work on cars since age six. He could swap valve springs in a small-block Chevy cylinder head before he could ride a two-wheel bike. When he was about nine, Jack had told him to go set the firing order on a neighbor's car. The neighbor had changed the distributor and the car wouldn't start. Shane got the car running in about five minutes. The neighbor never again asked Jack for advice, having got the point.

Shane read car magazine tech articles religiously and "The Kid," as he was called by his father's cronies, carried a respected opinion regardless of his age. He got decent grades -- a "B" average student -- because he refused to study for subjects he didn't like. He'd got A's in history, math and English, which most kids struggled with. He breezed through them, but he got C's in typing, health and science from goofing off. Had he worked hard he might have been valedictorian, but he didn't care about that. As long as he carried a "B" average his parents didn't gripe and he could concentrate on girls, cars and football.

He wasn't going to drive the Camaro to school until it was perfect. It was a six-cylinder, three-speed model -- not a hot rod to say the least. Shane though had a plan to build the ultimate street Camaro. He already had a 327 V-8 on an engine stand in the garage that his dad was helping him rebuild to replace the six, and a Saginaw four-speed transmission lay right next to the engine stand. He scoured junkyards for wrecked Z/28 Camaros or Pontiac Firebird Trans-Ams to salvage sway bars and other suspension pieces.

As usual, when he was working on the car, he lost track of time. His mother leaned out the door to the garage. She was wearing a long nightgown.

"I'm going to bed. Put the dog out when you go to bed," she said.

"Hold it," Shane replied, rolling out from under the Camaro. "You said you'd tell me about my grandfather tonight."

"You've been working on your car," Kate said.

"And you've been putting the little kids to bed, and watching TV with dad," Shane replied. "I'm not kidding,

I want to write a book about our family."

"All right," Kate said. "Come in the kitchen."

Shane sat down at the kitchen table across from his mother after she'd made coffee. He had a yellow legal pad and a pen to take notes.

"Where should I start?" Kate asked.

"At the beginning," Shane replied.

Kate began to talk and Shane began to write.

Rough and Ready California, 1901:

R ough and Ready was a mining town that boomed during the Gold Rush of 1849. On April 7, 1850 Rough and Ready "seceded" from the union of the United States in response to a new mining tax. After a couple months as an "independent republic" on July 4, 1850, our nation's 74th birthday, the residents "rejoined" the United States and once again saluted Old Glory. A lot of the people's fathers had fought in the War of 1812, and some of their grandfathers had fought in the Revolutionary War. They did not take shit from anyone, even the government, which in their eyes could be overthrown if the people were pissed off. The renegades had raised their children with the same attitudes.

Eddie Coyle was born in 1881. His grandparents left Ireland during the potato famine of 1848. Like a lot of immigrants, they settled in New York. His grandfather pulled the clan west during the Gold Rush of '49.

His mother was born in 1864, the last of seven children. In 1880 she married a gambler named Rafe Coyle. Although only twenty-six, he wore fine clothes and threw money around the pubs like he was rich beyond belief. He won a local mine in a poker game. Rafe later killed the man in a gunfight after the guy sobered up and realized he'd lost his mine. Eddie was the oldest of five children.

In June 1893, Rafe decided to open a horseracing track like in San Francisco. He sunk every dime they had into the venture, and even borrowed from some local mine owners and bankers to finance it. He was sure the venture would set his family up for life. It might have, but Rafe was kicked in

the head by a racehorse he was looking at and died a week later. The bankers
and mine owners called in the loans, and Eddie's mother lost everything.

He stood in the graveyard, looking at his father's grave. His little brother
John, who was only nine, was holding onto him. His mother kissed him on
the cheek and said, "I'm sorry, son, but you're on your own...take care of your
brother." She loaded his three sisters onto a wagon.

"How come we can't go with you?" he asked.

"You boys can handle yourselves, I don't know what I'm gonna do with
the girls," his mother replied and drove off.

Eddie held onto John and wouldn't let him run after the wagon.

Eddie convinced a local storeowner to give them room and board in
exchange for working in the store. Eddie had just finished sixth grade and
figured that was all the schooling he needed, so he worked full-time. John was
in third grade. Eddie figured he should stay in school until at least the sixth
grade as he had. John helped out after school and on Saturdays.

One day Eddie got a letter from his eleven-year-old sister Megan. It
was addressed to his old house, but the mailman knew Eddie lived with the
Hanson's. He cried when he read the letter, the first since his father's funeral.
It read:

Dear Eddie,

Mom left us at a convent in Sonoma. She said she couldn't
go on without dad, and she didn't want to ruin our lives with her grief.
I don't know where she is. The sisters here are very nice. We spend a lot
of time in school and church. I'll probably leave here when I get a little
older because I don't want to be a nun. At least the little kids will be taken
care of until they're old enough to take care of themselves. I miss you and
Johnny.

Love, Megan.

Eddie felt a hatred for his mother that chilled his blood. *She can't handle
Dad dying? How is a twelve-year-old boy and an eleven-year-old girl supposed to
handle it?*

Yet they were -- he caring for his brother and Megan looking out for his little sisters. He sometimes fantasized about his mother coming back to reunite the family, maybe married to some rich man. Then he realized she was never coming back. She walked away from five children because she couldn't handle her husband's death. He resolved that if she ever did come back, he'd tell her how much he despised her for abandoning him and his siblings. He also resolved to do better by his kids, if he ever had any.

Even at the young age of twelve, Eddie was a skilled negotiator. One Sunday James Hanson told them to pull some weeds in front of the house. John started outside, but Eddie stopped him.

"How much are you gonna pay us?" Eddie asked.

"Pay you?" James Hanson replied, incredulous. "Why would I pay you? You sleep here, you eat here, and my wife washes your clothes."

"We work our butts off in the store for that," Eddie replied. "The deal was we work for room and board. You want us to work outside the store, you pay extra. Did you ask Mitch to pull weeds on Sundays?"

"What?" Hanson said.

"Mitch Brown, who went to work in a mine. Before he quit, you were paying a grown man's salary and feeding us. Now you're just feeding us. We're doing all the work. The money you were paying that man every week is staying in your pocket. You're making more money because of us."

"I'll pay you a dollar," Hanson said.

"Each," Eddie replied.

Hanson and his wife laughed. "You're a tough negotiator, Eddie. A dollar each, if you mow the lawn too."

"Deal," Eddie said.

"Why'd you do that, Eddie?" John asked. "Mr. and Mrs. Hanson are nice to us."

"Mrs. Hanson is very nice," Eddie said. "I like her making cookies and stuff for us too. They don't have any children. All old ladies think little boys are the greatest. But I work twelve hours a day in that store, I'm not gonna be a slave on my days off too."

"I never thought of that," John said.

"Of course not, you're a kid," Eddie said, like he was a grown-up, which in essence, he already was.

He was nineteen and strong as an ox. At 5'10" and 175 pounds, he was lean and hard. He played on the mine baseball teams, even though he didn't work at the mine. Since he hit a lot of home runs, the league overlooked the minor detail. Jim Hanson had told Eddie that he and John could take over the business on his retirement. It wasn't heaven, but it was a living.

Then something happened that changed the course of his life. John was carrying some grain into the store when he bumped into a big miner.

"Watch where your goin', dummy," the miner sneered.

"Sorry," John said, and continued about his work.

"Don't you walk away from me, boy."

John put the sack of grain down. "What is your problem, mister?" he asked, "I said I was sorry."

The miner slapped John across the face hard enough to bloody his nose and knock him down. "I don't think that was a sincere apology. You better try again."

"Don't you dare apologize to this asshole," Eddie said in an icy tone, stepping in front of John. "Tough son-of-a-bitch are you? Slapping a sixteen-year-old kid.

Why don't you try that with me?"

Everyone in and around the store stopped and watched.

A dapper looking guy in an expensive suit, smoking a big cigar, was especially interested.

Not used to being challenged, the miner was a little unnerved. "Why do you care about that little bastard?" he asked.

"That little bastard is my brother. Now are you gonna step outside and fight like the big man you're pretending to be, or am I gonna drag you out and beat the dog shit out of you anyway?" Eddie growled.

The miner went out in the street. "Prepare for an ass-whippin', boy," the miner said, trying to intimidate Eddie with talk.

"Last time I had my ass whipped was by a midwife nineteen years ago, and I'm lookin' for her," Eddie quipped, drawing a laugh from the watching crowd.

The miner lunged forward, throwing a haymaker right at Eddie's head. Eddie stopped it and slammed a left into the miner's ribs, and then another left into his jaw. The miner staggered backward and Eddie came forward landing a right to the face, another left, another right, and a chopping left that drove the man face down in the dirt. He tried to get up, but Eddie hit him with a sledgehammer right uppercut that sent him sprawling flat on his back. He didn't get up.

"Who else wants some?" Eddie said, challenging the miner's friends.

"Hey, your beef was with him," they said, raising their hands in a conciliatory gesture.

"Can I talk to you for a few minutes?" the guy smoking the big cigar asked.

"I have to go back to work," Eddie said.

"Don't you agree, sir, that he needs cooling off?" the man said.

James Hanson and John were standing on the porch of the store. "Definitely," Hanson said, smiling.

"Way to go, big brother," John said, grinning from ear to ear.

"C'mon, I'll buy you a beer and we can talk. I'm Jack O'Hearn, but my friends call me 'Doc'."

"Eddie Coyle."

They shook hands and went into the saloon across the street.

"You beat the shit out of him," Doc said.

"He deserved it," Eddie replied.

"Of course he did. Have you ever considered being a prizefighter?" Doc asked. "You've got talent."

"Because I trashed some miner who pissed me off?" Eddie said skeptically.

"He was a big experienced fighter. I could tell from his attitude that he was used to winning fights. You destroyed him in seconds," Doc said. "I've seen pros like John L. Sullivan or Jim Corbett hit a guy once or twice and then hesitate. You chopped him down like a tree until he was done. You've got speed and instinct that few people have. You can make three or four hundred dollars on a fight in San Francisco or Virginia City. That's more than you'd make in six months working in a mine or that damned store."

15

"How would it work?" Eddie asked.

"I put up money to bet on you and negotiate odds. You fight. We split the winnings."

"I'm the one taking the beatings."

"You didn't today."

"I reckon I'll have to sometimes if I fight often enough."

"Look," Doc said, "I'll train you, keep you in shape, and I won't let you get hurt. If we lose a few, we lose a few. It's better to stay healthy to fight again another day. Plus I'll invest our money. What are you, twenty years old?" Eddie nodded. "How'd you like to be retired by thirty?"

"You got a deal," Eddie said and they shook hands.

Virginia City, Nevada 1901:

Doc and Eddie rode the Virginia-Truckee rail line into Virginia City. Although not quite as crazy with activity as it once was during the days of the Comstock Lode, when people like John Mackay made their fortunes and writer Mark Twain lived there, Virginia City was still pretty much a boomtown. It would remain so until the 1920's when the silver dried up.

Eddie walked into the Delta Saloon, pounded his fist on the bar and yelled, "I can beat any man in the house."

"I got twenty-five dollars says you can't," a guy at the end of the bar yelled.

"I got fifty says he can," Doc shot back.

"Have you got a hundred?" another patron yelled.

"I do," Doc said calmly.

"Have you got three hundred?" the bartender asked.

Doc and Eddie smiled at each other. "I do," Doc said.

The bar owner demanded they fight in his makeshift ring at the back of the bar. There was a curtain on one side. The local champion was a fat guy about thirty. Doc had warned Eddie about the scam that was used at carnivals all the time. People would bet obscene amounts of money on the fat guy against all comers. A local hard-ass would get in the ring expecting to make some money. The fat guy would use his weight to bull his opponent to the curtain, where a hidden accomplice whacked the guy on the head with a hammer. The fat guy would then throw a couple of punches and score a quick "knockout."

When the fight started, Eddie avoided the fat guy's bull-like rushes and gave him a left in the face every time he charged. Pretty soon, the fat guy was bleeding from the nose and mouth and breathing hard. After the first round, the fat guy's backers increased their bet to $500.00.

"Don't let him push you to the curtain," Doc said. "Keep boxing and cut his face to ribbons. Finish him if you can, otherwise keep beatin' him until he cries uncle."

By the end of the second round, the fat guy's face looked like hamburger and he couldn't hold his hands up.

He mustered one final rush and pushed Eddie toward the curtain. However, Eddie used the guy's momentum against him and, at the last possible second, spun the fat guy into the curtain. His accomplice cracked his skull with the hammer and the guy went face down in the dirt.

Eddie pulled the curtain back, exposing the guy with the hammer.

"You think that makes a damn bit of difference?" the bar owner sneered.

"You owe us five hundred dollars," Doc said, pulling his pearl-handled Colt .45 revolver.

"You can't get us all, tough guy," a big miner said, coming forward and pulling a knife as he did. Doc blew his brains out.

"Anyone else want to come up front with this brave man?" Doc asked. "Anyone else want to die for someone else's money?" The crowd dispersed quickly. "Our money," Doc said.

The bar owner pulled a wad of cash out of his pocket.

"That'll do fine," Doc said.

The bar owner tried to take the gun from Doc and got pistol-whipped into unconsciousness for his trouble. The guy with the hammer tried to get to Doc too, but Eddie cold-cocked him with a left-right combination.

They got on the train to Carson City. Doc had taken $1,700.00 from the bar owner. Eddie was remarkably unhappy for a man who'd just made $850.00 for five minutes' work.

"Save me your god damned innocent act," Doc said. "They hit you in the head with that hammer, and they don't care if you're dead or stupid the rest of your life. The guy with the hammer, what did he get, twenty bucks? They were willing to kill you or cripple you for a scam. They were willing to kill both of us when we beat their scam. Fuck 'em. If you're gonna be a prizefighter, Eddie, you gotta be a mean son-of-a-bitch. Otherwise these bastards'll use you up and take your money and leave you on the scrap heap with a bunch of other broken-down pugs. If we're gonna be partners I need to know right now: are you a choirboy or are you a mean son-of-a-bitch?" Doc finished.

"I'm a mean son-of-a-bitch," Eddie said and looked out the window.

Doc took them to a whorehouse outside Carson City.

They had a steak dinner and a bath, and then went to their own rooms with the girls they'd picked. The redhead Eddie picked did a trick with her mouth that she called "French."

He sent her to the bar for a bottle of whiskey and gave her some more money when she came back.

"Want me to do it again?" she asked seductively.

"Absolutely," Eddie replied.

As he enjoyed the sensations, he thought to himself, *I'm never going back to Rough and Ready. I'm gonna be bigger than John L. Sullivan. I'm gonna have lots of money and women falling all over me. I'm gonna retire young and have a bunch of kids.*

Doc had told him, "You've got gold in your fists." Eddie thought he did too and he was going to mine them for all they were worth.

San Luis Obispo, California 1930:

Twenty-seven-year-old Martin "Red" Sullivan walked along the docks of the San Luis Obispo Bay. He'd grown up in San Francisco, so the cold night air did not bother him. As he walked he was trying to decide whether or not to do the job, thinking about his life and how he ended up in this position. He carried two hundred pounds on his 5'11" frame.

He carried it so well that most people thought he weighed about 160. He had thick red hair and steel blue eyes. His face was handsome and he wore fine suits most of the time.

People who didn't know him thought he was some kind of soft dandy, but they were wrong. Some of the fools who'd tried to fight with him learned the hard way that he was much tougher and stronger than he looked. He had the gift of fury. In one second he could go from talking in a normal tone of voice to beating the shit out of somebody. As a kid growing up on the streets of San Francisco he'd learned exactly when to unleash that fury. To beat him in a fight, one had to kill him. To do that, one had to be willing to die also. Most street thugs weren't, which was why Red usually won. He didn't start fights, but if someone started one, he damn sure would finish it. It seemed like he'd had to finish too damn many lately. He couldn't remember when he'd not had to fight for everything.

He was born in 1902, the second of three children. His father always seemed pissed off -- pissed that there were five of them living in a tiny flat, pissed that he worked such long hours for such lousy money.

As Red got older, he was mostly pissed that he worked in an Italian restaurant down the street from their house, running errands and doing odd jobs for the men who ate there. He drank a lot and once in a while Red, or his older brother, took a beating. His little sister didn't get many because she was too little to aggravate anyone, and either Red or Kevin would step in front of her and take the brunt of their father's rage. He learned at a young age that everyone took a beating once in a while. At twelve, he started carrying paper and collecting money on a game called "Numbers" for the guys at the restaurant.

One day four older boys beat him and took the moneybag. A local priest broke up the fight. When they went to the restaurant, Red was scared. He was sure he was dead, but he wasn't punished at all.

The large Italian guy who owned the restaurant took two other big guys, found the boys who'd robbed him, and beat them within an inch of their lives. One of the guys took Red to a gym where boxers trained.

He told the guy who ran the gym, "Teach this kid how to fight. And not just Marquis of Queensbury rules."

For six months, every day after school Red went to the gym. The big Italian who ran the gym taught him how to throw punches with maximum impact, how to bob and weave, how to head-butt, and how to use his elbows. He also taught him how to hit people low, thumb them in the eye, jack their Adam's apple, and sweep their legs out from under them.

He schooled Red on using weapons at hand, like ashtrays, beer mugs, pieces of pipe, pool cues, etc. He was then assigned to collect numbers again. Occasionally others tried to rob him, but they were never again successful.

When he was fifteen, his older brother was sent to the war in Europe. An epidemic influenza virus hit San Francisco that killed thousands. His mother and little sister both caught it and died. Grief stricken over the loss of his wife and young daughter (she was only nine), his father became more sullen and angry. He didn't want them buried by the county, which was what happened to destitute people. At the funeral service Red told all the relatives to come back to the house afterward.

"What the hell's wrong with you, boy?" his father growled on the steps of the church. "In Ireland you're supposed to feed the relatives after a service. What are we gonna give 'em? A potato?"

"I've taken care of it, Dad," Red replied.

"With your dirty money that you get from your Dago gangster friends?" his dad sneered.

"The money doesn't know where it came from, Dad. I'm a delivery boy. I don't rob anyone and I don't kill anyone. I swore Mom to secrecy, but the only reason we've lived as well as we have is because of extra money I've been bringing in. She didn't want to hurt your pride. Well, I have pride too, Dad."

"You should have spent your money on a decent burial."

"I did. Mom and Jeannie are going to Holy Cross Cemetery, which is more than they'd get if they had to depend on you."

His father raised his right fist to hit him. Red put his fists up in a textbook boxing stance.

"You hit me and I'll whip your drunken ass. I put up with you for Mom. You've hit me and belittled me for the last time."

When they got back to the house, his father was surprised to see the kitchen table covered with food. There were large amounts of lasagna, spaghetti, Italian bread, prosciutto, salami and Parmesan cheese. There were several carafes of red and white wine.

"Not a pot of stew or leg of lamb anywhere," his father sneered. Guests began to arrive. "Nobody'll be eatin' your Dago food bought with your dirty money."

"Uncle Joe has a mouthful of it right now," Red said, pointing to the kitchen. "And it appears everyone else shares Joe's opinion. I've never known shanty Irish to turn down a free meal. You don't want to eat, don't. I'm done with you."

"I guess I've only got one son, if he survives the war," his father said.

"I haven't had a father for a long time, so that makes us even. You go to hell." Red resolved to leave home and make it on his own. And if he ever had kids, he'd do a lot better job than his old man did.

The guy who owned the restaurant got Red a job with a construction company. A lot of men were gone to fight the war, and companies needed strong men to work. He lied about his age and said he was seventeen. He was only fifteen, but now made more money than most grown men.

He learned just about every building trade. He was a pipe fitter, a carpenter, steelworker and a welder. He was such a good welder that he was requested on several big jobs for the city. Clawson Construction, Red's employer, usually got the big city contracts. Rumor had it that Clawson Construction got the contracts through payoffs and intimidation, because Anthony Maretti was a silent partner with connections to the New York mob, but no local prosecutor could ever prove it.

In 1929 he was asked to go to Rough and Ready to remodel an old gold mine. Apparently a new vein had opened up and the mine was once again profitable. Furthermore, someone had discovered oil near the mineand talk of building a pipeline was circulating. He should have seen the red flag when Tony Maretti asked him personally. Red had known Tony since he was a kid running numbers. It was Tony who took him under his wing and taught him how to do business. He refused at first.

"I don't want to go live in some shitty ghost town for a year," he'd said.

"I'll pay you extra," Tony said.

"There can't be enough 'extra' for me to go live in a dirt-street hellhole and do nothing but work," Red said.

Tony laughed. "I'll tell you a joke," he said. "A rich guy sees a beautiful girl on the street. He walks up to her and asks if she'll go to bed with him for a hundred dollars. She slaps his face, and says, 'Absolutely not.' He asks her if she'll do it for a thousand dollars. She slaps him again and says, 'What kind of girl do you think I am?' He offers her ten thousand dollars, and she says, 'Yes.' The rich guy says, 'I knew what kind of girl you were, it was just a matter of price.'"

Red laughed.

"I'll pay you a hundred dollars a week plus expenses, and I'll give you a company truck to drive." Since most men in San Francisco only made about $25.00 a week, and didn't have cars, he agreed. "I knew what you were, it was just a matter of price," Tony said, laughing.

"Nobody likes him very much," Red said. All the men at the meeting laughed. "I run the show. No bullshit from anyone," he added.

"You'll really only report to me," Tony said. "But you'll have to let the guys running the mine think they're in charge. I know you can handle it."

"Nobody likes you very much," Red said again.

Tony laughed. "Nobody but you," he said.

"I must be crazy," Red replied.

"I've known that since you were twelve. Crazy is sometimes confused with genius," Tony said.

"I'm really not liking you," Red said.

"But my money's still green. Pick up the truck and traveling money tomorrow. What else are you gonna do? You're family, even if you're not Sicilian," Tony finished.

Red drove into Rough and Ready. He saw dozens, maybe hundreds of people, even entire families living in tents on the outskirts of town. The company truck was a new Ford. It was like he stepped into a time warp that had transported him back to the Old West: one main, unpaved street through the center of town; a couple of stores, a couple hotels, and saloons and bawdy houses lining the street. The girls leaned out the windows and off the balconies waving to him. A man in a new truck obviously had money. He parked on a side street and went into the nicest-looking saloon, which was still a dive by San Francisco standards. He was thirsty and eager to see the lay of the land.

"What'll you have?" the bartender asked.

"Whiskey, the best in the house," Red replied.

The bartender produced a bottle of Canadian whiskey and poured Red a glass. Apparently, Prohibition wasn't rigidly enforced in Rough and Ready. Red laid a five-dollar bill on the bar and asked, "What's the skinny on this town?

"I don't gossip," the bartender replied.

Red laid another five out.

"Especially with strangers."

Red put a ten on top of the two fives.

"I think I've seen you before. Maybe you're not a stranger," the barkeep said. He saw that Red wasn't going to put out any more money so he stepped forward. "The Steeleys own the mine and one of the general stores. This was a ghost town until George Steeley found that vein. He was drunk and throwin' dynamite down a shaft. They go to clean up the mess and find gold everywhere. His brother, John -- he's the smart one -- hooked up with some big San Francisco construction firm to develop the mine for a percentage.

I don't know how much. They took out ads in papers from San Jose to Oregon. People showed up in droves to work. That's why you saw that tent city on the way in. They run that mine twenty-four hours a day. Some union guy from back east tried to organize the workers. Said he really improved things in the coal mines of West Virginia. Some company goons beat him half to death, but that only caused a bunch of union guys to retaliate."

Red noticed during the lecture that the twenty bucks had disappeared.

"It's a mean scene around here, buddy. Not for sissies or the faint of heart."

"Do I look faint-hearted?" Red asked.

"Maybe at first glance," the bartender said. "Now that I look at you, though, you don't. You look like a wolf in sheep's clothing."

"You're very observant," Red replied. "One more piece of information. I don't want to live in a god damned tent."

"Mrs. Thompson has a big boarding house up the road a fair piece. She used to rent rooms out, but she's been full for so long that people don't even ask anymore. I know an old lady that lived there died recently."

"Thanks for the tip," Red replied, downing the last of his whiskey. "I'll give it a try."

Red drove up the street until he saw a big yellow two-story house. He parked the truck and walked up to the house. As he got closer, he stopped in his tracks. His heart started to beat faster and his breathing increased.

He started to sweat more than he already was, as it was a hot summer day.

A woman was hanging laundry on a clothesline in the yard. She was tall, almost statuesque. Her black hair cascaded halfway down her back. She was barefoot and wearing a short white dress that was unbuttoned a little too much down the front and only went to just above the knee. It looked like her breasts were going to rip out of the dress at any moment, especially when she bent over to pick up laundry out of the basket. When she stood up on tiptoe to hang the laundry on the line, her bare heels lifting off the grass, her calf muscles and taut hamstrings beautifully displayed as the dress rode up her legs a bit, and the afternoon sun showed her smooth rounded behind like an x-ray.

"Oh, Christ," Red muttered to himself. His Sicilian friends called it "The Thunderbolt." Love at first sight, but more intense.

She knelt on the grass and began to scrub something on a washboard. The soles of her feet glistened from standing in the wet grass and the dress rode farther up, showing strong thighs. Red was totally smitten. He knew it was "The "Thunderbolt." He was awash with an overwhelming desire for possession. Nothing was going to stop him from owning this woman and from locking her in a house only for himself.

He knew she'd haunt his memory every day of his life if he didn't have her. He now understood the classic jealousy of the Irish male. He would kill anyone who touched this woman, or tried to take her away from him.

He went into the yard as the woman stood. "Hello," she said pleasantly.

"Hello," Red replied. "I was looking for Mrs. Thompson."

"You found her," she replied.

Red tried to keep his jaw from dropping. "I was expecting...."

"An old lady?" she said, cutting him off. "Sorry to disappoint you."

"On the contrary, I'm delighted. You're...."

"I'm what?" she said, interrupting him again. "You want to say something, spit it out."

Red laughed and decided to give her some of her own attitude, but politely. "You're the most beautiful woman I've ever seen. I thought Zeus must have sent a goddess down from Olympus."

All the bravado and the smart-ass answer she was preparing to give him seemed to evaporate out the top of her head. She smiled warmly and said, "That's the best compliment I've ever had. Could I offer you some lemonade?"

"Yes, thank you."

Red followed her in the house. She poured two glasses of lemonade and handed him one. She sat down at the kitchen table and casually propped her feet up on the table, crossing her ankles. Red sat down across from her. Red couldn't help looking at her feet.

"What's your name?" she asked.

"Martin Sullivan, but my friends call me 'Red.'"

"And why were you looking for me, Red Sullivan?"

"I was looking for a room," he said.

"What makes you think I have a room to rent?"

Red tried to act somber. "I don't want to seem to callous, but I heard about the recent passing of a resident of this boarding house and given the obvious housing shortage in the area, I thought I'd take advantage of the opportunity."

The woman laughed. "Red Sullivan, you are completely full of shit."

"How did you determine that?" Red replied.

"Mrs. Clanton died two months ago. What's a good-looking, educated guy like you doing in town like this?"

Red laughed, "Why do you think I'm educated?"

"The reference to Zeus and Olympus. Most laborers don't know Greek mythology."

Red enjoyed verbally sparring with her, it made her seem mysterious and exotic, like Mata Hari. He wasn't used to women being so bold, but he liked it -- it excited him.

"Why are you here?" she asked again.

"Came up from San Francisco to work on the mine," he said.

She continued her aggressive, sparring conversational style. "You a company goon?" she asked.

"No."

"You a union goon?"

"No."

"Then what are you?"

"I'm not anybody's goon, I'm just a guy trying to make some money."

"Why are you staring at my feet?"

The little bomb took Red by surprise, but he recovered and parried quickly. "Because they're on the table, and they're pretty."

She threw her head back and laughed while flexing her feet. "These? I'm usually barefoot all summer and they're always dirty."

"I still like 'em," Red said. "I was staring at your legs too."

She laughed again and patted her own right thigh. "All those years of dancing paid off."

"You were a dancer?"

"Sort of."

"How'd you end up here?"

"Just lucky, I guess."

"You are something else," Red said, chuckling.

"Would you like to see the room?" she asked.

"Yes."

The house had electricity, running water and a telephone. The room she showed him had a nice brass bed, a table and two chairs, a dresser and a fireplace. It was almost as nice as his apartment in the city.

"I used to charge two dollars a day, but because of the conditions in town I'll have to charge you five dollars a day," the woman said.

"That'll be fine," Red replied. With his salary it was reasonable, especially considering the alternatives.

"You can afford that much?" she asked.

"I would have paid ten," Red said.

"I would have settled for three," she retorted.

"Then I guess we're both content," Red said, and she gave him wry smile. Red pulled a hundred-dollar bill out of his pocket and gave it to her. "Let me know when that runs out. I'll trust you not to cheat me."

"Mr. Sullivan, I knew you were a fine man the minute I laid eyes on you."

"Now who's full of shit?" Red said, grinning.

"Just 'cause you've seen me barefoot with my hair down, doesn't mean you can get fresh with me. I haven't got fresh with you. Not yet," she said, winking as she turned to leave.

"Where is Mr. Thompson?" he asked.

"Dead two years," she replied.

"How did he die?" Red asked.

"Does it matter?"

"No."

"What's your name?" he asked.

"Mrs. Thompson in front of the other boarders."

"And when you're barefoot with your hair down?"

She smiled broadly. "Katherine, but you can call me Katy."

"Like Katie Elder?" Red said jokingly.

"Katie Elder was a whore and she ran with outlaws," she replied. "Let me make one thing perfectly clear. I do not run with outlaws."

Red burst out laughing. "I'm not an outlaw," he said.

"Good thing," she replied, looking over her shoulder as she left the room.

Even though he was alone, Red made a motion like he was having heart palpitations. *This might not be so bad after all.*

A hundred dollars a week, plus the good chance of sleeping in a wild woman's bed made him toss aside the apprehensions he'd had about the job. He decided to go see the mine people the following day. He'd had a long drive. He took his shoes and his shirt off, opened the window, and decided to lie down for a nap.

A couple hours later, he stirred. He thought he was dreaming, feeling the soft hand on his arm, the long-nailed fingers tickling him slightly. He opened his eyes and shook his head. Kate stood there. She wore a long dress and her hair was pinned up, exposing her beautiful neck. He couldn't decide which hairstyle made her look sexier.

"Mr. Sullivan?" It's dinnertime, if you're hungry."

"Oh, thank you," Red said, sitting up.

He could see Kate's eyes devouring him. He had hard muscles forged from daily hard work, plus he still went to the gym to box once or twice a week. He always joked, "A man with my personality has to stay sharp."

"Let me get dressed and I'll be right there," he said.

"You don't have to do anything on my account," she said, grinning. "But I guess my other boarders might object."

Red laughed. "You're crazy, woman," he said.

"Takes one to know one," she said as she left.

The other boarders were all women in their forties and fifties, and as much as Red could tell, either widows or spinsters. Everyone seemed quite excited to have a man in the house. He used all his manners and charm at dinner to show that he was a gentleman. The ladies all pleasantly wished him goodnight when he excused himself, saying he had to work early tomorrow.

The next morning he went to the mine. He walked up to an office with a porch. Two guys wearing rumpled pinstriped suits and fedora hats stood on the porch. Trying to look like wiseguys, they just looked silly. It showed the disdain Maretti had for the town and the union dispute. He thought second-raters like this would be adequate. Red dressed nice in the city, but it was at least ninety degrees already and he was going to work, not a dinner party. He wore jeans, a cotton shirt and an old hat.

"What do you want?" the one on the left inquired.

"See Mr. Steeley," Red said flatly.

"What's your business?" the one on the right asked.

"My business is with Mr. Steely."

"You lookin' to start trouble?" the one on the left sneered.

"If I wanted to start trouble, it would take a lot more than you two to stop me," Red said calmly.

Both men stepped off the porch and the one on the right tried to hit Red in the face. Red grabbed his arm and flung him into his buddy, knocking them both down. As the one tried to get up, Red slammed his right fist into his face and he fell backwards, his nose bleeding. The other one stood and reached inside his jacket as Red grabbed him by it.

"Skin it," Red growled. "Skin that rod and see what happens." The goon hesitated. "Throw down, boy," Red said. The guy hesitated, looking at his buddy with the bloody nose. "That's what I thought," Red said and threw the guy into his buddy, knocking them both down again.

"What the hell's goin' on here?" A gravel voice yelled. John Steeley had come out of the office.

"I asked to see you and these two attacked me," Red said calmly.

"Who the hell are you?" Steeley asked.

"Red Sullivan."

Steeley laughed. "Come on in, we'll have some coffee before we go to the job site. Maretti said you could handle yourself."

"Who is this son-of-a-bitch?" one of the two goons asked Steeley.

"The steel guy from 'Frisco."

"Why didn't you just say so?" the one with the bloody nose asked angrily.

"Because Mr. Maretti, who hired me said I had to report to him and Mr. Steeley here. He didn't mention two assholes in unpressed suits. Got the picture?" Red said contemptuously.

"Simmer down, boys," Steeley said and turned to go inside.

"Gentlemen," Red said, tipping his hat. When the goons looked at him, he mouthed the words "fuck you."

They bristled, but Red went inside and closed the door.

Steeley was a wanna-be gangster all the way. He kept talking about how tight he was with Maretti, but Red knew he had been sent there because Maretti thought it needed to be run better. Steeley was in over his head.

"What's Maretti's cut?" Red asked.

"Seventy percent," Steeley replied. "I sold him the mine and I still get to keep thirty percent. He puts up all the money, handles all the heat and I collect my percentage." He was proud of himself, like Red should be impressed at how he'd screwed Maretti.

Red kept his face impassive, but silently thought,

What an idiot.

He now had no recourse. If Maretti was grossly mismanaging the mine and its profits, and if this fool was smart enough to go to court, the court would rule that the man who owned seventy percent of the stock could do what he wanted with the company. The thirty-percent shareholder could sell his shares or go along. If Red owned a mine and wanted to sell to a developer to rejuvenate it and make it more profitable, he'd keep at least fifty-one percent, so he'd have control.

"I hear about problems with union organizers," Red said.

"What problems?" Steeley said, trying to act casual, but obviously surprised.

"Violence. Violence is bad for business," Red said.

"Nobody is gonna tell me how to run my business, or how much to pay my employees," Steeley growled.

Red silently groaned. *His business. That someone else owns seventy percent of. Steeley doesn't have a clue.*

Red knew that unions were the way of the future. People weren't going to stand for being treated like slaves in feudalistic Europe. Big business would have to come to the table and negotiate. He had helped Maretti make some businesses in San Francisco negotiate for unions that Maretti had a piece of.

Red decided he wasn't going to argue business sense or labor law with the idiot. It was so bad that he might as well get the whole picture before deciding.

"What do you and Mr. Maretti want to do?" he asked, probing for information.

Steeley produced architect drawings. "Reinforce the roof of the mine with steel girders to prevent cave-ins and lay railroad track throughout," he said. "That way the ore can be hauled out on rail carts instead of by hand. That'll more than triple production."

"But the mine's partially caved in," Red said.

"I've got a guy who was in demolition in the Army in the big war," Steeley said. "He can control the blasts. It's easier than digging."

"We'll have to dig and blast," Red said, looking at the blueprints.

"And we'll have to dig far enough away from finished areas that the blasts don't damage the areas we've already reinforced. It's gonna be a bastard."

"Let me look around, check things out for a few days, and I'll tell you my plan," Red said. "If you want my help, you'll have to let me work on it."

"I want your help, up to a point."

"Up to a point, I'll give it to you."

"Fair enough," Steeley said. "Let's go check the site."

Red knew he should run, not walk, but the image of Kate Thompson, barefoot in that white dress, lush hair cascading down her back, and sweat glistening on her olive skin clouded his judgment. If he left town without at least trying to land her, he'd never forgive himself.

"Let's go," he said to Steeley.

The mine and its operation were a complete mess. They tried to bring ore out of the one functional shaft, while still digging and trying to blast their way into the other shafts. Red had seen a talking picture, a comedy. The "Keystone Kops" were so inept, so bad, that it was cute. Even cops that Red knew liked the Keystone Kops, because it was so ridiculous. The Keystone

Kops were well organized compared to how the mine was run. After a week, Red called Tony Maretti and demanded to see him. He was told to come down the following weekend.

He asked Kate to go with him. She squealed with delight. "San Francisco with a handsome escort? Are you kidding? Mrs. Johnson will take care of the house if I drop her rent for the week."

"I hope people don't get the wrong idea," Red said.

Kate laughed. "Red, I am twenty-nine years old and I've been married twice. Once to a boy and once to an old man. I'd like to have a relationship with a man of the right age. This is a dirty little village in the middle of nowhere, and I don't much care what anyone in it thinks. I'm a woman.

I like men. If that means I'm not a lady, then so what."

"You're different that's for sure," Red replied. "But you're a lady, no arguing that. I've never liked the 'I'm going to faint' type anyway. The only thing worse than women being demure for men is them doing it for other women. I'd rather have a woman spit on the floor, smoke a cigar, and drink me under the table than play the helpless type," Red finished.

"Then I'm your girl," Kate said and they both laughed.

The drive to San Francisco was tough in the bouncy truck. Kate didn't complain, but Red could tell she was a little tired. He didn't feel like doing business when they arrived and decided he'd go see Maretti the following day.

He went to one of the finer hotels where they checked in and then went up to their room. Red tipped the porter who brought their suitcases up. The room had two double beds.

"I'm going to take a bath in that exquisite tub,"

Kate said. "Figure out which expensive restaurant you want to take me to and we'll go to dinner."

Red took her to Chez-Paul, a French restaurant that top wiseguys recommended. Red ordered frog legs and so did Kate. They came with potatoes *au gratin*. Red hadn't said much on the trip other than small talk, and he didn't said much in the restaurant. He wasn't a big talker. Even with his male buddies, he spoke if he deemed it necessary. Women thought he was the "strong silent type" and deep and mysterious, which he certainly used to his advantage, but in reality he was just a man of few words. He said what he thought when he thought it needed to be said, but he didn't rattle incessantly like a schoolgirl. Apparently Kate was used to people who did.

"How's your food?" she asked.

"Good," he replied.

"Are you tired from the trip?"

"Not really. I don't mind driving."

"Do you regret asking me to come with you?" she asked.

"Of course not. If I didn't want you to come I wouldn't have asked," Red replied. "What kind of question is that?" She hesitated and Red gave her the prodding she needed. "What is it that you think is wrong?"

"We're not getting along as well as I'd hoped," she said.

"Why would you say that?"

"You don't have much to say."

"What's to say?" he replied. "I'm in a nice restaurant, eating good food with a beautiful woman. Later I'm going to try to coax that same woman into bed with me. If she declines, I still had nice meal, stayed in a nice hotel and did some important business. Either way, it's okay."

Kate laughed and pointed her fork at him while smiling broadly. "Mr. Sullivan, you are a silver-tongued devil."

"I'll take that as a compliment," he said.

When they got back to the hotel, she undressed quickly and unceremoniously got in bed. He stripped down and got in with her. He'd been a while without a woman and already had an erection. Since the bed was slightly narrow, and being a polite man, positioned himself so it laid against her buttocks instead of poking her. After a few minutes she rolled over.

He pulled his hips back, because with all that female bone and flesh moving so fast, there was no telling what damage could occur. He kissed her and she kissed him back hungrily. She ran her hands down his body and squeezed his ass.

"For a big man, you don't have much lard on you."

Red laughed. "Why are you laughing?" she asked.

"Sometimes, in my profession, you have to get physical. I have a bit of a reputation for being very good at 'getting physical.' Most people that meet me, who have heard of my reputation, say, 'I thought you'd be bigger.' It's kind of a running joke among people that know me well. I better shut up or you'll think I'm not a nice guy," he said.

"I know you're not a nice guy," she replied. "And I don't care. You can put that thing inside me if you want."

"I want."

He tried to penetrate her, but had a little difficulty.

"I ain't had a man in so long, I done closed up tight," she said.

"Shhh, it'll be fine," Red replied. "It'll be fine.

They kissed some more and he enjoyed kissing, licking, and playing with her breasts. Apparently she did too.

Her breathing increased and she finally said, "Do it! Stop teasing me and do it."

He penetrated her slightly and she moaned. He sank as deep as he could and she moaned again. "Uuunnngh," she said, sounding like an animal. She held onto him and locked her ankles behind his back.

When they came to the end, they were locked together so fiercely and were straining against each other so violently, that falling away from each other was like the tremble before death. He rolled off her and caught his breath. She slapped his chest.

"You owe me," she said. "If I'd known you were that much of a stallion, I'd've snuck into your room the first night you were there. I've missed at least two weeks of prime humping and it's your fault."

"Every man thinks he's a stallion in the sack," he said. "And just how would a gentleman broach that subject with his landlord?"

Kate laughed. "I don't know. But you owe me," she said, rolling over on her stomach.

Red began kissing the back of her neck and rubbing her shoulders. "I'll give you an hour to stop that," she said, breathlessly. Red resolved to use the remaining fifty-nine minutes appropriately.

Red got dressed for his meeting with Maretti. "I have to do some business," he said.

"Go ahead," Kate replied. "Maybe I'll get my hair done. I haven't had my hair done in a salon in years."

Red met Tony in Louie's Restaurant, Tony's favorite hangout, partly because he owned it and partly because it had the best Italian food in the city. Red ordered spaghetti with extra Italian sausage. He loved spicy meats.

Red started talking after the salad. "You could increase production by double, even triple, if I could do it my way."

"I'm listening," Tony said, still wolfing down his lasagna.

"Steeley is stepping over dollars to pick up dimes," Red said. "Shut down the mine. Let me kick ass for six months, and the revenue you'll get in the following six months will boggle your mind."

"It takes a lot to boggle my mind," Tony said. "But I agree, we need to move faster and differently than we have in this area. We've known each other a long time. Tell me what you think, Red."

"Steeley is small-minded. He doesn't see the big picture. He's spending triple the money to show the union people that they can't tell him what to do, than he would if he just paid the workers a little more."

"Everyone there is an idiot," Tony laughed. "This is just between you and me," Maretti said. "John Steeley is probably worth a million dollars if he maximized his potential, yet he rides a horse, doesn't even have a car.

He buys suits off the rack at Sears. If you order a three-dollar steak in a restaurant, he'll tell you a two-dollar steak is just as good."

"If you don't know, you don't know," Red replied.

"I taught you well," Tony said. "Squash this union problem. Go see them, and if they're reasonable, give them what they want. Tell Steeley to negotiate, to give some concessions."

"That's the problem. He thinks you should help him kick the shit out of the union people," Red said.

"You know I can't do that. I've made money helping unions before. It would hurt me down here, if I did it differently anywhere else, even some jerkwater town. Convince Steeley that it's my idea. Work something out and I'll be forever grateful."

"I'm gonna hold you to that, Tony," Red said.

"I always pay my debts," Tony replied.

36

They shook hands and Red got up to leave, when Tony called his name. Red turned around. Maretti handed him a bag. Inside was a bottle of expensive Canadian whiskey, some Cuban cigars and a box of fine chocolates.

"I figured a man of your taste might miss some of the perks of the city workin' out in the boonies."

"Thanks, Tony. You're a class guy."

"As are you."

They said goodbye, and Red left to pick up Kate where she was getting her hair done.

Kate looked radiant.

"What do you think?" she asked.

"You're so lovely, I'm at your feet, I'm just at your feet," he said.

"A proper place for a mortal, beholding a goddess from Olympus," Kate quipped.

"Indeed," Red retorted. "When I see a mortal man I'll demand he assume the position."

Kate laughed out loud. "If you're not mortal, then you're...."

"Jupiter himself, or at least Atlas. I'd have to be to engage in relations with a goddess. Mere mortals aren't allowed that. However, once Jupiter or Atlas has possessed the goddess, she is his forever."

"I never heard that story," Kate scoffed.

"Then you don't know your mythology as well as you think," Red said.

"You are so full of shit," Kate said, laughing. "But I'm yours, whatever your name is."

Red kissed her passionately. "Want to go back to the hotel?" she asked.

"Absolutely."

They made love the rest of the afternoon and called room service for dinner.

On the way back to Rough and Ready the following day, they stopped at Russian River. They bought supplies at a store in Sebastopool and decided to go swimming and have a picnic on the river. Kate wore a black one-piece bathing suit that she'd brought along with the blue men's trunks that Red wore. She looked good.

"That's a nice bathing suit," Red said.

Kate smiled. "I suppose you'll be trying to shuck me out of it later, so I'll enjoy wearing it for now," she said.

They went swimming, then made sandwiches and ate them on the beach. They had a nice shady, secluded spot.

"So how'd you end up a big shot in construction?" she asked.

"My mother died when I was fifteen," Red replied.

"But I was already a tough little bastard while my mother was alive. I'd been working for some Sicilian guys in the neighborhood since I was eleven or twelve, running numbers, serving drinks at crap games, that sort of stuff.

I had a falling out with my father after my mother died.

My friends got me a job with a construction company. I did well and got promoted. I'm probably the only person, besides his wife and relatives and consigliore, Sicilian or not, that can call Tony Maretti by his first name."

"An Irish Mafioso. That's a twist," Kate said.

"I'm not a Mafioso. I'm the exception, not the rule. And only because a 'Don' took me under his wing when I was a kid, so I can be trusted with certain things that others aren't. You can't be a 'made man' unless you're one hundred percent Sicilian. Everyone else is 'Irish,' except for Jews, and they are more untrustworthy than Irish. 'Irish' of course, includes Germans, Swiss, English, any Anglo-Saxon descendants. I'm respected, but I'm still Irish, literally and figuratively. I use my connections to my advantage and they use me to theirs. It's strictly business. I know where I stand, I have no illusions."

"Wow," Kate replied. "We're always quoting Greeks to each other, and Plato said, 'Know thyself.' Apparently you do."

"I'd like to think so. What about you? You said you were married twice before. What happened?" Red asked.

"It's an epic saga. You sure you want to hear it?"

"Yes."

"I was kidding about the epic saga part," Kate said.

"I still want to hear it."

"I grew up in Sacramento. I was seventeen. This guy who'd lived in our neighborhood was twenty-one. He'd enlisted in the Army three years earlier. He came home on leave for Thanksgiving. When he left I was this tall, gangly, awkward fourteen-year-old that he paid no mind to. When he came back I was...."

"A gorgeous, full grown woman, and you had his full attention," Red said, interrupting her.

"Something like that. We got married before Christmas. We had Christmas and New Years together. He got some more leave around Easter. Then he got sent to the war in Europe."

"He never came back?" Red asked.

"Oh, he came back...in a pine box. How'd you like to be a widow at eighteen?"

"I wouldn't," Red said.

"Neither did I. My mother was Italian and my father Irish. I couldn't stand all the Catholic consolation I was getting from my mother's friends. My own friends avoided me like the plague because they didn't know what to say, and every boy or man in the neighborhood that wasn't married or going off to war was trying to get the hot young widow into bed. I left town, went into San Francisco and got a job dancing in the traveling show *H.M.S. Pinafore*. I did that for three years until the show closed.

"I went home to Sacramento and worked in a drugstore for three years. One day a guy comes in and asks me if I can dance. I say yes. He asks me if I'd like to make twenty dollars a day dancing. 'Just dancing?' I say. 'Just dancing,' he assures me. I go see him the next day. He's got this place downtown, with a band playing and maybe fifteen or twenty girls standing around. Guys come in and pay a dollar to dance with a pretty girl. The girl keeps fifty cents of that. He was right, if you danced with five guys an hour, in eight hours you'd make twenty bucks. I did that for a while. A guy comes in, he's in his fifties, a little shy. I ask him to dance. He spends fifty bucks on me that night. After that he comes in like clockwork, every two weeks. Always a perfect gentleman, always brings me flowers and candy. The other girls start jokingly calling him my boyfriend. One day he asks me to marry him. Says he inherited some land from his mother in a mining town, and wants to build a classy hotel as he knows mining is going to boom. Asks me to be his partner in the hotel. I figure, what the hell, all I'm getting on this job, other than the money I've saved, is older and calluses on my feet."

Red stroked Kate's pretty right foot. "You don't have calluses on your feet," he joked.

She kicked him playfully with her other foot. "That's cause I quit that damn job. Anyway, we built a first-class boarding house, and figured we might get a bank to give us capital for a big hotel." She made a motion with the fingers of her left hand, showing less than an inch. "We were this close to building the hotel, then he died. I found him slumped at his desk. He was sixty-one. Doctor said it was probably a stroke. The banks wouldn't finance a widow, especially a young widow. They figured I'd hook up with some man and they'd never get paid. Bastards, I want you to know something. I may have thought at first that it was a marriage of convenience, but I grew to love him. He was the kindest, gentlest man I've ever known."

"Why don't you leave that dump?" Red asked.

"I've thought about it," she replied, "but if I sold my property and went to some big city, eventually I'd have to work with horny men and catty women. At least here I'm my own boss. I figure I can make a living until I'm eighty if I live that long."

"Why haven't you got married again?" he asked.

"Two reasons," she replied. "One, no one's asked me. Rough and Ready isn't exactly a haven for eligible bachelors. Two, as I said, I did love my husband, and for a long time wasn't interested in starting over with a new man."

"What if someone did ask?" Red said.

"He'd have to be a helluva man. You know anyone?" she said, grinning.

"No," he said, deadpan. "Guys like that are hard to find."

"You damned jerk," she said, kicking him playfully.

"I love you, Katy," he said.

"Sure," she replied.

"No bullshit," he said. "You're all woman, anyone can see that, but you think and talk like a man. That's an irresistible combination. I don't say things lightly.

I hope you know that."

"Look," Kate said, "just because I make light of a situation doesn't mean I take it lightly. My humor is sometimes misunderstood. That aside, I love you too."

She pulled down the top of her bathing suit, exposing her large breasts. "Now show me how much you love me."

"Yes, ma'am," he said, and they made love on the beach.

When they got back to Rough and Ready, Kate insisted they sleep in their own rooms.

"I don't want to offend the Christian ladies that live here by openly sleeping with a man I'm not married to."

"I thought you didn't care what the people in this town thought," Red said.

"I don't. I do care about the money my boarders pay me. They'll look the other way a little, but I don't want to rub their face in it. I don't want them to move out because they don't approve of my conduct," Kate said.

"Why do you care what your tenants do or don't approve of?" he asked.

She gave him an exasperated look and spoke again.

"I'd rather have a bunch of stuffy middle-aged women for tenants than a bunch of transient miners. There's far less drunkenness and fights that way. And far less broken furniture and holes in the walls. It's strictly business, you understand."

"I understand," Red said. "When can I see you?"

"We'll work something out," Kate said, and kissed him as they unloaded the truck.

After they carried the luggage in, they went to their rooms. About three in the morning Kate sneaked in for a quickie and then returned to her own room.

He slept fitfully afterwards and was a little tired the next morning when the alarm clock went off. He wasn't looking forward to what he had to do. He knew Steeley would be pigheaded.

After breakfast he headed to the mine. *Might as well hit 'em between the eyes right off.*

John Steeley called his brother and several other guys who were foremen at the mine into his office. They sat down and waited for Red to speak.

"We need to shut down the mine while we remodel it," Red said.

"And whose brilliant idea was this?" John Steeley sneered.

"Maretti's," Red replied. "Look, you sold him seventy percent of your interest in the mine in exchange for development. Thirty percent of a million dollars a year is still three hundred thousand dollars. Maretti has the capital to remodel it and make it produce a million a year, you don't. The way you're going now, you'd be lucky to pull three hundred thousand dollars out in ten or fifteen years, much less one."

"Fine," Steeley said. "Shut it down, kick ass rebuilding and we'll make it up in the first few months of operation. I can live with that."

"We also need to cut a deal with the union," Red said.

"No way," Steeley replied.

"You don't have a choice," Red said. "Maretti owns seventy percent. He's the majority partner. He can do what he wants. If you try to take him to court, you'll lose. We cut a deal with the union, the fighting stops, everything runs smoothly and they go organize somewhere else. Everyone's happy."

"What if I don't go along?" Steeley said.

"You're gonna fight Maretti and the union people?"

Red said, incredulous. "We don't want another Matewan."

"What's Matewan?" one of the foremen asked.

"During the war, the coal industry boomed in Applachia," Red replied. "Some big shots back East unionized the mine workers in West Virginia and other eastern states. Working conditions and wages improved, and so did production. Matewan, Kentucky was home to one of the biggest coal mines in the nation. The union people decided to organize the workers there as well. However, the hillbillies in Kentucky that owned the mine and the company store didn't want anybody pulling their boot off the townspeople's throat. They brought in hired killers from Kansas City. They beat people up, raped women, killed people and burned their houses.

"The union brought muscle from back east to retaliate. Finally, in 1920, some union men and townspeople met the company goons in the middle of the main street in an all-out gunfight. It was all over newspapers everywhere. The last O.K. Corral type gunfight in the modern United States.

The townspeople won, but a lot of people were killed, the company lost their ass and anytime the union tried to organize somewhere people panicked. It set business and labor relations back twenty years. Nobody won. Let's not do that here," Red finished.

"All right, who's gonna negotiate with the union people?" Steeley asked.

"I am," Red replied. "You're the only person that knows I work for Maretti. If they think I'm an outsider taking their part that'll give me credibility. Especially if I make it look like I brought you and Maretti together. It's good business sense."

"Give it a try," Steeley said. "If they're not reasonable, then I'll do it my way, whether Maretti likes it or not."

"Okay," Red said, not commenting on Steeley's asinine bravado.

"Meeting adjourned," Steeley said, and everyone left.

Red went to see the union leader, Pete Jackson. He was about forty with a noticeable southern accent. When Red said he wanted to discuss the problems of the workers, for a minute Jackson's mouth went on automatic. Red could see soft touch was not going to work on the guy.

"I don't want to hear any more of Steeley's threats, or crappy offers. Maretti comes to the table, or it's all out war."

"Maretti is at the table," Red said.

"Really? I don't see him," Jackson said sarcastically.

"Who do you think I work for? That idiot Steeley?" Red said.

"At least we agree on something," Jackson replied. "You can speak for Maretti, no bullshit?"

"Would anyone be stupid enough to say he could if he really couldn't?" Red replied.

"Step into my office," Jackson said.

His "office" was a hastily built shack outside of town. Inside was a telephone, a desk, a couch, several chairs, as well as an icebox and a hot plate. Red spied a bottle of clear liquid on the desk.

"Could I have a little tap of that?" he asked.

"Of what?" Jackson said defensively.

"That's 'moon, isn't it?" Red retorted.

"This? It's water," Jackson said. "In Ireland they call it poteen. Of course, that's 'cause it's made from potatoes, not corn. I always wondered why it was called moonshine instead of 'cornshine' or something. A good ol' boy from Kansas City that was working out here explained it to me one time. It's called 'moonshine' 'cause it's made at night, by the light of the moon. White Lightning is another name." Jackson laughed. "You want a shot, have a shot."

Jackson poured him a glass. Red downed it in one gulp. He knew one had to do that with poteen, or their eyes would water and cough. He figured American home liquor makers were no better than Irish. He felt the burn like pure liquid smoke, but his eyes didn't water and he didn't cough.

"You're the first city boy to drink some of that and not get all red in the face and have a coughing fit. I'm impressed."

Red saw his intuition was correct, and his ability to relate to people on their own level again helped him get over.

"What can I do for you?" Jackson said.

"It's what I can do for you," Red replied.

Jackson poured two shots of moonshine. "I'm listening."

"I'm proposing, instead of having two twelve-hour shifts, that we run three eight-hour shifts. The mine'll still run twenty-four hours, but more workers'll have jobs and not be as tired at the end of the day. Everybody gets two days off. Some guys get Saturday and Sunday, some guys get Sunday and Monday. We'll close Sundays because most people want to go to church. We'll go to hourly pay rates.

I know people are getting paid by the day now, and sometimes those days are fourteen or fifteen hours. Now you work twelve hours, you get paid for twelve hours. A lot better than getting the same for an eight-hour day. That's the best I can do," Red finished.

"That's a helluva an offer," Jackson said.

Red turned on the charm. "I heard you were a serious man, to be treated with respect. I won't insult you by playing games. That's the bottom line."

"Everything you said, plus a raise to seventy-five cents an hour and you got a deal," Jackson said.

"Done," Red replied.

"I may have set my sights too low if you agreed that easy."

"Not at all," Red said. "I thought we'd cut the crap."

"We did. Why come to me with this great deal?" Jackson asked.

"It's good business. The mine will make money hand over fist once it's operational. Quibbling over a few cents per hour for workers is crazy, plus I see how committed you guys are to your cause."

"I'll tell you about commitment to a cause, my friend," Jackson said. "Before the war, I was already involved in the union movement. I killed a guy with an axe handle during a strike riot in Pennsylvania. I got charged with manslaughter. The statute says that although I didn't mean to kill the guy, I'm still responsible for his death. The jury didn't buy self-defense, which it was. I did forty-two months of a five-year sentence. While I was inside, I met some Amish guys who were there. They don't believe in war or violence under any circumstances. They were in prison because they refused to go to war. Their leader, who apparently was an elder in the church, had them all rip the buttons off their uniforms. Buttons are fancy, not plain. The warden had the guards handcuff them to the bars of the cell all day. Their fingers split open and began to bleed. They pulled the buttons off with their teeth when they were released.

"The warden decided if he could break the leader, he could break the rest of them. He sent the leader to the 'whipping house.' That's what they called this place that had been there since it was a plantation in the Revolutionary War days. The leader hung in the chains for five days. He had broken wrists, had bit off his own tongue from the pain, his whole body in shreds from being whipped incessantly. He died shaking his head 'no' when the warden asked him the last time to tell the others to toe the line.

"That's commitment to a cause. Big business, Mafia and unions all talk about commitment. They don't know shit about commitment. They all cave eventually. When I think about caving, I remember that Amish guy, who never did nothing to nobody, getting whipped to death over buttons on shirts. My resolve always returns tenfold."

"Guts are great," Red replied, "but guts will only take you so far, then they get you killed. A gambler told me once that you have to know when to hold 'em and when to fold 'em. It's always better to live to fight again another day than it is to go out in a blaze of glory. I don't want to die in a blaze of glory."

"Neither do I," Jackson said. "I'll need you to talk to the men with me. We need to convince them it's the right thing to do."

"I can do that," Red said.

"You should be an organizer. You could be huge with the union, maybe even national if you wanted to," Jackson said.

"I'm happy doing what I'm doing."

Jackson poured another round of moonshine. "Let's toast our deal."

"Indeed," Red replied, downing the burning liquor.

He still had a feeling of dread, however. He knew something was going to go bad somehow, no matter how easy things looked now. Red wasn't a pessimist, just a realist. If one prepared oneself for the worst, anything less than the worst was a pleasant surprise. He hoped for a pleasant surprise.

Lynchburg, Missouri 1929:

Lynchburg was a small settlement off the Gasconade River that originally was called Roubideaux, named after the French trapper who founded the trading post during the French and Indian War. The tributary of the Gasconade River that gave water to the town was call Roubideaux Creek.

After the Civil War ended, thing were rough in the "Reconstructionist" South. Missouri had been right on the line. Jesse James and his gang eluded capture for years because the stubborn people of rural Missouri would not give up one of their own. Carpetbaggers and others called small towns "burgs," which came from America's melting pot heritage. Germany came from the word "Germania." Germania was a nation of robust people dating back to 180 AD, when Marcus Aurelius was Emperor of Rome. Rome took Germania, but at great cost and the German people eventually won their independence. Germans loved good food and good drink. Beer makers were called "burgermeisters." Anywhere a burgermeister set up a brewery, a settlement usually ensued, called a "burg." This became part of American slang in the late 19th century.

John Lynch was a big man, 6'6" and 245 pounds. He was an ex-Confederate soldier who was elected sheriff of Roubideaux after the war. President Andrew Johnson didn't want another Civil War to break out. The Federal government gave bonuses to states with good law and order. State governors passed the bonuses onto the provinces. Anyone committing a crime in Roubideaux was summarily hanged.

It became so bad that the government sent the Pinkerton Detective Agency, which was the predecessor of the Secret Service, to investigate. Partly because of its history and partly because of the sheriff's name, the settlement eventually became known as "Lynchburg."

John Henry "Hank" Collins was born in Lynchburg in 1923. He was the oldest of four children born to Dan and Elizabeth Collins. Dan was the only child of Allen and Mae Collins. Allen had been born in 1851 in Jefferson City, Missouri. In 1863, the Union Army came through Jefferson City, killing anyone who got in their way, whether they were soldiers or not. They burned the whole town.

Allen's father hid him in the cellar before they burst in the door. He didn't have time to hide the other kids. They shot his father in the head and dragged his mother outside screaming. His little brother and sister had their heads bashed in with boot heels because the Army wanted to save bullets. Allen was basically destroyed that day.

He went and joined the Confederate Army. He lied about his age and said he was seventeen. Since he was already almost six feet tall, no one argued. Despite his young age, he became an exceptional soldier. His ferocity was legendary.

After the war ended in 1865, he wandered for more than ten years, searching for a man named "Swede Johnson." He was the commander of the unit that destroyed Jefferson City. He recalled another officer saying, "Swede, you don't have to kill the kids." Swede had said, "I don't want anyone 'fingering' me after the war."

He found Swede Johnson in Natchez, Mississippi in 1876. Swede was fifty-eight years old, retired from the Army and gambling on a riverboat. Allen was twenty-five, 6'4" and 235 pounds. He forced Johnson into an alley and beat him within an inch of his life, then he pulled his 1851 Colt Navy .36 caliber revolver.

"Jesus, man, what do you want?" Swede cried.

"I want your blood and I want your soul right now," Allen said coldly.

"You talk about souls, don't you have an ounce of mercy in yours?"

"My baby brother and sister never got to ask you that question," Allen sneered.

"I don't know your brother and sister," Swede wailed.

"Sure you do. Jeff City. Summer of sixty-three."

"That was war. The war's over."

"Not for me it isn't," Allen said and cocked the hammer.

Swede put his hands out in a pleading motion, but Allen blew his head off. "Now it's over," he said.

Allen walked towards the river and threw the revolver in it. He boarded the next riverboat that came by.

Allen got off the boat in St. Louis. He used the last of his money to buy an old horse. The horse died about five miles outside of Jefferson City and he walked the remaining distance to town.

His aunt and her husband had rebuilt his old house. Allen had sent her letters from the Army, but he wasn't sure if she'd received any of them. She welcomed him happily.

Her husband gave him a job, and eventually took him on as a partner in his blacksmith business. He got married in 1880 and had three children. He was happy and finally having a normal life. Then in 1892, tragedy struck again.

A small pox epidemic hit Jefferson City and the surrounding areas. His wife and children caught it and died.

Grief-stricken again, he wandered south. He built a cabin outside of Lynchburg and cleared a lot of wilderness away. He opened a sawmill and homesteaded, which eventually became over 400 acres. In 1898 he remarried to a half-Indian woman named Mae. She had a weird Indian last name he could not pronounce. His son Dan was born in 1900.

A fire in 1910 nearly destroyed everything, but he rebuilt and the business boomed during the war. When Dan married in 1922, Allen gave him 160 acres of farmland. There were two catfish ponds on the land, and some good timber on the back 40. Allen kept most of the timberland to support his business, which his son worked in when he wasn't farming.

His wife died of cancer in 1925 at the age of fifty-two. In 1926, the government tried to take his whole life away again. They said he owed "income tax."

Allen's opinion was since he'd built the business with his own two hands and rebuilt it after the fire without any government assistance, he didn't owe anything. He kept defying IRS agents until 1929, when they came with armed Federal marshals and shut down the sawmill.

He cursed them as they tried to arrest him. "Taxation without representation! Isn't that why we overthrew the god damned British? Maybe we ought to overthrow the greedy imperialist pricks in Washington!"

"Calm down, sir, we're just doing our jobs," one of the marshals said, in that annoying way that cops convey.

"Everyone watching heard me be nice, but I really mean fuck you and like it."

Allen decked the bastard. The marshal lay on the ground, moaning as blood squirted out his destroyed nose. The other marshal and IRS agents got a hold of him and handcuffed him as he cussed them.

His son bailed him out. Besides the income tax evasion charge, he was charged with obstruction of justice. The only reason he wasn't charged with assaulting a federal officer was the marshal didn't want to admit in a written report that he'd gotten his ass kicked by an old man.

He sat in his son's house drinking whiskey, which the god damned government said he couldn't drink. He got angrier and angrier. His life had been destroyed once by government men "just doing their jobs." He wasn't going to let them do it again. He was seventy-eight years old. He didn't care if he died trying or died in prison after, but the bastards were not going to get away with it.

He waited until everyone was asleep and walked silently down the hall. His six-year-old grandson was in the kitchen. The poor kid had been called "Baby" for the first month of his life because his parents couldn't agree on a name. Dan had wanted to Henry and Elizabeth had wanted John. Finally they agreed on John Henry, but now everyone called the boy "Hank."

"Hank, what are you doin'?" Allen asked.

"Sneaking some cookies," Hank replied with an impish grin. "You goin out, Grampa?" he asked.

"Yes."

"Can I go with you?"

"No. Enjoy your stolen cookies and go back to bed.

If anyone asks, I'll say I ate 'em."

"Thanks, Grampa. You're the best."

Allen went outside. He thought about driving his new Model A Ford, but starting the car would wake the family.

He went to the barn and saddled his son's horse. He took an axe and rode off.

Little Hank watched curiously from the kitchen window. He went to the barn and saddled the pony his grandfather had bought him for his birthday. Although he was only six, Hank weighed almost seventy-five pounds and could ride as well as most older kids. He followed Allen easily because the pony just followed the older horse's path.

Allen came to a clearing overlooking his sawmill.

He took one long last look and rode down to the mill. He cut the padlock off the gate with the axe. He went to the tool shed and got some cans of kerosene and gasoline that were used to run lights, chainsaws and the generator. When he was satisfied that he had enough accelerant poured around, he lit a match, threw it down and rode back to the clearing above. He watched until the fire was raging uncontrollably.

He heard a small voice say, "Wow."

He almost jumped out of his skin. "Jesus Christ!

You scared the shit outta me! How'd you get back here, Hank?"

"I followed you."

"Well, you shouldn't have."

"Why'd you burn your mill, Grampa?" Hank asked.

"Because the government wants to take it."

"Why do they want to take it, Grampa?"

"They say I owe them money that I don't believe I owe. If I can't have it, they can't have it. But you can't tell anyone about this, Hank. If the sheriff finds out, he'll put me in jail."

"That's not fair," Hank said. "If something's yours, you can do what you want with it. My dad doesn't punish me when I break my toys."

"The government doesn't see it that way, boy. This has to be our secret."

"Okay, Grampa," Hank said.

"Let's go home."

They rode home and quietly put the horses away. They went in the house and Hank got in bed with Allen. About an hour later, it started to thunder and rain.

The next day Allen was throwing a ball to Hank. Hank's younger sister, Laura, was playing with a doll on the porch. Elizabeth was cooking in the kitchen. Dan was working out in the field. Elizabeth came out of the house when she saw the police cars pull in the driveway. The local sheriff, two Federal marshals and two IRS agents came up on the lawn.

"You're under arrest," one of the IRS agents said.

"For what?" Allen said innocently.

"You know goddamned well what, you son-of-a-bitch!" the agent exploded.

Allen remembered his name was Flynn. "You use foul language in front of my daughter-in-law and her young children again and I'll knock you so flat you'll have to roll down your socks to shit," Allen said.

"You just said 'shit,' Al," the sheriff put in.

"So?"

"You told him not to swear and then you said 'shit.'"

"Never mind that!" Flynn yelled. "Are you gonna arrest this bastard or not?"

"On what grounds?" the sheriff said.

"He burned down his sawmill."

"No, I didn't," Allen said innocently.

"Where were you last night?" one of the federal marshals asked.

Elizabeth spoke up. "Gentlemen, I can assure you my father-in-law was here last night."

"All due respect, ma'am, but relatives are lousy character witnesses," the sheriff said. "Is there anyone else who can verify Al's whereabouts last night?"

"I can," Hank said.

"What do you mean, son?" the federal marshal asked.

"I got scared when the thunder and lightning started. Grampa got me some cookies and let me sleep with him," Hank said, unflinching.

"So that's what happened to those cookies," Elizabeth said.

"Then how did the fire start?" Flynn asked.

"Probably lightning. Lightning started the fire in 1910, so it probably happened again," Allen said calmly.

"You've lost everything," Flynn said.

"No, Uncle Sam has," Allen replied. "Ain't my property no more. It's Uncle Sam's. Remember how smug and happy you were to tell me that, Agent Flynn?"

"Arrest this bastard for arson and we'll work it out in court," Flynn said.

"No, you won't," Elizabeth put in. "My husband and I consulted a lawyer. He's filing a restraining order to stop the seizure of the land. My father-in-law is semi-retired. My husband wanted to keep that business. Why would he burn down a business that he was planning to pass on to his son, when his son was paying a lawyer to fight for it? Arrest a seventy-eight-year-old man for a crime he didn't commit. How do you think that'll play in the St. Louis and Chicago papers?" she finished.

"What's the lawyer's name?" Flynn asked.

"James Daniel from St. Louis. Have you heard of him?" Elizabeth asked sarcastically.

"Yes, we've heard of him," Flynn and the other agents said, almost in unison.

James Daniel was famous for beating the Feds in two high-profile cases. In the first, he got a moonshiner off by getting the search that netted five hundred gallons of whiskey ruled unconstitutional. Ten federal agents had surrounded the guy and demanded he open his barn. Daniel argued that since the agents did not have a search warrant signed by either a local or federal judge, the search was invalid under the Fourth Amendment, which protected people against unlawful search and seizure. The prosecutor argued that the man opened the barn of his own free will. Daniel argued that when one has been roughed up and have a twelve-gauge shotgun barrel poking you in the back and nine other shotguns trained on your wife and kids, "free will" kind of goes out the window. Daniel argued that the man never would have opened the barn door if not asked at gunpoint.

It constituted duress and made the search illegal, on top of them not having a warrant. The jury acquitted his client.

In the second, he got a rancher off who'd let his neighbors hunt deer on his land out of season. Daniel argued that one only needed hunting or fishing licenses on public land. If a man had wild animals roaming his property and let his neighbors hunt them, that was his perogative. Poaching was a federal crime on federal land. What about private land? Does a man have to ask the government if he can plant tomatoes? A man can do what he wants on his own land. The case was dismissed. Daniel loved cases where the government or big business was trying to screw the common man.

"Let's go," Flynn said. "We'll check with James Daniel. We can always come back."

A month later, Allen was acquitted on all charges. The trial was held in the Laclede County Courthouse in the town of Lebanon, which had been Fort Lebanon during the Civil War.

"Are you going to put my little boy on the stand?" Dan Collins asked.

"No, sir," James Daniel replied.

He always called his clients "sir" and "ma'am." They paid a pretty penny for his services and deserved the best both in and out of the courtroom. A southern gentleman educated at Harvard University, he had a unique style. While most lawyers had short haircuts and wore three-piece suits, Daniel looked like Wild Bill Hickock. Although he was in his forties, he wore his reddish-gray hair long. He wore tailored slacks and hand-tooled boots. He had a fringed buckskin jacket, under which he wore a crisp white shirt and perfectly tied western string tie. He wore a white Stetson hat, which he respectfully removed in the courtroom.

The courthouse dress code in most of the United States said lawyers had to wear a jacket and tie. He was. By pushing the envelope on the dress code and getting away with it, he knew it would give him additional latitude in presenting his case. If he used sarcasm or ridicule, he was viewed as a charming cowboy rogue making his point the only way he knew how. If his opposition did the same, they were viewed as pompous assholes. His down-home way not only swayed jurors, but sometimes judges as well.

"Don't worry, Mr. Collins, they'll be lucky if they don't end up owing you money."

Daniel shredded the testimony of the prosecution's star witness -- IRS Agent Flynn.

"When did you first meet Mr. Collins?" he asked.

"I first met the defendant in 1928," Flynn replied, all business, having testified in hundreds of previous cases.

"Were you coached by the prosecution, Agent Flynn?"

"Objection!" the prosecutor yelled.

"Overruled," the judge said. "Answer the question, Flynn."

"No, I wasn't coached." Flynn said angrily.

"That's strange," Daniel said, "that you called my client 'the defendant,' not Mr. Collins or even 'the accused.' The defendant is an antiseptic legal term. If you used his name, people might think he's a human being with emotions and problems like the rest of us. To you, he's just the nameless, soulless, evil defendant."

"Objection. Counsel is badgering the witness."

The prosecutor yelled, "Sustained. Move on, Mr. Daniel."

"And why were you sent to Mr. Collins' place of business?"

"Because he had ignored previous attempts to contact him," Flynn said.

"How did you try to contact him?"

"Through certified mail."

"Do you have a copy of the return receipt showing my client's signature?"

"No, I do not."

"And why not?" Daniel asked.

"He refused all of them."

"You have evidence of this?" Daniel asked. "You have Laclede County mailmen who will swear under oath that they personally saw my client refuse correspondence from the Internal Revenue Service that required a signature?"

"No, but you know damn well that he...."

"No, I do not, sir," Daniel said, cutting Flynn off. "And it's apparent that you don't either. Is it possible that his employees, many of whom were unskilled laborers, simply refused official documents not addressed to them?

Is it possible that your first face-to-face meeting was the first time my client found out that he was in tax trouble?"

"That's unlikely."

"I did not ask you what was likely or unlikely, sir. It's a 'yes' or 'no' question, Agent Flynn. Should I repeat the question?"

"I heard you the first time."

"Then what is your answer, sir?"

"Yes, it's possible that was the first time he had knowledge of any trouble. But he was belligerent and verbally abusive and threatening to everyone in the party," Flynn added.

Daniel led him exactly where he wanted him to go.

"What did he say and do specifically?"

"He said if we didn't get off his property he'd kick our asses," Flynn said smugly.

"How many were in your party, sir?"

"Five. Myself, another IRS agent, and three Federal marshals."

"Was anyone in your party armed?" Daniel continued.

"The three marshals were."

"Was my client armed with a shotgun or a pistol, say a Colt .45?"

"No."

"Was he holding a running chainsaw or a machete or a large stick?"

"No, he was not."

"How old are you, Agent Flynn?"

"Thirty-five."

"Were you the oldest man on the scene?"

"I don't know."

"I have records here showing that the other men on the scene were between the ages of twenty-two and thirty-three," Daniel said.

"Does that counsel have a relevant question, Your Honor?" the prosecutor asked sarcastically.

Daniel smiled. "I'm just wondering why five men between the ages of twenty-two and thirty-five, three of them carrying guns, felt threatened by and unarmed seventy-eight-year-old man."

The courtroom, including the jury, erupted in laughter.

"My daddy still threatens to spank me when he's drunk, but I don't take him seriously." More laughter.

The judge banged his gavel and the courtroom quieted down. "Any more questions, Mr. Daniel?"

"Yes, Your Honor, I have a few. Agent Flynn, were you aware that my client fought for the South in the latter part of the Civil War, after his family was brutally murdered in front of him by the Union Army when he was a boy of twelve?"

"Objection!" the prosecutor yelled.

"Relevance," Daniel replied. "Your Honor, the prosecution has talked a great length about my client's hatred of the Federal government. I think it's only fair for the defense to be allowed to show why he hates the government, if in fact he does. In doing that, I'll ask court for a little latitude."

"A very little latitude," the judge replied.

"Were you aware, Agent Flynn, that my client lost his first wife and three children in the small pox epidemic of 1892?"

"No, I was not."

"Were you aware that my client homesteaded his land legally, built his business, and rebuilt after a fire destroyed everything with his own two hands before there was Federal income tax?"

"Yes, that I knew," Flynn said.

"And how much assistance did Mr. Collins get from the federal government in rebuilding after this tragic fire?"

"None," Flynn said, wondering where Daniel was going.

"So, Agent Flynn, can you tell my why a man who built a business, hacking it out of the wilderness, burying his children along the way, with no help from anyone, would believe he owed anyone a percentage of his earnings?"

"He broke the law and he has to pay the price," Flynn said, bristling.

"Sending a seventy-eight-year-old man to prison is just?" Daniel said. "We both know that's a death sentence.

I don't think anyone should get the death penalty for not understanding modern tax law. Would you send your daddy or granddaddy to prison because he didn't understand modern tax law?"

"That's not the same," Flynn said. "And he burned the business down after we seized it."

"You have eyewitnesses to this?"

"No, but he did it the night he was let out of jail. I'm sure of that," Flynn sneered.

"Would that be the fifteenth, four days after he was arrested?"

"Yes."

"That would be three days after I first consulted with Dan Collins, his son. That would be two days after I filed a restraining order to stop the seizure of the land and sent a certified letter to the Internal Revenue Service requesting that no further action be taken until after this trial. Were you aware of that?"

"No, I wasn't."

"It appears the only thing you are aware of, Agent Flynn, is your obsessive hatred of my client and desire to convict an innocent man not with facts, but with supposition upon supposition."

"Objection!"

"Sustained. Any more questions, Mr. Daniel?" the judge said sternly.

"Just one," Daniel replied. "Why would he burn down a business when his son was paying a lawyer to fight for it?"

Allen was acquitted on all counts. He was allowed to keep his land, and didn't have to pay the three thousand dollars in taxes he allegedly owed. Allen lived another eighteen years, finally passing away in 1947 at the age of ninety-six. He was hale and hearty until his death, and never once complained about having to pay James Daniel $2,500.00 to win his case.

New York City, 1914:

Eddie Coyle was arguing with his manager Jack "Doc" O'Hearn. Having worked as a team for thirteen years, they sometimes bickered like an old married couple.

"Make the fight, Doc. I'm the fight guy, you're the money man, remember?"

"You're giving up too much weight," Doc said.

"Bullshit," Eddie said.

"And you're gettin' old for a fighter." Eddie was thirty-two.

"Bullshit," Eddie said again. "John L. Sullivan was champ for ten years until he was thirty-four. After Corbett took Sullivan, everyone said Gentleman Jim was unbeatable. Bob Fitzsimmons was thirty-five years old and one hundred and sixty-seven pounds when he knocked Corbett piss-limber and won the heavyweight title. He also held the light-heavyweight title, defended both belts and was champ of one division or another until he was forty-one. Tommy Burns, all five-foot eight and one hundred and seventy-nine pounds of him, was heavyweight champ for three years until Johnson cleaned his clock. Age and weight doesn't mean shit," Eddie said.

"Then why do you have so much trouble with it?" Doc retorted.

"Screw you."

"Screw you double."

Eddie knew what Doc was talking about. Eddie had started out as a light-heavyweight. The division weight limit was 175 pounds. The last few years they only took big money fights, usually against heavyweights, because Eddie couldn't make the weight anymore. He usually fought at about 185. It had

59

been a year since his last fight, and they were contemplating quitting when Doc negotiated a fight with the light-heavyweight champion. It was a non-title fight, as the champ wanted to see if he could compete in the heavyweight division without risking his title.

Eddie had been 210 pounds before starting training.

He trimmed down to 188 by the day of the fight. He still had a little rust from going so long without fighting. He took a bit of a beating for six rounds. In the seventh, he caught the champ with a sweeping left hook. The guy staggered backwards and Eddie bulled him into the ropes where he landed several more heavy wallops. The guy went down, but got up at the count of seven. He tried to retreat until he could clear his head, but Eddie knew this was probably his only shot at victory. Eddie plowed forward with both cannons roaring.

The guy tried to counter with an overhand right. Eddie's best shot was always a short left hook to the ribs. He buried his fist in the man's side like he was trying to rip out a lung, pivoting his hips, his left heel leaving the ground as he did. He heard an audible crack and the guy gasped. Eddie nailed him in the face with thunderous overhand right, followed by a vicious left hook. Eddie felt the weight of the punch down to his heels. The champion pitched forward on his face and was counted out. He had two broken ribs, a broken nose and a broken jaw from Eddie's blitz. The guy's manager accused Eddie of having plaster in his gloves. The commissioner cut his gloves off and found standard wraps.

The story of the fearsome light-heavyweight champion's destruction was in every newspaper in the country. Sportswriters started speculating, "Could Coyle beat Johnson?"

Johnson, of course, was heavyweight champion Jack Johnson, the first Negro to ever win the title. He was talented and tough, but his arrogant personality and affinity for white women made him immensely unpopular.

The search for a "Great White Hope" began almost as soon as he won the title. James J. Jeffries, who had been a fearsome champion, came out of retirement to give Johnson his comeuppance. Johnson gave him a savage beating.

After the "Could Coyle Beat Johnson?" story broke, Sam Landon, the number one contender, said Eddie would have to go over him to get Johnson. Jess Willard, the number two contender, refused to comment. According to his manager Johnson was touring Europe and fighting exhibitions to stay in shape.

The real reason was the authorities were trying to throw Johnson in jail for violating the Mann Act. The Mann Act was "transporting women across state lines for immoral or illegal purposes." The law was designed to deter criminals in Texas, Arizona and other southwestern states from kidnapping poor Mexican women and forcing them into prostitution. It was also to stop "dirty old men" and pedophiles from buying young girls from dirt-poor families in the South and taking them to states like Louisiana or Mississippi where one could legally marry a twelve or thirteen-year-old girl.

The woman in question was Johnson's over-twenty-one-year-old white wife, Lucille, who was with him in Europe. Grapevine had it that Johnson's mother was gravely ill and Lucille was homesick as well. Johnson's lawyer was negotiating a deal to allow him back into the States without a jail term. The deal included a stipulation that he would have one last big money fight, win, lose or draw, and retire into private life. Johnson's wily manager dropped hints that Johnson's finale might be against the winner of the Coyle-Landon fight. Sportswriters went nuts. The buzz grew and grew, until finally an offer was on the table -- $30,000.00 to fight Landon. Word was the winner would get double that to meet Johnson.

"I'll beat this guy, Doc, I promise. Then we get Johnson or Willard, and we'll retire filthy rich."

"You can't beat Johnson or Willard either one," Doc said. "And you've never thrown a fight in your life. You'll get killed."

"No, I won't. People will have to pay more than twenty dollars to watch my execution," Eddie quipped.

Doc laughed. "Bullshit aside, can you beat Landon?"

"I'll murder the bum," Eddie said. "I came out of that last fight at 188, which means no dieting or sweating in training. I'll eat good and I'll live in the gym until I can eat nails and shit steel wool. For thirty grand, I'd fight Landon and Johnson at the same time. For fifty, I'd whip their asses."

Doc laughed. "All right. I'll set the fight with Landon and make our usual side bets. Then we'll talk about the future. I know you want a title, Eddie. God knows I want you to have one. If I train one world champion, I can make a killing off the fight game until I'm a hundred if I live that long. But I don't want to do it at the price of my best friend's life. They say every great fighter has a last fight left in him. Problem is, you fuckers will never admit when that last one has come and gone."

"You tell me when that time comes, Doc, and I'll listen," Eddie said.

"I'm serious," Doc replied. "I don't want to see you with cauliflower ears, blind in one eye, slurring your words and begging some fuck of a promoter for one last fight at the age of forty-five."

"We've got enough money saved so that won't happen," Eddie said.

"It ain't the money, Eddie, it's the cheers of the crowd. Jeffries had a dairy and a government beef contract. He had a bunch of kids and more money than he could spend. He literally was fat and happy. I heard he was 330 pounds when he started training for his comeback. So he got down to 227. Johnson practically killed him. He's still disabled from that fight. But he wanted to hear the crowd one more time and his pride wouldn't let him quit when he saw it was hopeless."

"His manager should have thrown in the towel," Eddie said. "I'm hoping you'd do that if I was gettin' killed."

"I will. One more thing," Doc said.

"What?"

"Kick his ass."

Eddie grinned. "I'm a mean son-of-a-bitch, remember?"

"I remember," Doc replied.

Eddie trained like a man possessed. He quit drinking booze and went to bed by 10:00 p.m. every night. He ran five miles and did 800 sit-ups a day. He chopped down trees every day and stood in a swimming pool in water up to his neck and punched underwater. He sparred eight rounds a day with contenders. He whipped himself into a finely honed fighting machine. When he started out he had only youth and balls to get him through. Now he truly was a professional.

Five days before the fight, Doc made him stop training.

"You won't lose your edge in a week," he said. Doc didn't want him over-trained or fighting with a pulled muscle.

Landon had a well-deserved reputation as an excellent boxer. For five rounds, he moved around Eddie, stabbing him with his left jab, and occasionally landing a right. However, every time Landon threw that crisp left jab, Eddie slammed his right fist down on Landon's forearm. The jab was getting less crisp by the minute, and Eddie's relentless body attack was taking its toll. Landon was slowing down. Once in the sixth and once in the seventh Eddie brought the crowd to its feet with stunning flurries that nearly knocked Landon out. The crowd was still on its feet when the eighth round started.

From the eighth through the twelfth the pattern was the same. Eddie sunk both hands deep into Landon's midsection. He bulled him along the ropes, firing short rights and hefty hooks to the head, while Landon gamely fought back.

In the thirteenth round, Landon reverted to boxing and possibly could have finished the fight with a narrow decision, but his ego got the better of him. He wasn't going to be taken the distance by a puffed-up light-heavyweight, no matter how supernatural he was. Coyle was going down.

The fourteenth round went the same. Landon gamely trying for a knockout while Eddie landed wicked pinpoint rights over Landon's weakened left and slammed vicious hooks to the body. Before the fifteenth round, Landon was spitting up blood. Eddie's eyes were almost swelled shut.

"Open my eyes!" he growled at his cut man.

"Eddie, I'm stopping the fight," Doc said.

"You stop this fight and I'll kill you. Open my eyes."

"It'll leave a scar and need stitches," the cut man said.

"I've got scars and I've had stitches before."

Doc held up a towel to hide the squirting blood, while the cut man slashed Eddie's eyebrow with a razor blade. The pressure released, he could see better.

When the bell rang they met in the center of the ring like a train wreck. Each man was going for broke, and neither man gave an inch. Late in the round Eddie retreated and Landon bulled forward after him. Eddie stopped suddenly, planted his feet and launched a howitzer of a right hand. The timing was exquisite. He caught Landon coming in, dead on the jaw. Landon's head snapped back like his neck was broken, his knees buckled. Eddie slammed a left hook to the head and, as Landon staggered back, he fired a left-right combination to the head. Landon put both his gloves out in front of him, kind of feeling for direction. A final, savage left hook sent Landon through the ropes and out of the ring. The referee started counting and, as he reached eight, the bell rang. A man could only be saved by the bell in the last round, which it was. Landon was out for ten minutes.

The announcer announced the decision. "Ladies and gentlemen, we have a split decision." The crowd erupted in boos. "Judge Stevens scored it 143-142 for Landon." More boos. "Judge Greenwell scores it 144-141 for Coyle." The crowd erupted in cheers. "Judge Baylor scored it 143-142 for Landon."

The crowd started throwing things and several fights broke out. Eddie and Doc went to congratulate Landon's manager, only because they didn't want to look like sore losers in front the newspaper reporters there. Landon was still being attended to by the ringside doctor. Eddie saw Landon's name already engraved on the belt, which they weren't supposed to do that until after the fight.

"What the hell is this?" Eddie yelled.

Landon's manager appealed to Doc. "C'mon, Doc, you know how it is. Nobody expected a washed-up light-heavyweight to whomp the ass of the best fighter in the world."

"I've never seen a fight fixed so bad the winner needs an ambulance and the loser is standing here looking at a belt that's not supposed to be engraved until the next day."

"Well, there's nothing you can do about it now."

Doc grabbed the belt away from Landon's manager and took the microphone from the announcer. He told the crowd about the belt being engraved before the fight was over and threw the belt out into the crowd. A riot ensued, and Doc and Eddie barely got out. The arena was destroyed. Eddie went to the nearest hospital to get his eyes sewn up and be checked out. He bitched and swore all the way there.

At the hospital Eddie needed 21 stitches above his eyes, most of that damage inflicted by his own cut man before the fifteenth round.

"That right eye is damaged," the doctor said. "There's blood in it."

"No shit!" Eddie said sarcastically. "I just went fifteen rounds with the number one heavyweight contender."

"No, I mean there's blood in the eyeball. That's bad. We need to run some tests," the doctor said.

"How long will it take?" Eddie asked.

"We'll have to keep you overnight."

"No, I want to see my wife and kids."

"If you care about them, let him do the tests," Doc said. "Your wife and kids don't need you dropping dead of a brain hemorrhage a month from now. I'll take your wife and kids back to the hotel, champ."

"Who are you talking to?" Eddie said sullenly.

"I'm talkin' to you," Doc replied. "If anyone deserves to be called 'champ' more than you, he ain't been born yet."

The next morning, Eddie waited impatiently for the doctor to give him the news. His head was pounding and he'd been pissing blood all morning. He'd already taken six aspirin and the nurse wouldn't give him any more.

"You have a detached retina," the doctor said. "It'll heal, but you'll lose some peripheral vision. I recommend you quit boxing, because if the eye gets damaged again, you could go blind in it. We'll keep you today for observation to make sure you don't have other injuries. If everything checks out okay, you can go home tomorrow."

Eddie's wife came to see him. She was a petite twenty-year-old blonde with big blue eyes. He'd met her in 1910 on the Barbary Coast. He and Doc had come to town for a big money fight. Doc had wanted to get laid, so they went to the Red Garter Brothel. Doc took two girls back to the room and Eddie waited at the bar. He noticed a beautiful young girl sweeping the floor, emptying the ashtrays, washing glasses behind the bar and just generally cleaning up.

"Could I trouble you for a cup of coffee?" he asked.

"Whiskey or beer not to your liking?" she replied.

"I never get drunk before a fight," he said.

"You're a prizefighter?" she asked.

"Yes."

"You must be a good one."

"How would you know that just looking at me?" he asked.

"Your face and how you talk. Your nose is pretty straight, you don't have any vegetation on your ears, and you don't slur your words. That means you hit them a lot more than they hit you. That's the point isn't it?" she said.

"It is. What's your name?" Eddie asked.

"Why do you care? Don't you see any girls you like? Don't tell me a prizefighter's never been to a cat house before."

Eddie laughed. "I've been to these places before.

I only came tonight because my manager wanted to. I have women falling all over me all the time."

"Must be rough," she interjected sarcastically.

"You don't understand," he replied. "There's a certain type of woman that likes celebrities, baseball players, singers, rodeo riders, prizefighters, circus trapeze artists, whatever. They'll do anything just so they can say they had relations with you. If the guy wasn't a baseball player or a singer or a prizefighter, they wouldn't give him the time of day. Shit, excuse my language."

"I understand. You were just using them," she said.

"No, you don't," he replied. "It might sound funny coming from a man, but they were using me. They didn't like me, they liked the idea of me. My boyfriend's a big-time prizefighter, so that makes me big-time. Just once I'd like to meet a woman who was interested in Eddie the man instead of Eddie 'The Animal' Coyle the prizefighter."

"I'm interested in Eddie the man," she said.

"What's your name?" he asked again.

"Mary Nolan," she said, putting her broom down and starting to make a pot of coffee.

"Tell me about yourself, Mary Nolan."

"I was born in San Francisco sixteen years ago. I never knew my father. My mother didn't want to raise a little girl in a brothel, so she left me with my aunt and uncle. They lost everything in the earthquake of 1906. My mother brought me here and had me work as a maid. I'll be leaving pretty soon."

"Where will you go?" Eddie asked.

"I don't know. I won't be a prostitute because my aunt raised me a Catholic. I don't see myself being a maid here for the next twenty years either. I'll work something out."

"Want to come to the fight tomorrow?" he asked.

"Why would I pay to see a man I don't know get beat up?"

"Number one, I'm not gonna get beat up, I'm gonna win," Eddie said. "You said yourself, you knew I was good. Number two, it won't cost you anything. I'll have my manager get you a ringside seat. Number three, we're going to have coffee and get to know each other."

"Okay," she replied, and poured two cups of coffee.

They talked for forty-five minutes. Doc came out with two girls on his arm.

"Doc, will you get my lady friend a ringside seat tomorrow?"

"Absolutely," Doc replied.

"What time is the fight?" Mary asked.

"Four o'clock," Doc said.

"I'll be there," Mary said, smiling.

Eddie and Doc were waiting for the fight to start when Mary came up to them. Eddie thought she was pretty in work clothes, but when he saw her in a dress and her hair done, he was really smitten.

"Cinderella there cleans up nice," Doc said.

"Fuck you," Eddie replied.

"I mean it, she looks good."

"Thanks for coming," Eddie said.

"Thanks for inviting me," she replied, smiling.

"Give our gladiator here a kiss for good luck, and I'll show you to your seat," Doc said.

Eddie glowered at him, but she sidled up to him and kissed him lightly on the lips. "Good luck," she said and Doc led her away.

When Doc returned, Eddie was shadow boxing. "I thought you warmed up already," he said.

"I did. I just don't want to cool down," Eddie replied.

"You won't cool down in three minutes. You nervous 'cause your girlfriend's in the front row?" Doc asked.

Eddie rolled his eyes. "I'm nervous because this guy's a contender with fifteen straight knockouts." Doc punched him in the stomach. Eddie was in pretty good shape, but it hurt because it was unexpected. "What'd you do that for?" Eddie growled.

Doc grinned. "Now you're not nervous. Now you're pissed off."

"You really are a prick, Doc," Eddie said sullenly.

"Everybody's got to be good at something," Doc replied, and Eddie laughed involuntarily. They made their way to the ring.

Just before the bell, Doc spoke. "Oh, yeah, I forgot to tell you, I bet every cent on you winning in the first round."

"Shrewd," Eddie replied. "I love training for three months and then fighting for free. When I'm done kicking his ass, I'm gonna kick yours."

The bell rang. Eddie ran across the ring and engaged the other fighter in an immediate slugfest. The guy was taken back by Eddie's furious assault and tried to retaliate. The crowd was on its feet the whole first round. Near the end of the round, Eddie decked the fighter for an eight-count with a picture perfect left hook. He got up and, as Eddie moved in for the kill, the bell rang. The referee sent them to their respective corners.

"Don't you say a fuckin' word!" Eddie snapped as he came back to the corner.

"Can I say seven words?" Doc asked.

"Seven."

"I really bet you'd win inside three," Doc said.

"The whole purse?"

"No, only a grand, at ten to one."

"You're a genius," Eddie said.

"I know that. This guy had never been knocked down before a few seconds ago. That's how I got such long odds.

I know you still love me," Doc said.

"I still love you, and you're still a prick. And I may still kick your ass."

The bell rang and Eddie launched another furious assault. If the other fighter had been smart, he would have gotten on his bicycle and let Eddie wear himself out chasing him, but he wasn't smart. His manager had told him that very thing after the first round.

"Fireman" Jim Flynn had steamrolled his first twenty-nine opponents, winning twenty-five by knockout, nineteen in the first round. So the guy had landed a lucky punch. He was going to slug it out with the asshole regardless of what his manager said.

Big mistake. Halfway through the second round, Flynn's manager was screaming at him to disengage and box. Doc was smiling smugly. They screwed up. Eddie could be out-boxed, but he couldn't be outfought in a brawl. Doc knew the fight had gone into the trenches, where Eddie whistled while he worked. Eddie could be hit, but not easily or often. He bobbed and weaved, rolled his shoulders, and feinted left and right, and cut off the ring. Flynn came straight in and paid a terrible price, walking into power shots, which were Eddie's specialty. Flynn was dropped for another eight-count before the round was over.

"You can't slug with this guy!" Flynn's manager yelled between rounds.

"I can slug with anyone," Flynn growled.

"Yeah? Then how come you've been on your ass twice and he's still standin'?"

"I'll get him."

"Only if you start boxing or let me slip some cement in your gloves," the manager said.

"Finish this bum, and let's go celebrate," Doc said.

"He ain't a bum," Eddie replied. "I've hit him so goddamned hard, I thought it broke my hands and he still gets up."

"Then break your fuckin' hands!" Doc yelled. "I'll count the money we win while you're healing. This is it.

He lasts this round, and we might as well throw in the towel."

"You underestimated him," Eddie said.

"No, I overestimated you," Doc replied.

Eddie shot him a murderous look. The bell rang before either one could speak.

The third round started with the crowd still on its feet. Flynn started boxing, finally taking his manager's advice. Late in the round, Eddie was on flypaper legs, his nose bleeding. Flynn threw a somewhat lazy jab and Eddie whipsawed his right over it. The punch landed on Flynn's jaw with crushing force and his legs buckled. As he stumbled, Eddie landed another thunderous right to his head. Flynn's chin hit his chest and he fell facedown. The referee counted him out and the crowd went wild.

Doc climbed in the ring and hugged Eddie. They danced the jig in the ring. Mary climbed in and danced with them. The crowd cheered wildly, thinking they were happy over the victory. The crowd couldn't possibly know that Eddie and Doc were so happy because they'd quadrupled their prize money off Doc's bet.

Eddie went to the lockers and got dressed. After collecting from the promoter, Doc went back to the brothel, and Eddie and Mary went out to dinner. Eddie really liked her. She was smart beyond her years, obviously having gone to the school of hard knocks, and she didn't give a shit about boxing. She liked him for the man he was, not his image.

Eddie walked her back to the brothel. He kissed her on the porch. She melted into his arms, and her lips and tongue were incredibly soft.

"Oh, my," was all she said.

"I better be going," Eddie said.

"Thank you very much, this is a day I'll never forget," Mary replied.

"Neither will I."

"Where are you going from here?" she asked.

"I don't know, maybe Reno. Doc's negotiating a fight right now, but it probably won't happen for a month or two. I'd like to see you again," he said.

"I'd like to see you again, too."

"Let me know what your schedule is, maybe I'll come see you fight again," she said. She turned to go inside, when Eddie called her name. She turned back around.

"You want to get married?" he asked.

"When?" she asked, surprised.

"Right now, tonight," he said.

"You can do that?"

"Yes, you can. What do you say?"

"I say 'yes.'"

"Then go pack. I'll wait here."

Mary was packing her clothes when her mother came to the door of her room.

"Going somewhere?" she asked.

"To get married," Mary replied.

"To that prizefighter? What future do you think you'll have with him?" her mother sneered skeptically.

"What future do you think I'll have here?" Mary shot back.

"He'll use you and walk away."

"He wouldn't have proposed marriage if he wanted to do that."

"He might."

"Look, Mom, I'm sorry my father left you alone and pregnant. I don't think all men are like that, although you obviously do. I'm making my choice in life, just like you made yours. I'll write and tell you where I am."

"Good luck. And I hope I'm wrong about your man," her mother said.

"Thank you."

Mary kissed her mother goodbye and went out to meet Eddie.

They got married in a small ceremony in San Rafael, after taking a ferry ride. It was after midnight when they got back to the hotel Eddie was staying at.

Eddie went into the bathroom to piss. When he came out the room was dark. He made his way to the bed, undressed, and slipped in. He reached out and touched the silky bare skin of her back. She had not put anything on and this delighted him. He pulled on her shoulder so she would turn to him. He kissed her eager mouth and she wrapped her arms around his neck. Their bodies came together in one silken line of electricity. He rolled his muscled body on top of hers, crushing her breasts against him, still kissing her. She was surging against him in a virginal erotic frenzy.

She gave a little gasp when he entered her and her eyes became wide.

He took her face in his hands and said, "It's okay. I'll go slow."

She wrapped her satiny legs around his hips and kissed him again. "Go however you want," she said, her eyes shining with tears.

That night, and many nights that followed, Eddie Coyle came to understand the premium put on virginity by socially primitive people. It was a period of sensuality that he had never before experienced, a sensuality mixed with a feeling of masculine power. In those first days Mary became almost his slave. Given trust and affection, a young full-blooded girl aroused from virginity to erotic awareness was as delicious as an exactly ripe fruit. Eddie could not get enough of Mary's beautifully sculpted teenage body, her huge blue eyes glowing with passion. She had a fresh smell, a fleshy smell perfumed by her sex, yet sweet and exiting. Her virginal passion matched his machismo lust and it was often dawn when they went to sleep exhausted. Sometimes, spent but not sleepy, Eddie sat on the dresser and stared at Mary's naked body while she slept. Her face was lovely in repose, like those he had seen in art books.

Madonnas who by no stretch of artist's skill could be virginal. He remembered the morning after their wedding night.

Doc was pounding on the door. A bleary-eyed Eddie opened it. Doc stepped into the room.

"Where in the hell were you?" he said indignantly, like a father scolding a child who was late.

Eddie shook his head but didn't answer. Doc saw a small bare foot and the lower half of a slender female leg sticking out of the blanket. A mop of blonde hair stirred and the girl sat up, covering her breasts with the blanket.

"Hello, Doc," she said cheerily, completely unfazed by his presence.

"Hello, honey," Doc replied, recognizing the girl from the fight.

"I got married," Eddie said. "You remember Mary."

"Congratulations. Mary, would you mind if I took Eddie outside for a minute?" Doc said.

"No," the girl said flatly.

"Call room service and order some breakfast and champagne," Eddie said.

The girl eagerly picked up the phone as Eddie and Doc went out into the hall.

"Are you out of your fuckin' mind? How old is she?"

"Sixteen."

"At least that's the age of consent, thank Christ," Doc groaned. "Didn't I teach you anything?"

"Kiss my ass," Eddie retorted. "Your mamma, my mamma, and everyone else's mamma I know got married and had kids, the whole shootin' match by the time they were sixteen, or seventeen, or eighteen. You taught me, 'Don't be a whore chaser like me. Get you a young girl, straight from her mamma and raise her up like a good birddog.' You remember saying that? She ain't a birddog, she's a wonderful girl, and I don't need you tellin' me I made a mistake by getting married. I ain't the nice kid with the cast iron chin and sledgehammer left that you remember. I been around all these years too. I'm getting' goddamned tired of you tellin' me what to do."

"Maybe I oughta stop tellin' you what to do. At least personally," Doc replied. "I got two failed marriages, so I ain't one to talk. If you're happy, I'm happy. I just don't want...."

"Me to stop being a ruthless killer because I married a young girl?" Eddie said, cutting him off.

"Yeah, something like that," Doc said.

"Don't worry."

"Can I have some champagne?"

"No."

"Why not?"

Eddie grinned. "If women weaken legs, I'll have a noticeable limp by tonight." Doc laughed uproariously.

"Ed, are you listening to me?" his wife said, snapping him out of his reminiscence.

"I'm sorry, I didn't hear you," he said.

"I said I wish you'd retire. I don't want to be a widow or have to care for a vegetable because you got your brains beat out. We've got two little boys to look out for. We've got money. You said when we got married that you'd retire when you hit thirty. You're gonna be thirty-three in July."

Eddie closed his eyes and thought for a minute. His first son, Rafe, was born in 1911. His second son, John, was born in 1913. Like a lot of boxer's wives, the initial excitement of a man who fought for a living wore off quickly and she didn't like to go on the road with them. She wanted to see New York, however, so she and the kids came along on the trip.

"This is probably my last fight," he said.

She kissed him on the cheek. "I'm gonna hold you to that. You change your mind and you'll have the strongest legs in the world," she said. It was a myth that having sex before a fight weakened a fighter's legs.

"Point taken," he replied.

"I'll take the kids back to the hotel," she said. "Call me if they release you before tonight. Otherwise we'll bring you dinner. I know you hate hospital food."

The doctor said Eddie had to stay the night, until he stopped urinating blood. The doctor wanted to make sure his kidneys weren't damaged. Eddie grudgingly agreed.

Doc filed a grievance with the boxing commission.

The commissioner was fired and replaced with a member of the licensing board, but it didn't make Doc and Eddie feel any better. The commission ruled that although the commissioner had acted improperly in having the belt prematurely engraved, the rules clearly stated that a man could be saved by the bell in the last round. They further stated that if they reversed the decision, it might set a precedent that anytime the fans didn't like a decision, they'd riot.

"The hell with 'em," Eddie said. "We'll take on Johnson, and retire filthy rich."

"You won't live to spend the money," Doc said.

"Bullshit," Eddie replied.

"No, that's serious shit!" Doc yelled, slapping Eddie across the face with his left hand. Eddie glowered at him, balling up his fists. "You never saw that comin'," Doc said. "I'm a fifty-year-old hustler who's never set foot in a boxing ring. What do you think the heavyweight champion of the world would do to you?"

"Hurt me bad," Eddie conceded.

"No," Doc said. "He'd hurt you permanent."

"Permanent."

"You've got the heart, but you ain't got the tools no more. You've had your last great fight, Eddie. You said you'd listen when I told you."

Eddie started to cry. "I don't know how to do anything else. You took me out of that shit town and we've been ridin' high ever since. I don't want it to end. You've been like a father to me."

"I'm damn proud to call you my son," Doc said. "It doesn't have to end. You've got a helluva name now. We'll buy Murphy's Gym in San Francisco and remodel it. We'll have fighters beating down the door for you to train them and me to manage their money. We still get to go to big money fights and make a killing. Only difference is the blood we clean up isn't ours."

"I like that idea. I know Mary will like it," Eddie said.

"It's good business and it's the right thing to do," Doc said.

"If we're gonna be partners, I need to know right now, are you a choirboy or are you a mean son-of-a-bitch?" Eddie said, grinning.

"I taught you, didn't I?" Doc replied, laughing and hugging Eddie. "You're the toughest fuckin' choirboy I ever saw."

"And you're the most soft-hearted prick I ever knew."

Doc wiped his eyes. "Look at us, two mean sons-a-bitches crying on each other's shoulder. Now go call your wife and tell her about our new business venture."

"I should get more than half," Eddie said.

"Fuck you. You're wearing me out," Doc said laughing. "Tell Mary to bring me a steak too. I hate hospital food more than you."

"No one hates hospital food more than me," Eddie said, and dialed the phone.

Rough and Ready, California, 1930:

Kate Thompson propped her bare feet up on the ottoman in front of the chair. She sipped her tea and wiggled her toes. Sitting across the parlor, Red smiled and nodded, acknowledging her signal. Two of the ladies who lived in the house were also reading in the parlor. If she sat down to read and had socks on, it meant that it was a certain time of the month, or she was just tired. If she was barefoot, that meant she wanted Red to come to her room after everyone else was asleep. Occasionally, she'd sit down wearing socks, and then casually take them off as if her feet were hot.

It made a discreet, yet unmistakable signal. The system was Katy's idea, so not to offend the ladies living in her house.

It was after midnight when Red sneaked into her room.

"Who's there?" she said theatrically.

"The boogieman," Red replied.

She threw the blanket back to reveal her naked body. "I'm just a poor, helpless widow. Have your way, but don't kill me, boogieman," she said, trying not to laugh.

"I can't promise that," Red said.

"Why not?"

"I might screw you to death."

She spread her legs and put her hands over her eyes. "Do your worst, boogieman."

"Don't you mean my best?" he asked.

She burst out laughing. "Best or worst, I don't care, just get it over with."

"Turn over," he said.

"No, not that, boogieman," she pleaded in mock fear.

"Turn over," he whispered more forcefully.

She obeyed, it was her favorite position. She'd lay on her stomach with her ankles crossed. He'd mount her from behind. It drove her wild and he liked the feeling of his balls bouncing off her ass. She chewed on the pillow to avoid waking the house with her squeals.

Later, she was lying next to him, playing with his genitals with her hands. He got another erection.

"Can you be quiet?" he asked.

"I can't make noise if my mouth's full," she said.

"That's true," Red said, and enjoyed the feeling.

The next day started out like any other day. The day, however, would change the course of his entire life. The day would set in motion a chain of events that would change not only Red's life, but many others, and perhaps the course of the labor movement in the western United States.

Pete Jackson asked Red to come to a union meeting.

The man who owned the oil field wanted to develop it. As usual Clawson Construction was the front-runner to get the contract. Maretti wanted a percentage. The owner wanted to pay a flat fee. Negotiations were ongoing. The union was planning to organize the workers. Pete figured since Maretti would probably get the contract, and Red had successfully negotiated with Maretti before, perhaps he could help Jackson do something preemptively, before a big problem erupted. Red addressed the workers.

"Some of you are mine workers, some of you are transient laborers. I'll tell you a law of nature. Lone wolves are easy prey. That's why wolves run in packs.

I learned that on the streets of San Francisco. There's strength in unity. There's strength in number. However, a great military strategist for Napoleon once said that some of the greatest battles you win are the ones you don't fight. Let me and Pete try to work something out before getting yourselves all riled up for a fight. The owner of the oil field is a businessman. The owners of the construction company are businessmen. This battle may be fought in an office. Stick with Pete and let's see what happens."

The members applauded Red's speech, then Pete and Red answered the men's questions.

Kate was making dinner when George Steeley showed up at her door. He was a little drunk.

He said, "I have business with Red."

"He's at the union hall, go catch him there," she said and closed the door.

She went back into the kitchen. She started to continue making biscuits when someone hit the back of her head. She fell forward onto the table, dazed. He grabbed a fistful of her hair, pinning her head to the table. She felt him pull her dress up and heard him fumbling with his pants.

"I'm gonna get a little taste of what Sullivan's been getting."

"He's not getting anything here, but a room and meals," she said.

"Sure, honey, whatever you say."

Kate grabbed the bowl the batter was in and smashed it on his head. The man reeled backward.

"You fuckin' bitch!" he snarled.

She punched him in the face as hard as she could.

She then grabbed a butcher knife out of the rack and began swinging it at his head. "You bastard! I'll cut your god damned head off," she shrieked.

He staggered out the door. Kate stood by the table, shaking.

She was still holding the knife when Red came in.

"What's wrong?" he asked.

"George Steeley tried to assault me," she said.

"In what manner?" Red asked, shocked.

"In an unmentionable manner," Kate said forcefully.

Red got the drift and he started out the door. She went after him.

"Red, it's okay. I ran him off. He won't try it again," she said.

"You're god damn right he won't," Red snarled.

"Red, please, it's not worth it. This town isn't worth it."

"It's worth it to me," Red said, and went into the saloon he knew Steeley drank at.

George was too stupid to know when to be quiet. When he saw Red walk in, he said, "Hey, Sullivan, your bitch tell you I visited her?"

He didn't even put his hands up when Red walked up to him. Red punched him in the face and George fell off the barstool, twin jets of blood pouring from his destroyed nose.

"Yeah, she did," Red said as he grabbed George by the neck and his belt and threw him through the big window of the bar.

Steeley landed in the street in a shower of glass and blood. Red went outside and started kicking him in the face, the ribs, the ass, anywhere he could. George threw up and passed out.

John Steeley ran over and tackled Red. They wrestled on the ground for a minute or two before they stood. Red had pulled Steeley's shirt up over his head, pinning his arms. Red took advantage of the opportunity and punched Steeley in the face twice, knocking him on his ass. Steeley stood up, ripping his shirt off.

"Fuck Maretti and fuck you!" he yelled. "You're gonna die!"

"Not today," Red said as he came forward.

Steeley was a big man, 6'2" and about 240 pounds. About thirty of that was fat around his middle and he got winded quickly. However, like an old wounded lion, he was still dangerous and hit hard, even though he was taking three to land one because of Red's boxing ability. Finally, Red landed about five unanswered punches and Steeley went down. Red dragged him to a horse trough and started to drown him.

"Red, don't do it!" the sheriff yelled. He was on Maretti's payroll too. "You don't want to get the chair or do life for a piece of shit like him. I'll call Maretti and straighten this out."

Red threw Steeley out in the street. He coughed up water and gasped for air. "Call Maretti," Red said and stomped home, with Kate in pursuit.

Red was looking in the mirror at his bruised face.

"I don't recall getting hit that much," he said, almost to himself.

"He hit you a lot," Kate said. "But you walked through his punches and pulverized him anyway."

"Well, I've got to go straighten this out," he said.

"What's to straighten out? You won the fight," Kate said.

"You don't know anything about gangsters, or wanna-be gangsters."

"Then educate me," Kate said.

"I'm not afraid of any man," Red said. "Maretti knows I'd kill Steeley and his brother in a second if I thought they were coming after me. Normally, he wouldn't give two shits if I killed some Irish thug in a dump mining town. But if I do that, maybe the mine deal falls apart, maybe the oil deal falls apart. That he does care about and he'd have to do something about it or lose face with other Dons. It's real grease ball shit, going back to the old country. I'm in a perfect position. I try to negotiate peace. If Steeley's so stupid that he refuses, then I get Maretti's permission to kill him, or maybe Tony does it himself and I don't have to lift a finger. Either way I come out smelling like a rose. I grew up around these guys, I know how they think," Red finished.

"Be careful," Kate said.

"I will."

Red took his semi-automatic Colt .45 ACP pistol that his brother gave him when he returned from the war from under the bed. Red didn't normally carry a gun, but he figured it was better to have it and not need it than need it and not have it. *Steeley might be stupid enough to try to take Maretti on.*

He cocked it, put the safety on, and stuffed it in his pants behind his right hip. He kissed Kate and left for the meeting at John Steeley's house. Maretti had guaranteed his safety. Red knew it was the .45 that guaranteed it.

He always made sure he had an option, no matter what the situation.

Red arrived John Steeley's house and went into the living room. Maretti and two of his bodyguards were there. Steeley had one of his employees make everyone a drink.

"What is the problem, gentlemen?" Maretti asked. "The mine's finished making money hand over fist and then I get a call from the sheriff saying my two top guys in this town are trying to kill each other."

"His brother tried to rape my girlfriend," Red said.

"He left when she asked him," Steeley said.

"She 'asked' with a pot over the head, swinging a butcher knife," Red retorted.

"He tried to kill me."

"If I wanted to kill you, you'd be dead."

"Enough!" Maretti yelled.

"I'll tell you both something about running a business. In Sicily right now, the economy is shit. You only gain respect by killing other men, so nobody works anymore. Women do all the work because there's no men around. There's no men around because they're all dead from vendetta. The only business is foreigners who set up export businesses for products like olive oil and wine, and they get most of the profits. Anybody smart is over here or in Europe. You can't make a living there. I don't tolerate vendettas in the city and I won't allow them here. Red, you respect me as the boss. I expect you to be professional with anyone I ask you to work with. Steeley, I expect you to treat my men with respect. Taking a shot at a guy's girl is not a sign of respect. We'll put this behind us and continue working on the oil deal." Maretti pulled $300.00 out of his pocket and gave it to Red. "Take a couple weeks off, maybe take your woman somewhere. Be ready to work with no animosity when you come back."

"Thank you," Red said.

"You're welcome," Maretti replied. "I need to talk to John in private."

Red left and Maretti made sure he was gone before speaking again.

"Look," Maretti said, "you're on commission, remember? I'm a businessman. I look at assets and liabilities. The bottom line is all that matters. Sullivan is an asset. Your dumb-ass brother is a liability. Figure out the bottom line on that."

Maretti motioned at his men and they left without another word.

The problem that arose with the proposed oil pipeline came about because the owners of the oil field, unlike the Steeleys, were not desperate for capital. They made enough off the one functional well to pay for development without offering a percentage. Unbeknownst to Red, Clawson Construction got the contract by threatening off any other bidders. The union organized the workers who wanted to work on the pipeline. The owner of the oil field said they had to negotiate with the construction company because they were hiring the workers. Maretti refused to negotiate. Pissed off that he was only getting paid for construction, he wanted a bigger piece. He figured if people refused to work, he'd bring in his own people and get more profit from the project.

The plan backfired because the mine workers went on strike to support the oil workers. Maretti wasn't getting any revenue from the mine and he had to listen to John Steeley bitch all the time. He made more than enough from his other enterprises, so it didn't really hurt him financially, but it was hurting his image of invincibility with other mobsters. He had to do something.

He sent men to straighten it out. He had an "ace in the hole" if his union contacts in the city bitched. He'd had Red put a no-strike clause in the contract for two years to ensure he could make his investment back without labor complications. It hadn't even been a year since the deal. Since the union broke the contract before he did, he could do what he wanted to recoup losses. If the mine workers refused to go back to work, they did so at their own peril. It would be his defense to powerful labor leaders and other mobsters -- either a contract is valid or it isn't.

Pete Jackson asked Red to go talk to Maretti to avoid violence and even got the union to pay him a tidy sum for the service. Kate was pissed when he said she couldn't go with him.

"It's business, and it may get ugly. I don't need to worry about protecting you. You're not going and that's it," he said.

"I thought you grew up around these guys. I thought they were your friends?" she sneered with sarcasm in her voice.

"I did grow up around them. One thing I learned in the neighborhood was your murderer comes with a friendly face. They catch you off guard and send someone or suggest a meeting with someone you can absolutely trust."

"Why would he set you up to be killed?" Kate asked, confused.

"You don't know anything about this business," Red said, exasperated. "You can't learn it in school and you can't get a late start. There's no one you can absolutely trust, except yourself. Tony himself told me one time. All of our people are businessmen. Their loyalty is based on that, nothing else. On that basis, anything's possible, even the unthinkable. I don't think he'll try to have me killed. I've never failed him before and maybe I can work something out to avoid a long, destructive war with the union people. He knows that.

"On the other hand, he knows I've made a little on the side from the union and he looks at me as a smart, tough businessman that he personally groomed. In his mind that makes me smarter than anyone else around him.

He could figure I've decided to leave the fold and be a player for the union on my own terms. If he really thought that was the case, he wouldn't want to, but he'll have to set an example or lose face with the organization. I have to go see which way the wind is blowing. If he doesn't kill me, my refusing a meeting would be a slight. A slight is not the action of a friend. I'm damned if I do, and damned if I don't."

"If you're so god damned smart, how'd you get in this mess?" she asked.

"Because of you!" he exploded. "I knew the first god damned day I was here that I should have said no, not with a ten-foot pole will I touch a powder keg like this. But I meet you, half-naked in your yard with attitude to match, and I let it cloud my judgment. I wanted you so bad that

I would risk anything to have you. A man once said, 'beware of what you want because you might get it.'"

"What the hell does that mean?" Kate yelled. "I've disappointed you? You self-righteous son-of-a-bitch! You just finished telling me that you're a career criminal.

I've wronged you in some way? How?"

"You haven't wronged me, I'm just saying you took no risk. If I'd never come along, your life wouldn't have changed that much."

"But it has changed!" she yelled. "You made me believe I could have a life other than being a caretaker for old ladies. I thought I might even have children one day. You vain, self-centered bastard, it's all about you. I haven't risked anything? What if your gangster buddies decide to burn my house or kidnap or kill me to send a message to you? What if you die in a blaze of glory over this crappy town? How do I go on? Do I give the next handsome drifter a chance, hoping he'll be different, or do I become the best whore in town because I like sex and no one's proposed, and the bastard might as well be paying for it? Do I become a miserable old spinster because I went to a Catholic school when I was little? Just what are my choices here? How do I save face?"

"If I think the situation is untenable, I'll tell Maretti I quit, that I'm out. We'll get married, and do whatever you want to do. If I can work something out, we'll ride it out, and get married anyway. Maybe move to the city. I hate this dump except for you. But you're more important to me than any job, or so-called respect from gangsters. The only respect I really care about is yours," Red finished.

"You make up your mind this week," she said. "I'm not riding anything out. You want me, then I'm yours. You want to play mobster, you do it without me. I'm not moving into some big house and living the good life, and then being destitute with two or three kids because you disrespected somebody according to some weird Sicilian code. I'd rather resign myself to this town and no future at all than have a taste of a good future and have it taken away. I've been there and done that, twice. Now go sleep in your own room. I'm not in the mood."

Red met Tony Maretti in San Francisco in the private room Tony had. There were several other big shots there, all mob men or San Francisco labor leaders.

"So, what does labor want from management?" Tony said theatrically.

"Since when do I have to ask your permission to tell someone, if I could, would you?" Red replied. "I stayed loyal to you all these years. Yeah, I made what I could on the side, but I never stole from you and I stayed loyal. I saved you a truckload of trouble over the mine. You owe it to me to at least listen to the proposal before dismissing it."

"Don't tell me what I owe or don't owe," Tony said.

Red stood up. "I'm outta here," he said. "I'm not gonna stand here and play Sicilian pissing match for whoever's here. You're the boss. Blow the whole goddamn town off the map, I don't give a shit. Become a legend like Capone. Except we both know that everyone's basically written Chicago off. There's no business there, just a bunch a cowboys killin' each other. Your reputation was made years ago, you don't have to prove anything to anybody. You're the one who told me violence was bad for business and should only be a last resort, not a reflex. It's a dirty little village in the middle of nowhere. It's not worth fighting over. I quit." Red started toward the door.

"Sit down," Maretti said.

One of Maretti's men came over. "You heard the man," the guy said.

"I'm not in the mood," Red said.

"Hey, fuck your mood," the guy sneered, reaching inside his jacket.

Red kneed him in the groin, head-butted him in the face and smashed his right elbow into the man's jaw. The thug dropped like a stone. Another one pulled out a gun.

"Jumbo, put the gun away," Maretti said calmly. "Red, come outside for a moment." Maretti stood up, motioned at his men, and then went into the public bar area of the restaurant with Red.

"You're all fucked up, aren't you, *amigo*?" Maretti said. "I'm playing with you, breakin' your balls a little, and you fly off the handle. Anybody else would be dead on the floor right now. I've known you your whole life. What's the problem?"

"I've met a woman and I want to settle down with her.

I don't want to get killed in a dispute over this deal," Red said.

"Is that all?" Maretti said. "You want to settle down, have kids? Come back here and I'll get you a pizza place with a numbers book next door. You run the pizza joint and take a silent piece of the book. Pizza guys don't get killed that much."

Red laughed. "You'd do that?" he asked.

"Sure. Even if you're not Sicilian, you're still like a son to me. You want a change, no problem. What a Don you'd have made if you weren't Irish," Tony replied. "Now come back in, act reprimanded, and tell me what you'd do for the record."

They went back to the private room. "I apologize for my outburst, Don Maretti," Red said. "I've been under a lot of strain lately. I meant no disrespect."

"God damned Irishman," Maretti said. "I'm breakin' the guy's balls a little and he flies off the handle. If

I wasn't his godfather, I'd have to shoot him. What do you do with an insolent Irish godson?"

Laughter pealed around the table. Red instantly caught Tony's drift.

"All due respect, Godfather, but you don't always sound like you're kidding," he said.

"No one's ever told me that before," Tony said, deadpan. "Is that true?" he asked his consigliore.

"I'm sorry to say, 'yes.' I don't know how many guys I've shot over your misunderstood jokes."

More laughter pealed around the table. Maretti knew he had control of the meeting once again.

"Give me your proposal," Maretti said.

Red began to speak. "A gambler once said, 'You have to know when to hold 'em and when to fold 'em.' Cut a deal with the union. Take your profit on the construction and your percentage of the mine. In a few years the gold and the oil will dry up again and it'll be a ghost town again. You don't need the bad publicity you'd get by making it a grudge fight."

"What about the next project, or the one after that?" Maretti asked.

"Take it on a case by case basis," Red said. "Screw those big shots back East. Do you tell Luciano how to run New York? Would he listen if you did? I know the street is watching. That bitch always is. She loves turmoil and feeds on it. The street is saying that Don Maretti's weak for not kicking ass at the slightest provocation. He's slipping. A used to be bad guy. People might even think they could take you down because you didn't immediately act like a savage." Red noticed some nervous fidgeting around the table. "Savages aren't businessmen. Savages don't look a year ahead, five years or ten years ahead. Businessmen do. You've always been a good businessman. Now if you'll excuse me, Don Maretti, I'd appreciate it. I'm not feeling well after the long drive."

"You're excused," Maretti said, almost imperceptibly nodding at Red.

Red caught it although he was sure no one else had.

Red left, satisfied with the events and knowing that Maretti wanted to talk without him around, but didn't want to make it obvious. The nod meant everything was okay, but that same old-country shit that he didn't need to be involved in was about to happen and that Tony was grateful for Red being smart enough to exit gracefully.

"What are you gonna do with that guy?" one of the other Capos asked.

"I'll tell you something about that guy," Tony replied. "I've know him since he was eleven. As you can see, he needs a wheelbarrow to carry his balls around in." Laughter pealed about the room. "Like a lot of things, we laugh because it's funny, but we also laugh because it's true. If he was Sicilian he'd have his own family. It's much better to have guys like that working for us instead of against us. We have to get away from this fourteenth century 'never question the Don no matter what' mentality if we want to survive in the modern world. I should whack the guy for stating irrefutable facts? That violence is bad for business? That people, maybe even some in this room, are saying unpleasant things about me? That Capone's an idiot? That I don't need to waste my time and money on some shitty little burg up north that doesn't make in a month what I lose on a weekend at the track?" More laughter. "I'll remind him which side his bread's buttered on."

"I think he knows that," another Don said. "I think that's why he was ill."

Maretti knew he had maintained control of his empire without firing a shot.

France, 1944:

John Henry "Hank" Collins lay in a foxhole somewhere outside Versailles. After the successful invasion of June 6th at Omaha Beach, Normandy, the Allied forces had marched steadily into France. He was sweating his ass off. It wasn't really any worse than a typical Missouri summer, but it was hot.

He'd left Lynchburg in 1939 at the age of sixteen. While the coasts had pretty much recovered from the depression then, the rural south and Midwest was still pretty poor. His family did all right because they owned farmland free and clear and could raise their own food. He heard that General Motors was opening a new car plant near St. Louis, so he went there looking for work. He lied and said he was eighteen. He got a job at the car plant and was doing all right.

Then in December 1941, Japan attacked Pearl Harbor and America entered the war. He got drafted in 1942. At that time, they called up men twenty-one to thirty-six years old. He was only nineteen, but he thought if he complained and revealed his real age he'd lose his job or go to jail, so he went in the Army. He actually turned twenty-one in France.

The day before he left for basic training he called his grandfather for advice. Hank always admired Allen and cherished the memory of Allen getting away with burning down the sawmill. Allen was ninety-one years old, but still sharp as a tack.

"Damn, boy, I hate that they got you," he said. "I was about sixty-five or sixty-six when America entered the First World War. Because some son-of-a-bitch shot the Archduke of some little shit European country in 1914.

88

The Archduke -- he wasn't even the fuckin' king! I remember all the political experts I used to argue with. Their main argument was that the British were involved so we had to help. Didn't we fight two wars with the English because we didn't want to do what they wanted? People I knew lost sons and husbands and brothers. The ones that came back were shell-shocked and all fucked up. It didn't change life in America one ounce except for the poor bastards that died and their families.

"Shit. Now it's happened all over again. I tell you, Roosevelt did the right thing by trying to stay out of this mess. Even now, it was Japan who attacked us. We should blow the shit out of Japan and let Hitler, Stalin and Churchill fight over Europe till there's nothin' left. You should have seen the idiots the week after Pearl Harbor leavin' their farms and their families to go die thousands of miles from home. At least you were drafted. These fools signed up."

"So what should I do, Grandpa?" Hank asked.

"I'll tell you," Allen replied. "The Confederacy was already losing by the time I joined up. I was fueled by rage and pain. All I wanted to do was kill as many Yankees as possible. I'll tell you straight, I killed a lot of 'em. My goal besides that was to hunt down and kill the bastard that had killed my family. To do that, I had to survive. I made sure, regardless of orders, that I had a way out, that I would come out alive. Dereliction of duty? Shit. At least I'd be alive to be court-martialed. Death and honor are not always the same thing. I searched for that man for ten years after the war, and I blew his head off while he pleaded for his life. I'd dreamed of that for years. Sometimes I think that goal was the only thing that kept me going. But when it finally came, it didn't feel anything like I thought it would. No great weight was lifted off my shoulders. I still felt like shit and my mom and dad and sister and brother were still thirteen years dead.

"I was drunk on the street in St. Louis after that and a Quaker preacher offered to buy me a meal. He wouldn't give me money, because he didn't want me to buy booze, but he said I looked hungry and that he'd buy me food. I hadn't eaten in two days, so I took him up on his offer.

I'd renounced God after my family's murder. What kind of god would let men do such things? He asked how I got in such a state. While I ate, I told the preacher about my life. He surprised me. He said, 'Even if you don't want to turn to the Lord, you owe it to yourself and your family to go on and try to make a decent life. Otherwise you may as well have died with your family. You're on your way to being a casualty of that war, no matter the time of your death. Don't let tragedy and the horror of war consume you. Don't be guilty because you survived and others didn't.'

"I thanked him and told him I was going to go on. He gave me a couple bucks, which I gambled and won enough to buy a shitty horse with. The rest is history. My point being, you always look out for number one, no matter what. And no matter how many times you see your buddies blown to bits or how many bastards you have to kill, you make it home. And when you get home, go buy a new car, marry some pretty gal, start a business, whatever. Don't mope around and be a casualty of war, even after it's over. That preacher was a wise man."

"Thanks, Grandpa, that helps a lot," Hank said.

"You can thank me by coming home in one piece," Allen replied.

"Collins!" Lieutenant Taylor's booming voice snapped him out of his reminiscence.

"Right here, sir," Hank said, raising his hand.

"Colonel Monroe has a job for you. Get two day rations and meet me at the colonel's table in five minutes," Taylor said.

"Yes, sir," Hank replied, saluting. Taylor returned the salute and walked off.

Hank went to the supplies tent. He got some food and extra canteens. For some reason he thought he needed more ammo for his pistol. Oddly enough he didn't worry about his rifle. Hank long ago learned to go with his gut feelings.

"I need six extra pistol magazines," he said to the guy running the supply tent.

"Issue's three. You've got three," the guy said without looking up.

Hank long ago learned how to pull rank without getting caught. "Lieutenant Taylor told me to get extra supplies for a special mission for Colonel Monroe. Either give 'em to me or call Lieutenant Taylor," Hank said, acting pissed off.

The guy looked at Hank for a moment, obviously thinking. Taylor was
a tyrant. If Hank wasn't bullshitting and the guy questioned Taylor's orders,
he'd wish he was never born. He handed over six magazines loaded with 230-
grain military hardball. Hank hid them on his person.

Hank walked up to the colonel's table, where he was consulting with
Taylor. "Master Sergeant John Henry Collins reporting for duty, sir," Hank
said, saluting.

"At ease," Colonel Monroe said.

"We have a very sensitive mission, Collins. Lieutenant Taylor says you're
the best man for the job. And I can't find fault with that statement."

"Thank you, sir."

"Don't thank me yet, until you know what it is,"

Monroe said, matter-of-factly. "I assume you're aware of the situation
here."

"What situation is that, sir?" Hank said.

"Hauser," Monroe said, referring to the name of the German commander
they were facing. "His guns are bigger than mine and he has a lot more of
them. We keep our heads down while his men dig thirty yards of trench a day.
In three days they'll be in range and pound us into dust. We sent a courier to
Marseilles two days ago. I know there's a crack airborne unit there. Apparently
he didn't make it. We're sending another courier, but we want you to go with
him, protect him. If we don't get reinforcements or air cover, we're toast."

"Deliver the message no matter what, Sergeant," Taylor said.

"Yes, sir."

"Dismissed," Colonel Monroe said.

"Collins," Taylor said as Hank turned to leave.

"Sir?"

"If you die on this mission, I will shoot myself and come after you."

"Yes, sir."

"Will they get the message, Sergeant?" Taylor asked.

"Either that or I'll see you in hell, sir," Hank said.

Colonel Monroe got coffee up his nose laughing.

Hank left the camp in a jeep driven by another soldier. The driver had the
colonel's dispatch in his breast pocket. The road was so rough that they could

only go about twenty or twenty-five miles per hour. It wasn't really a road, just a trail, but the French resistance had told them about it. The French resistance was outmanned and outgunned, but they gave the Nazis fits and were helpful in setting up the D-Day surprise attack.

Hank thought about what would happen if an enemy army tried to get him and his friends around Lynchburg. The locals knew where there a fallen tree was, or a washed out bridge, or a cave to hide in, and a million other things no map showed. It was hard to beat a proud people on their own turf.

They'd been puttering along for about an hour when the windshield exploded and the driver stiffened in an odd way. Hank jumped out of the jeep and rolled into the ditch. He saw the jeep flip and the driver thrown out. The jeep finally stopped on its side a ways down the road.

Hank quickly got his bearings and thought. *I heard the report of the rifle after the bullet hit. That means the shot was fired from a long way away. A sniper. A sniper that waits to see what the survivor will do. I will have to outwait the sniper before making a move.*

He lay in the ditch absolutely still for an hour. He was so still that a deer could have walked right by him. It was a God-given gift he had that came without training from some inner pool where stress never reached. Before he left home, even at the age of sixteen, Hank was legendary as a hunter in Lynchburg and the surrounding areas. He learned from hunting with his father and grandfather about "buck fever." Guys would be surprised by a deer and in that first moment of surprise, jerk awkwardly and miss the shot.

He'd learned in war hunting men, that men were stupid. They farted and yakked, and smoked and stepped on things and gave themselves away long before they should have. Not the old Ozark bucks. Like a superior visitor from another planet, they would just appear out of nowhere, thundering out of the brush past the dumbfounded hunter. They were superior in one way. Their senses were razor-sharp and the old bucks weren't worried about their girl or their taxes or their job. They put first things first, like their personal safety. So did professional snipers. So when the man suddenly materialized out of nowhere on the side of the road, Hank's reaction was nothing that his body showed.

He reached for his .45 on his hip; he'd lost his rifle in the crash. He took the safety off. Hank always carried "cocked and loaded." He figured if he was in a bad enough situation that he needed the pistol, he needed it to fire the second it left his holster. Like now.

The sniper stood on the edge of the road, coolly surveying the scene. Hank felt the sniper's gaze fix, unerringly it seemed, on him and wash away.

You can't see me, Hank thought to himself. *Here I lay and you can't see me. Just like an old Ozark buck, these guys looked for any sign of abnormal motion.*

Hank put the front sight of the .45 in the center of the man's chest and squeezed the trigger twice. The .45 roared twice and the man looked down at the holes in his chest and, like a marionette whose strings had suddenly been released, collapsed to the ground.

Hank waited a couple minutes to make sure the sniper was dead. He went over to the corpse, kicked the man's rifle away and relaxed a little. He was dead. Hank took the orders out of the dead driver's pocket and put them in his own. He heard a movement behind him and spun around and almost fired, when he saw another American.

"Jesus Christ! I could have killed you," Hank said.

"Yes, sir, I believe you could have," the soldier said in a southern drawl even more southern than Hank's. "But I think we're both glad you didn't. Good work. I got his spotter yesterday. I knew he was dug into those trees like an Alabama tick. I guess the jeep was too good a target to pass up. I crawled across the road in the dust from the crash. Sucker walked right by me, lookin' for you.

I was gonna shoot him in the back when you got him from the front."

"What the hell are you doing out here all alone?" Hank asked.

"Five of us were sent from the camp at Marseilles. There's a bad siege there. The radio doesn't work worth a shit in these mountains. We were hoping to hook up with the French Underground, maybe use their telegraph system or their couriers to send a message to Versailles for help. Anyway, he got my four buddies before they could blink.

I lied in that ditch all night. Yesterday morning he sent his spotter down to check and I nailed the bastard. The sniper shot back, but I couldn't make the muzzle flash in the light, so I spent another afternoon and night in the ditch until he went for the jeep."

"Fuck!" Hank cursed. "God damned fucking son-of-a-bitch! I was sent out to get reinforcements from Marsielles because our god damned radio system was shot and we were being pounded."

"You got any water on you, buddy?" the other soldier asked. Hank tossed him a canteen. "You got any food?"

"Do I look like a walking supply tent?"

"No, you don't. But like I said, I lay in that ditch for two days and my food and water ran out yesterday."

Hank tossed him a canned C-ration from his pack. The soldier wolfed it down quickly.

"Thank you, Jesus, thank you, Lord," the man said.

Hank was curious. *Here we are in the middle of nowhere, the jeep is probably fucked, and this guy is thanking Jesus.* "What are you thanking Jesus for?" Hank asked.

"For sending you to me. I surely would have died from dehydration if you hadn't showed up."

"I was sent by Colonel David R. Monroe, U.S. Army. Jesus had nothing to do with it. Help me turn this jeep over. If we're lucky, maybe it'll still run," Hank said.

"It sure will. God is on our side," the guy said.

"Do me a favor and don't say another fuckin' word okay?" Hank said as they turned the jeep back on its wheels.

Hank tried to start the jeep, but it wouldn't start.

He punched the dashboard, which didn't do anything except bruise the side of his hand. The other guy was looking at him.

"What? You got something to say, spit it out."

"You said not to say another word."

Hank punched the dash again. "I meant don't say another word about that Jesus-is-with-us shit! If you can fix this fuckin' thing, then do it or tell me what I need to do to help," Hank said, exasperated.

"Engine's probably flooded from being upside down," the guy said. "These things usually have a small toolkit under the backseat in a little compartment. If it does, we can pull the spark plugs out, clean 'em, and it'll probably run."

Hank pulled the toolkit out from under the seat and handed it to the soldier. He opened the hood and went to work. Hank's job at the car plant was installing fenders, but he didn't know much about engines.

"Yup. Look how black and wet they are," the guy said, showing Hank the plugs. Hank nodded like he knew what the guy was doing.

"What's your name, buddy?" Hank asked.

"Orris John Simpson, but you can call me 'Rabbit.'"

"Why Rabbit?"

"I was the fastest runner in basic training and the name kind of stuck."

"I'm Hank Collins." They shook hands and Hank said, "Hey, I'm sorry I got shitty with you, it's just -- I'm on edge too."

"Everybody is. Forget it," Rabbit said. He put the plugs back in the jeep. "Try it now. Hold the throttle wide open until I tell you to let off."

Hank cranked the jeep over. It coughed and spit, and the starter groaned, but it finally caught. Black smoke poured out the tailpipe and the engine sputtered and knocked. It finally cleaned out and really revved up.

"Okay, let off the gas," Rabbit said. The engine was still knocking.

"What's that noise?" Hank asked.

"Probably doesn't have any oil pressure from being upside down. It'll quiet down," Rabbit said. Almost on cue, the engine stopped knocking and sounded normal.

Rabbit closed the hood and jumped in the passenger side. "What do we do now?" he asked.

"Go ahead toward Marseilles, see if we can find some French fighters, or maybe see what the commander there wants to do," Hank said. "Unless you've got a better idea."

Rabbit shook his head no and they drove off.

They talked a little on the road. Rabbit was from Mississippi. His family were real Pentecostal crackers, the kind that used poisonous snakes in rituals and spoke in tongues at revivals. A few years before, Rabbit had a falling out with the church and the local preacher. Apparently, from what Hank could tell by reading between the lines, it was violent. Rabbit got sent to the military by a sympathetic local judge in Mississippi. It was that or the prison farm at Thebes. He figured if he had to go to war, he wanted the best training and the best chance to survive, so he signed up for Airborne Ranger school, which didn't take draftees. Basic training for them was two years instead of eight weeks like everyone else. His marksmanship was so amazing that he was made an American sniper. Rabbit boasted of taking out another German sniper in Belgium from a thousand yards out in a driving rainstorm.

"There's only maybe eight, ten guys in the world that could have made that shot. It's the only thing I was ever good at."

Hank patted Rabbit on the shoulder and smiled. "I'm glad you're with me," he said.

"What are you smiling about?" Rabbit asked.

"I was thinking about a play on a Bible passage that applies to you," Hank said.

"What is it?"

"Yeah, though I walk through the shadow of the valley of death, I fear no evil, for thou art with me, and thou art the meanest son-of-a-bitch in the valley."

Rabbit laughed heartily and Hank laughed with him.

They stopped in a clearing above a small town and looked down. A group of Nazi soldiers was rounding up the townspeople. Rabbit started humming some gospel tune. It was familiar, but Hank couldn't name it.

"What are you doing?" Hank asked.

"We're screwed now," Rabbit said. "I hear *Amazing Grace* whenever I'm in danger."

"You're shittin' me," Hank said.

"I am not. This is bad."

The townspeople were mostly women, little children and old men, since all the men and boys were fighting the war. The Nazi leader took a young girl and a young nun and gave them to four others. They dragged the girl and the nun screaming into the church. The remaining Nazis lined up all the women of the town against a barn facing the church, then they shot every other one.

"Oh, Jesus Christ!" Hank groaned. "Oh ,shit! They fuckin' killed 'em."

Hank was chilled to the bone. He'd heard Allen's horror stories, but that was eighty years before. *Surely men are not that barbaric now. Apparently they are.* Rabbit was praying. "Lord, I ask you to guide my hand and the hand of my Christian brother next to me so that we may avenge the deaths of these innocents. Amen." Rabbit stood up and said, "Give me all your M-1 magazines."

"Why?" Hank asked.

"Because we're goin' in," Rabbit said coldly.

This is so bad. Hank knew if he walked away that he'd never be able to live with himself. "I'm sorry, Grandpa," he said to himself and tossed Rabbit his rifle magazines. Rabbit tossed Hank his .45 and extra magazines.

"Here's the plan. I'm an ace with a rifle, and you showed you're good with a pistol back there. They'll be posted to lookout for another group. One man can slip through, however. You go into town and smoke anybody that gets in your way. I'll cover you from long range. All you go to do is not miss. Don't look back until you get to the church. I'll meet you there," Rabbit finished.

Hank worked his way stealthily down the hill. As he entered town two Germans who were smoking by a Duesenhaf truck stared at him in disbelief for a second. Hank shot the one in the chest twice. The .45 slugs slammed him back into the truck, leaving a bloody smear on the body as he fell.

As the second one went for his rifle, Hank shot him in the head. He fell back as his rifle erupted into the air. The gunfire brought other soldiers. Hank faced overwhelming odds in the street. He fired furiously, a pistol in each hand. Out of nowhere bullets took out adversaries who should have had him. Hank ducked behind a building and reloaded. Lieutenant Taylor had taught him a trick to reload a .45 with one hand, while shooting with the other. It looked like a weird dance, but it worked.

Hank felt like he was inside a pinball machine as he raced around town. He made it to the outhouse by the church, but found it surrounded by nine soldiers. He took four out in a blazing gunfight, and Rabbit obviously felled three from afar. Hank was furiously trying to reload when the other two stepped into view.

"Time to die, Yankee," one said in a thick German accent.

Suddenly they both stiffened as Bowie knives from nowhere stuck in their throats. Rabbit stepped into view as the men drowned in their own blood. He was almost talking to corpses, but he got in, "We're not Yankees, you Nazi bastard."

Rabbit took their Walther P-38 pistols and spare magazines. He tossed Hank one and kept one for himself.

"In case we get low on ammo, these'll cycle this European shit. We definitely don't want to be unarmed."

Hank and Rabbit went into the church. A young girl was lying on the altar in an odd position. As they got closer, Hank could see she was tied up. She couldn't have been more than fourteen or fifteen. Her clothes were ripped and the dress was too short, obviously a hand-me-down. She was barefoot and the soles of her small feet were dark with dirt. They'd tied her up as tight as a meat bundle. They'd tied her wrists and elbows behind her back, and her ankles were crossed and tied, her heels resting in her upturned palms. There was a rope around her neck, and a little blood trickled out from under the rope. Her eyes stared unblinkingly at the wall. It was obvious she'd been strangled.

Rabbit said something Hank couldn't understand and started dancing. It was a sad dance, obviously some Pentecostal rite for the dead. Hank sat down and tried to think.

He heard moaning from one of the confessionals. He opened it and inside was the young nun. She too was tied up unbelievably tight. They had pulled her arms up behind her like someone was "twisting her arm," crossed her wrists and tied them into a noose around her neck. If she moved her arms, she choked herself. They'd also tied her ankles to her thighs and balanced her on her knees on the bench of the confessional. Her face was purple and her breathing was labored. It was a painful and impossible predicament.

Bastards! Hank pulled her out and cut the ropes off her with his k-bar knife. She was talking a mile a minute in French, which Hank didn't understand.

Rabbit came over and said, "I wonder if she can tell us why this village is important."

"I can tell you," the nun said in perfect English.

"You speak English?" Hank asked.

"And French, German and Spanish," she said proudly.

"Why do you think this town is important?" Hank asked Rabbit.

"Killing everybody does no good. Killing half the people puts the fear of God into 'em. They'll turn on their neighbor to save themselves. At least that's the reasoning behind it," Rabbit finished.

"Where did you learn that reasoning?" Hank said, disgusted.

"From Genghis Khan, Attila the Hun, the Spartans and Alexander the Great," Rabbit replied. "We studied legendary military tyrants in Ranger school. Leaders who see themselves as mythical tend to study other mythical leaders and emulate them. Hitler certainly sees himself as mythical."

Hank was stunned and looked at Rabbit in a new light. However simple and annoying he seemed at first glance, he was much deeper. He fixed the jeep and got them through the battle with the Nazis. Now his theory made sense. He had obviously learned a lot in Ranger school. Hank resolved to really listen to what he said from now on.

The nun spoke up. "This town is important because the resistance sometimes uses the church to pass messages. I guess the Nazis found out."

"No kidding," Rabbit said. "We have to go."

"Let me look after her," the nun said, pointing at the altar where the bound peasant girl was.

"Why did they kill her?" Hank asked.

"For sport, to try to scare me," the nun replied. "The German commander thought we were pretty. He said he'd let us live if we'd service him and his men. I said I'd rather die. They strangled the girl in front of me. It was horrible. They'd choke her until she was almost dead and then let her breathe a little, then they'd choke her some more. The last time, she didn't breathe again. She kept saying, 'Sister, don't tell them anything, and don't let them dishonor us.'

I asked the commander why didn't he and his men just take us by force since we were already tied up. He leered at me and said, 'An Aryan always wants a non-Aryan whore to willingly submit.' I kicked him in his privates and bit the one holding me. He had them throw me in the confessional and said they would see me later after I'd had time to think.

99

I heard gunfire outside, and then you guys showed up. Would you gentlemen excuse me for a few minutes?" she asked.

Hank and Rabbit went outside. They saw the townspeople regrouping. Several of the old men saluted Hank and Rabbit. They returned the salute.

Rabbit again surprised Hank with his intelligence and depth of character. "The Nazis deserve to burn in hell," Rabbit said. "They are evil incarnate. I know now that God is on our side."

"How do you know that?" Hank asked skeptically.

"I know what she meant by service. I know nuns are married to Jesus, which is why they don't have Earthly husbands and children. Anyone who would rape or kill a nun will have to face the vengeance of the Lord. I know you and I just killed twenty men, but that was our duty. You and I wouldn't go into a German village and execute a bunch of women and children. That's what makes us better. That's what makes us right. People will say we're evil like them. Not true. We are the necessary evil that opposes the other evil, so the good and the meek can inherit the earth. The warriors fight for those who can't fight. The warriors die and kill so others can live. We're fighting the good fight."

"I agree with you," Hank replied. "Let's go back inside."

Inside the church, the peasant girl was laid out onthe altar dressed in the nun's habit. Her hands were folded in front of her holding rosary beads. Candles were lit all around her. The nun appeared dressed in the peasant girl's clothes.

"I did what I could for her under the circumstances."

Hank looked at the nun for the first time. She was robust, but extremely pretty. Some women were exotically gorgeous, all sultry and rich like Marlene Dietrich, and some were just pretty like Katherine Hepburn. The only way to describe the nun was extremely pretty. She was tall, almost statuesque. Her shoulders and arms looked strong, as did her legs. She had medium-sized breasts, but they looked extremely firm. The peasant girl was smaller, so the clothes fit really tight, accentuating her body. Hank noticed she was barefoot and that she had small feet for such a big girl.

"Where are your shoes?" Hank asked.

"The peasant girl didn't have any."

"What about yours?" Hank asked.

"I didn't have any either," the nun said indignantly. "The church has to make sacrifices in wartime."

"We need to talk to the leaders of the resistance," Hank said.

"I can show you," the nun replied.

"Let's go," Rabbit said impatiently.

They drove the jeep until it ran out of gas, then they started walking. The terrain was grassy for a while, then it became rocky. Hank saw the nun gingerly trying to walk over the rocks. Her bare feet were already bleeding.

"Sister, let me carry you," he said.

"I'm fine. I'm doing God's work," she said.

"So is Rabbit," Hank replied, "but he's got combat boots on." He picked up the nun, threw her over his shoulder over her protests and kept walking.

They reached a grassy knoll. Hank put the nun down and she started to get up.

"Sit down," Hank said, and she did.

He rummaged through his pack and found what he wanted. He took one of his canteens and gently washed the nun's feet.

"That isn't necessary," she said, unnerved by the big American gently washing her feet.

"It is," Hank said as he put some disinfectant on the cut areas.

"Unnngh," the nun groaned.

"Sorry. I should have warned you that would sting," Hank said.

He then took some bandages out of his pack and bandaged her feet. He took some medical tape out and taped over the bandages. Her feet and ankles were taped like a football player's.

"We need you, Sister," Hank said. "You're our guide here. One thing they drilled into us in basic training was take care of your feet. A soldier that can't walk or run is no good to himself or anyone else. If you get gout or a fungus or an injury, you're done. Ain't that right, Rabbit?"

"That's right," Rabbit replied. "You can walk when it's smooth, but when it gets rough, either me or Hank will carry you. No argument, Sister. You can't help the resistance if you die or get an infection or if they have to amputate your feet from gangrene."

"No argument," she replied. She realized they were right. They needed someone who knew the terrain and spoke the language. She needed to get to the resistance stronghold. The only way she'd get there was if she was escorted by men with guns. They needed each other.

Hank took some C-rations out of his pack and gave them to Rabbit and the nun. He also passed the nun a canteen.

"This is quite good, considering it's cold in a can," the nun said. "What is it?"

"Deviled ham," Hank replied.

The nun burst out laughing. She laughed so hard that Hank thought she was going to faint. Hank and Rabbit laughed at the nun's laughter. She finally composed herself.

Rabbit then said, "Maybe she can have some angel food cake to make up for it."

They all had another laughing fit. The jokes seemed to make everyone feel better. Hank and Rabbit picked up all the debris from their little picnic and put it in their packs.

"Why did you do that?" the nun asked.

"No sign of a trail," Hank and Rabbit said, almost in unison.

They trekked on. The terrain became rough again and Hank and Rabbit took turns carrying the nun.

Rabbit was carrying her when she started to gripe. "Gentlemen, this is ridiculous."

"You said you wouldn't argue, Sister, now stop griping or I'll...."

"You'll what?" the nun said challengingly.

Hank pulled the roll of medical tape out of his pocket. "I'll tape your mouth shut," he said.

"Tape can be pulled off."

"I'll tape your hands behind your back too."

"You wouldn't, would you?" she said.

"Yes, I would."

"Fine, break your backs. I don't care," she said.

Gabrielle Cerdan was twenty-three years old. Her mother Irina was sixteen and working in a vineyard when she fell in love with Gabriel Cerdan, the son of the vineyard owner. She soon became pregnant and Gabriel offered to marry her. Even if they hadn't been in love, it was a no-brainer. She could be a noblewoman with respect or a whore with a bastard child.

Gabrielle was born in 1921. They had a son in 1923, and another one in 1925, and a third in 1927. Contrary to the usual European thing about sons, Gabrielle was always her father's favorite. He'd spank the boys and berate them verbally when they screwed up, but he rarely even yelled at her. She had her mother's raven hair and green eyes, and her father's lean physique. When she told her father she wanted to enter the covenant at seventeen because she felt the calling, her father was crushed. She was so smart and so beautiful, even in 1930's Europe, she could have been anything she wanted. He supported her decision, however, and she became a nun. She worked hard for the church, helping the poor, and when the war broke out she worked with the resistance.

When the Nazis took France, she had to be very careful, but her commitment to the cause was strengthened. She passed messages through the church and hid resistance fighters. After the massacre at the village, she became really angry.

The Nazis must be stopped. I'll lead these two Americans to the resistance and perhaps they can call in more Allied forces.

She hoped she wasn't leading the two brave young men to their deaths. The huskier one, called Hank, always had a longing look when he looked at her. He'd said twice that he wished she wasn't a nun, which got her to thinking.

He is handsome and strong, as is the other one, Rabbit, although that is obviously a nickname. For a fleeting moment she thought about leaving the church, leaving the war and this place and bearing children for Hank. For the first time, she realized the sacrifice she made in her vow of chastity, but she wouldn't let them see her cry.

Near dusk they came to the foot of a rocky hill.

"This leads to the resistance stronghold," the nun said.

They drank some water and Hank picked up the nun. Rabbit went up the hill first. They saw a large stone wall. It was obviously a back way in, known only by insiders.

When they reached the top, they saw six armed men. The men brought their rifles up to bear. Rabbit shouldered his rifle and Hank dropped the nun and drew one of his .45's.

"Don't shoot!" she yelled at Hank and Rabbit in English, and then began yelling in French. The men lowered their weapons as did Hank and Rabbit.

"Tell them we want to talk to the leader," Hank said.

"I already did," she replied.

She took Hank and Rabbit by the hand and led them into the compound. It was well designed with several buildings, and surrounded by what looked like lush farmland. There were grapevines everywhere. Several times the nun spoke French to people, and they nodded and went on their way. A petite barefoot woman in her thirties said something to the nun, and she followed her, motioning at Hank that everything was okay. Hank and Rabbit were soon surrounded by several armed men.

"I hope the leader's here," Rabbit said.

"I hope he speaks fuckin' English," Hank replied.

A tall dark haired man in his thirties stepped forward. "I am here, and I do speak fuckin' English," he said.

"He speaks English," Rabbit said.

"We've already established that," the man said. "Why did the Sister bring you here?"

Hank told of the massacre at the village and their exacting revenge.

"The two of you took out an entire Nazi unit?" he said, incredulous.

"It wasn't a whole battalion, only about twenty or twenty-five," Rabbit said.

The leader made a sweeping motion with his hand and said sarcastically, "Only twenty or twenty-five." The rest of the group laughed.

"I didn't come here to be insulted," Hank said. "If you don't want to help, then the hell with you. Take good care of the Sister."

"You misunderstand me, my American friend. We heard that Americans saved half the townspeople. We were expecting a whole battalion. Our joking was out of respect. Please stay and talk, perhaps I can help you," the leader said. "I'm Marcel Dupré."

"Hank Collins. This is Rabbit," Hank said.

The three shook hands.

"Come, my friends, we shall eat and then discuss military strategy," Dupré said.

Hank and Rabbit sat with the other soldiers. They had roasted a pig for dinner. In addition to the roasted pork, and green beans and potatoes with cheese on them. Hank couldn't remember the last time he'd had a hot meal.

He ate ravenously. Several women, including their nun friend, served the men dinner and then ate themselves.

After dinner, Dupré took Hank, Rabbit and several other men to a room in the compound. Dupré gave them a drink he called "cognac." It tasted like whiskey, but was a lot smoother. Rabbit abstained.

"What can I do for my American allies?" Dupré asked.

"Right now, it's like we're between a rock and a hard place," Hank said. "I was sent to get reinforcements from Marseilles, and he was sent to get reinforcements from Versailles because we were both under terrible siege."

"The problem at Versailles has probably been solved," Dupré said. "An American soldier came into the church gunshot. His last words were, 'Versailles, need help or fort will fall to Krauts.' I sent two hundred men there day before yesterday. I had no idea there was a siege at Marseilles. What do you suggest?"

"Send some men to help, send telegrams, couriers, whatever to get more Allied help," Hank replied.

"I told you, I just sent two hundred men to Versailles. It takes twenty to protect this compound. Right now I have twenty-eight. I can only spare eight," Dupré said.

"Eight's enough," Rabbit said. "Do you have a map of this area?"

Dupré produced a map.

"The siege is here," Rabbit said, pointing to a spot on the map. "This hill is perfect."

"Of course," Dupré replied. "Two sides of it face the open end of a draw. That means you only have to defend two sides."

"Exactly," Rabbit replied. "Do you have a good sniper rifle and a machine gun?"

"Come with me," Dupré said.

He led them to another room in the compound. He showed Rabbit a .308 chambered scoped rifle. He also pulled out a Thompson 1927 A-1 submachine gun with a fifty-round drum magazine.

"We get the best that American and English weapons craft can offer," he said proudly.

"Ammo?" Rabbit asked. He was shown a case of .308 and of case of .45 ACP, which not only worked in the Thompson, but their pistols as well. "Do you have mortar here?" Rabbit asked.

"Yes, plenty," Dupré replied.

"Here's the plan," Rabbit said. "You put a sniper and a spotter on this hill. The other eight guys go down near the Nazi camp and start lobbing mortar into the camp. The German commander will order everyone to engage. The eight guys retreat to the hill, still lobbing mortar. The Germans will follow. The sniper and the spotter shred 'em. The Americans in the besieged fort can come out, and we'll catch 'em in a crossfire. That's our only chance."

"We don't have a sniper that good," Dupré said ruefully.

"Sure you do," Rabbit said, smiling.

"The spotter?" Dupré asked.

"I want Hank watching my back. I trust him."

"Leave before dawn, so you can surprise them," Dupré said. "Anything you need tonight, gentlemen, is yours, within reason."

"That sounds like a warden giving a last meal order for someone on death row," Hank said.

"We're all dead men, *Monsieur* Collins. It's just a matter of when and how," Dupré said and then left.

"That's a defeatist attitude if I ever saw one," Hank said.

"That's the right attitude for a soldier," Rabbit replied.

"How do you figure?" Hank asked.

"We studied Japanese Samurai warriors in Ranger school. The Samurai were legendary and regarded as invincible. The way of the Samurai is death. He does not fear it or welcome it. He lives with it every day, the deaths of his friends, the deaths of others by his hand, the prospect of his own death. In a fight, the Samurai has already thrown his life away. To defeat him, you have to kill him. To do that, you have to be willing to die yourself. The Samurai wants to die with honor. He will take you with him if he can. That is what makes the Samurai dangerous. That's why I personally think the Japs are a bigger problem than the Germans. The Japs will never surrender," Rabbit finished.

The next morning, Hank and Rabbit set up on the hill, while the resistance fighters prepared to lob the mortar into the Nazi camp. Rabbit set up sandbags and spent a considerable amount of time adjusting his position.

"Just like the village, you do your part and I'll do mine," Rabbit said. "Except I want you to work my side with me first."

"Why?" Hank asked.

"Because it'll take 'em a while to reach the other side of the hill, if they do at all. We may shred 'em before they get the chance."

"We're gonna die on this hill, aren't we?" Hank asked.

"Not necessarily," Rabbit replied. "Tactically we could make it. We shouldn't have been able to take that village, but we did. You're a Samurai, Hank, just like me."

"I'm a country boy, afraid of death," Hank replied.

"You been saved?" Rabbit asked.

"Yeah," Hank replied. "Baptized in the river by the Baptist church when I was thirteen."

"By the Pentecostal church when I was ten," Rabbit replied. "We've got nothing to worry about. Our place in heaven is made. What are you worried about?"

"What if Darwin was right, that we are all animals, what if there is no afterlife? What if this world is it?" Hank asked.

"I don't believe that," Rabbit said.

"I don't care what you believe or don't believe, what if this is all there is?"

"We are where we are. Let's take as many of the bastards with us as we can, and hope Darwin's wrong,"

Rabbit replied.

"Okay, let's do it," Hank said.

The resistance fighters started lobbing mortar into the camp with the desired effect. It created chaos and the Germans were running everywhere. Their commanders ordered them to engage. The Frenchmen retreated towards the hill, lobbing mortar, and the Germans followed. Rabbit started firing. He was so good with the scoped rifle, it was scary.

He shot fast to break their charge.

The Germans only knew an all-out "blitzkrieg." They hoped to maneuver and fire, take casualties, but still move in for the ultimate kill. Not today. In the "O" of the scope, Rabbit became God's avenging angel. He saw them coming, six times their normal size, six times more disillusioned and scared, six times more desperate for leadership, and he destroyed them.

He killed five men in seven seconds. He then pulled the bolt back, reached into the ammo case beside him, rolled five more shells into the breech and resumed firing. Each time he took out an officer, they'd scramble in a different direction. They tried to set up a machine gun team to their left.

"Now, Hank, now!" Rabbit yelled.

Hank took up a position next to Rabbit on the sandbags.

He took out the gunner with the Thompson. The loader tried to take the weapon from his stricken hands and Hank rewarded him with a three-shot burst to the chest. A private stood up to try to shame his comrades into advancing. Hank cut him in half too.

"Check our flank!" Rabbit yelled.

Hank checked the other side of the hill and saw enemy soldiers advancing up the hill. He fired furiously with the Thompson. He shot until the gun was empty, then reloaded and shot some more.

Rabbit was in an almost trance-like state. He was in a zone. He saw the enemy soldiers so clear and he moved fluidly -- aim, fire, throw a bolt; aim, fire, throw a bolt. They were all so damned brave! They were all so damned dead!

He felt a presence over his shoulder. He knew it was Death, and he knew Death was pissed, because he, Rabbit, was giving the orders. *Stick with me, man in black, because some customers are about to be made that should have been made a long time ago.*

Rabbit heard Hank yelling, "I'm hit, god damn it, I'm hit." He turned around and saw Hank lying on his back, bleeding from his left leg. The last time he'd tried to reload the Thompson, it had jammed. While trying to clear the malfunction, he got hit. Rabbit took his belt off and fashioned a tourniquet on Hank's leg.

"Cover me while I fix this bitch!" Rabbit growled.

Hank drew both his .45s and crawled to the edge of the hill. He fired furiously down the hill, kind of "spraying and praying," but it had the desired effect. The enemy soldiers hit the dirt. Hank reloaded, hobbled to the other side and did the same. Rabbit fixed the machine gun.

They had a tag-team rhythm going. Rabbit fired the machine gun until it was empty, then Hank fired his pistols while Rabbit reloaded, and reloaded while Rabbit fired. They did so down both sides of the hill. The American troops came out of the besieged fort and started kicking ass. It seemed they were getting help from behind the besieged camp. On the other side, away from the camp, the Nazis began to retreat. Rabbit picked up his sniper rifle.

"Come on," he said, handing Hank the Thompson.

"They're retreating, they're broken."

"He ain't broken," Rabbit said, pointing down the hill.

Hank used his binoculars and saw who Rabbit was talking about. A full-bird German colonel, if not a general, judging by his uniform, was shouting at the soldiers to reengage.

He even started firing at his own fleeing men.

Rabbit took out four men around the commander while Hank sprayed the rest with the Thompson. With his last shot in the breech, Rabbit nailed the commandant in the chest.

He flopped on the ground like a fish. The survivors fled at a dead run, only to be met by French fighters.

"Now they're broken," Rabbit said. His face and hands were black with gunpowder and he was bleeding from underneath both shoulders.

"Can you walk?" he asked Hank.

"I can hop."

"Then let's go."

Hank and Rabbit worked their way down the hill. As they neared the bottom they saw Americans and French resistance fighters taking prisoners and tending to wounded. Hank and Rabbit held on to each other, and then both fell down.

Hank knew he was being put on a stretcher. He thought he was hallucinating. He was sure Lieutenant Taylor was standing over him, a .45 to his own head, saying, "I mean it, Collins, you die and I'll come after you." He laughed himself into unconsciousness.

He awoke in the resistance infirmary. He heard voices outside. They sounded familiar.

"Have you ever seen anything like that?" one of them said.

"I've never even heard of anything like that," the other one replied. "How many did they take?"

"Eighty-seven dead, forty-four wounded. We've got another fifty-five prisoners. Saved sixty of our men from certain death. They both deserve the Medal of Honor."

"If Eisenhower gets our letter and sends it on to the President, maybe they will."

Hank saw two men come into view. He swore it was Colonel Monroe and Lieutenant Taylor. He rubbed his eyes and shook his head. They were still there. He tried to sit up.

"Save your strength, soldier," Colonel Monroe said.

"How'd you guys get here?" Hank asked.

Taylor spoke. "We got overrun and had to flee the camp. About that time, a couple hundred French Resistance fighters show up loaded for bear. With their help, we retook the camp and got several prisoners. One of the German officers cursed us, saying after their comrades destroyed our men at Marseilles, they'd come and destroy us. We came as fast as we could. We got here in time to help you guys, and I'm glad we did. You and your partner did a hell of a job."

"How is Rabbit?" Hank asked.

"Crazy son-of-a-bitch had two bullets in his chest and didn't know it. He was singing *Amazing Grace* when we put him on the stretcher. If he doesn't get an infection, he'll be all right. He's going home, and so are you. It was a pleasure serving with you, Collins. When I talk about integrity and guts to new recruits, I'll tell them to aspire to be half the soldier you are. I'm glad I didn't have to come after you."

"Me too, sir."

"I'd say something, but I don't have the words," Colonel Monroe said. "Good luck, son." They both saluted him and Hank tried to sit up to return it. "Don't waste your strength saluting us," Colonel Monroe said.

They both left.

A while later, Dupré came to see him. "*Monsieur* Collins, I have a gift for you," he said.

He handed Hank a wooden case. Hank opened it. Inside was a gorgeous Browning Hi-Power 9mm semiautomatic pistol. The frame was parkerized, but the slide was nickel-plated. The grips were exquisite French walnut, and it had oversized target sights. The letters "FN" were engraved in its walnut grip, which stood for "*Fabrique Nationale.*" The Belgian Armory had produced them early in the war.

"There are two, they were a matched set," Dupré said. "I gave one to Mr. Rabbit also. They were a gift from my men for showing exceptional valor when the Nazis took Paris. But I have never see valor on the level of yours and Mr. Rabbit's."

"I can't take this," Hank said, flattered.

"I will be insulted if you don't," Dupré replied. "My mother and sister live in that village. You could have just walked away. You didn't. I owe you a debt I can never repay, my friend. What you did for our people, and the war effort, was a lot. If you ever need me, anytime, anywhere, I'm there, no questions asked."

"Thank you, Marcel, you're a warrior and a patriot.

I'm honored to call you my friend," Hank said. "Where's the Sister?"

"She wants to see you," Dupré replied.

"She is something else," Hank said.

"I agree," Dupré replied. "Her father is very rich.

She went to the best girl's schools in all of Europe. This used to be one of his vineyards. He let us use it as a base, and another unit has one up north. He also gives us money to buy weapons and information. The English work with us mainly because of him. His work, and his daughter's, have been invaluable to the resistance. I'll send her to see you."

"Thank you."

Hank felt an outpouring of love and respect for the nun. She could be vacationing in the Greek Islands or touring America. Instead she was helping the war effort and cursing soldiers for not letting her walk barefoot over jagged rocks. He resolved to tell her of his feelings for her before he left.

The nun came in. She sat down by the bed and held his hand. Her hands were tantalizing to him. They were a little soft, just because they were female, but they also showed signs of hard work. She was unique.

"I wanted to say goodbye," she said. "I hear you'll be leaving tomorrow."

"Sister, you are the most amazing person I've ever met," Hank said. "I wish you weren't a nun. Under different circumstances, we could...."

"We can't," she said, starting to cry. "I've thought about it too, and I can't. But I will never forget being carried up a mountain and fed devilled ham by a handsome warrior."

"I'll never forget bandaging the feet of an angel in a grassy meadow," Hank said.

She cried harder and Hank held her. She held onto him tightly. Tears ran down Hanks unshaven cheeks as well. She looked up at him and Hank kissed her. She kissed him back urgently. Finally they broke the kiss and looked at each other.

"I'm never gonna see you again, am I?" Hank said.

"No," she replied. "But I'll never forget you."

She removed the gold cross she wore around her neck and gave it to Hank. Hank took his dog tags and gave them to her. She hugged him again and then stood to leave.

"Sister?" he said. "I never even knew your name."

"Gabrielle Cerdan," she replied.

"Well, Gabrielle Cerdan, it was a pleasure knowing you," he said.

"And you as well, Hank Collins. I'll pray for you and Mr. Rabbit," she said and she walked out of his life forever.

Rough and Ready, California 1930:

Unbeknownst to Red, John Steeley had decided to end the strike. He hired muscle to come in without Maretti's knowledge. Since the thugs were there, Red assumed Maretti had allowed it.

When he returned to Rough and Ready he saw Kate standing on the lawn arguing with four guys. He took the .45 out from under the seat and stuffed it in his waistband. He went over to the house.

"Problem, gentlemen?" he inquired casually.

"Nothing that concerns you, pal," the apparent leader said.

"I beg to differ, sir," Red replied, trying to be polite and annoying at the same time, and succeeding. "Since this is my place of residence, anything that happens here concerns me."

"She's evicting her boarders, including you," the guy said, showing a .38 revolver in his belt. His three buddies did the same.

Red pulled his coat back, showing the .45. "Like I said, I beg to differ."

"Wyatt-fuckin' Earp, huh?" the leader said. "You think you can take the four of us?"

In a lightning move, Red grabbed the guy by his shirt with his left hand, pulling him closer, while drawing the .45 with his right. Red put the barrel in the middle of the man's forehead.

"Probably not," he said in a conversational tone, which made it more menacing. "But before your friends get me, I'll turn your head into a fuckin' canoe. You understand me, you son-of-a-bitch?"

"I understand," the guy said as his pals drew their guns. "Put 'em away, boys. This bastard's dumb enough to kill me."

"Or smart enough, depending on your point of view,"
Red replied. "Don't come around here again."

They left hurling threats.

"What the hell was that?" Red asked.

"They said they were strike breakers. They demanded
I evict my tenants and give my rooms to them. I told them to go to hell.
That's when you showed up. Bastards," Kate said. "You scared 'em."

"No, I didn't," Red replied and went in the house.

Kate followed him. "How did your meeting go?" she asked.

"I quit," Red replied. "Tony said he'd set me up in a restaurant in the
city."

"Are you gonna do it?"

"I'm thinking about it. I'd want you to go with me."

"Damn it," Kate said. "I love you and I want to be with you, but I'm leery
about putting all my hopes on a man. Like I've said before, been there and
done that. I was hoping you'd leave your friends behind completely."

"If the stock market hadn't crashed and things weren't shitty all over, I
could," Red said. "But not now. Besides, like Tony said, pizza guys don't get
killed that much. Think about it."

"I will," Kate said.

"I love you, Katie," Red replied.

"Why do you love me?" she asked.

"Your intelligence, your spunk, your quick wit," Red replied.

"Go ahead, dig a hole," Kate said. "When a man talks about a woman's
spunk and intelligence you know what that means. Any other reasons you
love me?" she said challengingly.

Red realized she was messing with him. He decided to mess with her
back. "Yeah," he said. "Those tits, that ass, and that thing you do with your
mouth."

She burst out laughing. "I almost had you, you son-of-a-bitch!" she said
gleefully. "You may fold under questioning, Mr. Sullivan."

Red laughed. "I'll hire you as my attorney. No man in his right mind
would take you on."

"You did."

"And who said I'm in my right mind?"

Kate laughed. "Want a reminder of why you love me?" she asked.

"Absolutely," Red replied.

He followed her to her bedroom. No matter how many times they'd been together, when she dropped her dress and stood naked in front of him, it always took his breath away.

This woman is gonna be the death of me. What a way to go, he thought as he pushed her onto the bed.

The strike raged on. The union accessed their emergency fund to feed the striking workers and brought in hired muscle of their own to combat the strike breakers. There were fistfights, stickfights and gunfights almost every day.

Maretti grudgingly agreed to help Steeley when he saw that it wasn't going to be resolved quickly. His position was still, "A contract is a contract." He knew he had to do something to avoid losing face with other Dons, and to keep unions in the city from believing they could fuck with him.

He sent men to help.

The Steeleys had closed their general store to spite the union, but the other one remained open. Union men and sometimes the owner, John Coyle himself, would sit on the roof of the store with a shotgun to discourage vandals and looters. Armed union men escorted shipments of supplies to the store.

Red was in the store one day when three wiseguys came in. He drew his gun and took a solid ash sledge handle out of a bin. He worked his way over to the men. Red liked John Coyle, who'd run the store for over twenty years.

Red respected him for not buckling under to Steeley's and Maretti's threats.

One of the thugs pulled a revolver, pointed it a John Coyle and said, "You're out of business, pal."

Red brought the sledge handle down on the man's forearm full-force. He dropped the gun and Red smashed him in the face with the stick. The thug fell, blood spurting from his destroyed nose. Red stepped forward, his .45 pointed at the other two. Coyle pulled out a sawed-off 12-gauge from under the counter. The goons hesitated.

"Get the hell out of here!" Coyle yelled.

"You might as well kill me, 'cause if you don't,

I'm gonna fuckin' kill you," the one on the left yelled.

"Okay," Coyle said, and triggered the shotgun.

The sound was deafening in the store. The shot slammed the thug backward into some shelves, knocking down the stock. Blood oozed onto the floor like maple syrup. The one Red had hit with the stick started to get up and Red kicked him in the face. He fell backward and was quiet.

"What are you gonna do, tough guy?" Coyle asked the third one.

He was so sure of his buddies that he hadn't even drawn his gun. He mistakenly tried now.

"No!" Coyle yelled.

The man drew the pistol anyway. Coyle triggered the shotgun a second before Red fired. The goon was lifted off his feet and slammed into a stack of flour bags. Red put his gun back in his belt.

The sheriff came in the store and asked, "What happened?"

"These guys tried to rob me," Coyle said.

"Is that right?" the sheriff replied skeptically.

"That's right," Red said. "I saw the whole thing."

"So did I," another customer, a union man Red recognized, put in.

"You two have to come to the office and give a statement," the sheriff said, pointing to Red and the customer.

"I'll give my statement here," Red said, knowing the sheriff was corrupt. *He could still be working for Maretti, or he could be working for someone else.* Red figured, *There'll be guys at the office wanting me to change my view of the events.*

"You want to be arrested?" the sheriff asked.

Red pulled his coat back. "I don't think I'll let you arrest me today," he said.

The sheriff put his hand on his gun. Red did the same.

"You want to die for Steeley's greed, or Maretti's, or whoever's pulling your strings now?" Red asked. "I don't want to kill you and you don't want to be dead. Let it go."

"That goes double for me," John Coyle said, still holding the shotgun.

The sheriff stormed off and returned later with men who worked for the undertaker in town to pick up the bodies.

Red told Kate of what happened at the store. "Coyle wouldn't have been able to kill Maretti's goon if I hadn't intervened. I'll have to answer for that. I have to get out of this town. Are you coming with me or not?"

"I'm coming," Kate said. "Let me send a telegram to my cousin in Seattle. She and her husband can run this place and send me a percentage. Just be a couple days till she gets back to me. You can play kept man and I'll spoil you. Then we can do whatever you want to do."

"Sounds like a plan," Red replied.

Red stood at the window of Kate's room looking out the window. She was lying on her stomach on the bed, naked.

Her ankles were crossed, the soles of her pretty bare feet facing him. He'd always liked her feet, her legs and her ass. The view was wonderful.

She must have sensed his stare, because she turned her head over her shoulder and said, "What?"

He walked over and slapped her ass playfully, once, twice and then a third time.

"What are you doing?" she asked in her "I won't ask, but I'll go along" voice.

"Just thinking. If I have to spank our children, they'll have plenty of padding," he said.

"Screw you," she retorted, getting up and starting to get dressed.

"You just did," Red replied.

"Cheeky bastard," Kate said, smiling.

"I'm gonna take a bath," Red said.

"Soak your sore muscles after all that work?" Kate said.

"Yes, thank you," Red replied and he went to the bathroom.

It started to rain. Kate wanted to go to the store and get some groceries. She didn't want to walk in the rain, however, so she went to Red's trousers that were thrown over a chair and found the keys to his truck.

Red heard the explosion and was hit with glass as the percussion broke the windows in the house. He looked outside and saw his truck burning. The flames were about ten feet high.

"Katy! Katy!" he yelled as he ran through the house. She didn't answer. He ran outside and he knew. The bastards wanted him and they'd killed Kate.

You want me, you got me, he thought to himself as he got dressed. He got his gun and started for the door, then he thought again, *You go off half-cocked and you'll get killed. You will bring no justice to Kate by dying today.*

He couldn't imagine that Maretti would allow a hit on him. He remembered a proverb he'd read in a Sherlock Holmes novel: "Once you've discounted the impossible, then whatever's left, however improbable, has to be the truth."

Whether Maretti was involved or not, he knew what his course of action would be. After the stock market crash the previous October, things were bad all over. The only things of value were land and gold. The mine was especially valuable now.

He was patient and waited. He had the funeral for Kate two days later. It was attended by the town preacher, the ladies who lived in Kate's house, Pete Jackson, John Coyle and Red.

He got a telegram after the funeral. It read:

"I'm terribly sorry for your loss. If you need anything please let me know. My deepest sympathies, Tony Maretti."

Red would not let ambiguity deter him from his mission of vengeance. He remembered what he'd told Kate about friendly faces in bad times.

Maretti might be genuinely sorry for Kate's death and may have had no part in it. If he did, however, he'd still offer condolences to throw me off. Screw, Tony. He should have made it clear to Steeley and everyone else that I was untouchable. If they acted without his knowledge, he should have made that clear to me. Screw 'em all. I am going ahead with my plan.

He waited until three o'clock in the morning and went to the mine. There were picketers at the front entrance, but the guard at the back fence was asleep. Red climbed the fence quietly and entered the tool shed where he found the explosives and detonators. He set the charges at strategic locations to ensure maximum damage by going off in a domino effect. He did it exactly the way the demolition expert had shown him. He'd taken great pride in showing Red how to arrange blasts. He set the timer and returned to the fence. The guard was startled and jumped up, but Red quickly beat him unconscious. He took side streets through town.

The first explosion woke the whole town. All of the charges went off perfectly. A crater six miles wide and three miles deep was now where the mine used to be. At the edge of town, Red saw Pete Jackson and John Coyle.

"Nice work," Pete said. "You sent your personal message, but it'll help us in the future with other bastards. Where are you gonna go now? They'll be looking for you all up and down the coast."

"I'll call my brother in San Francisco," John said.

"He's a big-time boxing promoter, and he has a piece of a lot of other things. I owe you for saving my life the other day. He'll help you."

"And we'll get you to San Francisco safely," Pete said. "That's the last place they think you'd go."

Anthony Maretti had been an American Mafia chieftain since 1909. He was born in Palermo, Sicily in 1878. In 1895 at seventeen, his father Mario Maretti was murdered for an insult to the brutal local Mafia chieftain. His older brother, Enzo, swore revenge and was also murdered.

Tony did his reconnaissance and took his time before making his move. He knew the tyrant, called Don Ciccone, had lunch every Thursday at a little cafe in the mountain village of Sirigusa. He did so partly because he liked the wine the cafe owner made and wanted to buy a few jugs to take home, and partly to collect from the shepherds, farmers, and merchants he strong-armed. He always went with two of his men, who carried shotguns. The Don himself was never armed.

Tony took his father's horse and his double-barreled shotgun he used for hunting quail and other game birds.

He didn't load it with birdshot, though, he used No. 4 buckshot. He put it in the rifle sling on his saddle and rode to Sirigusa.

He casually rode up to the café and dismounted. The café owner smiled at him.

"Did you have a good hunt?" he asked pleasantly.

"Yes, thank you," Tony replied and shot the bodyguard sitting to the left of Ciccone. The impact threw him backward, knocking over two tables behind him. The Don put his hands over his face as Tony swung the barrel past him.

The guard on the right had jumped up and grabbed his own shotgun, but he wasn't fast enough. The blast of buckshot at point-blank range almost cut him in half.

The bodyguard's blood sprayed onto Ciccone, who stood, knocking the table over and was trying to pick up the fallen man's gun.

Tony was on him quickly with a large hunting knife in hand. He cut Ciccone from his groin to his collarbone.

The Mafioso wailed like a wounded coyote, making gurgling sounds as a rank gas came out the gaping wound in his torso.

"You've killed me. Why?" the dying man asked in a death-rattle voice.

"Mario Maretti says hello," Tony growled, and kicked the man in the face as he breathed his last.

Hearing the gunfire, the cafe owner's sons ran out with *luparas* (Italian for shotgun) of their own. They saw the dead bodies and their father still standing, and hesitated.

"My problem was with Don Ciccone, not you, sir," Tony said. "I apologize for disrupting your business."

"Fine. Now leave," the taller of the man's sons said, pointing his shotgun at Tony.

"Would you not point that gun at me?" Tony asked.

"You're leaving, one way or the other," the boy said.

"I'd like to think it was my idea," Tony said. The father motioned and they lowered their guns. Tony picked up his own shotgun and mounted his horse. "Thank you, gentlemen," he said and rode off.

Tony knew the cafe owner would tell Ciccone's men what he'd said and that they'd come after him. Paul, Ciccone's son, would come after him with everything he had, but Tony wasn't waiting for them.

He rounded up some friends and some men from the town who'd had fathers, sons, cousins or brothers killed by Ciccone. That night they went to Ciccone's villa and lit it on fire as well as the barn and the guest house.

Then they shot the men as they ran from the flames.Ciccone's consigliere survived, and fearing that other

Mafia chieftains in the area would try to take over after their misfortune, set up a meeting with Tony. He proposed that if Tony and his friends were loyal to him and helped him fend off the others trying to take Ciccone's territory, he'd make Tony the second-in-command. Tony agreed.

Afterwards, Tony was treated like a king. Fruit vendors in the street gave him goods at no charge. Farmers and workers gave him gifts of homemade wine, hand-sewn clothing, and home-cooked food. Tony told everyone he appreciated their hospitality and would gladly help them any way he could. He said that men like Ciccone were a disgrace, preying on poor people. He pointed out that there wasn't much law enforcement in Sicily and what little there was, was corrupt. If a peasant had a beef with a rich man, the peasant was screwed. "But if you come to me and Don Vario in friendship, your enemies will become our enemies. And then they will fear you."

For five years, Tony was the "power behind the throne." If people wanted a favor from Don Vario, they went through Tony. If Don Vario wanted someone killed, or wanted to negotiate peace, he had Tony handle it. He learned something valuable that would serve him well in later life. He realized that while Vincent Vario was officially the boss, Tony held all the respect of the peasants and other gangsters because he was on the street. He had told people, "Don't worry, I'll fix your problem. Don Vario won't be angry."

Vario was a private man who hated meetings. He didn't like anyone hearing what he said or what he was being told. For a man that hundreds of people depended on, he didn't talk to three people a day. Everything went through Tony. People worried more about what Tony thought than what the Don thought.

Tony resolved that when he was the boss, he'd be accessible. The lowest man in his organization could talk to him, and the little old lady griping about her neighbor's dog could do the same. He'd be loved by the people in his territory for being so friendly and open. His credo that he told all his underlings was: "Be nice. Until it's time to not be nice."

Other mobsters wouldn't try to fuck with him because he'd be around to see the slightest thing. Tony's father had told him before he died, "Son, many men ask, 'Is it better to be loved or feared?' If you have to choose between the two, it's better to be feared. But a man that is both loved and feared is almost invincible. A man once said, 'You get more with a kind word and a gun than you do with just a kind word.'" Tony always had a kind word for people and he always had a gun.

Vincent Vario had a massive heart attack in 1900. Since his sons were dead, Tony took over. Other Mafia chieftains were polite but cool at the funeral. Tony knew instantly what was going to happen. All the other Dons were men in their forties and fifties who came to power by staying loyal to a tyrant until he died. They resented Tony, being barely older than many of their sons, yet having power equal to or in some cases greater than their own.

Tony had long ago befriended a pair of brothers -- one a blacksmith, the other a livery stable owner. The blacksmith had made beautiful wrought-iron gates for Tony's villa and the stable owner tended Tony's horses. One day a rich parliament member brought in a horse that had been bitten by a rattlesnake.

"Can you take care of him?" he'd asked.

"I can keep him cleaned and fed, but he's been sickened," the stable buck said.

Two days later the horse died. The parliament member was furious. He demanded the stable owner pay him 5,000 Lira for the horse, or he'd have the corrupt sheriff arrest him and thugs burn down his place. The stable owner went to see Tony.

"Don Maretti, you said you'd help me if I was ever in trouble."

"What kind of trouble are you in?" Tony asked.

The man told him the story.

"Honestly, how much is a good horse worth?" Tony asked.

"A thousand Lira," the stable owner said.

"Don't worry, my friend, I'll take care of it," Tony replied. "Just remember that I did you a favor."

"Always, Don Maretti," the man said and left.

Tony went to the parliament member's house with six of his men. He confronted the man in front of his son and wife and two daughters.

"I apologize for the misunderstanding on my friend's behalf. Apparently his employee wasn't clear with you.

The horse was basically dead when you brought it in. Nonetheless, I'm prepared to give one thousand Lira, the market value for a good horse."

"I told that peasant I wanted five thousand!" the man exploded. "I'll kick your ass into the next county!

Do you know who I am?"

"I was about to ask you the same question," Tony replied. "Take my offer. I won't make another."

"You're a dead man, and so is your friend," the man snarled.

"No, you are," Tony replied and blew the man's brains out. Two of his men held the son at gunpoint while the others stripped his crying mother and sisters.

"A horse isn't worth your whole family. If you want, it ends right here," Tony said. "Try to retaliate, and next time they won't stop. Don't be an arrogant fool like your father, challenging people whose capabilities you don't know."

The poor people adored him after the incident. Tony gave money to the church and lent people money to start businesses at reasonable rates. If they didn't pay, he might take a horse, or depending on the debt, maybe someone's business or house, but family was sacred. Tony wouldn't go after people's families, and he wouldn't widow women or orphan children unless absolutely necessary. The peasant population that was much larger than the rich and they were fiercely loyal. Never before had a Don take the part of a peasant over a nobleman and not hurt people's family for leverage.

They told him when other Mafiosos were plotting against him. No one wanted another tyrant to take over. Thus, every attempt by other Mafia chieftains to usurp him failed and usually only increased his power base. In 1905 there was a terrible war. Five other families lined up against him, and still Tony out-generaled them and came out stronger than ever. Then an underboss from America came to see him.

Vito Calabrese was a member of the Genoa family of New York. Tony was curious as to why someone would come all the way from America to see him. He rolled out the red carpet when the man arrived at his villa.

"Mr. Calabrese, it's a pleasure to meet you," Tony said.

"Thank you, Don Maretti," Calabrese said, surprised at Tony's young age.

"Fabrizio," Maretti said, addressing one of his men, "if Mr. Calabrese wants food, the chef will cook for him special. If he wants wine, give him the best from our cellars. If he wants a girl, get that peasant girl, Angela, for him. You've had a long journey. We'll talk tomorrow, after you've rested."

"Thank you, Don Maretti," Calabrese said. "You are every bit the businessman people say you are."

The following morning, Tony waited for Calabrese to show up for brunch. He knew Calabrese had drank two bottles of expensive wine and slept with Angela. Slept being the key word because he was drunk. Angela left before the morning light.

Calabrese was red-eyed when he came to Tony's table.

"Good morning," Tony said. "The girl Angela is amazing, is she not?" He saw Calabrese think quickly.

"I would like to see her again tonight, if that's possible," Calabrese said.

Tony smiled. *Bastard wants to know what he missed.*

"Why did you come all the way from America to see me?" Tony asked.

"I thought we could help each other," Calabrese said.

"In what way?" Tony asked.

"We buy wine, olive oil and other products from here. We recruit men from here. It seems every other month, we're dealing with a different guy," Calabrese said.

"How does this concern me?" Tony asked.

"Underbosses in America are thinking they can achieve what you've achieved here. It's hurting business."

"Your business, not mine," Tony said. "Why do I care what happens in America?"

"Because you could be big in America," Calabrese said.

"I'm sure you've heard the saying that, 'It's better to be the big fish in a small pond than a small fish in a big pond.' It's always better to be the big fish," Tony said.

"I knew you'd say that," Calabrese replied, smiling. "How'd you like to be the big fish in a big pond?"

"Talk to me," Tony said.

"You come to America," Calabrese started. "There's an underboss we're unhappy with. He won't be in charge much longer. You won't have to work your way up. You'll start as a boss. I'll sponsor you. You make your bones, do what

I think you can do, and the sky's the limit."

"Why do I deserve this generosity?" Tony asked. "Don't you have a son?"

"No," Calabrese replied. "I have five daughters. I know that's why I haven't risen higher. There'd be a war over my succession if I had too much power. You be my son and we'll have power the New York Dons never dreamed of."

"How so?" Tony asked.

"I have a plan," Calabrese said. "I heard a saying once. 'Go west, young man, haven't you been told, California's full of whiskey, women, and gold.' Everybody's fighting for control in New York. Chicago and Kansas City aren't much better. But California's wide open for someone with balls and organization."

"You'll have the most expensive consigliere in history. But it'll be money well spent," Tony replied.

Calabrese stayed another week while he and Tony worked out their plan to the tiniest detail. Tony's territory would be split up among his underbosses and enemies. Tony went to New York with Calabrese. He hired a woman to teach him English, because he couldn't negotiate properly or command respect through an interpreter. He married Calabrese's youngest daughter, which further cemented his position, but he didn't do it for that, which is why the older man didn't object.

He was hit with the thunderbolt the second he saw her. She looked more Greek than Italian, with lush black hair, huge brown eyes and exquisite olive skin. She had large breasts, but her waist and hips were trim, and her legs were long and slim. Her mother had raised her like in the old country where women were taught to be pleasing to a man.

She was completely submissive. If he wanted sex, she was eager and willing. If he was hungry, she cooked. She never questioned him about where he went or what he did. If he was gone on business for her father, she always welcomed him back with open arms and open legs. Tony's fearsome business reputation was exactly that -- just business. He was always very loving and gentle with his wife.

He rose through the ranks quickly, until he became the top underboss for the family. Don Domenico Genoa, in the midst of a turf war with two of the other six families in New York, secretly allowed Tony to build his own regime, although he wasn't officially given the title of Capo.

Don Domenico was impressed. Every man Tony recruited was a little too good for the job he was doing and paid a little too much. Don Domenico was dying of cancer, and didn't think his own son, who was only twenty-five and studying to be a lawyer, and who had never worked in the family business, could keep the empire together. He told his son that he wanted his power to pass to Tony. However, he died before he could officially announce it to the other caporegimes.

The son, Dino Genoa, called Tony and Calabrese into his father's study at the funeral reception.

"Gentlemen, we have a problem," Dino said. "Santino Morrone, and his pal, Costanza, think I'm the head of the family now, and have asked for a meeting to solve our problems. I need your help, Tony. I never worked the street, that's true. But I've seen how my father did business and I listened and learned a lot more than he ever thought I did. He had this dream that I'd be a prosecutor or a congressman. If he'd lived longer, that dream might have come to fruition. May he rest in peace.

"I'm Sicilian, just like you. You wouldn't just hand over an empire to someone who wasn't blood to honor a deathbed wish that only two or three people knew about.

I'm taking over the family. However, I'm not a fool. Here's my offer. I know I'm supposed to be assassinated at this meeting. I know this, because it's what my father would do. It's a smart move. You kill Morrone and Costanza and cement my power, and you can form your own family, with my blessing and full support."

Tony thought for a moment before responding. He owed Calabrese for bringing him there. *A deal's a deal. Plus, trying to break off from the Genoas would be hell. The war won't end it though, it will get worse.* He proposed Calabrese's plan.

"I'll settle your business with Morrone and Costanza," Tony said. "Then meet me and my father-in-law, and my regime will move to California, with your blessing."

"Why California?" Dino asked.

"Vito proposed it to me before I ever came here. Everybody in New York is fighting over turf -- their little piece of turf. In California, it could all be my turf. However, I may still need a favor from you now and then."

"My father taught me to never refuse an accommodation for a friend. Agreed?" Dino said.

"Agreed," Tony replied, and the three exchanged hugs.

The meeting was supposed to be at Vesuvio's in Brooklyn. It was a small family place with good food.

The owner was being strong-armed by Morrone's gang for protection, plus his men had run up a tab totaling nearly $3,000.00. Tony said if the owner worked with him, the Genoa family would pay the debt and he would be protected by the Genoas, but wouldn't have to pay anything except occasionally to cater a wedding or funeral for Don Dino Genoa's immediate family. The owner readily agreed.

The meeting was set for 6:30 on a Thursday night. At 5:00, the regular waiters were sent home and were replaced by Tony's men. Tony waited in the building across the street.

Morrone and Costanza showed up in two new Ford cars at 6:00. No horses and buggies for such important men. They also arrived with two hitters and several Brooklyn cops as bodyguards. One of the "waiters" took a break and came to see Tony.

"What do you want to do, boss?" he asked.

"Just what we planned," Tony replied.

"But they're cops."

"Just like the dirty constables in Sicily," Tony replied. "You get mixed up in the rackets, sometimes you get killed. This is better than I thought. We kill a bunch of dirty cops that were posing as mob bodyguards and no one will dare fuck with Dino, even after I'm gone. It's perfect."

The "waiters" served drinks to everyone while Morrone's men set up. Then they came out of the kitchen blasting. Three of the "waiters" were killed, but Morrone, Costanza, their hitters, and all except one of the cops were killed.

A wagon came by and the surviving waiters got in and rode off.

Don Dino Domenico's power was undisputed and the war ended quickly afterwards. The cops cracked down for a while and a few wiseguys from every family were beaten or shot in the head resisting arrest, but eventually everything returned to normal.

Tony and Calabrese moved to California. They decided on San Francisco because it was a port city with a lot of business, and it was close to Oakland, another port city. Once they were set up in San Francisco, they did the usual, gambling, whores, loan-sharking, and so forth. Tony had learned from his time in New York that such illegal empires could easily be toppled by rivals or fanatical lawmen. Real power that couldn't be usurped easily came from having powerful friends in politics and some legitimate businesses.

San Francisco was still rebuilding from the devastating earthquake of 1906. Tony, himself, was having an old mansion remodeled for his family. The Irishman who was doing work, James Clawson, was affectionately called "Big Jim" by his employees. It fit, as he stood 6'4" and weighed 250 pounds. One day he asked Clawson to lunch.

"If I wanted to take over construction in San Francisco, how would I do it?" Tony asked.

"Partner with me," Clawson said unflinchingly. "If I had money, I could own construction in the whole Bay Area, not just here. I'm talking Oakland, San Jose, all up and down the coast."

"If money is all it takes, why should I back you?" Tony asked.

"Because I grew up here. My father was a builder. I know everyone. People will give me what you'd have to take by force with someone else."

"Did I say anything about using force?" Tony asked.

"Look, Mr. Maretti, I'm not dumb. It's obvious you're a powerful man. That's none of my business. I don't care how my customers make their living as long as they can pay the bill. However, it looks to me like you want to invest in local business. Why, I don't know and I don't care. But if you invest in mine, I guarantee you won't be sorry. I'm under-capitalized like a lot of small businessmen. I can't go after really big jobs, or government jobs, because the work has to be done before you get paid. I don't have the money to pay a crew and buy materials for months at a time with no income. Yeah, the profit is great, when you finally get it, but little guys don't have the cash to wait that long to get the profit. If I had the cash to do that, the sky'd be the limit."

"I'll give you all the cash you need," Tony said.

"But don't ever cheat me or think you can push me out."

"Why would I kill the goose that lays golden eggs?" Clawson asked.

"I believe we've come to terms," Tony said. "If you don't have a lawyer, get one. I want this as legal as possible."

"Yes, sir."

Construction proved to be lucrative. Tony had a daughter in 1910 and a son in 1912. In 1915, he had another son. He invested in restaurants, bars, grocery stores and other businesses. He backed people who were running for office, sometimes with money and sometimes by convincing popular rivals to drop out of the race. When Prohibition was enacted, he really hit the mother lode. Running tequila out of Mexico and whiskey from Canada was lucrative beyond anyone's dreams. When it was finally repealed in 1933, his power, both criminal and political, was beyond anything he and Calabrese had ever dreamed of.

However, he got nailed by the Feds for tax fraud and racketeering, and went to jail in 1935. He left his twenty-one-year-old son, Anthony, Jr., in charge with strict instructions to consult his grandfather, Vito Calabrese, on anything. Tony was sure the kid would obey the old man, and when he got out nothing would have changed much. The kid though was headstrong and didn't always consult the old man. The street soldiers didn't argue. It was better to apologize for making costly mistakes if the kid turned out to be a bad Don than it would be to face an angry Tony, Sr. about not following his son's orders while he was incarcerated.

San Francisco, 1930:

If Irish men had "consiglieres," Jack "Doc" O'Hearn certainly would have been one. Now sixty-six years old and three times divorced, he was a happy old bachelor. If he wanted to get laid he could certainly find a younger woman to indulge him. "Younger" usually meant some fortyish ex-hooker or showgirl who smelled money.

Eddie had asked him one time when they were drinking, "Why do you go out with those forty-year-old women?" He meant, of course, that Doc should socialize with women his own age.

"Because thirty-year-olds won't go out with me any more," Doc quipped.

Eddie laughed. "Why don't you socialize with women your own age?" he asked.

"Who wants to screw an old lady?" Doc asked, aghast. Eddie laughed again. "Go ahead, laugh. I don't need the sanctimonious opinion of 'Mr. I have a pretty thirty-six-year-old wife, even though I'm almost fifty.'"

"That's not the same," Eddie said.

"Bullshit," Doc replied. "If I had a blonde thirtyish chippie that did whatever I said, I wouldn't be a whore chaser either. Fuck you! You're wearin' me out," Doc said as he always did when he and Eddie teased each other.

After they settled in San Francisco in 1915, their business really boomed. As Doc said, Eddie had a great reputation. Because sportswriters played up the fixed fight angle so much, he actually had more guys lining up for training than guys who'd won titles. Through the '20's their power and influence grew. By 1930, Doc and Eddie owned the fight game on the West coast.

They had a guy who gave them a percentage of the sales if he was the only guy allowed to sell soda pop at fights. They had the same deal with a Jewish deli owner who was the only person allowed to sell hot dogs and sandwiches at fights.

When radio got big, fights were not only broadcast locally, but sometimes nationally. Radio station owners came to see Eddie. His fighters were too good. Fights had to last at least five rounds for the radio stations to make money on advertising. Eddie had never thrown a fight and he wouldn't ask his fighters to. However, if they won by knockout in the fifth or sixth round instead of the third or fourth, what harm was there in that. The radio stations were appropriately grateful.

They were getting ready for an unsanctioned fight.

A Dago kid, named Sergio, was undefeated and ranked fifth by the WBA. His backers, mob guys of course, didn't want to compromise his ranking should he lose officially. They were, however, willing to bet ten thousand dollars unofficially that Sergio could beat Cash Williams, Eddie and Doc's hottest prospect, who was a big Negro kid. "Cash" was short for Cassius, his given name. Doc had told him it would sell tickets. Cash was also undefeated.

Doc and Eddie stood to make another thirty thousand off street bets if Cash won. They'd promised him half the purse if he won. Five thousand dollars was a lot of money, so Cash was extremely motivated.

Eddie's brother, John, called and said a guy was coming in who needed help. Doc said he would handle it. Just before the fight, one of their employees came over with a stocky red-haired guy.

"This guy needs to see Eddie," he said flatly.

"After the fight," Doc said. "What's your name?" he asked.

"Red," the guy replied.

"Well, Red, you're in for a treat. Everyone else paid twenty dollars to be here, whether they bet or not. You want a sandwich?" Doc finished.

"Yes," Red replied, and Doc gave him a pastrami and swiss from Klein's Deli.

The fight occurred in a makeshift ring in the attic of the Century Theater. The "referee" took off a coat and tie before getting in the ring. In the first round, Cash ran into a punch and was dropped for a five-count, with every

Italian in the room jumping up and hollering. After that the fight was one-sided. In the fourth round, Cash landed a picture perfect right. Sergio dropped to his knees. The referee counted to eight and allowed the fight to continue. Cash moved in for the kill and landed several more heavy wallops. Sergio went down and was counted out.

Everyone except the boxer's handlers and the money men left. Eddie went over to collect from the Italians. They griped about a short count.

"You picked the referee," Eddie said.

"Fuck you."

"Pay me."

"No," the leader of the Dagos said, expecting a verbal argument, where he'd say how powerful his backers were.

Eddie turned over the table they were sitting at. The bodyguard of the arrogant little underboss came forward. Eddie grabbed him by the throat and the belt, and threw him down the attic stairs. When a second bodyguard came forward, Eddie slipped a wild right and slammed a hook to the ribs, a hook to the head, and a right uppercut to the jaw. The thug dropped like a sack of potatoes. A third one came forward, swinging a lead jab. Instead of backing off, Eddie stepped forward, grabbed him by his shirt, head-butted him in the face, kneed him in the groin and smashed his right elbow into the man's chin.

"Tough bastard, isn't he?" Red said admiringly.

"He'd have been champ about five times over if the mob hadn't fucked him," Doc said calmly. "You lose the legs and the wind, but you never lose the punch or the heart, even if you are forty-eight years old."

Eddie grabbed the leader by the throat and held him up against the wall. He pulled a wad of cash out of his pocket and gave it to Eddie.

Eddie came over to where they stood, breathing a little heavy.

"God damned Wops," he said. "You give an Irishman, or an Indian, or a Negro, or a Mexican a good beatin' and he never forgets it. Fuckin' Wop needs to a reminder about every three months." Everyone laughed.

"This is the guy your brother called about," Doc said, pointing to Red.

"I'm Eddie Coyle."

"Red Sullivan."

They shook hands and Eddie said, "Let's get out of here. We'll talk business at the gym."

They went in three cars to the gym. As some guys started to clean up, Red, Eddie and Doc went into an office at the back.

"You want a drink?" Eddie said.

"Yes, thank you," Red replied.

"Doc?"

"You need to ask?" Doc said. Everyone laughed.

Eddie pulled a bottle of Irish whiskey and three glasses out of a cabinet. He poured the drinks and served them.

"What can I do for you?" he asked.

"I've run afoul of the Maretti family," Red replied.

"Blowing up a half-million dollar investment can do that," Eddie retorted. "But hell, in your place I'd have done the same thing. My brother told me what happened to your girl. That's really the shits. You have my condolences."

"Thank you," Red said flatly.

"What can I do for you?"

"Obviously, I need to get out of town," Red said.

"I'm gonna help you," Eddie said after thinking for a moment. "For two reasons. One, I hate Dago gangsters. I probably had two hundred fights if we counted all the barrooms, barges and county fairs."

"At least that many," Doc said, laughing.

"Officially, I had sixty-four fights. Forty-four victories, thirty-eight by knockout," Eddie said. "Of those twenty fights I supposedly lost, I really only lost about five or six. The others we got robbed on because some gumba owned the other guy. One time, they already had the belt engraved with the other guy's name. Remember that, Doc?"

"How could I forget?" Doc retorted.

"The second reason is you saved my brother's life. Call the soda pop guy," Eddie said to Doc. "He's got to have a load going away from here." Eddie spoke to Red again. "After you do what our guy says, you get on a train and go to New York. Go to Mickey's Gym in Hell's Kitchen. Ask for Mick. Tell him I sent you. My brother says you have balls of steel. Even if Mick can't find you work, he can set up some fights for you. That's better than being in the bay wearing cement shoes."

"Thank you," Red replied.

"Good luck," Eddie said as they shook hands.

Doc made the calls and the arrangements were made.

Red met the soda pop guy at his warehouse. Since Prohibition started, besides selling soda pop, he made a pretty penny running booze.

"You work for Coyle?" the guy asked.

"He's doing me a favor," Red said.

"You a prizefighter?"

"No."

"You sure as hell could be. Coyle always has muscle for hire. One prizefighter can take out three or four street goons. You want to make some money?" the guy asked.

"I want to get out of town," Red said.

"Sure, sure. I'll buy you a train ticket to anywhere you want," the guy said. "I'll pay you two hundred bucks."

"For what?" Red asked warily, "killing somebody?"

"No, just driving a truck. You take this load of soda to San Luis Obispo. You pick up another truck on the dock and bring it back here."

"What's in the truck?" Red asked.

"You don't want to know."

"Yeah, I do, if I'm gonna risk my ass for it," Red said.

"Tequila," the guy replied. "Disguised in soda pop bottles. No problem."

"If there's no problem, why are you willing to pay two hundred dollars for one run?" Red asked.

The guy was crestfallen that he couldn't sucker Red. "Sometimes people try to hijack the loads," he said sheepishly.

Red hadn't saved much money from his stint in Rough and Ready, as he spent it on spoiling Kate and stuff he liked.

"Three hundred dollars up front, the train ticket, and you got a deal," Red said.

"One hundred and fifty up front, and the train ticket when you get back," the guy said.

"Agreed," Red replied.

He drove the truck to San Luis Obispo without incident.

It was dusk when he arrived. He left the truck at the designated site and then walked down the docks, thinking,

I could get prison time for running liquor. On the other hand, it was in soda pop bottles, in a soda pop company truck, so I might be able to play dumb if I get caught. I am just a guy who took what I thought was a legitimate job. I could take the guy's one fifty and run. To where?

He decided to do the job and went back to the warehouse.

"You the driver?" the guy asked.

"Yeah," Red said flatly.

"Sometimes you need a negotiator on these runs," the guy said. Red showed him his .45. "Hello, Mr. Speaker. You'll do fine. Here's some money for gas. You know San Francisco?"

"Yeah."

"Go to the Popco warehouse on Church Street, there'll be guys waiting there."

Red got in the truck and drove off. He put the .45 on the seat next to him.

He cruised along for several hours with no problems.

He gassed up a couple of times, the last time outside San Francisco. While he was waiting, four guys came over. Red figured them for wiseguys -- nice suits, bad attitudes.

"What's in the truck?" the apparent leader asked.

"Soda pop, like the sign says," Red replied casually.

"Mind if we take a look?"

"No, if you're cops and have a search warrant."

"I keep it in my shoe!" the leader snarled as he tried to kick Red in the balls.

Red blocked it with his right leg, stepped forward, and slammed his forearm into the man's throat. He fell, gagging, as the other three converged on Red. They got in the first half dozen blows to his head and body. Besides his boxing training, Red had the deep muscles and strong hands of a man who worked with his body all is life. Pain didn't ruin him, and the sight of his own blood didn't bother him. He rose up, slamming one in the balls with an uppercut. He drove a savage right into another one's solar plexus and followed it with a hook to the jaw. Both fell. The last one swung wildly and Red nailed him with a picture perfect left hook.

The first one he'd hit was up and pointing a .38 at Red. "Goodbye, asshole," he said just as Red slapped the barrel with his right hand.

The gun discharged and Red felt his arm go numb. He slugged the guy in the face with his left. The thug fell as the others were trying to get up. The gas jockey had run back into the station. Red grabbed the pump nozzle out of the tank and dosed them all with gas. They backed off, but drew their revolvers. Red's .45 was on the seat of the truck. He sprayed more gas at them as one took aim.

"That's suicide," Red said calmly. The thug hesitated, looking at his buddies. "You can put a cigarette out in raw gasoline, under the right conditions," Red said, "but have some fumes and you're fucked. Like a muzzle flash igniting this whole block." He sprayed some more gas. "You might get me, but you'll take yourselves and everyone else around here with me."

They backed off. Red got in the truck and drove off.

He saw headlights behind him. He couldn't imagine the assholes from the station were following him, but it could be. They were gaining on him. With the heavy load, the truck would only run about 40 or 45. He had to give them the benefit of the doubt, as much as he hated it. He didn't want to kill some poor bastard who was just trying to pass a slow truck. The car pulled alongside. Red put the .45 in his left hand and gripped the steering wheel with his injured right, even though it hurt. The passenger in the car rolled down the window and stuck a sawed-off shotgun out the window.

Red emptied the clip into the car. The car veered off and flipped into the ditch. Red kept driving.

He dropped the truck at the warehouse and collected his money and train ticket.

"Jesus Christ," the guy who paid Red gasped. "Come with me."

He took Red to a house on 30th Street. The guy who lived there wasn't a doctor, but he had been a medic in the big war, and treated people who couldn't go to a hospital.

"You're lucky," he said.

"Do I look lucky?" replied Red sarcastically.

"Yes. It's a nasty stripe, but it didn't hit bone.

It also missed an artery, which is why you didn't bleed to death. You may lose some feeling in the elbow, but you should have all your strength back once it heals. It's gonna leave an ugly scar. Keep it clean and change the bandages every twelve hours for the first few days. You don't want gangrene," the guy said. He gave Red a bottle of rubbing alcohol. "It'll sting like hell, but it'll probably save your arm. Pour it on when you change the bandages."

The soda pop guy drove Red to the train station. Three hundred dollars would take care of him for a while. He bought a first-class ticket and boarded the train. He went to his private cabin and went to sleep, despite the pain in his arm.

Lynchburg, Missouri 1945:

Hank Collins stood on a street corner in Waynesville, which was just outside Fort Leonard Wood. After a truck convoy had taken him and Rabbit to Paris, they were flown to an airbase in England. Hank's injury wasn't life-threatening. The bullet hadn't hit bone, only thigh muscle, and eventually he was able to limp around. He did the exercises the doctors at the base told him to do. Eventually, except for an ugly scar, he was as good as new. Rabbit got an infection and had to stay longer. It was touch and go for a wile, but he recovered. Hank went to see him before he left.

"Goodbye, brother," Rabbit said.

"Goodbye," Hank said, shaking hands. "Thanks for everything. What are you gonna do now?" he asked.

"I'm not goin' back to Mississippi," Rabbit replied. "My mamma and daddy are both passed on. My uncle owns a bar and restaurant in San Francisco. He said he'd give me a job after the war. It's called 'Jerry's.' It's on Sixteenth Street. If you're ever in San Francisco, look me up."

"I might do that," Hank said. "I just might."

"I think about Sister Gabrielle," Rabbit said.

"So do I," Hank replied. "Good luck."

"You too."

After he left England, he was flown directly to Washington D.C. He wanted to call his parents or send a telegram to let them know he was coming home, but it all happened so fast and he didn't know what to say. Now he stood outside the Oval Office, waiting for the President with several other guys who were being hailed as heroes.

He was nervous as hell. He and Rabbit had taken the village on sheer adrenaline and rage, without having time to think. He was thinking now. He was actually more nervous than when they were on the hill overlooking the besieged camp. It seemed funny that accepting an award would be harder than facing death. The government had a reception for them, and because of his nervousness, he'd had four shots of whiskey to try to calm his nerves. He didn't want to face the president drunk, so he stopped though he certainly would have liked another drink.

The band started playing "Hail to the Chief" and the President came in. Each man was called up individually. The president put the medal on the soldier, shook hands and talked for a minute with the soldier while pictures were snapped. The soldier was then ushered out and the next man called. Hank was fourth out of ten. He looked at the dapper little man in a cream-colored suit with pale skin. But he pulsated with vibrant life. He was very confident and dignified. Hank was reminded of a proverb he'd once heard. "It's not the size of the dog in the fight, it's the size of the fight in the dog." Harry Truman exemplified the proverb. Since Harry was kind of short and Hank was 6'2", the President had to go up on tiptoe and Hank had to stoop so the Congressional Medal of Honor could be placed around his neck. Harry pumped his hand with a firm grip.

"Congratulations. You're a fine American. Where you from, son?" Harry asked.

"Missouri," Hank replied.

"Well, I'll be go to hell! So am I!"

"I knew that, sir," Hank said.

"I guess everyone does, now that I think about it.

What kind of whiskey were you served at the reception?"

"Jim Beam, sir," Hank said, more nervous than ever.

Harry leaned forward and whispered in Hank's ear, "If all these damn reporters weren't here, I'd invite all you boys to the office for a drink."

Hank laughed nervously.

"Yes, sirree, it's men like you that are gonna keep this country great in the future. We're really gonna roll now. Industry, small business, everything. I'm sure of it. What do you plan to do now?"

Hank was stunned and at the same time proud to be an American. The most powerful man in the world was asking him what he wanted to do and seemed genuinely interested.

"I haven't decided, sir. Go see my mom and dad, get my bearings, then decide," Hank replied.

"Well, you've earned it. Good luck in whatever you do," Harry said, and pumped his hand again.

Flashbulbs went off until he saw stars and then he was ushered out.

"We'll have a car take you anywhere you want," the President's aide said.

"The train station, I guess," Hank said.

He was put on a troop train and went to Fort Leonard Wood. He walked out of the fort after getting his final discharge papers and kind of walked around Waynesville for a while still wearing the medal. A military car stopped.

"Where you headed, soldier?" the driver asked.

"Lynchburg, sir," Hank said.

"Don't 'sir' me, I'm just a recruiting officer. Hop in," the man said. Hank got in. "I'm happy to give a ride to a Medal of Honor winner."

"Thank you," Hank said.

Neither spoke again until Lynchburg.

Hank got out in front of his house and gave thanks to the man. He walked up the rock driveway. His father met him halfway.

"I'll take it here, my wife's already cryin'," Dan Collins said.

"Why is Mom crying and what are you gonna take?" Hank asked.

His father recognized the voice. "Hank? Holy shit! We saw the military car and the uniform, and thought the worst. Good to see you, Son," Dan said, hugging him.

"Good to see you, Dad," Hank replied.

His father stepped back, his eyes tearing. "Is that the...?"

Hank cut him off. "Congressional Medal of Honor. Yes, Harry Truman was happy that I was from Missouri."

"How come we weren't notified? I'd have loved to see the President give that to you," Dan said.

"I don't know, Dad," Hank replied. "I left England and went directly to Washington. I wanted to send you a telegram or a letter and I kind of wanted to see you in person. I guess it's my fault."

"That's okay. You're home and that's all that matters. What did you win the medal for?" Dan asked.

"Killin' a bunch of Nazi bastards that needed killin'. You know someone with a worse war story than Grandpa's," Hank said.

"You can tell me and Grandpa about it when your mother's not around."

"He's still alive?" Hank said, both surprised and happy.

"Yes, and just as full of piss and vinegar as he ever was," Dan replied.

Elizabeth came out of the house. "Is that Hank?" she said excitedly.

"Yes, Mom, it is," Hank said.

She hugged him and started crying again. "I thought...."

"I know, Dad told me. Don't cry, Mom," Hank said.

"Look at that medal," she said. Dan shook his head at her and she got the drift. "Come on in and see Grandpa. He'll be happy to see you. The boys'll be home soon and we'll have supper."

"Thanks, Mom," Hank said and kissed his mother. They all went in the house.

Allen stood up when he saw Hank. "Smart boy, always takes his granddad's advice. I told you to come home in one piece and you did," Allen said proudly.

"How are you, Grandpa?" Hank asked.

"Mean as cat shit, like always," Dan said.

"Lizzie, remind me to slap him when I can reach him," Allen said to Elizabeth. Everyone laughed. "This calls for a drink," Allen said.

"Just about everything calls for a drink with you," Elizabeth said.

"Nobody asked you, woman," Allen snapped. "Anytime a man's grandson comes home a hero, that's celebratin' time."

"I'm not a hero, Grandpa," Hank said sullenly.

"Bullshit, bull...shit," Allen said sternly. "They don't give the Medal of Honor to candy-asses. You mamma's cryin' 'cause you're home. A lot of other people mammas are cryin' 'cause their boys ain't comin' home. Stop feelin' sorry for yourself and have a drink with me and your dad. That's an order, soldier."

"Yes, sir," Hank said, happy to see Allen as ornery as ever.

Allen poured three glasses of Kentucky bourbon. "They call that 'Wild Turkey,' son. Has a right nice bite to it," Allen said.

Hank felt the burn and liked it. "That it does," he said.

Allen and Dan downed theirs, and Allen refilled their glasses.

Hank's little brothers came home. He could hear his mother scolding them from the kitchen. "Take those muddy shoes off!" she yelled. "Your father'll clean those fish later. Come in and see who's here."

Robert, who was ten, and affectionately called "Bobby" and six-year-old Jack came in from fishing.

"Hank!" little Jack yelled, outracing his older brother and jumping on Hank. It made Hank feel good. A child's love is unconditional.

"How are you, little man?" Hank asked.

"Good," Jack said. "I caught four fish today. Are you back from the war?"

"Yes, I am."

"Did you get shot?" Jack asked.

"Yes, I did," Hank replied.

"Did it hurt?" Bobby asked.

"Yes, a lot," Hank said.

"You kill a lot of Germans?" Bobby asked.

"Yes."

"But you guys don't need to worry about it," Dan put in.

Hank started tickling Jack, who called to Bobby for help. Soon Hank had them both on the floor, giggling.

"Daddy, spank him!" Jack yelled.

"He's too big," Dan said.

"I thought you said nobody's too big to be spanked," Bobby said indignantly.

"Did I say that? I meant too old," Dan said. "Hank's twenty-two. Your parents can't spank you after you're twenty-one."

"Daaad," Bobby groaned.

Allen slapped Hank on the ass and Hank theatrically yelled, "Ouch!"

"The rule doesn't apply to grandparents," Allen said. "They can spank anybody they want."

"Grandpaaa!"

"Don't you sass me, boy, or you'll get one." Bobby and

Jack squealed with laughter.

"You boys stop that horseplay and come to supper," Elizabeth yelled from the kitchen. "And that goes for Bobby and Jack, too."

Everyone, including the little boys, caught the joke and laughed as they went to the kitchen.

"Where's Laura?" Hank asked after everyone started eating.

"Didn't you get my letter?" Elizabeth replied. "I wrote and told you, she married Everett Hodge and moved to California."

"He has a forty Ford coupe with a souped-up flathead in it," Bobby said admiringly.

"I hope that's not the only reason she married him," Elizabeth said, annoyed. Hank could tell his mother didn't completely approve of his sister's husband.

Dan spoke up. "I recall a certain preacher who wasn't overjoyed with his daughter's choice of men either. After twenty-three years he agrees it might work out."

"That's different," Elizabeth said.

"Different, how?"

"Oh, shut up."

Everyone had blackberry cobbler for dessert. Hank went into his sister's old bedroom and unpacked. He put his medal in a drawer.

Six-year-old Jack was watching him. "Aren't you gonna wear your medal tomorrow?" he asked.

"No," Hank said.

"I'd wear it all the time," Jack said.

"Why?"

"It says you're brave and honorable."

Hank pulled the medal out of the drawer again. "A lot of good men died in this war that didn't get medals. This says you're brave and honorable," Hank said, pointing to his chest. "This says you're lucky," he finished, pointing to the medal. "You understand what I'm saying?"

"I understand," Jack said. "I'd still wear it all the time."

"You can hang it on your wall if you want," Hank said, handing Jack the medal.

"Thanks, Hank!" Jack yelled, hugging him. "You're the greatest big brother in the world!" He ran down the hall yelling, "Mom! Dad! Guess what Hank said?"

Hank put his face in his hands and cried.

His dad came in and put his arm around Hank. "What's wrong, son?" he asked.

"I keep seeing this girl," Hank replied.

"A friend of yours?" Dan asked.

"No, I never knew her name," Hank said. "Me and Rabbit -- he was another soldier I met in France -- we came upon this village. It was all women and kids and old men. The Nazis lined all the women up against a wall. Then they shot every other one in line."

"God damn," Dan said, aghast.

"Yeah, me and Rabbit took revenge. We killed every single German there. We went into the church. This little peasant girl, she was maybe fourteen or fifteen, was tied up on the altar. She was barefoot and her feet were dirty.

I remembered church hayrides and picnics. The girls wearing cutoff jeans, no shoes, teasing the boys. How at the end of the day their feet would be dirty, maybe even a little green on the heels from playing in wet spring grass. Then it hit me. Her feet were dirty because she didn't have any shoes, not from being on a picnic. The Nazi commander strangled her to frighten a nun that was helping the resistance. She was someone's daughter, someone's sister. Because of the whim of one evil man, this beautiful little girl would never play in grass again. Her eyes were wide open. I keep seeing her, like she's the spokesperson for a lot of others."

"You did what you had to do," Dan said.

"If we'd got there five minutes earlier...," Hank started, but his father cut him off.

"You might have died with the townspeople. You can't agonize over could've, would've, should've. You've got to go on."

"I don't know how, Dad."

"If Grandpa had lain down and died after his war experiences, I wouldn't be here, and neither would you,"

Dan said. "I'll tell you a story I haven't told your mother. A friend of mine was a couple years ahead of me in school. He was a straight-A student, a great athlete, a star baseball player. Married the prettiest girl in school. Worked for Grandpa for a while. Made foreman in less than two years. Then he got drafted and sent to World War I. He came back alive, but he was different. He wasn't the happy-go-lucky guy I remember. He was very melancholy. Grandpa gave him his job back, but had to fire him for showing up drunk all the time. He got in fights in bars, beat up his wife. He was always in trouble.

"One day, I'm fishing off the bridge over the Gasconade by Nebo. He comes staggering across the bridge and tells me how his wife's leaving him and life isn't worth living. I said I'd talk to Grandpa and get him his job back if he'd quit drinking. That I'd talk to his wife, maybe she'll reconsider if he quit drinking and promised not to hit her anymore. I even offered to go to the town preacher with him, whatever he needed to straighten out. He said, 'You can't help me. No one can. I'm goin' to Hell anyway, it might as well be sooner than later.' Then, before I can say or do anything, he jumped off the bridge. He was dead as soon as he hit the water. He was twenty-two. A stone waste of life. Because he did something, or saw something, that he couldn't live with. I know the Army has counselors for vets having problems adjusting. Talk to one, or at least me or Grandpa."

"Thanks, Dad," Hank replied. "That helps a lot. Don't worry, I won't be leaping off any bridges. I just need to get my bearings and decide what I want to do."

"We all love you."

"I know. That's what got me through."

Hank spent the next couple of days wandering around his home area. Because of his brothers talking at school, everyone knew about him being awarded the Congressional Medal of Honor. The way people acted, one would have thought Gary Cooper was in town. Everyone wished him well.

He borrowed his dad's '37 Chevy and went to St. Louis. He went to the plant where he had worked. Since he didn't have a suit, he wore his dress uniform. He waited in an office for the manger to come in.

Hank didn't like the manager the minute he saw him. Hank's old boss had been drafted too. The new guy wore a crisp black suit and a white shirt. He also wore a yellow tie, tied perfectly into a double-Windsor knot. Hank got one of those involuntary full-body shudders.

He remembered his maternal grandfather, a fire-and-brimstone preacher. Seven days a week, regardless of weather, he put on a crisp white shirt, a tie and a black suit. He apparently ran a tighter ship at home than he did at church. Hank recalled a dinner he went to at the home of a friend of Allen's when he was about ten. Allen's friend was running for the state legislature and invited everyone he knew to a campaign dinner. A Missouri senator's wife commented on his mother Elizabeth's impeccable table manners. She thanked the lady and went on.

But Hank was awake and heard his mother talking to his father later that night. Apparently, his great-grandmother was a noblewoman in England. His maternal grandfather was fiercely intent on raising a lady. He had tied Elizabeth's left hand behind her back at the dinner table to make her eat properly and not push food with her fingers. He taught Hank how to tie a tie. He drilled Hank mercilessly on it, so one of the useless things Hank knew too much about was the proper tying of a double-Windsor knot for a necktie. Others were how to make a bomb out of soap and other household products, and how to clear a jam on an M-60 machine gun in a sandstorm.

The man enjoyed clothes, took pleasure in clothes, and had that snake-oil salesman look. He'd never done a day's work in his life. Hank tried to hide his contempt, but wasn't sure if he was successful or not.

The man spoke. "I see you're a decorated veteran. Congressional Medal of Honor. That's impressive."

"Thank you," Hank replied.

"Do you have any other experience?" the man asked.

Hank seethed. *What other experience do I need, you fucking arrogant prick,* Hank thought to himself. He mentally bit his tongue, though, and said, "I worked here three years installing fenders on cars before the war broke out."

"I see," the man said.

Hank wanted to kick him in the balls so hard that he'd have to part his hair differently. The man had that preacher's way, the druggist's way, the sheriff's way, the banker's way. It was the way that said, "I'm smarter than you, but I'm not going to say it." He then smiled that pitying smile bankers do when denying a loan, or preachers do when they say your faith isn't strong enough, or cops do when they say, "I'm just doing my job." It was all he could do to not jerk the guy up and slap the shit out of him.

"We're making airplanes now. And we're fully staffed. I'm sorry," the man said with the finality of a first grade teacher telling a student to clean the erasers.

He waited for Hank to stand up and leave. Hank sat there until the man became uncomfortable.

"I think we're done," the man said, trying to intimidate Hank with his uppity manner.

"I don't think we are," Hank said. "I don't care if you don't have any openings. You could have been nicer telling me."

"I'm sorry if I offended you," the man said in that I'm-apologizing-but-I-really-mean-fuck-you voice. "I'm going to have to ask you to leave," the manager said.

"And if I don't, you'll do what?" Hank asked. "You have your job because men like me went to war and fought and died. I'm glad you told a bunch of women what to do while I stormed a beachhead under fire. The war'll be over soon and men, not pansies like you that fear real men, will be back in charge. It will matter that you fought in the war and want to work. You disgust me, sir. You can go to hell," Hank finished.

"We might have an opening on the night shift," the manager said nervously.

"Let me reiterate. You can go to hell," Hank said.

"I don't want charity or pity, and I don't want you telling me later that you did me a favor. Kiss my ass."

Hank left and went to a bar down the street.

"What'll you have, soldier?" the bartender asked.

"Whiskey. Smooth, but with a bit of bite," Hank said.

"That'd be Jack Daniels from Tennessee," the bartender said.

"I'll have it," Hank said, pulling a five-dollar bill out of his wallet.

"Your money's no good here," the bartender said. "I'm proud to give a drink to our servicemen. The Army made a man of my son. He was a worthless layabout before the war. I'm told he stood up at Omaha Beach. Only time in his life. The Army made a man out of him. Killed him, but made a man out of him."

Hank shuddered. He remembered coughing up salt water, not knowing if the blood was his or not, so many good guys screaming for their mammas, their guts hanging out, and the endless noise and fire coming in.

"Only good thing he ever did was stand up to the Germans at Omaha Beach," the bartender said.

Hank lost it. "I was at Omaha Beach. Mister, if you say one more word about a man that fought and died on Omaha Beach being worthless, I will knock your fuckin' teeth out."

The bartender was a big man and so was Hank. He wasn't used to being challenged in his own place.

The bartender spoke. "My son was a worthless piece of...."

Hank grabbed him by the shirt and pulled him over the bar. Hank hit the man in the face four times, let him fall to the floor and said, "Told ya."

He put a five-dollar bill under his glass and started out the door. The other patrons of the bar let him leave without incident.

Hank was disillusioned. He couldn't imagine a man talking that way about his own son. Hank loved his father. However, he just couldn't see himself working the farm for the next forty years and looking out for Mom after Dad died, or vice versa, and never trying for something more. He had to know. The grass may not be greener, it may just be mowed differently, but he had to know.

He told of his plan to look up Rabbit on the coast.

His father was supportive of his decision.

"Since your sister's out there, maybe after Grandpa dies I'll come out to California too," Dan said. "I promised I wouldn't sell the land in his lifetime."

"I understand," Hank said. "Will you drive me to the train station?"

"Sure," his father said.

San Francisco, 1922:

Tim and Tom Conway were eleven months apart. Because their mother was busy with four other children, she enrolled them in school at the same time, even though Tim was almost a year older. Tim did well in school and the nuns liked him. They told him to help his brother, who didn't adjust well.

In second grade they met a boy named Martin Sullivan. One day at recess, two fourth grade boys were beating up Martin. He was holding up all right, considering that it was two against one. Tim ran to get Sister Mary Thomas, who was in charge of the schoolyard. Tom waded in like Jack Dempsey.

When Tim and Sister Mary Thomas returned, Tom and Martin both had bloody noses, but were standing over their crying, vanquished adversaries, who also had bloody noses and the beginnings of shiners on their eyes.

"Anytime you sissies want to try again, come and get it," they said.

After the incident, Tom and Martin were inseparable. Tim played with them a lot and liked Martin, but not as much as Tom did. When they got older, Martin got a job at an Italian restaurant in the neighborhood. The big Italian guy that owned the restaurant called Martin "Red" because of his red hair. All the businessmen who ate there did too. Martin called the restaurant owner "Uncle Tony" or "Godfather."

Martin and Tim and Tom went to ball games and ate all the hot dogs and soda they wanted, all paid for by "Uncle Tony." When they hit junior high, their relationships changed. Red started working a game called "Numbers" for Tony. He had more money than other kids in the neighborhood. People didn't park in his family's driveway, even though they didn't have a car. When they went to the bakery on Sunday, the owner would come from around the counter and serve Red, no matter how many people were in line. Older boys carried Mrs. Sullivan's groceries home from the market and refused offers of tips. Respect for people Red worked for. Tom started working "Numbers" too.

Tim didn't tell their father because he loved his brother and knew Tom would get a beating for running numbers. Tim helped out at church and at school. He said he wanted to be a priest, and Father Tommasino took him under his wing. The nuns wondered if Tim might be the next bishop. They also wondered what prison Tom and Red would go to.

One Sunday, Tim got a quick education in the ways of the world. Tom came running into the rectory, bleeding from the nose and mouth, and breathing hard. "They're gonna kill Red!" he yelled. "They're gonna kill him!"

Tim and the priest followed Tom. Four older teenagers were beating Red. Father Tommasino broke up the fight. Red looked like he'd been hit by a truck.

"Martin, you need to go to the doctor, or at least home to see your mother," the priest said.

"No," Red said stoically. "They took the money bag, Tom," Red said, depressed.

"Shit!" Tom yelled, and then said, "Sorry, Father."

"Help me up, Tom," Red said. "We need to see Tony."

Tom nodded and picked Red up.

"Tony who?" the priest asked warily.

"Mr. Maretti," Tom said.

"Don Maretti?" the priest said, incredulous.

"Yes, Don Maretti," Red replied.

The priest took them to the restaurant.

"Thank you for your help, Father Tommasino," Tony said respectfully. "These are good boys who run errands for me. I'm saddened that hooligans would assault them.

Have you contacted the police?"

Tim was stunned. Father Tommasino seemed nervous.

"The boys said they wanted to see you, Don Maretti, so I brought them directly here," he said sheepishly.

"You did the right thing," Tony said. "Is there anything I can do for you, Father? And don't be shy, you're among friends."

"The church could use a new kitchen and a reception hall for weddings and funerals," the priest said.

"Done," Tony replied. "I'm always happy to help the church."

"Thank you, Don Maretti," Father Tommasino said, bowing like he was addressing the Pope.

"Tom, Red, stay here, I want to talk to you," Tony said. "Don't worry, Father, I'll get the boys home."

"I hope to see you next Sunday," the priest said.

"You will."

Father Tommasino ushered Tim out.

They didn't see Red a lot for a while, but when they did, he and Tom owned the neighborhood. Nobody messed with them. If they did, Red told Mr. Maretti and they didn't do it twice.

Red and Tom played football in high school. Tom was a star defensive end and Red was a star linebacker, until he quit school after his sophomore year because his mother died. After that Red worked construction. He made more money than most grown men in the neighborhood. He was generous, always taking his friends out to dinner or to ball games, or to boxing matches, where they had ringside seats.

Now grown men, nineteen or twenty, their paths were almost what the nuns had predicted. Tim was studying to be a priest. Red had set Tom up with an older woman who "did the business." He made the same offer to Tim. Tim declined at first, but gave in after merciless ribbing from his brother and his friend.

"Look," Tom said, "at least you'll know what you're missing. If you still want to be a priest, great, this'll only strengthen your resolve. If you don't, at least you didn't throw your whole life away because the nuns liked you in grade school."

Tim was twenty, the woman was twenty-seven.

"Everyone's nervous their first time, baby," she said soothingly. "I'll help you."

He was disgusted that women would do such things with men they weren't married to, with men they barely knew. He was disgusted because his body betrayed him and he physically enjoyed it, and couldn't bring himself to stop her. His brother wouldn't let it rest.

"How was it?" Tom asked.

"Nice," Tim replied. "It was fun. I'm still gonna be a priest."

"Why?" Tom asked. "Do you still need to be called a 'good boy' that much?"

"I'm not like Red, and I hope you're not," Tim said.

"What's wrong with Red?" Tom asked. "All he ever did was include you and stick up for you, you self-righteous prick. I remember you going to all those ball games. I don't recall you questioning Father Tommasino accepting a new kitchen and reception hall. I do recall you dropping Red's name, and mine, when those thugs said they were gonna beat up a bunch of sissy seminary boys -- you and your friends."

"I like Red," Tim responded. "And, yes, I've used the fact that my brother and his best friend are bad-asses on occasion. Maybe I shouldn't have. But the neighborhood is the neighborhood. Since you brought it up, Father Tommasino understood that and so do I. Just because I can negotiate my way through things doesn't mean I approve of them. I like Red, I really do, but he's gonna end up in prison or dead. And so will you."

"Wrong again, brother," Tom said. "I'm gonna be a cop! The most feared made man in the world has to take it if the lowest patrolman decides to slap him around. Nobody can kill cops and get away with it. I'll be the law."

"And selling it to people like Red and Maretti," Tim said.

"What is your problem?" Tom asked. "Red is our friend, who in your own words is negotiating his life the way he has to. Red has never pretended to be anything other than what he is, which is more than I can say for some people, present company included. As for Maretti, there was a man before him and there'll be a man after him. There'll always be a man. And the cops will always have to work around that. If you don't believe that, you're more naive than I thought. Go ahead and hide from life behind the church, I'm living it."

"Have you told Mom and Dad?" Tim asked.

"They're happy," Tom replied. "A priest and a cop in the same family? Are you kidding? If one of our sisters becomes a nun, no one's going to hell for three generations. I'm tired of you being the good one and me being the bad one."

"Then stop being the bad one," Tim said, a little too sanctimoniously for Tom's taste.

"I don't care if you become the fuckin' Pope. I know you wet the bed and were afraid of the dark. You're still my asshole brother to me."

"Asshole or not, I still worry about you," Tim said.

"Don't. You're preaching to the choir," Tom said.

San Francisco, 1932:

Haimer Reinhardt was born in 1901. He left his native Germany at the age of fifteen for a life at sea. In 1920, he came ashore for good in San Francisco. He quickly realized that hatred of Germans after the war was rampant all over America. Since he'd been all over the world, he didn't have a German accent. When he spoke he sounded slightly European, but nothing one could put your finger on. He changed his name to make finding work easier. He took the names of two heroes of the American Revolution, Ben Franklin and Thomas Jefferson. He experimented with Frank Thomas and Ben Jefferson, and finally settled on Tom Franklin.

At the time, San Francisco was known as the most productive port in the entire world. The waterfront held seventeen miles of berthing space, 82 docks capable of berthing 250 vessels at one time. It was a port of call for more than 118 steamship lines, with more than 7,000 ships arriving and departing yearly. In 1929, freight tonnage in and out of the Golden Gate amounted to more than 31 million tons. San Francisco shipping and stevedoring companies took pride that San Francisco had one of the most cost-efficient longshore workforces in the nation. A gang of sixteen men could move, by hand, upwards of 20 tons an hour and a crew of a hundred men could load a 3,000-ton steamer in just two days and a night, stowing enough cargo to fill a train of freight cars five miles long. The American-Hawaiian Steamship Company calculated that during the years 1927-1931 their agents paid, on average, $0.99-1.03 per ton for loading in San Francisco, compared to $1.85-1.99 in New York and $2.17-2.43 in Boston. The port of San Francisco was also known for the worst working conditions in the world -- and the deadliest.

By 1919, the waterfront and maritime unions that had first organized in 1858 and made San Francisco the premiere union port in the world were violently suppressed. Legal protections for maritime workers were nonexistent. For centuries law and custom had regarded maritime workers as less than human, more chattel slaves or pack animals.

As late as 1897, the Supreme Court had denied seamen the protections of the 13th Amendment banning slavery and involuntary servitude. The court ruled that they were "deficient in that full and intelligent responsibility for their acts which is accredited to ordinary adults."

With the employers now firmly in control, working conditions declined to their lowest point in history.

Longshoremen were selected like cattle in the humiliating ritual of the "shape-up" where thousands of desperate men circled up for hours in all weather to beg for a job. The chosen few were required to kick back a portion of their pay for the opportunity. It might take a man three or four days to connect with a job, sometimes as long as a week. Once on the job, they worked under the speed-up, a killing pace enforced by the walking bosses, sadistic bastards who made Southern chain-gang guards look progressive by comparison. These company foremen held the threat of blacklist for any man who fell behind or complained. Crews were often forced to race against the other to see which might load the faster. A man might hunt for days for a job that lasted only a few hours, but work shifts often ran as long as 24 or 36 hours without rest. Even longer shifts of 58 and 72 hours were not uncommon.

The longest longshore work shift ever recorded ran for 110 hours straight. Two men died on the job and five others were never able to work again.

Those who dropped from exhaustion or heart attack or were injured or killed on the job were easily replaced from the pool of hungry men at the pierhead. It was not unusual for a man to obtain work through a fellow worker's misfortune.

Throughout the 1920's three to six working longshoremen were disabled for every eight hours on the job. Yearly, the number of accidents reported equaled the number of workers. Since reporting an accident meant running the risk of blacklist, many accidents were never reported. The death rate for longshoremen through industrial accidents and job-induced disease was the highest for any occupation in the world, 62 percent above normal. On average, a longshoreman could expect to die before his forty-seventh birthday. The pay averaged $10.45 a week.

Out of these deplorable conditions grew one of the most democratic and progressive labor unions in the United States and, in later years, one of America's most revered labor leaders. Tom would start an insurgent labor movement that would transform the lives of workers from San Pedro to Ketchikan and into Canada, over to Hawaii, inland to Chicago and Baltimore, and as far south as New Orleans.

In 1925, Tom had tried to revive the Dockworkers Union that had been broken in 1919. During a strike on Pier 38, he'd fought with company goons and accidentally killed a man. Some witnesses said he kicked the man's face in after he was unconscious. Others said he hit the man a couple times and the guy hit his head on the curbstone. He did six years for manslaughter. A lot of guys hook up with other criminals in prison and others tried to get bigger and stronger. Tom read, mostly Machiavelli and Dumas. He especially liked the *Count of Monte Cristo* where a wrongly imprisoned man wreaked vengeance on his tormentors.

After his release, the only work he could find was collecting for a loan shark on the docks. He ran afoul of his boss one day when he showed some sympathy for a down-on-his-luck worker. Tom had refused to break the guy's leg. If the guy had a broken leg, he couldn't work and he couldn't pay, Tom reasoned. The loan shark didn't see it that way. He couldn't have street guys being lenient. He decided to make an example of Tom.

Four guys accosted him on the street. Tom got his blood up and pulled out a knife. "I'll cut you up!" he yelled.

Two of them pulled guns. Tom ran down the street. The goons shot at him, breaking windows in cars parked on the street. He ran into a boxing gym on the corner.

A dapper looking guy in his sixties said, "What's your fuckin' hurry?"

"Some guys are trying to kill me."

"Great," the guy said, making a motion with his hand.

Several boxers stopped what they were doing and came and stood behind him. The four goons came in.

"We're gonna kill this fucker," they sneered.

"Not in here you're not," the older guy said, showing a revolver, while the boxers scowled.

"We don't have a problem with you, Doc," the apparent leader said.

"And I don't have one with you," Doc replied. "You want to kill this guy, kill him outside. A murder happens in here, and the cops close us down while they investigate. That could take weeks. We could lose thousands of dollars. That I do have a problem with. Now get the hell out here." Doc drew the pistol and the boxers started to move forward. "I'm not gonna ask you again."

The four goons left.

"Thanks, boys," Doc said.

"Any time, Doc," the boxers said, almost in unison. The men were willing to die for "Doc" whoever he was.

"Thanks a lot," Tom said.

"Fuck you," Doc replied. "In my office." Tom followed him to an office.

"I appreciate what you did," Tom said.

"Fuck you," Doc said again. "I give a shit what happens to you? No. But like I said, I have to do what's right for business. I let them kill you in here and that hurts business. Now I have to call their boss and apologize for not letting them kill you."

"I'll make it up to you," Tom said.

"How?" Doc asked skeptically.

"I have a business proposition for you, since you obviously have juice around here," Tom said. "Make you a hundred grand a year, easy, all legal."

That got Doc's attention. He gave Tom a business card. "My partner'll be back day after tomorrow," Doc said. "Call me Thursday morning, we'll talk. And buy a firearm if you're gonna go around like a hard-ass, pissin' people off."

Tom sat in a coffee shop down the street from Murphy's Gym. As he ate breakfast, he was a little aware of the four inch barreled .38 caliber Smith & Wesson Model 10 revolver under his arm in a shoulder holster. He'd have to get used to it. He agreed with Doc. Monday was the last chase on him. He would carry his own piece from now on. He paid the bill and walked down the street to the gym.

When he arrived, he walked directly back to the office. A huge Negro kid stepped in front of him.

"What's your business?" he asked.

"I have an appointment with Doc and his partner," Tom replied.

"Mr. Coyle?" the kid asked.

"Yes. Mr. Coyle," Tom replied, not missing a beat.

The Negro kid knocked on the door to the office and then opened it. "Man here to see you, Mr. Coyle," he said.

"Thank you, Cash," a voice said. "How's your mamma?"

"Better. Thanks for asking, sir," the Negro kid said.

"You ready to fight now?" the unseen voice asked.

"Yes, sir. I won't let you down," Cash replied.

"You never have. Can you eat nails and shit steel wool?"

"Yes, sir."

"That's what I want to hear. Send the man in."

Tom went in and shook hands with Doc.

"This is my partner, Eddie Coyle," Doc said. They shook hands.

Tom was curious. "What the hell was that?" he asked brazenly.

Eddie didn't flinch. "Cash is undefeated in thirty-six fights. He's getting a title shot this month. It was supposed to happen a couple months ago. His mother got sick and he wasn't training worth shit. We knew he'd lose if we made him fight. We lied and said he broke his hand in training and got the fight postponed. His mother recovered and now his mind's right. I've got too much invested in that kid to blow it now. He's gonna be the next champ. Never mind that, Doc says you have a proposal for us."

"That I do," Tom said.

Tom told of the deplorable conditions on the docks.

Tom always read and talked to people. He was well informed of world events and more informed of local events. With the coming of the Great Depression, the shipping companies seized the opportunity to squeeze out even more profits. Even though the construction of their fleets had been ninety percent subsidized by taxpayers, and even though they received millions of dollars yearly carrying U.S. mail overseas, the ship owners took advantage of the sudden pool of unemployed. To the critics of the subsidies they had claimed the necessity of paying "good American wages," yet they now drove these wages down so steeply that desperate seamen were forced to pay $5.00 and up for jobs that paid once cent a month plus room and board. The jobs were called "workaways." The men worked 16 or 18 hours and the food was so bad it would reportedly make a billy goat puke.

"It can't be that bad," Doc said.

"It's worse than that," Tom replied. "You complain and you don't work. You complain twice and you're dead. Even though they charge guys a couple bucks a day to be on the work list, if the decide to call a work stoppage and strong-arm some merchant who buys perishable goods like bananas from Brazil say, you lost what you paid to be on the list, even though you didn't work.

"Any given day there's what -- six thousand workers on the docks that are being screwed daily. Start an honest union, don't charge to be on the work list, limit days to ten or twelve hours, and you'd clean up. If you only got one third of them to sign up with you, payin' three bucks a month in dues, that's seventy-two thousand dollars a year, legal. Then it would go up."

"The shipping companies broke the Dockworkers Union in 1919 and again in 1925," Doc said.

"That's because the leaders of the union weren't properly organized. They didn't have any backup and they weren't willing to do what was necessary."

"And you are?" Doc said.

"Yes," Tom replied. "Freedom is not given by the oppressor, it is taken by the oppressed. This tyranny isn't going to blow over by itself. Somebody's got to huff and puff."

"How does this concern us?" Eddie asked.

"Roosevelt just unveiled a huge new economic reform plan," Tom said. "I hear they're going to build bridges over the bay to make commerce easier. The government is planning a bunch of new roads and other projects."

"Yeah, but any union will have to negotiate with the construction companies. That means Maretti," Doc said.

"Not necessarily," Tom said. "Start your own construction company. Go after the contracts yourself.

The mob always adds at least thirty percent for Blue Sky, to cover their payoffs. It would be easy to underbid 'em. Maretti can't intimidate Uncle Sam."

"He'll try to intimidate us," Doc said.

"'Try' being the key word," Tom replied. "You don't need the mob for muscle. You've got your own. Ten prizefighters can take on twenty street goons and kick ass. He pulls a knife, we pull a gun. He sends one of ours to the hospital, we send three of theirs to the morgue. If the mob gets these government contracts it'll get worse than ever for the working man."

"It'll be a fight," Doc said.

"It's a fight we ought to make," Eddie replied.

"He's right. These Dago gangsters get the government work contracts and they'll have a stranglehold on this town like never before. Then they'll try to take over other things, like the fight game. I'm too old to start over, and I know you are too, Doc."

"It'll cost more than we bring in, at first," Doc said.

"So did Cash, and Sharkey, and Simmons," Eddie replied.

"How much have we made off them?"

"Enough," Doc acknowledged, not wanting to divulge financial information to a newcomer. "He can't do it alone," Doc said, pointing to Tom. "We'll need another organizer who absolutely is not afraid of the mob or anyone else.

Do either of you know anyone like that?"

"I know someone," Eddie said. "We sent him to New York a couple years ago. Maybe it's time he came back."

Hell's Kitchen, New York, 1933:

Red Sullivan sat in Mahoney's Bar in the Irish section of Hell's Kitchen looking at the telegram he'd received. After prohibition had been repealed, bars sprang up everywhere. New York, with the Statue of Liberty standing over Ellis Island, was supposedly the light of freedom for immigrants the world over. The light shined only on the ones with balls enough to fight for it. As it had been throughout history, when the first group of Cro-Magnons that took on the first group of Neanderthals, discovered that the group that had the most people that threw the most rocks faster won, there was safety in numbers. Hell's Kitchen housed all kind of poor people. There were Italian sections, Irish sections, German sections and Polish sections. Harlem was considered the Negro section. Outside one's neighborhood, one was a stranger and enemy.

Red had gone to Mickey's Gym like he was told when he arrived two and a half years earlier. He dropped Eddie Coyle's name. Mickey must have thought he was a boxer, because he ordered Red to get in the ring with a contender training there.

"You don't understand," Red protested.

"Maybe I don't," Mickey said. "Get in the ring or get the hell out of here." Red got in the ring.

The contender was showing off. He stuck his chin out, wound up his punches and verbally taunted Red. He wanted Red to get mad and go after him, so he could destroy him and look good.

Red stood flat-footed in the center of the ring, making "come on" motions at the contender. The guy came forward, throwing a lazy jab. Red countered with a right. He missed the guy's jaw, but the punch landed flush on the guy's left cheekbone and snapped his head back. Red followed with a nice hook off a jab that also caught the guy flush in the face.

He retreated and respectfully nodded at Red. The nod meant, "Okay, you're not an amateur. No more foolin' around. Now I'm gonna have to hurt you."

The contender came forward, serious now. He flurried hard and Red countered. Red had boxing training, but the guy boxed every day. Still, Red held his own. He got out punched about five to two, but he didn't fall down and he didn't back off. Late in the round, they clinched and Red threw the guy on the floor. The guy got up and head-butted Red in the face. Red hit him in the balls so hard he almost lifted the guy off the floor, then he tackled the guy and hit him in the face until other boxers pulled him off.

"All right!" Mickey yelled. "Let go of him. Low blows are illegal."

"So are intentional head-butts," Red retorted. "Fuck him!"

"Okay, I should have known. Coyle never sends no pansies. Come back tomorrow about eleven."

Red had 24 or 25 club fights over the next year or so, fighting under the mane of Mike McBride, since his middle name was Michael and his mother's maiden name was McBride. He didn't want to use the name Sullivan. He won all except one. After a while, Mickey figured out that Red had a knack for talking to people. He paid Red a percentage of the gate on fights that Red negotiated for Mickey's guys. It wasn't paradise, but it was a living.

Then he got the telegram. It read: "I have a business deal for you that's too good to believe. Pick up $500.00 in traveling money from Eastern Union tomorrow. Come to San Francisco and talk to me. Call the gym from the train station and we'll pick you up. Your friend, Eddie Coyle."

Red bought a first-class ticket and ate steak every night in the elegant dining car. He called the gym from the train station and Doc O'Hearn picked him up in a huge Dusenberg.

"You look like you're ready for a title shot,"

Doc said, commenting on Red's muscles bulging under his suit.

"I was twenty-three and one," Red replied. "Nineteen by knockout."

"Mick made you fight?" Doc said.

"At first, then I became kind of a trainer/promoter.

I still sparred with the guys though. I liked being in shape," Red replied.

"Christ. You were a mean son-of-a-bitch before," Doc said. "I pity the guy that takes a shot at you now. Let's go."

The gym was empty except for a few guys cleaning up.

Doc led him back to a lavish office. He shook hands with Eddie.

"Doesn't he look like he's ready for Baer?" Doc said.

Baer was heavyweight champion Max Baer, who killed Frankie Campbell in the ring a couple years earlier. Frankie Campbell was a local fighter that Eddie and Doc had a piece of. Baer had also destroyed Primo Carnera for the title. Carnera's mob backing didn't matter because Baer floored him eleven times before the referee mercifully stopped the fight.

"Nobody's ready for Baer, except maybe Joe Louis," Eddie said. "Give it up, Doc, you're never gonna get back at Baer for Frank. You do look good, though. Did Mickey help you out?"

162

"Yes, he did," Red said. "Thank you."

"You want a drink?" Eddie asked.

"Yes."

Eddie produced four glasses and a bottle of expensive Irish whiskey. After he served the drinks he said, "This is our new business associate, Tom Franklin."

Red shook hands with a tall blond-haired guy.

"Tom, tell Red about our plan," Eddie said as he sat down with his drink.

"We're starting an honest labor union for dockworkers," Tom said. "And we're starting a construction company to go after government contracts to build bridges over the bay."

"It's a big play," Red replied. "Tony Maretti still run things in this town?" Red asked.

"Pretty much," Doc put in. "He's gonna line up with the shipping companies so he can continue to bleed the corrupt so-called union they have now."

"You open the ball on him and you have to go all the way. If I'm gonna go against the Maretti family, I need to know that I have total commitment to the cause. You're a family man, right Eddie?" Red asked.

Eddie nodded his head yes.

"Total commitment means that when thugs try to burn your house down, you go to a hotel while your house is being rebuilt and burn down the bars or places you know these guys hang out. It means when thugs threaten your wife and children, the thugs that threatened them turn up in the bay the next day. It means busting the heads of dirty cops on the mob's payroll and fighting off their cronies when they retaliate. It means risking your life every single day. I want to help the working man, but I'm not gonna get killed, or get a bunch of other people killed, and then see the movement die because you guys don't have the stomach for it. I saw that happen in 1919 and in 1925. I'm not starting a fight I can't win."

"I thought you said this guy was tough," Tom sneered.

"There's a difference between tough and stupid," Red said. "Apparently you haven't learned that yet."

Tom stood up. "How 'bout I just kick your ass?" he sneered.

"You feel froggy, jump," Red replied flatly.

Eddie started to stand, but Doc grabbed his arm. Tom tried to hit Red. Since he'd worked out with boxers the last two years, Red's reflexes were lightning-fast. He slipped the punch, grabbed Tom by his jacket, and drove him to the wall. Red had never lost his street instincts. He snaked his left hand inside Tom's jacket and pulled out his gun before Tom could reach for it.

Red stuck the man's own pistol in his face and cocked the hammer. "Now that I have you full attention, I'm gonna educate you. I blew up a million dollar mine over a union dispute. As you can see, I'm willing to go to extremes to make a point. But those extremes don't include suicide or taking a bunch of innocent people with me. Now, you ever threaten me again and I'll break every bone in your body and shove your gun up your ass. You understand me?"

Tom looked at Eddie and Doc. "Oh, I like him," Tom said.

"I like him too," Doc said, grinning.

"He's gonna do fine. I apologize for insulting you, sir. Now let's talk business," Tom said casually.

After unloading it, Red gave Tom his gun back and sat down.

Tom spoke, "Ten dollars for every man you sign up and ten percent of the first year's dues."

"That's what you make?" Red asked.

"No, that's what you make. What I make is none of your business. There's over six thousand dockworkers in this city. If you only get one-third of them to sign up the first year, that's twenty thousand dollars a year. Plus ten percent of the seventy or eighty grand we collect in dues. You won't make that kind of money doing anything else."

"The money's fine," Red said. "We all agree that I'm tough and I'm smart. But I'm only one man. What if I go to some big company or construction site to organize and a bunch of company goons are there?"

"Doc and Eddie have agreed to let us use their non-champion or contender boxers as muscle on the bigger sites," Tom said.

"What about the smaller sites or a bar or a restaurant I ask guys to meet me at?"

Eddie spoke up. "If you let us know where you were going beforehand and had trouble, you might see me or Doc or Tom and seven or eight boxers standing behind you."

"No retreat, no surrender, no matter what," Red said. "We go all the way."

Eddie said, "All the way."

"All the way," Tom and Doc said, almost simultaneously.

"We're in business," Tom said, hoisting his glass. The others did the same, and Eddie refilled them.

At first it was tough, because people were afraid to go against the corrupt hiring bosses and the mob. After Prohibition was repealed, the soda pop company owner had branched out into wholesale liquor distribution. He brought in whiskey from Canada and tequila from Mexico, as well as wine and cognac from France and Germany. He got American whiskey from Tennessee and Kentucky via the Gulf of Mexico. He brought California wine from the Napa Valley across the bay. He was waiting for a huge shipment of Canadian whiskey. The corrupt mob-controlled walking boss had called a work stoppage. If the soda pop guy didn't cough up two grand in 24 hours, they'd start breaking cases and throwing them in the bay. The man came to see Eddie, asking to borrow the $2,000.00. Tom, Red and Doc were present as well.

"You know I'm good for it, Eddie," the man said.

"We've always treated each other right. I'm just cash-poor at the moment. I had to pay the rent on my warehouses, all my employees, and taxes. As soon as I sell this load I'll pay it back."

"What about the next load, or the one after that?" Eddie asked.

"I don't want to lose this load and I don't want to give this fucker two grand that I don't have. What do you want me to do, Eddie? Tell me what to do and I'll do it."

It was the break they'd been looking for.

"You heard the man," Eddie said. "Go get his goods unloaded."

"You got heat in case we need it, Red?" Tom asked.

"It's better to have it and not need it, than need it and not have it," Red replied.

"Amen," Tom replied. "Doc?"

"Covered. I'll send ten or twelve of my meanest club fighters to mingle in the crowd. Any shit goes down, they'll back you," Doc assured them.

Tom and Red showed up on the waterfront with a box load of sandwiches from Klein's Deli. Tom blew a whistle to get everyone's attention.

"We gotta get this booze unloaded. Any man who wants to work gets a sandwich and a day's pay. Even if it only takes half a day."

About twenty guys ran over.

"Eat first, then work," Tom said.

Red passed out sandwiches while Tom took down names. Three wiseguys strutted over.

"What the hell do you think you're doin'?" one of them asked.

"Giving work to honest laborers with families to support," Red said.

"Well, do your social work somewhere else," the thug snarled, showing a .38 revolver in his waistband.

In a lightning move, Red grabbed the goon's own gun and hit him in the face with it four times. When the thug fell to his knees, Red hit him twice more and threw the gun in the bay. The other two drew guns, but Tom had already drawn his and so had Red.

"A Mexican standoff," Red said calmly.

"What do you want to do, boys?" Tom asked tauntingly.

The goons picked up their wounded comrade and left, hurling threats.

"You know where they went," Red said.

"Reinforcements," Tom replied. "We're covered. I got faith in Doc's men."

About twenty minutes later a flatbed truck with wooden sides pulled up. About 25 wiseguys got out, carrying ax handles.

"It's on now," Red said.

The boxers Doc had sent came up behind Red and Tom. The boxers and the goons clashed. The boxers slipped the thugs' wild swings with the sticks and knocked them out, sometimes with one punch. They picked up ax handles from fallen goons and used them. The boxers kicked ass.

Two guys got out of the cab of the truck carrying shotguns. Red and Tom let them pass and then caught up.

They came down the dock and aimed into the crowd. They didn't fire because Red had stuck his .45 in the ear of the one on the left, and Tom had stuck his .38 in the ear of one.

"Let's keep this fair," Tom said.

Red took the shotguns and threw them in the bay. In a matter of minutes, every mob goon was laying unconscious or bleeding on the dock. The boxers had minimal injuries, no more than they got in a ten-round fight.

"Now get the hell off our dock and don't come back," Red said to the two they'd taken the shotguns from.

"Your dock?" the one on the left said contemptuously.

"You're saying we're not in charge?" Red replied.

Tom had picked up an ax handle. He smashed the guy in the mouth with it. The goon fell, spitting out blood and teeth. "My associate is too polite sometimes," Tom said. "Now, once again, who's in charge here?"

"You are," the other goon said, not wanting free dental work.

"Now get your boys out of here and don't come around here again."

The mob goons who could stand loaded their wounded comrades onto the truck and left.

Red spoke to the crowd watching. "We represent the new Dockworker's Union. As you can see, we aren't easily intimidated. You want to work every day without paying to be on a list or putting up with corrupt hiring bosses, sign up with us."

About twenty additional men came over. Red passed out business cards with the address of the building they'd rented to be the union hall.

"There's a meeting tomorrow night. I hope to see you all there. Tell all your friends."

The workers applauded and went back to unloading the shipment.

"That was relatively painless," Tom said.

"It'll get worse before it gets better," Red replied. "This is gonna be a long haul. What the hell, somebody's got to do it."

"Somebody's go to pay somebody to do it," Tom corrected. "You're not here for free."

"That's true."

Tom and Red organized more workers each day. There were several clashes with mob goons and shipping company enforcers. Tom and Red's planning was impeccable. Whenever the companies sent thugs, there always seemed to be a group of boxers there ready to oppose them.

Red's childhood friend, Tom Conway, was now a police sergeant. Sometimes a group of cops mysteriously showed up at a job site and stopped a problem before it happened. Tom and his cop buddies were well compensated by Doc.

In the meantime, Doc had hired experienced construction workers and architects. "Bayside Construction" made bids on both the Golden Gate and Bay Bridge. Doc had erred on the side of caution. His top construction consultant had worked in New York and Chicago. He'd come out west and had a falling out with the Maretti family. He told Doc how to proceed.

"The other companies are almost all gonna be mob fronts. They'll figure in blue sky, and more to cover corrupt politicians. You underbid 'em so badly that even a corrupt official couldn't award anyone else the contract without losing his job and going to jail. You get the job. Halfway through, there's unforeseen cost overruns. As long as it's still less than the other bids, the government will okay additional funds. I've done this before."

Doc also put a lawyer on retainer. One of his and Eddie's fighters had used his ring winnings to go to law school. Tom's words of "Maretti can't intimidate Uncle Sam" came back again and again. Doc wanted everything as legal as possible.

Red, Tom Franklin and Tom Conway were having lunch in Klein's Deli when two wiseguys and a cop came in and sat down at their table. They were completely unfazed by the fact that Tom Conway was in uniform.

The cop spoke. "Our employer is unhappy with what you've been doing," he said.

Red played dumb. "I haven't even had a parking ticket since I've been back in the city. Certainly my friend and lunch companion could tell me what I've done to offend the police department."

"You assaulted a man on the docks a month ago with a pistol," the cop said.

"It was his pistol," Red retorted.

"Do you know who Don Maretti is?" the cop asked.

"Since I was eleven. He's my godfather," Red replied. "How is Tony? I've been out of town. I'll have to stop by Louie's and catch up."

The statement threw everyone for a loop except Tom Conway, who tried to keep a straight face.

"Tell Tony I have no problem with him, that I'm just doing business the way he taught me. Tell him he still has my respect and friendship, bygones being bygones."

The wiseguys and the dirty cop were dumbfounded. They looked at each other for a moment, and finally the cop spoke again. "What if Don Maretti asks you to withdraw your bid to the government, to step down?" Red spoke in what little Italian he knew from his childhood.

"What did he say?" the cop asked the other two wiseguys.

One of them nodded respectfully at Red. "It's a Sicilian proverb. It doesn't translate well, but it basically means: 'Don't ask for what you can't take.'"

The cop bristled. "I'll tell him you said that."

"Please do," Red replied.

Tom Conway spoke up. "Tell them that applies to Sergeant Conway as well. He'll get a kick out of it."

The three men left.

"Ballsy," Tom Franklin said. "Stupid, but ballsy."

Red and Tom Conway laughed.

"Tony's a businessman," Red said. "He understands that you sometimes have to step on toes to advance your cause. He also only goes all-out on something personal.

And regardless of what he tells his underlings, Tony takes everything personal. If one of his friends gets struck by lightning on the golf course, he takes it personal. If his eggs are overcooked in a coffee shop, he takes it personal. But he's known me and Tom since we were kids. He knows we're not targeting him, that we're just advancing ourselves."

"What about the mine you say you blew up?" Tom Franklin asked.

"I took something personal. I'm pretty sure he understands that."

"If he doesn't?" Franklin asked.

"Then it's gonna get ugly," Red replied. "Real ugly."

The following day Red went to Louie's at lunchtime when he knew Tony would be there. Tony stood up when he walked in.

"Red, you son-of-a-bitch, you look great!" he roared. "Come here. I haven't seen you in what, two, three years?" Tony hugged him. "Sit down and have lunch." Red sat down.

"I didn't know you were back in town," Tony said. "But I figured it out when this lieutenant on payroll comes back and says he was told, 'Don't ask for what you can't take.' That's my line. Then he says my godson and Sergeant Conway send their regards. I almost puked I laughed so hard."

"I wanted to straighten things out," Red said.

"What's to straighten out? That shit on the dock.

That's part of doing business," Tony replied. The other wiseguys at the table were awestruck by the conversation. They'd never seen Tony so casual with anyone.

"I meant Rough and Ready history."

Tony said, "It pissed me off, but I understood. In your place I'd have done the same thing. The Steeleys killed your woman by mistake, trying to get you without my knowledge.

I thought you knew. I thought you were smart. If you killed 'em, they're only dead, but to make paupers of 'em, that's brilliant. I was hurt that you didn't come back here."

"I thought...."

Tony cut him off. "That I was involved. God damned Irish, they never learn. Didn't I teach you to think like a Sicilian? If a Sicilian thought I put a contract out on him, that Sicilian would have come after me, not left town. I knew you were working at that boxing place in New York. I've got friends in New York. If I wanted you dead, you'd be dead. I've known you your whole life. You're like a son to me. A loveable, pain-in-the-ass son, but a son nonetheless." Everyone in earshot laughed. "You want to be a labor leader, fine. As long as your interests don't conflict with mine."

"They might," Red said. Everyone at the table froze. "That's why I'm here. We're gonna organize a lot of workers besides longshoremen in the future. I know companies will ask you for muscle to help quash strikes and disputes.

My partners are not gonna back down. They're gonna stay the course. I'm asking for help, Godfather."

"How can I help without giving you a blank check to do whatever you want at my own people's expense?" Tony asked.

"I don't need anything from you," Red said. "I have my own muscle and money to back me. All I'm asking is if we're in some epic struggle with a huge company, that you don't take their side and you don't take ours. Let it play out.

I don't want to have to choose between my loyalty to you and my commitment to my new job."

"Apparently you already have," Tony replied. "I'm proud of you, though. It takes guts to make your own way, and to do it when it's not easy. That's the way I came up. I won't hinder you, not on purpose. I expect you to do me reasonable favors from time to time, and I'll always accommodate any reasonable request of yours. Our friendship isn't over, it's just changed." The other men in the room hung on their every word. "I remember the boy you were, and I admire the man you've become. You have my blessing."

"Thank you, Godfather," Red said. "But I'm still sticking you for lunch."

"You've been doing that since you were eleven. It's good to have you back," Tony said.

"It's good to be back," Red replied, smiling and finishing his lunch.

Donald James "Blackie" Wilson was twenty-one years old. His mother was Italian and his father was Russian. He'd left his home in Salinas at fourteen. He was the third of seven children. His father worked for the railroad. When his father was killed in a railroad accident, the company didn't even pay for the funeral. His mother washed clothes and cooked pies for a laundry service and a bakery down the street to make ends meet.

He didn't want to work for the railroad and he didn't want to be a lettuce picker or work in a fish cannery, which were the only jobs in Salinas. He hopped a freight train to San Francisco and made money by shining shoes in the train station. Businessmen called him "Blackie" because of his jet-black hair.

When he was nineteen he went into construction at the urging of a friend who worked for a large San Francisco firm. Clawson Construction paid well when they worked.

The work, however, was largely seasonal, even though San Francisco had mild winters.

Work stoppages irritated him. They weren't usually strikes over real problems, but attempts to strong-arm some poor bastard who was trying to make an honest living.

He quit and went to work on the docks. He figured the waterfront was the city's lifeline and it had to be less corrupt. He was wrong.

The docks were horrible. The hiring bosses were assholes who ruled with an iron fist. The shipping companies regarded the workers as the enemies of profit, although they obviously needed the workers to make a profit. One day a walking boss fired a guy for being five minutes late. The guy's wife had had a baby the night before. He had three other kids. He was a hard worker, a good family man.

Blackie told off the boss and rallied the workers. "Jensen doesn't work, the rest of us don't work," he said.

"Then you're all fired!" the walking boss roared.

"Tell me something," Blackie said calmly. "How are you gonna unload twenty tons yourself, tough guy?"

"I'll call the company," the guy said.

"And tell them what? That you fired a whole crew and cost them thousands of dollars because one guy was five minutes late? I didn't know you had that kind of juice.

I'm impressed," Blackie finished.

"All of you get to work!" the boss yelled.

Blackie was a hero to the working men.

The next day when he went to work, three guys were waiting for him. Don was 6'3" and 215 pounds of solid muscle, forged from painting anchor chains for the Navy and turning them, and hauling sheetrock for the construction company before he became a longshoreman. He'd had a few fights in his time. He wasn't afraid to fight.

Three guys had brass knuckles and left Don behind a warehouse bleeding. His ribs hurt terribly. He knew two or three were broken from the cutting pain in his chest. He took his belt off and cinched it around his chest. It became a dull ache, but the pain stopped cutting. He knew his nose was broken too. He blew blood out of it until he could breathe better.

He went to his locker and got his crowbar. He used it to turn anchor chains when he was in construction. Thirty inches long and three-quarters of an inch thick, it was a nice piece of steel, which was why he kept it.

He walked back to the dock where the walking boss and the three goons were telling the workers to never think they could pull what he'd pulled yesterday. Blackie hit the first goon in the back of the head so hard that it split his skull like a watermelon. The goon knocked down six workers as he fell.

He hit the second one in the face before he could blink, destroying his nose. The third one tried to pull a gun, but Blackie slammed the crowbar down on his forearm full-force. The guy dropped the gun and howled in pain, and the arm of his expensive suit soaked with blood. Blackie hit him in the face with the crowbar, and then started walking toward the walking boss.

"You touch me and I'll...."

"You'll what?" Blackie said. "Send more of these morons after me?"

Blackie hit the walking boss in the knee with the crowbar. The man fell screaming. Blackie started kicking him and talking, "I'm kicking you to show you and your bosses that we won't be intimidated and beaten any longer. I'm kickin' you to send a message. The dock workers will fight back from now on."

Blackie kicked him until he was an unconscious, bloody mess. He then threw the crowbar into the bay and walked off. He took a cab to the hospital.

He had three broken ribs and a broken nose. The doctor said he needed six weeks to heal.

After a month of not working, he'd spent his savings and had to go back to work. It was Blackie who led the first twenty or so men to work the day Tom and Red came to the waterfront. Blackie was the only worker who fought alongside the boxers and Tom and Red, although they didn't notice in the confusion of the fight. It was Blackie who convinced almost fifty more guys to go to the first meeting. After another brutal fight on the docks with company goons and a murder of a popular but outspoken worker, Red and Tom called another meeting. Hundreds attended.

"It's not easy," Red said. "I can't guarantee that every one of you will be protected. Let's not make his sacrifice in vain. If we give up now, they've won. They killed one guy and scared a thousand. Which is what they wanted to do. We have to show that you kill one guy, a thousand will be angry and retaliate. Unity is the road to ultimate victory."

"At what price?" one worker asked.

Blackie stood up. "You ungrateful bastards!" he yelled. "You want to be god damned sheep to slaughter? Are you too dumb to see what's happening? These guys don't make it, and seamen and longshoremen are fucked forever. We might as well be slaves in Europe under feudalism. We might as well be Communists, working for the state like in Russia. The companies win and there won't be any working class. There'll only be rich and poor. And most of us will be poor. I don't like being poor. I'm gonna fight until hell freezes over for workers' rights. Now who's with me?"

"We are!" the workers yelled.

Red put his arm around Blackie. "What's your name?" he whispered.

"The men call me 'Blackie,'" Don whispered back.

"What are you doin'?"

"Work with me," Red whispered. "You guys stay the course. We'll keep Blackie informed and he'll keep you informed," Red said to the crowd. The crowd of workers applauded. "Come with us after the men leave," Red said.

Blackie was hesitant. Red handed him his .45. Blackie checked to make sure it was loaded. He was bewildered.

"You can hold that until you see we're on the level," Red said. "You've got a gift for getting through to the men. They listen to you. We need an organizer like that. Tom and I are overloaded anyway. You coming?"

Blackie got in the car with Tom and Red. He gave Red his gun back.

"Why'd you do that?" Red asked.

"I figure if you were gonna kill me, I'd already be dead. Since I'm not, that means you're on the level, and

I should trust you. If we're gonna get the workers to trust us, we have to trust each other."

"Good point," Red said. "What's your real name?"

"Don."

"Nice to meet you, Don," Red and Tom both replied.

Red, Tom Franklin and Blackie went into Eddie's office.

"This is Blackie," Red said. "We think he'd be a good organizer. The men listen to him. He could be a big help."

"Tom?" Eddie asked.

"I agree. He's got a gift."

"Then hire him. We'll need all the help we can get," Eddie said. "Bayside Construction got the contracts to build the bridges."

"All right!" Tom said, pumping his fist in the air.

"That opens a whole new can of worms," Eddie said.

"But we'll manage."

"Manage, hell!" Tom said. "We're gonna roll!"

"I agree with Eddie," Red said. "The light at the end of the tunnel is probably the headlamp of an oncoming train. If not, great, but let's not break our arms slapping ourselves on the back just yet. Let's see what happens."

Construction began on the Bay Bridge. It was a massive project, employing thousands of workers. Tom, Red and Blackie had organized thousands of workers in Oakland and San Jose as well. Doc and their lawyer set up bank accounts to manage the dues they collected. One fund was a strike fund, so workers would have income in the event of a strike. Another was to pay doctor bills if the worker or his children got sick. A third was a pension fund, so workers could get retirement benefits when they had more than twenty years in.

In February 1934, the previous union contract expired. Tom and Red demanded sweeping changes. The shipping companies refused. In their eyes they didn't have to give anything. The salaries of corporation officials, largely paid out of subsidies, reached staggering figures: Four stockholders of the Dollar Line received from 1923 to 1932 a total in salaries, profits and bonuses of $14,690,528.00! When Tom threatened a strike, the corporations laughed. If there was a strike that stopped shipping, the corporations anticipated no great loss -- the government paid the deficit. The corporations sat back and waited.

At the union hall Tom fumed. Red, Eddie, Doc and Blackie were also there. Red came up with an idea.

"These companies are national, right?" he said. Everyone agreed. "If we close the port of San Francisco, they'll use Oakland. If we manage to close both, they'll use trucks and the railroad to bring stuff in from other port cities. Stopping them from doing business in San Francisco won't hurt them enough. If we could stop them from doing business on the whole West Coast, that would hurt. They'd have to come to the table or go out of business."

"Sounds good in theory," Eddie said. "But how would we accomplish it?"

"We go see union leaders in other port cities," Red replied. "We set up a board of directors, composed of three delegates from each union, elected by the rank and file guys. We propose that no union settle or arbitrate its demands until all other unions have received agreements satisfactory to their members. We pledge to have everyone hold out for a coast-wide agreement. We'll call it the 'Joint Marine Strike Committee.' We have to get the Teamsters behind us," Red said.

"They're assholes," Blackie put in. "When I worked construction, if you told a Teamster driver to drop a load over here, they'd drop it over there," he said, motioning to opposite sides of the room. "If you bitched and demanded he move it to where you asked him to put it in the first place, the guy would call his union rep, who'd call a work stoppage. No freight would be delivered for a couple of days, while someone kissed their ass enough for them to start delivering again. They are complete assholes."

"They're assholes that are the highest paid and best benefited workers in the country," Red replied. "They control a lot of other workers besides truck drivers.

We ask them to not cross dock worker picket lines, and not to take freight to or from the docks. We promise to back them in the future if they have a problem. We also organize Negroes and migrant Mexican farm workers."

"Why?" Tom asked.

"Scabs," Red replied. "If all the other unions agree, they'll try to find replacement workers to break the strike, pit worker against worker along racial lines. If they're with us, the companies won't have a source of scabs. A coast-wide strike will break them."

"How do we get all the unions together?" Eddie asked.

"By talking to the workers. Blackie can stay here and be the day-to-day rep to the men. That's no reflection on him, the men trust him. Tom and I will go to San Diego and Los Angeles, and San Luis Obispo. We'll go to Portland and Seattle. Local by local, we'll build support and then we'll strike -- both literally and figuratively."

"Blackie, you tell the men to stick with us, that things are being negotiated that will solve their problems. If you can keep the men patient and working, letting the shipping companies think they're in charge, while building support, it'll be huge."

"That's a big job," Blackie said.

"You're a big man," Eddie said. "Doc and I will back you just like we have Tom and Red. This is just like when

I had to take Flynn in the third round or lose out on ten grand. It's do or die. And we're not going to die. Red has a great plan, if we can make it work. Just like boxing, strategy is only good if you execute it. Let's execute this and make history."

"Amen," everyone said.

Red and Tom went to churches and meeting halls in Negro neighborhoods in San Francisco, Oakland, San Jose, San Pedro, all up and down the coast. They acknowledged the injustices that had plagued colored workers for so long and promised that in the union they were trying to create there would be no color line. The union would open full membership to Negroes, based not on the hue of their skin but solely on the strength of their hearts for the struggle ahead. Red nailed them with a few sentences.

"I'm Irish. As blue-eyed, lily white as you can get," he said. "I remember when businesses used to have signs in the window saying, 'No Irish need apply.' I ran numbers for the Mafia when I was a kid to help out at home, because my father couldn't get a decent job. All workers must stand together," he said. "There can be no discrimination because of color, creed, nationality, religion or political belief. Discrimination is the secret weapon of the boss."

There was no lack of heart. During the hard months ahead, the Negro community stood by the longshoremen and the longshoremen stood by their promise.

They left San Francisco and as planned went to all the port cities on the West Coast. In some areas Tom connected with the workers; in other areas, Red did. What mattered was they connected. A meeting was set up in Seattle. Delegates of every local on the West Coast attended. They resolved that the committee would be composed of five men from each union, and Tom was elected chairman. For the first time in American labor history, both licensed and unlicensed personnel cooperated on an equal basis, breaking down craft jealousies that had riddled the marine industry. Also for the first time in history the rank and file fully controlled the conduct of a major strike.

On May 9, 1934, after months of fruitless negotiations, the longshoremen struck for recognition. The Teamsters agreed to not cross picket lines and every port on the West Coast shut down. Not long after, the beleaguered seagoing unions joined the strike. Seamen also worked under terrible conditions. It was the first industry-wide strike in history. It was unionism built by the members and run by the members.

Contributions flooded in from everywhere -- from other unions, organizations, and private individuals up and down the coast. Farmers sent truckloads of produce to the strikers' relief kitchens.

The ship owners and their allies were also prepared. They believed the strike was the opportunity to deliver the final blow to organized labor on the docks. Banker William H. Crocker called it, "The best thing that ever happened in San Francisco. It's costing us money, certainly, but it's a good investment, a marvelous investment. It's solving the labor problem for years to come, perhaps forever. When the men have been driven back to their jobs, we won't have to worry about them anymore. Labor in San Francisco is licked."

Arrayed against the strikers were the ship owners, the Associated Farmers of California, and the Employers Industrial Associations up and down the coast, the American Legion, and several vigilante groups which, in connivance with the police and employers, unveiled an unrestrained reign of terror. Unionists were assaulted on the streets and in their homes. Meeting halls were destroyed and organizations friendly to the strikers were raided and their members beaten. After one such raid on a small pro-union group, the hallways and staircases were found slippery with blood. In one particularly disgusting attack on strikers by company goons and San Francisco police, 250 high school students were clubbed bloody on National Youth Day. In San Jose, fifty miles south of San Francisco, a score of workers were kidnapped by vigilantes, beaten and driven three hundred miles down the coast.

Despite the unprecedented savagery, the maritime unions maintained their picket lines up and down the coast. Vigilantes, none of whom were arrested, continued to terrorize the city. Employer-inspired violence broke out in San Pedro, Portland and Seattle.

Newspapers, led by William Randolph Hearst, condemned the strike. His papers censored all strike news published in the press and dictated editorial policy to every Bay Area newspaper.

Edward McGrady, a government "troubleshooter," arrived and set to work to break the strike. He got nowhere.

"I've been able to crack other strikes," he complained. "But I can't crack this one."

At McGrady's suggestion, Angelo Rossi, mayor of San Francisco, summoned Joseph P. Ryan, the international president of maritime unions. However, Ryan lacked authority. In 1911, when the Pacific Coast District rejoined the national association from which it had previously seceded, the association granted the district complete autonomy and agreed that national officers should have no jurisdiction in coastal affairs unless their assistance was specifically requested.

When he arrived in San Francisco in May 1934, Ryan strutted and wheedled, bullied and argued, and finally signed a secret pact with the employers ending the walkout.

The newspapers rejoiced at the strike's termination.

When the longshoremen read the terms which failed to provide any improvement in conditions, and in addition violated the pledge entered into by all striking unions that any settlement must include any union involved, they repudiated Ryan and the agreement. The "President" hurriedly left for the East, miserable over the miscarriage of his most zealous, corrupt strike-breaking. All hope of the shipping companies ending the walkout by bartering with corrupt union officials melted away.

With Hearst leading, the press attacked Tom Franklin as a communist and an alien, and demanded his arrest and deportation. Contrary to Red and Eddie's advice, Tom was defiant.

"I neither affirm nor deny that I am a communist. Political beliefs have nothing to do with the strike."

The workers only drew their lines tighter around the docks.

The Department of Labor investigated. Tom had twice taken out first citizenship papers and had allowed them to lapse twice. At the time of the investigation, he had again obtained his first papers. Moreover, he had entered the United States legally. The Commission of Immigration and Naturalization could find no lawful grounds for deportation.

In addition, fear of repercussions on the waterfront that deporting Franklin would arouse caused many industrialists to counsel caution. Furthermore, stories of the fabulous fortune amassed by Tom, $100,000.00 banked in some secret place, completely misfired. His ego caused him to play big shot with people, but he made what Red and Blackie made, commission on men organized. A good living, more than the average working stiff, but he was nowhere near as affluent as the media moguls who were slandering him. He became the poster child for immigrants. He came here and tried to make his fortune, living the American dream, and people conspired against him.

When William Randolph Hearst suggested that the strike was "Moscow made" and financed by "Red Gold," and that a violent revolution was forthcoming if the dock workers strike in San Francisco was not broken, union leaders all over the country laughed out loud. Tom and Red became nationally known, although Red did not receive as much celebrity status as Tom. He was born in the United States and didn't have a prison record. Red appeared to be an all-American guy. The press couldn't slander him much, so they concentrated on Tom.

After more than two months of a stalemate employers nationwide decided to open the docks. The key port of San Francisco was their target.

If they crushed the revolt in San Francisco, then the coast-wide strike would collapse.

What followed on July 3rd was brutal street fighting between thousands of strikers and police. An uneven struggle, angry and bloody, pitting the fists and boots of unarmed union men against clubs and revolvers, nausea gas, and riot guns. Everyone on both sides took the Fourth off. July 5, 1934, the seventy-sixth day of the strike, a desperate twelve-hour battle raged up and down the Embarcadero. The date is remembered as "Bloody Thursday."

It began with 5,000 striking workers lining the inland side of the Embarcadero, facing off against the thousands of armed policemen and vigilantes who guarded the docks. Pier 38 was to be opened. The longshoremen knew full well what that meant. Their children would remain hungry, their wives old before their time, their own lives cut short and brutalized. They were determined never to see that day.

Red, Tom and Blackie were there to support the workers and advise caution. At 7:45 a police car pulled up.

Tom Conway came over and spoke to Red. "You better get the hell out of here. This is gonna be ugly. I'm not gonna participate, I'm gonna make sure I'm away from here, but I don't want to see you get killed."

"I can't desert the men in their most desperate hour. What kind of leadership is that?" Red replied.

"Hey, I'm looking out for my best friend since second grade, not giving political advice. I'm risking my job and my ass even talking to you," Tom said. "I gotta go."

"Thanks," Red replied.

"Cover your ass," Tom said, and sped away.

At 8:00 a.m., a prowler car pulled between the lines.

A police captain rode the running boards. He called out, "Let 'em have it, men!"

The police emptied their riot and gas guns into the line of strikers. The unionists recoiled, but held their ranks. The next moment they surged forward and the battle was on.

Witnesses of the day claim the men fought and fell in silence. They only sounds to be heard were the crack of clubs against skulls, the report of gunfire and exploding gas canisters, and the wail of sirens. Scattered groups of men slugged it out against the swinging clubs, while others retreated under the onslaught only to regroup and join the fray again.

Tom Franklin stayed on the waterfront. Red and Blackie led several hundred men up the slopes of Rincon Hill, then under preparation for anchorage of the Bay Bridge. They threw up barricades from the debris of demolished building to protect themselves from gunfire. From their positions they hurled brickbats down the slope at the police.

Three assaults were mounted against the men on Rincon Hill. The first was a wave of policemen on foot, the second on horseback. Both were driven back by the strikers.

The third was also on horseback, but prepared for with a sustained volley of gunfire and a curtain of gas laid across the crest of the hill. The exploding canisters ignited the dry grass and the slopes were soon a raging inferno. The police pounded up the hill, but there was not a striker in sight. Red and the men had simply slipped away. Police surrounded the hill to avoid it being retaken.

All morning long the battle raged. The possibility of maintaining a picket line on the Embarcadero in the face of gunfire and gas seemed hopeless. At noon, in an almost surreal moment, both sides broke away for lunch. It was as if a whistle had blown and all had retired to observe a time-honored ritual. Policemen headed for their lunch buckets and strikers from all positions drifted back to their headquarters at the corner of Steuart and Mission where they had established a mess hall.

Most of the fighting had occurred in an out-of-the-way industrial district along the south end of the Embarcadero, but the striker's headquarters was in the heart of downtown, a block off Market Street and a stone's throw from the busy terminus of the Ferry Building. Thus situated, it had long been considered by the longshoreman as a neutral zone.

Thus, when shortly after one o'clock, the police staged their most crushing attack, the strikers were taken entirely by surprise.

A police car pulled to a halt in the middle of the intersection. Tear gas shells were fired through the windows of the union hall and thick smoke filled the rooms that were already filled with injured people. The men emptied the building and scattered in confusion, only to encounter lines of policemen driving them toward the downtown area. Then the shooting began. Riot guns and pistols. Men fell. Streetcars were abandoned as stray bullets crashed through the windows. One woman fled a stalled trolley only to be dropped by a glancing shot to the head. A man in a business suit ran to her aid. He too was felled by gunfire. Ironworkers clinging to the towers of the Bay Bridge scrambled down their ropes and jumped into safety nets as sporadic rounds flew around them. The battle swept onto Market Street.

Women shopping in downtown stores stepped into an inferno. With screaming children clinging to them, they found themselves in clouds of tear gas. Guns cracked. Men fell, screaming as they went down. Police clubs cracked against skulls of bystanders and strikers alike. Smothered and blinded by the gas, women and children staggered about helplessly. Police grabbed them and sent them to the hospital where they were horrified by the sight of men dripping with blood and moaning from bullet wounds.

The fight raged until mid-evening. Thirty-three men and women had been shot, strikers and bystanders alike. Two men lay dead, Howard Sperry, a longshoreman and veteran of the big war, and Nick Brodoise, a cook who had volunteered at the mess hall. Both men had suffered multiple gunshot wounds to the back. The total number of injured was unknown, but estimated in the thousands.

In the midst of all the bloodshed, Tom Franklin led a contingent of strikers, fighting tooth and nail all the way, to the office of Mayor Rossi.

"You've got to call off the cops," Tom pleaded. "People are dying out there. Innocent people."

The mayor, whose last campaign was financed by big business, didn't care. "You started this, Franklin. Now live with the consequences."

"No, you son-of-a-bitch, you're gonna live with them on election day. You call me a communist? And then you send police after unarmed protesters with tear gas and shotguns? You bastard. You go to hell."

That evening, Governor Merriam, whose campaign fund was immediately enriched by a $30,000.00 "voluntary" contribution from the ship owners, ordered the National Guard onto the waterfront and declared martial law along the Embarcadero. 2,000 troops marched into the area armed with Browning automatic rifles, .30-caliber machine guns, and bayoneted Springfields. Along with them came a squad of small tanks known as Whippets. They occupied the entire waterfront and mounted their machine guns atop the piers and along the Embarcadero in sandbagged nests.

The union had a meeting at the church where Tim Conway was pastor. It was held in their reception hall.

"We can't fight the police and the machine guns, and the National Guard," Red said.

"Let's see how big Mayor Rossi's balls are, and Governor Merriam's," Tom Franklin said. "We'll walk down to the docks in a peaceful demonstration. Let them explain having soldiers shoot at civilians making a protest. I'll personally lead the march." The workers cheered. "Pretty soon Roosevelt's gonna have to take notice. We've come too far to back off now. Every port on the West Coast is watching with bated breath to see what happens here. The shipping companies chose this. They decided to make this the key battleground. If we lose, everyone loses."

Red spoke up. "We need to get the rest of the unions in the city to have a general strike to support us. Now nobody does anything. Rossi's such a bad-ass, let's see how he likes it. Everybody marches tomorrow. They can't gun down ten thousand unarmed people. Tom and I will approach the other unions tomorrow. This is not over," Red finished.

The workers applauded wildly. Everyone agreed to march at 7:00 a.m. Friday.

Up until then, being under Hearst's boot, the San Francisco newspapers had been firmly in the camp of the employers. But on July 6th, their very headlines seemed to recoil at the choice: "S.F. Waterfront rocked by Death, Bloodshed, Riots." "BLOOD FLOODS GUTTERS AS POLICE BATTLE STRIKERS."

"Murder! Murder on the waterfront!" Newsboys cried at the top of their lungs.

Reporters who had been in the thick of the fight all day had been beaten along with the rest. The newsmen had seen so much that day. Blood was the word that ran through their copy. Blood with all its variants of motion and color. "Blood ran red in the streets yesterday." "San Francisco's broad

Embarcadero ran red with blood yesterday." "The color stained clothing, sheets, flesh." "A run of crimson crawled to the curb." "Most of us came to hate the sight of red." "There was so much of it."

"Bloody Thursday." The events of that day vibrated through the city. Homes, meeting places and bars ran loud with talk. Eyewitnesses recounted over and over what they had seen. Doorbells and telephones rang. Questions were asked, opinions voiced. Citizens of San Francisco had been shot down in cold blood. The city was boiling with anger.

A general strike was fermenting.

The old-time conservative labor leaders were determined to block a general strike at all cost, yet the demands from their membership was so overwhelming they dared not oppose it too frankly. They quickly formed themselves into the "Strike Strategy Committee" whose duty it was to work out a common program for all San Francisco labor. The maritime unions were carefully excluded from representation.

"We are not considering a general strike at all," the chairman told reporters. "There is no danger of a general strike at all."

At that moment, however, the rank and file of fourteen unions were voting overwhelmingly in favor of a general strike. More than 2,000 Teamsters crowded shoulder to shoulder into Dreamland Auditorium. Mike Casey, their conservative leader, warned that a strike was contrary to union rules and they would lose benefit funds from the international if they took such action. Their AFL chapter might be forfeited and the union could be ruined. His protests were drowned in laughter.

Voices cried out, "Franklin! We want Franklin!" Catcalls and whistles split the air. "We want Sullivan!

We want Franklin!"

Casey's voice was swamped by the noise. Several Teamsters ran out to where Tom and Red waited with the maritime workers. The salaried officials had not even bothered to invite them to the meeting. They entered the hall to a deafening ovation.

Tom spoke to the men in his direct way, reminding them of the lessons learned from the failed strikes of 1901, 1916, 1919 and 1925. "The entire labor movement faces collapse if we are defeated. I think, deep down, you all know that. You will double our power if you join us."

Casey called for the "yes" votes and all 2,000 hands went up. The Teamsters would join the general strike no matter what the Strategy Committee decided.

The success of a general strike would depend on more than the solidarity of organized labor. Without the support of ordinary citizens, any such action faced tough sledding indeed. Public opinion was crystallizing rapidly at opposite poles. San Francisco was a city divided.

On Sunday, Tom, Red and Blackie led a delegation of longshoremen to the offices of Police Chief Quinn. They requested permission for a funeral parade on the following day to bury their dead.

"You keep the cops away and we'll maintain order and direct traffic," Tom said.

Quinn was well aware of the public resentment that had been aroused and wanted to placate it. "Okay," he agreed. "But no union banners, no inflammatory speeches. We'll hold back as long as you keep order. You don't and...."

"I got it," Tom said. "Thank you."

Monday was July 9th. In the early morning, crowds began to gather in front of the longshoremen's headquarters at Steuart and Mission. By noon, a living sea of people crowded Steuart Street from one end to the other. More than 40,000 men, women and children from every trade and profession stood silently with hats off in the hot sun, waiting for the procession to begin.

The two coffins were loaded onto trucks. A union band struck up the slow cadence of Beethoven's Funeral March. Slowly, the trucks moved onto Market Street. The procession followed, headed for Dugan's Funeral Parlor near the corner of 17th and Valencia. The mourners marched ten abreast.

A great mass, moving silently, their heads bared. The sidewalks were crowded with citizens.

Hours passed, but still the mourners poured onto Market Street, until the entire length, from the Ferry Building to Valencia, was filled with silent marching men, women and children. Streetcar men stopped their cars along the march and removed their caps. On the sidewalks, businessmen in suits doffed their hats. Parents pushed their children to the front, instructing them in whispers, "Remember this.

Don't ever forget it."

Newspapers described it. "A river of humanity flowed up Market like lava...the solemn strains of dirges and hymns...uncountable thousands of spectators lining the streets with uncovered heads...overhead a brilliant sun in a cloudless sky."

The reporters commented on the men in the coffins.

"In life they wouldn't have commanded a second glance on the streets of San Francisco, but in death they were borne the length of Market Street in a stupendous and reverential procession that astounded the city. Even the hostile Industrial Association bowed to the power and dignity of the march. It was one of the strangest and most dramatic spectacles that has ever moved along Market Street. Its passage marked the high tide of united labor action in San Francisco. As the last marcher broke ranks, the certainty of a general strike, which to many had appeared as a visionary dream of a small group of radicals, became for the first time a practical reality."

On July 12th the general strike began. At 7:00 a.m. all transportation of freight and merchandise halted as the Teamsters joined the 25,000 maritime workers now on strike. Two hundred butchers walked out of the slaughter houses, 1,500 more from the retail stores. Light rail and cable car drivers braked their cars to a halt.

Cabbies returned their taxis to the barn and walked home. Boilermakers walked out of sixty shops. Bartenders, cooks and waiters, shop girls and secretaries, shoeshine boys and newsies all joined. 2,600 laundry drivers and workers walked out.

Pressed by reporters on what action the Strike Strategy Committee would take, their spokesman refused to elaborate, but said, "Do you guys need to see a haystack in the air before you know which way the straw is blowing?"

Placards were plastered in the windows of Mom-and-Pop stores all over town. "No business until the boys win!" "Closed for the duration."

The citizens of San Francisco had joined with organized labor. With one voice they said, "No business until this wrong has been made right."

In Oakland, upwards of 47,000 workers joined the 50,000 on strike in San Francisco. In all, more than 125,000 citizens from all walks of life, union and non-union alike, participated in the general strike.

Later in the day, a reporter stopped his car in the middle of Market Street. "It was as if the entire city was asleep," he wrote in his column.

Governor Merriam sent an urgent telegram to President Roosevelt, then observing naval maneuvers off the coast of California. "Bolshevik Army has invaded San Francisco," the wire read. "Federal troops needed. Urgent."

Reportedly, FDR replied to his secretary, "Wire the governor not to excite himself. There is no invading army. You tell him that's just Franklin and Sullivan."

The reaction from the Waterfront Employers Association was inevitable and predictable. Ship owner Roger Lapham was their spokesperson in a phone call to Madame Perkins, the Secretary of Labor.

"We can cure this thing best by more bloodshed," Lapham told her. "We've got to have bloodshed to stop it. It's the best thing to do."

"Isn't that a pretty dangerous outlook? And a pretty dangerous and illegal thing to rely on?" replied the secretary.

"I think it's the best thing that could happen," said Lapham. "The best way for all of us."

The employers believed all their troubles would be solved if they could be rid of two troublemakers -- Tom Franklin and Red Sullivan. Tom because he was head of the strike committee and testifying before the National Longshoreman's Board, an attempt by the Federal government to gather the facts necessary to a peaceful settlement.

Tom spoke at length, extemporaneously and without notes.

His presentation was so powerful that even the employers later remembered it as "extraordinary," recalling his astonishing command of the facts and his command of the language. A reporter would write, "Employers were for the first time to understand something of the hold which he had been able to establish over strikers both in his own union and in the other maritime crafts."

They knew if Tom was gone, the men would look to Red for leadership and the first thing on the agenda would be avenging and honoring Tom. The captains of industry frankly and openly discussed Tom and Red's murders.

The first attempts on Tom and Red's life then occurred. Red was warned by Tom Conway who actually heard talk in the police station. Tom was so incensed he said he would quit being a cop and volunteer to be their bodyguard. The other cops made a joke out of it, saying it was just hearsay that probably wouldn't happen.

Red and Tom Conway went to see Tony Maretti. They figured any hits that were okayed, even out-of-town ones, he'd know about. Tony questioned his underbosses. One admitted being approached by the ship owners, but refused the offer, figuring it to be cops trying to railroad him to jail. In his eyes, killing key union delegates during an epic strike was stupid. They'd be martyrs and that would redouble the strikers' resolve. Business-wise it was equivalent to shooting yourself in the foot, the underboss said, sure Tony was going to whack him.

"Why didn't you tell me about this?" Tony asked.

"I said no, Godfather. I thought it was bullshit, a setup. If I was a pimp, I wouldn't expect my girls to tell me every time they walked a john they thought was a vice cop. I wasn't trying to hide anything, I didn't think it was important enough to bother you with."

"I want you to take the job," Tony said. "You play big shot, like you're not even telling me. You set them up with Joe Vallinari."

"The target's sitting right here, boss, plus... Vallinari hasn't pulled a trigger himself in fifteen years," the underboss said.

"I know," Tony replied. "But he was one of my best men for years. He just got out of an eight-year sentence.

He could have only done three, or maybe walked, and he never once mentioned my name. He's a true Sicilian, the last of a dying breed. He's dying of cancer and he's got seven kids. He makes the attempt, which fails. He takes the rap and rats out the shippers who hired him. The union pays his wife a one-time union death benefit and gives his two oldest boys union jobs. You pay his lawyer fees and funeral expenses," Tony said to the underboss, "for not brining this to my attention sooner."

"Thank you," the underboss said, relieved he wasn't going to be killed for his mistake.

"That acceptable?" Tony asked Red.

"Fine. Let me know where the payments need to go and I'll have it handled," Red replied. "I owe you one, Tony."

"That you do," Tony replied.

Red informed Tom of the plan. Vallinari would carry a sawed-off shotgun loaded with birdshot. He'd accost Red and Tom outside Louie's Restaurant and shoot over their heads. Tom Conway would be cruising by in his police car at the exact moment and arrest Vallinari, who would confess as Maretti instructed.

The "hit" went off perfectly. Red had grabbed the barrel of the shotgun and Tom tackled Vallinari as the gun erupted. Conway pulled up and jumped out with his partner, both with guns drawn. Vallinari didn't struggle as he was arrested. He named Roger Lapham's driver as the man who hired him. The story was on the front page of the newspapers the following day. Laphman nor his driver were ever indicted, but the damage was done. The shipping companies now looked so bad that they made Genghis Khan look like a philanthropist. The governor demanded action.

Three days after the start of the general strike, both sides agreed to arbitration by the National Longshore Board. The industrial interests had been pressured by their bankers, who frankly suggested, "Give them the closed shop."

The Board awarded the longshoremen all of their demands, including a jointly managed hiring hall, with the all-important position of dispatcher to be appointed by the union to ensure the work was distributed among the men fairly and without prejudice and the hiring hall could not be used to dispatch non-union men to the job during a strike.

The seamen won their demands as well. Maritime workers at sea and on shore no longer had to work under the worst conditions in industrialized America. Now they and their families had a future.

Afterwards, everything was not roses though. Workers had won substantial gains in the strike, but without rigid enforcement, the concessions would prove meaningless.

From the moment work resumed on the docks, the ship owners tried every ruse to circumvent the arbitration award. Provocation, increasing the weight of the sling loads, blacklists, dismissals of militants on faked charges.

The union met the violations with job-action strikes, or "quickies." When the straw boss fired without cause, the gang affected quit-work until the union investigated and made a settlement. When scabs appeared on boats, quickies scared them off. When slings were consistently overloaded, the longshoremen laid down their hooks. The "quickies" provided an immediate, powerful means of enforcing conditions without calling a strike of all longshoremen and other members of maritime unions. It impressed upon companies they could not chisel on the awards. Employers raged, but the "quickies" continued as union workers retaliated against employer cheating.

The ship owners protested "quickies" violated agreements. The unions replied that if the ship owners did not abide by the contract, then workers didn't have to either. Gradually the owners realized they were dealing with a resolute group of rank and file leaders far different from the usual AFL officials who tolerated any and all employer abuse and talked "sanctity of contract," which bound only the workers. The industrialists in San Francisco learned while they could trust Tom and Red to keep their word, they could not violate an agreement without facing countermoves by the union.

By the fall of 1935, the docks were solidly organized; not a single member of the San Francisco local was on relief. Unemployment was practically abolished on the Pacific waterfronts. The rank and file demanded the spread of unionization to all categories of workers.

Early in 1936, the Maritime Unions "march inland" began in earnest. 4,500 more workers enrolled the first month and had obtained substantial wage increases, a forty-hour week and other major concessions. Tom, Red and Blackie, and several other hired organizers rolled.

They organized all the wholesale coffee houses, wholesale grocery, hardware, drug, hay fuel and feed firms, as well as cold storage plants and the general warehouses. Bakery wagon drivers in various parts of California unified their locals. The retail clerks, affected by the upsurge of militancy in other unions, invaded department and chain stores. Striking lettuce pickers in Salinas, one hundred miles south of San Francisco, turned to the dock workers for financial aid when vigilantes attempted to forcibly break their union. In the Northwest, lumber workers set up an alliance similar to the Maritime Federation and pledged to cooperate with the waterfront unions. Industrial workers rallied to the support of the Newspaper Guild in Seattle, with the result that the success of the *Post-Intelligence* strike caused every major newspaper in the Bay region to enter into agreements with news writers. Even Los Angeles, the stronghold of the open shop on the West Coast, was invaded by the union with increasing success.

The Industrial Association watched the spread of organization with helpless fury. One *Chronicle* reporter wrote, "'The march inland,' as it is termed by the maritime unions, is part of a well-laid plan by Tom Franklin and his fellow radicals to exert control over the movement of all merchandise in San Francisco as well as the waterfront."

What they really dreaded was Tom and Red might coordinate all unions as they had on the waterfront. Tom had said publicly in 1936, "Of course we oppose splitting the labor movement. But as yet the possibilities of industrial unionism on the West Coast is still hard to predict. The first job here is to organize the unorganized on an industrial basis. I think the real drive in the future must start in the mass industries -- in steel, autos, and rubber."

Tom was a celebrity and Red had more money than he ever had in his life from the union's success.

Red bought a boat-tailed Cord Speedster in 1936. He only drove it on weekends, using the '34 Ford the union supplied for business. He picked up the tactic from a rich guy in New York who used to come to big money fights. He was in construction. After a couple of record years, he thought he'd reward himself and bought a new Cadillac. Business dropped off. His accountant told him, "Guy gets a Cadillac, poor people think he's making too much money. They don't want to do business with a fat cat." The guy sold the Caddy and bought a Packard, which cost almost as much. Business picked up.

"Perception," the guy had told Red. "Only automobile aficionados know that a Packard is expensive. Everybody knows a Caddy is expensive. Nobody says you can't enjoy life. Wear one-hundred fifty-dollar suits if you want to.

Only drink twenty-dollar bottles of whiskey, or smoke five-dollar cigars. But don't rub the poor man's face in it, then he'll hate you."

Red never forgot, which was why he used the Ford for union business. He bought a nice house in Glen Park, a nice upscale family neighborhood. Even though he wasn't married, he wanted a house, having lived in rented flats his whole life. However, he was smart enough to not buy a mansion in Pacific Heights. If he was to continue to connect with the working man, he couldn't look like a fat cat. He couldn't convince Tom Franklin of this.

Tom held the opposite opinion -- that he set an example for the men to aspire to. Tom dressed like a wiseguy and drove a Cadillac. He went out on the town sometimes with two women . Red knew that Tom had also branched out into loan sharking and gambling, and muscle for hire.

When Red cautioned him, Tom griped, "How is me loaning some poor slob money different from Eddie giving a guy fifty thousand dollars out of the pension fund to open a hotel or restaurant?"

"Because unions making loans to advance their pension or strike funds is legal, and loan sharking isn't. You want to be a legendary gangster, go be one. You want to be a labor leader, do that. But you can't be both," Red finished.

"Why not?" Tom asked.

Red was disgusted. Eddie and Doc said they didn't care what Tom did on the side as long as it didn't hurt the union. They contended that since he'd been instrumental in building the union, if he was forced out, it would look bad. Employers might question the rank and file's solidarity and try union-busting practices. Kinky or not, Tom was too important to the union to kick out. They'd deal with his vices on a case-by-case basis.

"When your gangster shit threatens the integrity of this union, you and I are gonna have a problem," Red said.

"That's friendship for you," Tom said.

"We were never friends. We were business associates," Red replied.

"Okay. Fine," Tom said.

"Eddie Coyle" in the book. This photo was taken in 1909. He's the darker-haired boxer.

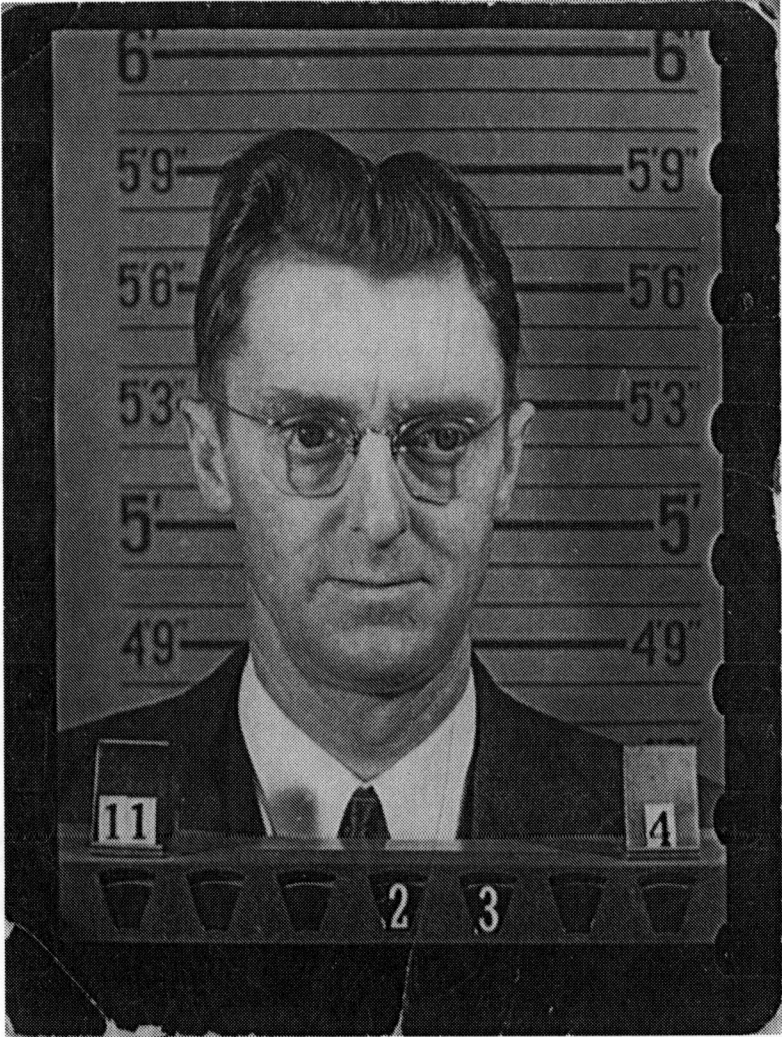

"Red Sullivan" after the famous "Bloody Thursday" 1934 strike riot.

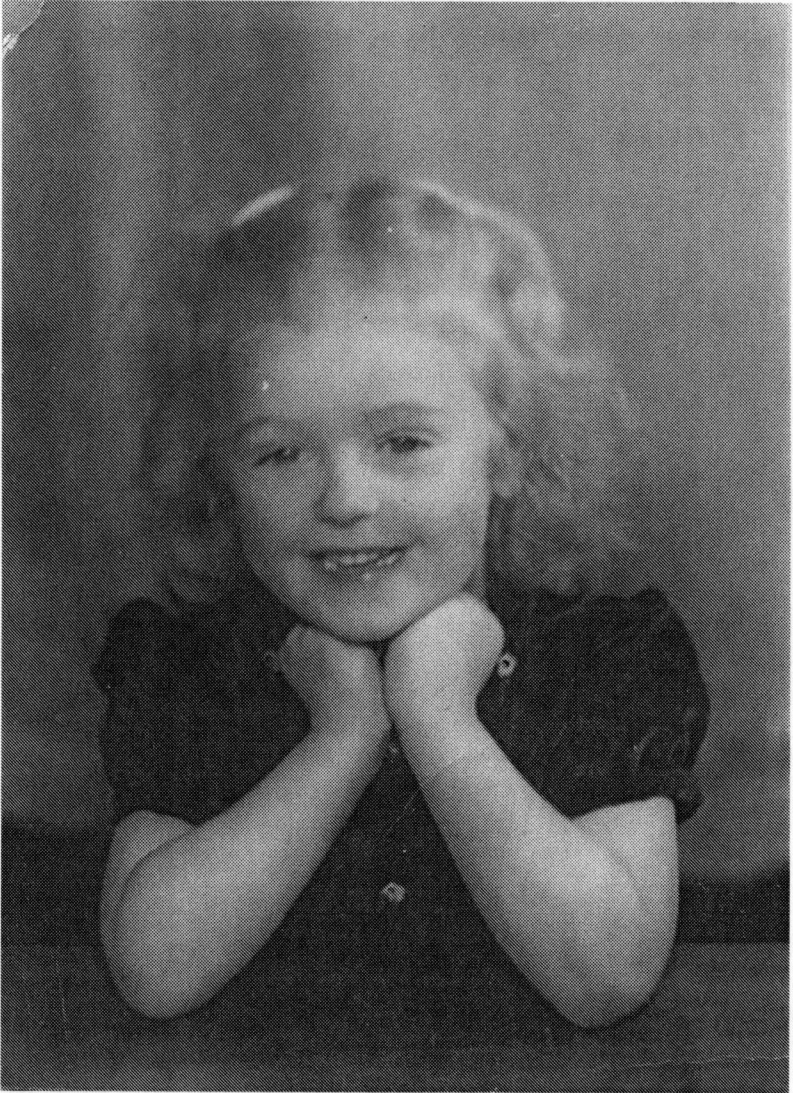

"Katie" around 1950

"Hank Collins" his father "Dan" and little brothers Jack and Bobby. This photo was taken in 1945 after my uncle's discharge from the military.

Jack And Kate Collins, at their senior prom in 1960.

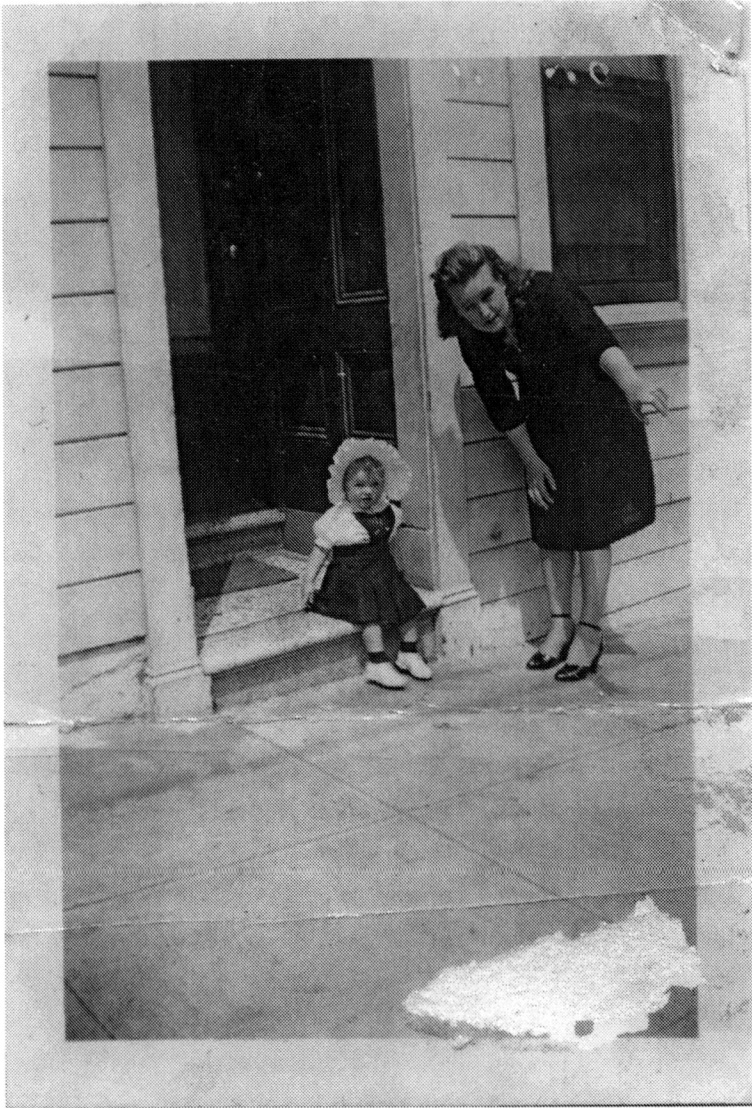

-"Ellen and "Katie" circa 1945

San Francisco, 1945:

Hank Collins got off the train and took a cab to 16th and Mission. He walked into Jerry's and asked for Rabbit.

"Who?"

"Orris," Hank said. "Orris John Simpson."

"Orris!" the bartender yelled. "Someone wants to see you."

Rabbit came out of the back room and his face lit up when he saw Hank. He came over and hugged Hank. Hank was happier to see him than he thought he'd be.

Rabbit took him into the back room. Rabbit lived in a room behind the bar. He had a bed, a dresser, a radio and a card table.

"Where's your bathroom?" Hank asked.

"I use the one in the bar to piss and shit in," Rabbit replied. "I shower at the YMCA down the street. It's only a couple bucks a month."

"What do you do here?" Hank asked.

"I cook hamburgers and hot dogs, ham-n-egg sandwiches, and stuff. I coordinate deliveries, help my uncle with bookkeeping. I don't serve liquor," Rabbit replied.

"Where you stayin'?"

"Nowhere yet. I just got off the train and came here," Hank replied.

"You can stay here until you get on your feet. Maybe my uncle will give you some work. He's always looking for help," Rabbit said.

"You're a good friend, Rabbit."

"I gotta look out for my spotter," Rabbit said, winking.

"That's true," Hank replied, laughing.

200

They went to an Army surplus store and bought Hank a cot to sleep on. Rabbit introduced Hank to his Uncle Jerry.

"I need an opening bartender. This is kind of a rough neighborhood. The ability to jump over the bar and kick somebody's ass is sometimes more important than mixing drinks. My nephew says you can do that. Is that a problem?"

"No, sir," Hank said.

"Ten to six, Tuesday through Saturday. You get Sunday and Monday off. Thirty dollars a week, you keep your tips."

"Yes, sir," Hank replied.

"I know you just left the Army," Jerry said, "but calling me 'sir' is like putting an elevator in an outhouse. Dumb and not necessary. Jerry's fine."

"Yes, sir," Hank said, reflexively, and the three of them laughed.

"Took me a while to drop that too," Rabbit said.

Hank stayed with Rabbit and he showered at the YMCA as well. Hank took to his new job like a duck to water.

He didn't have any problems with customers. Hank was one of those guys who scared others just by being there, even if he didn't do or say anything. He didn't have to put on an act or play tough. Jerry joked with another bar owner about it. The other bar owner said he was afraid the city was going to close him down because the cops had been called to his place too many times.

"We don't have that problem," Jerry said. "We never have to call the cops. When Hank tells them to leave, they leave."

About two months after he arrived, an incident occurred -- an incident that changed his entire life. Hank met "The Man" -- Tom Franklin.

About five o'clock one day the bar was unusually busy. The night bartender, who usually came on at 4:00 p.m., had called and said he was going to be late. Hank was doing his best to keep everyone's drinks full, and Rabbit had a grill full of hamburgers and sandwiches for the late afternoon crowd. A tall guy in an expensive suit came in with three others. He went to the end of the bar near the grill and addressed Rabbit.

"Why don't you help your friend so some men can do some drinkin'?"

"I don't serve liquor," Rabbit replied coldly.

"My boys and I say you do."

Rabbit calmly walked toward the bar. "You and your boys are mistaken. Now act like gentlemen and wait for the bartender. Otherwise, I'll have to take action that I don't want to take."

Hank came over. "How can I help you, gentlemen?"

"You can fire your cook," the leader said.

"Can't do that," Hank said. "His family owns the place."

"I think it's time for you gentlemen to leave," Rabbit said, taking off his apron.

Hank saw the look on Rabbit's face. He put his arm around him and walked him back toward the grill. "I'll take care of it. It's not worth it," Hank said. "I know you could kill all four of them in the blink of an eye."

"He doesn't know that," Rabbit sneered, pointing to the apparent leader.

"I'll convince him," Hank said. "You don't need to go to prison for killing some lout. I have to look out for my sniper."

"Okay," Rabbit said.

Hank went back to the bar. "I'll have to ask you gentlemen to leave," he said. "Like the sign says, we reserve the right to refuse service to anyone."

"Do you know who I am?" the guy asked, standing up to his full six-foot height, which was still two inches shorter than Hank.

"I don't give a shit who you are," Hank replied, stepping around the bar.

"Why are you backing your mouthy cook?" the guy asked.

"I'm not," Hank replied casually. "I'm protecting you idiots from him. I'm not gonna tell you again. Get the hell out of here."

Tom Franklin had won most of the fights he'd had in his life -- on the docks, in prison, and with the cops during the 83-day strike in 1934. He was going to teach the bastard a lesson. He swung his right fist, knowing it was going to destroy the guy's nose. The guy, however, blocked it with his left arm and drove a sledgehammer right of his own into Tom's solar plexus. Tom's knees buckled and every ounce of air left his lungs. The bartender had a hold of his coat with his left hand, trapping Tom's right arm. The bartender hit Tom in the face twice with his right hand and threw him down. Tom watched the rest of the fight from the floor, trying to catch his breath.

Two of Tom's men attacked the bartender, raining blows on his head and body. The bartender picked up a barstool and whacked each in the face with it. They reeled backward. Hank hit them both several more times until the stool broke, and they fell.

Tom heard a blood-curdling scream and everyone in the bar froze. Tom's third man had a butcher knife embedded in his right forearm and his gun was on the floor. The cook came around the bar, twirling large knives in each hand.

Tom got up. "Could I have a few minutes of your time?" he asked the bartender.

"You've taken up too much of my time already."

Tom handed the guy a twenty. "Give me a few ticks," he said. "Wait outside, boys," he said to his wounded men.

The night bartender came in.

"Take over for me, will you, George?" Hank said.

"No sweat," George replied.

"It's okay," Hank said to Rabbit, who put the knives away and went back to the grill.

Tom and Hank had a beer. "I could really use a man like you," Tom said. "I want you to be my personal bodyguard eventually."

"Why do you need a bodyguard?" Hank asked.

"You're not from around here, are you?" Tom asked.

"No," Hank replied. "Got here from Missouri a couple months ago. Before that I was fighting the Nazis in Europe. Before you make me an offer, let me make one thing clear.

I don't want to kill anybody. I done enough killin' in the war."

"You don't have to kill anyone, unless they're stupid enough to try to kill you. I'll start you out at one hundred fifty dollars a week. You do what I think you can, and later you'll make three or four hundred dollars a week."

"What about Rabbit?" Hank asked, pointing behind the bar. "He's twice the soldier I am."

"Sure. In combat in a war zone, I don't doubt it. I see now what you meant about protecting us. But you tried to avoid a fight. When a fight

203

became inevitable, you kicked ass. That instinct will keep you alive on the street. You have it, and he doesn't," Tom replied.

"He comes with me," Hank said. "You can use him for backup when you think you need it."

"We'll pay him well on a job-by-job basis. If he works out, fine. But I want you full time. You got a piece?" Tom asked.

"Yeah," Hank said. "I thought you said no killing?"

"I did," Tom replied, quoting something Red had told him years ago that he'd heard from someone. "You get more with a kind word and a gun than you do with just a kind word." Tom pulled a wad of cash out of his pocket and gave it to Hank. "That's a little advance. Buy yourself some nice suits and show up at my office Monday about nine." Tom gave Hank a business card and left.

Hank showed up on time on Monday wearing a nice cream-colored suit. He'd also bought a black one, a blue one, a brown one, and a blue pinstriped one. He also bought several white shirts and ties that the salesman said would match the suits. He bought two pairs of shoes, one black, one brown, and both shiny. He also bought a holster for his gun. It was designated for a Colt .45, but since they were similar in size, the Browning would fit nicely.

A few minutes after nine, Tom Franklin showed up with a big guy in an expensive suit, more expensive than Hank's.

"You look professional, good job," Tom said. "Come in the office. "You want some coffee?" A woman brought them coffee. "Let me see your piece," Tom said.

Hank pulled his jacket back. Tom was impressed. A Browning 9mm semi-automatic. It held thirteen shots and its large grip fit perfectly in the guy's bear-like paws. One couldn't really kill a man with one shot, unless it hit him in the head, but one could hurt him bad. Two more would finish him and there were still ten shots left for anyone else who was around.

"Mr. Franklin, I've been thinking," Hank said.

"About what?" Tom asked.

"I don't feel right about living at the bar with my friend if I'm not working there. I need to get my own place. I spent all the money you gave me on suits like you said.

If you could see fit to...."

Tom cut him off. "I like your style. Pay you what you're worth, right?" Tom said. He pulled a wad of cash out of his pocket. "Consider this a signing bonus, like they do with star baseball players. Get yourself a nice apartment. There's a car out back, belonged to a guy who no longer works for me. I think it's a Ford. It needs a new battery or something. It's yours. After you've made some money, if you get tired of it, feel free to trade it in on something else. I believe in paying a man what he's worth. And, like a star baseball player, I think you're worth a lot. But I demand absolute loyalty."

"You say jump, Mr. Franklin, and I'll say 'how high?'" Hank replied.

"That's what I'm talkin' about!" Tom said, banging an open palm on his desk. "If I had ten guys like you I could rule the world. Or at least San Francisco. Mike here will show you the ropes for a couple weeks, and then you'll work with me most of the time," Tom said, pointing to the big guy in the expensive suit. "You're gonna make more money than you've ever dreamed of."

"How do you know what I've dreamed of, Mr. Franklin?" Hank said.

"I love this fuckin' guy!" Tom said, pounding the desk again. "Can the 'Mr. Franklin' shit. Call me 'Tom' when we're alone, or 'boss' in front of the other guys. Got it?"

"Yes, boss," Hank replied, knowing Tom was right.

Hank couldn't believe how easy his job was. He was the kind of guy that scared other guys by his very presence.

Tom said he only knew one other guy like that and he didn't mention a name. Hank's first job was collecting on the docks. One day a guy named Bob French was short and Hank made a judgment call. It was the right call. Bob French owed Tom Franklin $200.00. He hadn't made a payment in two weeks. He ran when he saw Hank. Hank caught him in less than a block. The guy started begging.

"I got a wife and kids. The bank said they'd take my car if I don't pay them."

"Bob," Hank said emotionlessly. "I have a brother we call 'Bob.' I have a personal weakness for 'Bobs,' but I can't get emotionally involved. You want to dance, you pay the bank, you want to borrow, you pay the man. I'm supposed to hurt you if you don't pay. I don't want to hurt you. You don't want to be laid up with a broken leg. Do us both a favor. Give me some money, Bob," Hank said.

Bob coughed up $75.00.

Tom Franklin saw it when Hank turned in the day's receipts. "What's eatin' you?"

"I saw Bob French today," Hank said. "I got seventy-five dollars out of him. I think he's good for the rest."

"Sure, Bob's good for it," Tom said. "You did the right thing."

"I feel like I let you down," Hank said. "On one hand, I fuck the guy up, he can't work and he can't pay.

On the other hand, he's a grownup. He knew the terms when he borrowed. I feel bad for him and I feel like I didn't do my job."

"No, you sent a message," Tom said. "Certainly Bob thinks you would have hurt him if he didn't pay. It's perfect. He believes you would have kicked his ass if he didn't cough up something. He'll tell his friends. Inadvertently, that'll increase business. Guys will know they can't fuck us over, but they'll also think, 'Hey,

Bob said these guys are reasonable, they'll negotiate under certain circumstances.' We won't under most, but the men don't know that. Perception is everything."

"I thought you'd be mad," Hank said.

"Mad? I'm proud of you," Tom said. "You had balls enough to make a decision and you had balls enough to tell me of that decision like a man. That's the way to do business."

After a year and a half, Hank was well known. He was Tom's top man and had a well-deserved reputation as the union exec's most feared enforcer. He got that rep largely from two unrelated incidents.

In the first one, he had foiled an attempt on Tom's life. Tom and Hank had come from a dinner meeting with some people. Hank's car was at Tom's house. Tom pulled into his garage and they got out of the car. A man came out from the shadows, carrying a shotgun. He raised the weapon to his shoulder and pointed it at Tom. "Kill 'im, kill 'im," a voice outside urged, which distracted the gunner for a split second. Hank grabbed the shotgun's barrel and ripped it from the man's grasp. It went off as he did so, blowing plaster out of the garage ceiling. Hank slammed the rifle's butt into the startled goon's forehead, which immediately split open. The goon made a sighing sound as he fell.

Hank saw the other gunner lean around the corner with a revolver in hand. His soldier's instincts came back -- eliminate the threat. Hank drew his pistol and shot at the gunner in the head just as the guy crouched to sneak into the garage. As the 9mm slug blew his hat off and laid a stripe across the top of his head. The gunner fell down clutching his scalp and screaming, "Fuck! Fuck! I'm hit!"

Hank saw three more guys get out of a sedan across the street with pistols. He opened up on the car. The Browning bucked in his fist as it spit twelve rounds out lightning fast, breaking every window in the car. When the slide locked open, Hank smoothly released the empty magazine, slapped a fresh one in place, hit the slide release and resumed firing.

The other three ran down the street, abandoning their car. He didn't hit any of them, but he had fired twenty-five rounds so fast they must have thought there was a whole team of hitters in Tom's garage.

Tom was kicking the guy with the scalp wound and talking to him. "Attack me in my house, you son-of-a-bitch? I'll beat you to death right here and set fire to your corpse!"

"No, you'll call the cops," Hank said. "Maybe they can get him to roll on who hired them. You kill him and you'll never know."

"Good point," Tom replied.

Tom went into the house to call the cops, although the neighbors probably had already.

Hank wasn't arrested. It had cost over a thousand bucks and Tom had to call in some favors, but Hank had a permit for the gun. It made things easier and kept him out of jail in case he was hustled by a cop in a bar being rousted or during a traffic stop. The papers had a field day with the failed assassination attempt.

In the second incident, he had defended himself from what he thought was a belligerent drunk, but in reality was the toughest cop on the force. Hank had bought a new Lincoln convertible and had double-parked in front of Jerry's. He had gone in to get Rabbit, as they were meeting some women at a club across town. When they came out, a guy was sitting on the hood of Hank's car. Three others were leaned against a car that Hank had pinned in.

"Is this your car, asshole?" the guy on the hood growled. He was Clark Shaughnessy, the most feared cop on the force. He hadn't risen higher than patrolman because he had so many brutality complaints against him. Everyone who worked the streets feared him.

He was off duty and out of uniform. Hank had never met him before and thought he was a jerk-off who needed an attitude adjustment.

"Get off my car, shithead," Hank said calmly.

Shaughnessy jumped off the car and lunged at Hank.

They clashed like NFL linemen during a goal-line stand. Shaughnessy's three buddies thought it was funny until Hank got the upper hand.

Rabbit stepped in front of them. "Let's keep this fair," he drawled in his Mississippi way.

"You gonna stop us, hillbilly?" one of them asked, laughing.

"You done been stopped," Rabbit said calmly.

The three of them came forward. In a flash, Rabbit had slammed the one on his right in the nose with the heel of his left palm and hit the one on his left in the adam's apple with the web of skin between the thumb and forefinger of his right hand. They fell almost simultaneously, one gagging and the other holding his destroyed nose. It had happened so fast that the third one was still advancing. Rabbit spun around with a vicious sidekick, caving in three of the man's ribs. It had taken Rabbit six seconds. By now Hank had knocked the other guy out with a thunderous right.

"What took you so long?" Rabbit asked Hank.

"Screw you," Hank said, laughing. "Let's go before somebody calls the cops." They got in the car and left.

Word traveled fast on the street that Shaughnessy and his posse had gotten their asses whomped, and who did it. Curiously, as it happens sometimes with such incidents, Rabbit's presence was not mentioned, even though he took out three and Hank only one. Hank got the credit. From then on, he was King Kong with the street guys.

He was smart, though. He kept as low a profile as he could and paid for cops' lunches if they were dining in the same place as he was. He sent mob guys and other union people bottles of wine if they were having dinner where he was. Except for his car and fine clothes, Hank saved most of his money.

Women were always around union dinners and boxing matches, and he took advantage of their hospitality. He didn't fall in love, he just had fun. Sex was a fun release, nothing more. He actually liked the club girls and the hustler types. They knew what one wanted and didn't care, as long as they got what they wanted. Everyday girls were a pain in the ass. They wanted you to meet their parents and date them for months before they put out, if not marry them. Not Hank. He had the perfect attitude. Women were fine until they got tired of him, then he found another.

The same with work. It was a good job. He didn't get bogged down in the politics of street life like a lot of other guys. He enjoyed the money and the fun for a couple years until he was pulled kicking and screaming into a mob war.

San Francisco, 1948:

Captain Tom Conway sat in his office fingering three envelopes filled with betting slips. He wished he could decode the notations on the slips. It was very important for him to do so. The envelopes were the betting slips that his raiding party had picked up when they hit one of Tom Franklin's top bookmakers the night before. The bookmaker now had to buy back the slips so the players couldn't claim winners and wipe him out. It was important for Captain Conway to decode the slips because he didn't want to get cheated when he sold them back to the bookmaker. If there was fifty grand worth of action, then maybe he could sell it back for five grand. But if there were a lot of heavy bets and the slips represented a hundred grand or maybe even two hundred grand, then the price should be considerably higher.

Tom fiddled with the envelopes and decided to let Franklin and his underlings sweat a little bit, maybe even make the first offer. It might tip off what the real price should be. He called his wife and told her he was going to be late. He never confided in her on anything. She thought they lived the way they did on his policeman's salary. Tom snorted in amusement. His first partner's wife had thought the same thing.

John McCluskey had taught him early. McCluskey even had the balls to bring his seven-year-old son with him on collections, usually on the last Saturday of the month.

He'd walked through the precinct and to all the businesses, say, "This is my little boy." The storekeepers shook John,

Jr.'s hand and compliment him extravagantly and open their registers to give him a gift of five or ten dollars. At the end of the day, "Little John," as he was called, had seven or eight hundred dollars in his pockets, proud that his father's friends liked him enough to give him a gift every month they saw him. Of course John, Sr. kept all the money and "Little John" got maybe a five-spot for himself.

Prohibition really drove it home for Tom, especially after McCluskey made lieutenant and he was made sergeant.

He remembered when McCluskey told him "the law of the land."

"Shit. Who really cares if someone wants to lay a bet, or a broad, or a base for a three-day drunk? If Tony Maretti or some other bootlegger comes in here and puts his paper bag full of money on my desk, and I spread it around to all them men in my precinct, who don't make enough off the taxpayers to buy their children shoes or maybe take them to a ballgame, or take their wives on vacation, like every American family should do, what harm is there in that? We're not letting bank robbers go and we're not letting murderers go. In the senate, it might be illegal, on Nob Hill it's hospitality."

Conway had been a good cop, a brave cop. The tough young punks terrorizing street corners fled when he approached and finally vanished from his beat forever. He was a very tough cop and a very fair one. He never ducked into movie houses or goofed off in restaurants when he was on foot patrol as some of the other cops did, especially on winter nights. He always made his rounds. He gave his stores a lot of service and a lot of protection. When winos and drunks filtered up from Third Street to panhandle on his beat, he got rid of them so roughly that they never came back. The tradespeople in his precinct appreciated it and they showed their appreciation.

He also obeyed the system. Maretti and other players knew he would not make trouble to get an extra payoff for himself being content with his share of the station house bag. His name was on the list with the others and he never tried to make extras. He was a fair cop who only took clean graft and his rise in the police department was steady if not spectacular.

During the time he raised a family of four sons and a daughter -- none of the boys became policemen. The boys went to private schools and one to Cal-Berkeley. He rose from sergeant to lieutenant to captain, and his family lacked for nothing. Conway thought there was nothing wrong with clean graft.

Why should my boys go to city college, or no college at all because the police department doesn't pay its people enough to live on and take care of their families properly?

He protected the people with his life and his record showed his citations for gun battles with stickup men, strong-arm protection guys and would-be pimps. He had hammered them into the ground. He'd kept his corner of the city safe for ordinary people and he was entitled to more than a lousy c-note a week. He wasn't indignant about his low pay though. He knew everybody had to take care of themselves.

The point was driven home during Prohibition. A friend was shotgunned to death on a liquor raid in 1933. The next day, Congress repealed Prohibition. He died for the "law of the land," which wasn't a law the next day. Tom never lost perspective on "law and order."

San Francisco, 1938:

After the gala opening of the Bay Bridge in 1937, with construction on the Golden Gate Bridge ongoing, business in San Francisco was doing well. The Golden Gate Bridge was scheduled to open in 1938, and could open sooner if everything went according to plan. The dock workers union's membership was at an all-time high. Red, Eddie and Doc had seen Joe Louis demolish Max Schmeling in the first round in New York, much to Hitler's dismay. Jesse Owens had humiliated him at the 1936 Berlin Olympics, winning nearly every track medal. Not only was he American, he was a Negro. A real slap in the face to the "superior" Aryan race. Hitler thought Schmeling bringing the title back to the Fatherland would be redemption.

Schmeling had knocked out Louis in the 12th round a few years earlier, when Louis was still an up-and-coming contender. The young Louis had a habit of dropping his left after jabbing. Schmeling, a noted right-hand puncher, had a field day. Joe Louis had since matured into the "Brown Bomber" who would hold the title twelve years, have an incredible twenty-five defenses, and retire as champion in 1949. Louis came back in 1950-51 due to tax troubles and won eight fights before being demolished by Rocky Marciano. The Louis who Marciano fought was a shell of his former self.

In 1938, however, Louis was a razor-sharp, fast, ruthless killer, with knockout power in either hand, who could only be topped in ferocity by the legendary Jack

Dempsey. Boxing writers said if Dempsey in his prime had fought Louis in his prime there would be two possible outcomes. If the fight were held in a

213

boxing ring, Louis would win. If it were held in a phone booth or the street, Dempsey would win. Schmeling was nowhere near the caliber of either one.

Hitler boasted that Schmeling would destroy Louis. Louis, the reigning champion, had said, "I ain't really champ 'til I beat Schmelin'."

The fight was held at Yankee Stadium. People cheered when the *Star-Spangled Banner* was played and the flag waved, and booed loudly when the Nazi flag was unfurled for the German national anthem.

Schmeling never had a prayer. He was over thirty and on the downside of his career when he fought Louis the first time. The victory was one of those "any given Sunday..." flukes. After beating Louis, however, Schmeling was promoted heavily by the Third Reich. He rolled over the tomato cans he was matched against. Hitler saw his chance to prove the superiority of the Aryan race. Big deal that Jesse Owens could run faster than any one in the world. If a German could become world heavyweight champion fighting, he would feel redeemed after the debacle of Berlin.

When Louis became the first black man since Jack Johnson to win the title, the Third Reich's propaganda machine went into overdrive. There were quite a few viable contenders who would have made a much better opponent for Louis. Former champ Max Baer was still fighting and ranked in the top ten. He was still winning and could still hit as hard with his right as any man in history. Baer's close friend, Maxie Rosenbloom, was a superb boxer and a ranked contender. "Two-ton" Tony Galento was a feared brawler, who boasted if he fought Louis, he'd "moider the bum."

Hitler kept taunting boxing promoters from afar, and finally, the American public wanted to see Louis fight Schmeling, and the other contenders were passed over.

Schmeling's corner was attended by his manager and several German soldiers. Schmeling looked nervous. He was a smart man who knew he was in a lose-lose situation. If he won, he would further the Nazi's madness. If he lost, he'd very likely see problems back home in Germany. He did not want to carry his nation's pride on his broad shoulders.

Louis entered the ring and Doc said, "This'll be over in less than three. Did you see the look on Schmeling's face when he saw Louis?"

Louis always had a "poker face" in the ring, but his eyes spoke more hatred than any words could. Jesse Owens just did his job and was proud to be an American. Louis wanted to kick Hitler's ass. He wanted to smite his tormentors in Biblical fashion. He paced and snorted like an enraged bull in a rodeo chute.

When the bell rang, Louis rushed out to meet his opponent. Louis jabbed and Schmeling threw his famous right. It landed on Louis' left glove instead of his jaw. Louis drove an uppercut to the midsection, followed by a hook to the head and bulled Schmeling to the ropes. Louis unleashed a barrage unseen before or since in boxing. He sunk both hands deep into Schmeling's midsection and bulled him along the ropes, firing short rights and hefty hooks to the head. Schmeling tried to fight his way out, but Louis would not be denied. Max tried to cover up, but it was futile.

Sportswriters at ringside said they actually heard Schmeling's ribs crack. When he tried to spin away, Louis hit him so hard in the kidneys people ringside said they heard Herr Max scream in pain, even above the din of the crowd. Louis crashed blow after unanswered blow into him. Max fell to the canvas and lay in a queer position, writhing in pain and screaming. It was thought that the hook to the kidneys damaged his spine, as even after the referee counted him out at barely two minutes into the fight, he continued moaning and clutching his lower back.

To the utter disgust of the crowd, before the knockout was officially announced, German soldiers came into the ring and picked up the injured Schmeling, getting in a shoving match with Louis and his seconds, who were trying to see if Max was badly hurt and offer assistance. The Nazi men refused to let the ringside doctor examine Schmeling and carried him from the ring without a stretcher, even though the doctor said he might have a back injury.

Schmeling was not taken to the dressing room or the hospital, but directly to the airport to be flown back to Germany. Max recovered and was inducted into the German Army and fought in World War II. After the war, he and Louis actually became friends. When Joe was broke and having medical problems late in life, it was Schmeling who paid the doctor bills. In 1938, however, they were mortal enemies and America was happy that Louis destroyed him, but disgusted with the Germans' conduct. It was not the first or last time representatives of the Union would witness or participate in a major political event.

The big strike of 1934 had been the first. Partly because of Tom's troubles of being called a communist, they were more attuned to world affairs and constitutional issues. They had blocked the shipment of supplies to the rising Fascist nations in Europe and Asia, and had supported the fledgling Republic of Spain in its uneven struggle against the Axis powers. In 1938, the Union now refused to load scrap iron destined for Japan or Germany, presciently claiming the iron would return as bombs against the United States. The winds of war were brewing in Europe. They were also brewing on the streets of San Francisco and within the union itself.

In 1933, a young upstart prosecutor named Fred J. Walton had decided to go after the Maretti family. After nailing Capone, the Feds and other law enforcement agencies realized they might be able to put previously untouchable gangsters in prison for income tax evasion, fraud and other crimes, even if they couldn't get them for murder and other heinous crimes. If they were off the street and out of circulation, it didn't matter why.

Walton managed to prove, like they did with Capone and countless other gangsters, that Maretti lived like a movie star, yet officially had no income. He also proved that Clawson Construction took taxes out of their workers' paychecks, but had not paid the Feds and Maretti was a silent partner. Maretti's lawyers negotiated a plea bargain. He would plead guilty to tax fraud and racketeering and pay a large fine if Clawson Construction wasn't implicated. Tony was sentenced to ten years, but everyone on both sides of the law knew, with his clout and time off for good behavior and so forth, that he'd do maybe three. Both sides could claim victory. Walton put a heretofore untouchable mobster behind bars, regardless of time. Tony knew everyone takes a hit now and then, and he could ride out his incarceration if he played it right.

He went to jail in 1935, leaving his son, Tony, Jr. in charge, with strict instructions to consult his grandfather, Vito Calabrese, on any major issues. The kid was headstrong and the old man was dying of lung cancer. Tony had to deal with problems his whole term and had to re-exert himself as King of the Jungle after his release.

Tony's two capos, Dante Fresca and Rocco Lampone, spent nearly the entire three years fighting over who should be top dog and trying to carry favor with Tony, Jr. Business suffered. Tom Franklin had branched out into loansharking and took territories quietly. Tony, Jr. favored Fresca. Fresca and Franklin's people had got in a huge fight in front of Louie's. Louie's was destroyed and seventeen people were injured. Fresca requested permission to go after "these union fucks that are chiseling our business."

Tony, Jr. agreed, assuming he meant Franklin. Fresca went after everyone. A Molotov cocktail was thrown through the front room window of Tom's house, but he wasn't home.

Red, Doc, Eddie and Blackie were going to lunch at the St. Francis on 24th Street. They had good soup, good sandwiches, homemade ice cream and hand-dipped chocolates. Doc always bought a pound of vanilla creams whenever they went there.

"I have to stop by my house," Eddie said. "I accidentally took the keys to the other car when I left this morning. My wife and daughter want to go shopping.

I'll drop the keys off, just take a minute."

When they arrived at Eddie's house, the front door was open. Eddie ran inside. He saw his twenty-year-old daughter Ellen in the hall.

"Where's your mother?" he asked.

"In the bathtub," she said shakily.

"Why?"

"Some guys threw paint on her," Ellen said.

"Paint?" Eddie asked, incredulous.

"Paint," Ellen repeated.

Eddie went to the bathroom. Mary was in the tub, crying and washing paint off herself.

"What the hell happened?" he asked.

"I thought it was you bringing the car keys. I opened the door and these two guys were standing there. One of them throws red paint over me and says, 'That's what you'll look like dead. Tell your husband and his union cronies to stop messing with the Maretti family.' Are you messing with the Maretti family?" she asked.

"I am now," Eddie said coldly, and stormed out the door.

Red saw his expression when he came out. "What's up?" Red asked.

"Junior Maretti just committed suicide," Eddie growled.

"Are you comin' or not?"

Everyone got back in the car. Red tried to talk to Eddie as he drove, but Eddie only got more agitated.

"Let's talk about this," Red said.

"I'm not talkin'," Eddie growled. "I'm doin'. Little bastard can make moves without his father's approval, he can pay the consequences without his father's involvement."

"What is wrong? What happened?" Red asked.

"They threatened my family. Now they're done for."

They pulled up in front of Louie's. Tony, Jr. and six men were coming out. Four went to a Cadillac and got in.

Eddie got out of the car and started yelling, "Hey, Junior! You want to fuckin' fight, come over here and do it like a man!"

Red got out, as did Doc and Blackie. The two on either side of Tony, Jr. came up to Eddie.

"Whatever he's payin' you, it ain't gonna be enough," Eddie said.

The one on the left threw a wild right at Eddie's head. Even though he was fifty-six years old, Eddie still worked with boxers every day, sometimes getting into the ring with them and saying, "If you can't beat an old man, how are you gonna beat a contender?"

Thirty years into his retirement, when he was well into his sixties, two toughs tried to mug Jack Dempsey outside his restaurant in New York. He dispatched them both quickly, and they demanded a witnessing cab driver call the cops and stay until the cops arrived to protect them. Like Doc said, "You lose the legs and the wind, but you never lose the punch or the heart."

Eddie slipped the punch and slammed a textbook double-hook into the goon's ribs and face, who fell facedown on the pavement. The second one rained several blows on Eddie. Instinct rushed back and, even though it looked like the thug was doing damage, he really wasn't. Eddie took the blows on the top of his head, shoulders and elbows. He exploded out of the crouch with three lefts and two rights that sent the second goon to dreamland.

The other four tried to get out of the car. Red knocked out the driver before he could. He kicked the door shut on the guy in the backseat's arm, and then pulled him out, punched him in the face twice and banged his head on a telephone pole.

Blackie ran around to the car's rear and popped the guy getting out of the backseat on the right in the back of the head with his brass knuckles. The goon fell. The fourth one tried to pull a gun. Blackie slammed both the goon's arms with his brass-knuckled fists, which paralyzed the thug's arm for a split second. A final shot to the face destroyed the man's nose and put him down for the duration. Everything had transpired in less than a minute and a half.

"Come on, Junior!" Eddie yelled. "You afraid to fight a man your daddy's age?"

Tony Maretti, Jr. was 6'1", big for an Italian. He'd had his share of fights on the street. He'd proven that people feared him for reasons other than his family name.

He was an accomplished street fighter and his rage usually sealed him off from pain until hours later.

"I'm gonna kick your ass, old man. I'm gonna put you through the street," Tony sneered as he came forward.

Junior had worked out with his father's boxing trainers before. He threw a textbook right hook that would have pole-axed the average jerk. For a second he felt the soaring pleasure of triumph in battle, knowing your opponent is destroyed.

But the old guy was fast, faster than anyone at any age had a right to be, and slipped the punch. Eddie countered with a left hook that hit like Thor's hammer. It actually broke three ribs. Tony felt the air leave his lungs and felt unbelievable pain. He burped and his lunch came up.

He fell, making death-rattle sounds, and curled up into a fetal position, gasping for air. He felt something he'd never felt in his whole life -- fear.

The old guy talked to him. "I only hit you half as hard as I know how," he said. "I want to see your father soon. I don't care how he does it, or how you do it, but he talks to me or I'll give you a war you won't believe."

The two goons who Eddie had cold-cocked got up and drew pistols. Doc had stopped carrying his .45 Peacemaker. He realized that young toughs might be able to take a pistol from an old man. A career tough guy, he wasn't going to change his attitude late in life. He carried a cut-down 12-gauge pump shotgun loaded with double-aught buck in a custom-made sling under his coat. Even in the hands of an old man with poor eyesight, it was a formidable weapon. If you hit the floor in front of your assailants, they'd lose their legs, at least temporarily.

The thugs pointed their guns at Eddie. He couldn't let them kill the only son he'd ever had.

"No!" he yelled and triggered the shotgun.

He had held the shotgun low and hit the first goon in the torso. The report seemed to stop everyone. Red and Blackie made sure the goons near the car didn't try anything. The second goon started moving again.

"Don't do it!" Doc yelled.

The thug continued to raise his gun. Doc pumped the slide and stroked the trigger. The thug was lifted off his feet and slammed to the pavement.

"Fuck!" Doc yelled. "Didn't you hear what I said?"

Eddie seemed unfazed by the gunfire over his head.

Mario Maretti, Tony's younger brother, was watching from the doorway of Louie's.

"Talk to your brother. Tell him your dad needs to settle this. You understand?" Eddie said.

"Yes, sir, I understand," Mario replied.

"Thanks, Doc, I know you've always got my back,"

Eddie said.

"I'm too old for this shit," Doc replied.

"Apparently not," Eddie said.

They got in their car and left.

Tony Maretti was paroled a month earlier than scheduled. Vito Calabrese was gravely ill. Ten grand to a District Court judge got him released so he could arrange and attend his father-in-law's funeral, provided he stayed under house arrest the final thirty days, except for the funeral. He summoned his two sons in his private study when he got home.

"What caused this problem with the union people last week?" he asked.

Mario spoke up. "Some of our guys threw paint on Coyle's wife."

"Why?"

"To send a message."

"What message?"

"That we're insane?" Mario laughed.

"Who okay'd this?" Tony asked.

Mario pointed to his brother, who was still nursing his wounded ribs.

"You authorized something that stupid?" Tony said to his eldest son with disgust.

"Not exactly," Tony, Jr. said.

"Either you did or you didn't. 'Not exactly' is not an answer."

Tony, Jr. sighed and spoke, dreading the fact he screwed up and his father knew it. "Tom Franklin has been quietly taking over a lot of territory with loansharking, numbers, crap games and stuff. His people and Dante's got into it the other day."

"I heard. Go on."

"Dante asked me if he could take care of the union fucks that are chiseling our business. I said yes. I thought he meant Franklin."

"And why would you think that would be okay?" Tony, Sr. asked.

"Listen, Pop, I know Red is your godson. He's not a made man because he's Irish, but there still has to be a sit down before anyone can touch him. Everybody knows that. But Franklin, the hatred for him on both sides of the law is unbelievable. The government is still trying to deport him and prove he's a commie. And he's fucking with us. I figure if Dante whacked him, it would fall under DSAF -- Did Society A Favor. I got no beef with the union. Hell, I like Doc and Coyle. They've given us ringside seats at every big fight for years. I had no idea Dante would go after anyone but Franklin. Honest, Pop."

"All right," Tony said. "It's not your fault. Dante screwed you. Mario, go get Rocco and Sonny."

Tony, Jr. stiffened. Sonny Lauria was Rocco Lampone's right hand man and the smoothest, most reliable, most feared hitter in the family. Obviously his father was considering a big move.

Mario came back with Rocco and Sonny. "Sonny, I want you to take out Dante Fresca," Tony said.

"Done," Sonny said stoically. "Do you want him cowboy'd or done discretely?"

"You decide," Tony replied. "You're not surprised?" he asked.

"A little. I'm surprised it took you so long," Sonny replied.

Tony saw his son's reaction and decided to run with it. He could allay Rocco's apprehension and teach his sons a valuable lesson at the same time.

"The whole time I was in Alcatraz, Rocco came to see me regularly, as did all our people. Dante never once came to visit me. All I heard was Dante's neglecting business, he's trying to go on his own. All he's interested in is smack and cocaine, and he leaves the gambling to last. He's using our people to run dope in Oakland. He's partnering up with Provenzano from Oakland. I knew he didn't respect me anymore when he attacked Coyle's wife. We don't go after women and children. He's daring me to respond," Tony said. "I'm going to. It might get ugly for a couple years here. Other families may move against us. These things gotta happen every five years or ten years or so. It's been ten years since the last one. Gets rid of a lot of the bad blood."

"Are you sure, Pop?" Tony, Jr. asked.

"I'm sure." Tony continued, "You have to learn to think as people around you think. Dante didn't know I was getting out, no one did. He figured if he started a war with the union people, they'd do his work for him. Maybe they'd kill you or Mario, or both. I'm in prison, so my hands are tied to some extent. He takes over the family. At the very least, I have to negotiate from jail, and have to acknowledge his leadership of the street guys. The union guys are gonna want peace. They're labor leaders, not gangsters. They don't want violence in the streets. The peace Dante would want would be a piece of the union and the right to run drugs through the docks. I know Red and Coyle, and they'd never allow that. They'd fight until hell freezes over, but Dante doesn't know that.

"Business-wise, it's a smart move, if I was doing twenty years, if Rocco was as dumb as Dante thinks, and if Coyle was stupid, but he blew it. I'm out. Rocco stayed loyal to me and Coyle isn't stupid. He kicked your ass in a rage and demanded a meeting with me. That I can understand; if someone threatened your mother, I'd be as mad as hell too. I'll give him a meeting and work out any grievances.

As mad as he was, he had the presence of mind to tell Mario to tell me to negotiate. But he didn't cross the line Dante hoped he would. If he'd killed you, it'd be all-out war, no negotiation. He didn't want that. He wanted me to know he was pissed and that shit was going on that shouldn't be.

He sent his message clearer than Dante sent his. Sonny, do it this week and surprise me," Tony finished.

"Yes, boss," was all that Sonny said. Rocco was smiling from ear to ear.

Dante Fresca was having lunch is Sausalito. One had to take a ferry to get there. The restaurant was close to the beach and had great seafood. Dante liked their New York style pan roasts. It was hard to get New York style pan roasts in California. Dante was stunned when he saw Sonny.

"What the hell are you doing here?" he said, genuinely surprised.

"Tony says nice try," Sonny replied and blew his brains out with a .38 revolver.

He walked out fast, but he didn't run. Sonny got in a car outside the restaurant and immediately went to the train station where he was sent to New York. In New York, Tony's contacts treated him like a king. He had money, booze, broads, anything. He returned six weeks later, happy and ready to go back to work.

Dante Fresca's killing was never solved. Witness reports were conflicting. Reports said that the man was between 5'8" and 6'2", dark hair, between twenty and forty, between 160 and 220 pounds, and may or may not have had a mustache. About 150,000 men in the greater Bay Area qualified. The police were stymied.

Tony took Mario and Tony, Jr. to see their grandfather. Vito Calabrese was seventy-eight years old. He'd run a long, hard race with death. Now, vanquished, he lay exhausted on the raised bed. He'd wasted away to little more than a skeleton. Tony had always affectionately called the older man "Dad" even though they weren't blood. It had been a running joke for many years, a sign of their relationship.

"Look, Dad, I've brought your grandsons to see you," Tony said with sadness in his eyes.

The old man clasped the young men's hands and thanked them for coming. He then grabbed onto Tony with both hands. With a Herculean effort, he raised his head and spoke, "Please help me, son. I can feel my flesh burning off my bones and the worms eating my brain. I gave you my youngest, prettiest daughter. I helped you get started.

I loved you as a son. I know you have the power to save me from the Reaper."

Tears rolled down Tony's cheeks as he tried to retain composure. Tony, Jr. and Mario remained quiet.

They had only seen their father cry once before. They were children and their older sister's dog been run over by a streetcar. Their sister and mother were inconsolable. Tony comforted the women and cried himself. Not that he cared that much about the dog because he used to kick the shit out of it when it pissed in the house. He cried because people he loved were hurting and he was absolutely powerless to do anything. Nothing he did could bring that stupid dog back. It was the same now. Tony couldn't help the old man at all, so he cried in front of his sons.

"Don't fear the Reaper," Tony said reassuringly. "I'll stay and meet him with you. I'll have Mass said for you every day, and your daughters and widow will pray for you every day. How can God be vengeful when there are so many pleas for mercy?"

The old man seemed animated in his delirium, almost happy. "It's been arranged then, you'll handle it?" he asked.

More tears flowed and Tony fought to keep his voice strong. "Yes, I'll handle it," he said.

"Thank you," Calabrese said, breathing heavily. "I knew you wouldn't fail me. We'll beat death just like we've beat all the other bastards over the years." He closed his eyes and was still.

Tony held his hand and a half-hour later he was gone. Tony stood, looking as if he'd come to a monumental decision.

"Tell Coyle I'll se him at the funeral. After Grandpa's funeral, I want to talk seriously to both of you about the family's future."

"We can talk now, Pop," Tony, Jr. said.

"After the funeral," Tony said, and walked out of the hospital room. The younger men followed, knowing when to be quiet.

Red, Tom Franklin, Doc and Eddie sat in Eddie's office. Red was furious.

"I warned you about this bullshit!" he yelled. "Now we have to have a sit-down because of your shit! Starting a war with Tony Maretti. That's shrewd. What the fuck is wrong with you?"

"Fuck you," Tom replied contemptuously. "His people beat up my runners and take my money and I'm starting something?"

"You chiseled his territory while he was in jail,"

Red replied. "Did you think he'd allow that?"

"It wasn't him, it was his piece of shit underboss," Tom replied.

"That was mysteriously killed last week, just after Tony got released," Red said. "Figure it out. You can't learn it in school and you can't get a late start. You're not a labor leader anymore. Now you're a gangster. You make peace with Tony or you fight him, but this is the last time the union suffers from your personal business."

"Is that how it is?" Tom asked.

"That's how it is," Eddie replied. "I have a plan that I think will work for everyone, and be in the union's best interests."

"I'm all ears," Tom said.

Red made a motion with his hand and Eddie spoke. "Tom, what you've helped us accomplish is amazing. The men on the street respect you. The men also respect Red. I can see that a working relationship with the two of you is now impossible. I propose that we split the union into two factions. Tom takes the Dockworkers Union, and Red takes the Steelworkers Union. Officially we'll say that this will allow us to better serve both unions by specializing, and giving each a strong leader. Unofficially I'm doing damage control.

"Tom, I don't agree with what you're doing on the side, but it would hurt the union, maybe irreparably if you were fired. Your hold over the public and the men is too valuable to lose. Red has the integrity this union needs. Regardless of his past, he's committed to the labor movement and he sees things down the road, not just the moment. I thought about holding an election and having you both run for president, but whoever lost would be a lame duck, and either way we'd lose a powerful man that we need. I think this is the best solution. We need to show the public and press a united front," Eddie finished.

"I can live with that," Tom said.

"So can I," said Red.

"What about this meeting?" Tom asked.

"You weren't invited," Red said coldly. "You have to deal with Tony on your own terms, big shot."

Tom shot Red a murderous look, but didn't say anything.

Eddie's plan was perfect. The rank and file members loved the plan. Blackie was ecstatic. "Now I can tell the men how much clout I have with the president of not one, but two locals. Beautiful."

Even the press lauded the decision once it was made public. They were sticking to their man-on-the-street roots, not becoming a huge conglomerate that only cared about the bottom line. Only insiders knew how tense the days preceding and immediately following Calabrese's funeral were.

At the same time, Mr. Fred J. Walton was eyeing a run for Attorney General. He thought his success as a prosecutor would get him the job and with any luck in a few years he could be the youngest man to ever become governor. He had asked for and received the union's endorsement in 1936. Now that he was going on to bigger things, he was worried there might be a conflict of interest with Eddie and company running a labor union and owning a construction company. Further he worried that Tom's continued trouble of being called a communist might hurt him if he accepted the union's continued endorsement, although he didn't think he could get elected without it. He wanted their help, but didn't know how he could accept it under the current circumstances.

Doc was utterly furious. "Arrogant little son-of-a-bitch! We get him re-elected and now he's casting reflections on how we do business, because it might hurt him politically? He's threatening us? If I wasn't a religious man, I'd kill this fucker myself."

Eddie spit coffee across his desk and got some up his nose as well. Red and Blackie tried to keep straight faces, but couldn't. They roared with laughter

"What's so god damned funny?" Doc sneered, sulking.

Eddie spoke up. "Doc, the only time you talk to Jesus is when you're bent over the toilet after a hard night of drinking."

Doc had to laugh. "Okay, maybe the religious thing was a little over the top. But don't tell me you don't see a veiled threat," Doc said. "We don't come up to his standards, and he's not our friend anymore. If we're not friends, then he can start a witch-hunt investigation."

"Here's how we can get him by the balls," Red said.

"We sell the construction company to the highest bidder."

"We know who that'll be," Doc said.

"Who hates Walton and doesn't mind doing favors for us," Red retorted. "We've already agreed to split the union. The Steelworkers Union endorses Walton. We ask Tom to have the Longshoreman's Union endorse his opponent."

"Brilliant," Doc said. "Absolutely brilliant."

"I don't follow you two," Eddie said.

"Neither do I," Blackie said.

Red motioned at Doc, who took the cue. "Here's how it is. There's no conflict of interest if we don't own the construction company anymore. We can sell it to whoever we want. Maretti's money is as green as anyone else's, and he's smart enough to buy it through a front. That'll chap Walton's ass, but he won't be able to do anything about it. He was worried about affiliating with a union with an accused communist leader. As far as the AFL is concerned, Red's a model citizen. The Steelworkers Union endorsement looks good politically.

"Tom, the accused commie, of course endorses Walton's enemy. On paper that looks like a stalemate, one cancels out the other. But in reality, no one's forgotten Tom's leadership during the 1934 strike or his persecution by the government. The split is semantics to all union men. Most union men will go with what Tom does. The Dockworkers Union endorsing his opponent is the kiss of death, but he can't say anything about it. He'll lose and he'll know we made him lose. If he decided to run for D.A. again, or Attorney General again, he'll be a lot more humble. It's perfect," Doc finished.

"I agree," Eddie replied. "But how can we be sure Tom will do that?"

Red spoke up. "We don't ask him, we tell him. We tell him what Walton said about being associated with him. That should be enough. If not, Tom still has to make peace with Tony. Tony asks him the same favor as terms of peace."

"Can you guarantee that?" Eddie asked.

"Is a pig made out of pork?" Doc put in. "It's done. Fuck Walton! I feel better already." Everyone laughed heartily.

Red bought the most expensive funeral bouquet that Frigosi's on Mission Street offered. He sent it to Tony's house, not the funeral home. He paid extra to have a sealed envelope delivered with it. The note inside read: "I can't say I know what you're feeling because I don't. I didn't get along with my father, and I know yours died in your teens. I do know it would be very painful to lose a mentor, a friend, and someone who taught you to act like a man. I hope I'm never in that position. Red."

Calabrese's funeral was a lavish affair. After leaving the funeral home, guests went to Tony's estate on Nob Hill. Mob power nationwide was represented. Heads of families came not only from California, but from Portland, New York, Kansas City, Chicago, Cincinnati, New Orleans, Pittsburgh and Atlanta. Tony, Jr. discreetly spoke to powerful guests about staying for a meeting after the relatives and neighbors left. Red, Eddie and Doc were invited. Even thought they were "Irish," they were too powerful to ignore. Plus, they had business to address.

Eddie was at the bar, becoming impatient. Red was circulating and Doc was arguing boxing with a promoter from New York. Tony Maretti put his arm around Eddie.

"Eddie Coyle, my most valued friend," he said.

"I'm sorry for your loss," Eddie said politely.

"Thank you. I'm sorry my underlings were stupid while I was incarcerated. I never would have allowed such tomfoolery. I apologize to you and your wife."

Eddie was surprised. His face must have shown it, because Tony said quietly, "When I'm wrong, I say I'm wrong."

"Apology accepted," Eddie said, extending his hand.

Tony shook it. "My younger son says his brother couldn't sit up straight for two days after you smacked him."

"In my prime it would have been a week," Eddie said.

Tony laughed. "That I believe," he said.

In spite of his hatred for Italian gangsters, Eddie found it hard to not like this guy. *Maybe Red is right.*

"Never make an Irishman mad," Eddie said.

"And don't trust a Wop," Tony replied.

Eddie laughed uproariously and he and Tony had a drink.

The guests ate and drank and offered their condolences to Tony and his wife and children. People played bocci in the backyard and the women cleaned up and traded stories about babies and other things. People began to leave, little by little. Tony thanked each individually and wished them well. His sons discreetly moved all the big players into the basement gameroom where large tables were set up, and pitchers of water and wine sat on each table.

Finally Tony was able to go downstairs and do business.

Tony came to the head of the long table.

"Gentlemen, I want to thank you all for coming and offering your respects to my father-in-law. Now that my state-sponsored vacation is over, I can get back to business." Muted laughter was heard. "First, I have some local business to take care of, and then I want to propose something that affects all of us," Tony said. No one disagreed, so Tony spoke again. "Mr. Coyle, you had a problem that you wanted to discuss?"

Eddie deferred to Doc, who began to speak. Doc told of the situation involving Fred J. Walton.

Tony thought for a moment and then spoke. "I will buy Bayside Construction under the name of one of my other companies. Further, I will ask some prominent local people I know to contribute to his opponent's campaign. I do this because it's good for business and because I have a personal interest in Mr. Walton's professional demise."

"We need a favor, also," Doc said. "An associate of ours made a mistake a couple weeks ago. He's valuable to our business, so we don't want anything to happen to him. He'll make amends for his mistake and maybe able to do valuable favors for you in the future."

"You agree with this, Red?" Tony asked.

"Yes," Red said flatly.

"Done," Tony said.

"I bet that hurt to say," Doc whispered to Red.

"You'll never know," Red whispered back.

"Anything else?" Tony said.

"What dollar figure are we talking about for the construction company?" Doc asked.

Tony wrote a number on a slip of paper and had Mario take it to Doc. Doc showed it to Red and Eddie. "That's more than fair," he said.

"That's fuckin' great," Eddie whispered. Red nodded his agreement.

"Now for the next order of business," Tony said. "Mario," he said, addressing his son for everyone's benefit. "You will now be the so-called mayor of the North Beach enclave. You will supply all the soldiers for the family. But also, I have just bought you a construction company business, a large one. This business is assured, but I expect you to drive it to new heights. The soldiers will have legitimate employment and you will make plenty of money."

Tony continued. "You will serve an apprenticeship under the man who now runs it, to learn the business. But your primary duty is to supply and command soldiers of the family."

He turned to Rocco Lampone. "Rocco Lampone will be my new Consigliere."

Rocco was overcome with pride and surprise. He stood up. "Don Maretti, I thank you for your confidence in my abilities. I assure you and everyone else here that my loyalty will set a new standard. I accept this with pride and humility, Godfather." Everyone applauded.

Tony continued. "Sonny Lauria will take Rocco's place as my top Caporegime. He has all my confidence."

Sonny stood up and raised his glass. "Thank you, Don Maretti, and salud. At the risk of sounding arrogant, may

I say that you have made the right decision. I will never let the family down."

"You never have," Tony said. Everyone applauded.

"Tony, Jr., you will train to be my successor. You will no longer take part in the muscle end of the family that invites danger. Your children, my grandchildren, must not grow up in this world. We're rich, we don't have to risk our lives to earn a living."

Tony, Jr. was obviously ecstatic, though he didn't speak.

"Gentlemen, I didn't ask you here to hear my personal business, but it pertains to what I'm about to propose. My proposal is this. I retire from all my interests with the exception of gambling. I yield all my interests in the rest of the country to your families. This includes the union, transportation, alcohol, tobacco and drugs." Several people involuntarily gasped. "All my access to the law will be available, including my influence in New York. What I ask in return is that you let me handle your earnings. The Maretti family will serve only as financial advisors to the other families. We will serve as their political support and mediate quarrels. We will protect everyone's money.

It will be safely held and available. You will not have to worry about the government tracking down the money.

For this I ask only a ten percent commission."

It was a dream deal for the men at the meeting.

Tony was retreating when he could have gone forward to reestablish himself as King Kong. The men held their glasses up and toasted Tony's deal.

San Francisco 1940:

"Big" Jim Clawson was fifty-nine years old. He owned the most successful construction company on the West Coast. His third wife was thirty-seven and had two kids from a previous marriage, however, she was still stunningly beautiful and the daughter of a congressman.

Jim had flourished in construction with the Maretti family's infusion of money. He was one of those people who was much smarter than others thought he was, but not so ambitious as to get in trouble. For example, he employed Maretti family soldiers without question for years. He was making more money than he'd ever dreamed of, so why would he mess it up? He had contributed to political causes over the years, most of them philanthropic. He built schools and churches at a considerable discount.

After the events of 1934, Angelo Rossi's career was over. The puppets that big business tried to put in his place didn't fare well. He thought the time was right to run for mayor.

He had a huge Fourth of July barbecue party to announce his candidacy. It was held at his lavish home in Pacific Heights. A perfect opportunity to see where the real power in the city was. It looked like a princess was having a wedding. Huge tables were set up all over the backyard. The back of the patio had an open bar and a buffet. Every fine restaurant in San Francisco had been called upon to cater the food. Besides the usual American fare, guests had their choice of Italian, Mexican, Chinese and French cuisine.

A band was playing and part of the cement patio had been made into a dance floor. Jim greeted everyone personally.

Red arrived and surveyed the scene. Judges and politicians were there as well as lawyers and businessmen. He saw muscle everywhere. Maretti wasn't there, but his capos and his sons were. Other union leaders nodded at Red as he entered. He despised these events, people showing up to parties they didn't want to just to curry favor. That was how it was though -- if one wasn't there, then they have slighted someone or missed out on something. Red had promised to meet Eddie and to make sure the Steelworkers Union was represented. Tom was invited, but Red didn't see him.

He saw Eddie at the bar, so walked over and tapped Eddie on the shoulder.

"How are you, buddy?" Red said pleasantly.

"I hate these fuckin' things," Eddie replied.

"Me, too."

The bartender came over and Red held up two fingers. "Whiskey. And for my friend, too."

"Irish, American or Canadian?" the bartender asked.

"I've always liked Canadian whiskey, but I'm feeling adventurous, what do you suggest?" Red replied.

"Jack Daniels from Tennessee," the bartender said.

"I'll have it." Red tried the drink and liked it. It had more bite than the Canadian blends he usually drank, but it was still smooth and eminently drinkable. He handed the bartender a twenty. "Keep 'em comin'. For my friend, too."

"Yes, sir," the bartender replied, happy.

He'd worked dozens of such affairs. The rich fucks who attended usually didn't tip shit at an open bar, but this guy had class. He made a mental note to take care of them.

Eddie downed his whiskey and the second one the bartender had brought him quickly.

"That's nice whiskey. Look at those gumbas," Eddie said, pointing to some Maretti family soldiers at the buffet. "Give 'em a free meal and they come out in force." One waved at Red and Eddie. Eddie waved back and yelled, "Hi!" He added quietly, "You greaseball bastard. Tony's not here, so they have to eat his share?"

"What the hell do you care, you're not paying for it," Red put in.

"It's the principle."

Red saw Eddie was working himself into being pissed off. Doc had long ago warned Red. "Eddie will give you the shirt off his back," he'd said. "He's the best friend you could ever have. But when he gets in a certain mood, look out. Don't let that lion out of the cage unless you're sure you can get it back in."

"What's eatin' you?" Red asked.

"You see that blonde girl in the blue dress?" Eddie said, pointing at the dance floor.

Red had certainly seen her. Tall and slender, she resembled Jean Harlow. He'd looked at her when he came in and she looked back. She didn't play cute and quickly look away, nor did she flirt brazenly. She was just acknowledging that they'd looked at each other. He'd made a mental note to investigate.

"That's my daughter," Eddie said.

Red almost spit out his drink. He didn't know Eddie's children, except for Rafe, who ran the local in Oakland and did a good job. When he saw Eddie socially it was usually just the guys, or Eddie and his wife along with whatever woman he was dating at the time. He knew Eddie had an adult daughter, but they'd never met. Before Red could think or banish the thoughts he'd had about her in that fleeting moment from his mind, Eddie spoke.

"Look who she's dancing with," he grumbled.

"Mario Maretti," Red said flatly. Red didn't see a problem. They were both attractive and about the same age.

"He's got his hands on her ass!" Eddie grumbled.

"I believe those are her hips," Red replied. "They're just dancing, having fun. What's wrong with that?" Red asked honestly.

"Do me a favor. Go cut in," Eddie said. "I don't want a Wop-gumba son-in-law."

"C'mon, Eddie, just because they danced at a party doesn't mean anything. I know Mario's reputation; he wants to get laid. If you raised your daughter the way I think you did, there's no problem."

"Are you gonna help me out or not?" Eddie snarled.

Red saw the lion was getting out of the cage. He never thought he'd see the day when he felt forced to hit on a pretty girl.

Red walked over to the dance floor as the song was ending. He shook hands with Mario. "How's your dad?" he asked.

"On vacation in the old country," Mario replied. "Thanks for asking."

"I decided I couldn't let you hog this pretty lady for the entire party. May I have the next dance?" Red said.

Before the girl could respond, Mario stepped back and said, "By all means. Good to see you, Red. I'm gonna get a drink."

Mario headed to the bar. He wanted to get drunk and get laid, but maybe not in that order. He had only met the girl ten minutes before, and though she seemed promising, he wasn't going to make a beef with a player like Red over a dance with a pretty girl at a party. There were many more promising prospects for him to explore.

"You're a bit older than the suitor you ran off," the girl said.

"Age and treachery will overcome youth and exuberance every time," Red quipped.

The girl laughed. "I'm Ellen," she said.

"I'm Martin, but people call me 'Red,'" he replied.

Ellen Coyle was twenty-three years old. Although she still lived with her parents, she wasn't the typical Irish spinster aunt type. When she went out, heads turned and beer bottles clicked on teeth. She recalled her conversation with her father on the way to the party. Her mother didn't want to go, but Ellen pleaded and griped until Eddie relented. It was going to be the party of the year and she didn't want to miss it.

"I want you to be careful at this party," Eddie said, cautioning her.

"I'm a big girl, Dad, I can take care of myself," she replied.

"You're a kid."

Ellen laughed. "Dad, Mom had three kids and was helping you and Doc run a business when she was my age. You need to stop treating me like I'm eleven."

"Those guinea hoods are gonna try to get in your pants," Eddie said.

Ellen laughed again. "I've got a news flash for you, dad, it doesn't matter if they're Irish, Italian, Jewishor whatever. All guys want to get in your pants.

It's not a race thing, it's a guy thing. Don't worry, I won't do anything stupid like elope with a guy I meet tonight."

Eddie looked at her, surprised she'd thrown his own life back in his face. He opened his mouth to read her the riot act and realized she was right, he had no room to talk. He sulked the rest of the way to the party.

"Let's get some food and sit down," Red said as the song ended.

Ellen followed him to the buffet. Although he was at least ten years older than her, he was very handsome and carried himself with supreme confidence. Powerful men at the party greeted him politely, politicians, cops and even as her dad said, "Guinea hoods." The Mafioso she'd been dancing with backed way off when he came over and asked to cut in. He knew how to handle it and wasn't arrogant or self-absorbed. He was really down-to-earth for such a mover and shaker.

"Your father never told me he had Jean Harlow for a daughter," Red said.

"How do you know my father?" Ellen asked.

"Martin 'Red' Sullivan, president of Local 372 of the Steelworkers Union," he replied.

"You're the 'Red' my dad talks about. I've heard of you."

"Eddie tends to exaggerate if he likes someone," Red replied.

"No, he doesn't," Ellen said with a fiery look in her eyes.

They talked and danced for a lot of the party. Ellen indulged herself in a third and fourth glass of wine, and became a little tipsy. On a slow dance, when she knew her father was in the bathroom, she kissed Red passionately.

She was her father's daughter. Her mother had raised her to act like a lady, and she did. However, she could go to a baseball game, eat hot dogs and drink beer, and yell with the men. She could go to a boxing match, sit ringside and not be bothered by the blood.

She decided she was going to marry Red Sullivan. She was a good judge of character, and she had never seen such force in one man, not even her father. She suddenly realized that was the problem with all the guys she'd dated. None of them could measure up to her father. Red stacked up.

She thought she played it exactly right. She knew he'd be hesitant because of his business relationship with her father. She wanted him to know she was interested, but she didn't want to come off as a forward hussy without manners or upbringing. She had drank enough that he could file it under youthful indiscretion if he wasn't interested, or he could take it as the go-ahead that it was if he liked her.

As such affairs go, the party reached a point where the band was rocking, people were dancing, the booze was flowing, and everyone was having a wild time. When it started to taper off, people began to leave. Her father didn't want to stay until only the hardcore partiers were left.

Before she left, Red discreetly asked to see her again and she readily agreed. She knew if she played demure and said "no" that he'd take it as "no and never ask again." The normal rules of teenage and early 20's dating didn't apply with a man of his caliber. She had to say and do what she meant, no games. That was just her game.

"Did you and Red have a good time?" Eddie asked her.

"Lovely," she replied. "He's a charming man."

"He's not always charming," Eddie said.

"Neither are you, Dad, according to Mom."

Eddie laughed. "You should marry Red," he said jokingly.

"I might," Ellen said.

"I could think of worse things," Eddie said.

Ellen smiled all the way home.

Doc O'Hearn died in August at the age of seventy-six. He had always said he wanted to go one of two ways -- in a blaze of glory or in his sleep. He went in his sleep.

Eddie was devastated, but took it upon himself to arrange the funeral. Eddie knew Doc had wanted a bash, not a somber affair. Except for Clawson's party, Doc's funeral was the event of the year. Union people and wiseguys showed up in force. Sportswriters and boxing promoters came from all over the country. Members of the New York, Nevada and Illinois boxing commissions came to pay their respects. All the promoters and sportswriters got up and spoke about their dealings with Doc, some of which had the crowd in stitches.

Eddie was the final speaker. "Today I have to say goodbye to the best friend I ever had. To a man who was like a father to me. I was only nineteen years old when I met Doc. He was the world. He was Wyatt Earp and Ernest Hemingway and P. T. Barnum all rolled into one." The crowd laughed in acknowledgement. "He taught me that anything's possible if you put your mind to it. He took an orphan from a mining town and damn near made him heavyweight champ. He helped that kid build an empire around boxing and he helped the most powerful labor union in the West get started. He taught me everything I know, and not all of it can be told in mixed company. I know Doc wouldn't want me to give a long-winded speech and keep everyone from the food and booze, so I'll just say this: I'm sure he's negotiating with God and Saint Peter right now, and they're getting the short end of the stick." The crowd laughed. "Let's go drink to Doc and not lament that he died, but celebrate how he lived."

The crowd roared with applause. Eddie received a standing ovation.

As Eddie left the funeral home, Doc's fourth wife, a woman named Sheila, stopped him. Sheila was fifty-three, but still attractive. Ten years before, she'd probably been a stunning beauty. She was slightly overweight now, but she had big tits, big hair and a big attitude, which was what mattered to Doc. Doc had achieved his goal of never having to screw an old unattractive woman. Eddie stopped to talk to her.

"What am I gonna do, Eddie?" she sobbed. "Doc was all I had."

"Don't worry," Eddie replied. "Doc had in his will that you got half his end. The other half went to my children, if he didn't have any. You'll be well taken care of, Sheila."

"Very well. Eddie, I didn't mean it that way, I just...."

"I know," Eddie said, cutting her off. "You and Doc each knew who the other was when you got married. Neither of you had any illusions. He was happier these last ten years than I've ever seen him, honest. You earned it."

"He was a son-of-a-bitch, but I did love him," Sheila said.

"So did I," Eddie replied. "Doc didn't apologize for his life. You don't have to apologize for yours. The lawyer will contact you next week."

"I'd still like to see you and your family sometimes," Sheila said.

"Call or drop by anytime," Eddie said.

Sheila hugged him and kissed him on the cheek. "He told me he never had kids because if he had a son, he didn't want the boy to walk in your shadow. You cast a big shadow, Eddie. Doc loved you more than anyone."

Eddie hugged her again because he didn't want her to see him cry. He composed himself and released her. "Thank you," he said.

"Thank you, Eddie, for being his friend, and mine," Sheila replied and then walked away.

The reception was held at Murphy's Bar, Doc's favorite watering hole. They had tables set up outside to accommodate the many guests. Additional grills had been set up to make steaks, hamburgers, chicken, fish -- anything guests wanted. The bar was open, and a second makeshift bar had been set up outside to sate the mourners' thirst. Eddie took up Doc's usual seat at the end of the bar to greet people.

Kenny O'Donnel, an old sportswriter who had over the years been both a friend and enemy of Doc's, depending on circumstance, came over. Kenny was one of the few who could say to Doc or Eddie's face that Eddie would never have beaten Jack Johnson.

"'Twas a fine funeral, Eddie," Kenny said in his Irish brogue. "Himself would be proud."

"I wish he could have been here," Eddie replied. "Doc hated to miss a party."

"He's here," Kenny said. "I can feel him. But I'm not saying you could have took Johnson to appease a ghost."

"He wouldn't want you to," Eddie said, laughing.

By osmosis, Kenny was moved away as other mourners came in and offered their respects and condolences. Tom Franklin came in and shook hands with Eddie.

"I'm sorry for your loss," he said.

"Thank you," Eddie replied.

"I liked Doc," Tom said. "You always knew where you stood. The Dockworkers Union is setting up a memorial fund that benefits schools in Doc's name. I know you two were close. I'm sorry, Eddie. If there's anything I can do."

"Thanks, Tom," Eddie replied. "I appreciate it."

"Give Red and Blackie my condolences, I know they liked Doc too," Tom said.

"I will. Have a drink or some food," Eddie said.

"I will," Tom said and walked away.

Tony Maretti, Rocco Lampone, and Sonny Lauria came in, as did Tony, Jr. and Mario. Tony did all the talking.

"I liked what you said at the church," he said.

Eddie hadn't seen them, but the place was so full it was understandable. "I know how hard it is to lose a trusted consigliere, a friend and a man you looked up to like a father. I'm sorry for your loss," Tony said, opening his arms.

Every wiseguy in the room was watching. Eddie was quick on the uptake as Red had told him about mob etiquette. Eddie hugged him and they shook hands.

"If you need anything during this time of trouble, just ask," Tony told him.

Eddie could feel the eyes on him. He believed Maretti was genuinely sorry that Doc was gone, but somehow felt a message was being sent as well. Eddie decided he'd go along.

"Don Maretti, my most valued friend," Eddie said.

"You understand everything. I know I can always depend on you."

"And I know I can depend on you, and my godson. I'll leave you now, because I know you have many mourners to greet."

They hugged again and Eddie shook hands with Rocco, Sonny, Tony, Jr. and Mario. They left, and parts of the crowd whispered and scrambled.

Blackie came over. "That was nice," he said.

"That was a show of force for somebody," Eddie replied.

"C'mon, maybe he was being sincere," Blackie said skeptically.

"If it was just him and his boys, maybe. But Rocco and Sonny? They didn't have to show, unless they were told to. Go get Red," Eddie finished.

Red returned with Blackie and listened to the story.

"You're absolutely right," Red said. "You played it perfect. You're gettin' good in your old age."

"But why?" Eddie asked.

"Think," Red replied. "One of the principals that started two of the most powerful unions on the West Coast dies, that leaves a power vacuum. Other people, who have pieces of other unions, might think they could move in or buy Doc's successor. If not, they may try to use force. Street warfare is ugly and brings down unnecessary police action or maybe even feds, it it's bad enough. Tony was saying subtly to all the wiseguys here, 'Fuck not with me or the status quo in my territory. If you do, you're making a big mistake. Everyone here is in agreement. All you'll do here is lose money and men.' He did us a favor, but that was definitely self-serving, although he probably meant it when he said he was sorry about your loss. Now nobody'll fuck with us for a while, or ask if we need help in reorganizing."

Red and Blackie ordered a drink as a promoter from New York came over and offered his condolences to Eddie. He talked about a guy named Mike McBride who was a real ass-kicker that fought in New York a few years ago. He could have been a real contender if he'd had a manager like Eddie or Doc, but just disappeared. Red spit out his drink and got it up his nose.

"You ever see this McBride fight?" Blackie asked.

Red waved him off and went to the bathroom, laughing and coughing.

Eddie was still at the bar at Doc's favorite seat.

He wondered who would start singing *Danny Boy* and who would throw the first punch. He'd never been to a funeral for a great Irishman where there wasn't a fight or someone singing.

Red and Ellen were eating food and laughing together. Red seemed so relaxed around her, and she seemed so animated around him. Mary had been concerned, but Eddie told her, "He's not any older than her than I am older than you. You know how Ellen is. Maybe an older guy will have a little more patience, cut her some slack."

"And if he doesn't?" Mary asked.

"Look at it this way, he respects me. Not many girls are lucky enough to have an ex-heavyweight contender for a father." Mary laughed.

After Doc's funeral, Eddie semi-retired. He was depressed for a while after Doc's death. He had no interest in running the unions and gave Tom total control of the Dockworkers Union, and Red total control of the Steelworkers

Union, although he still drew a salary from both, which was fine with Red and Tom. They paid him as an "independent consultant."

He became motivated again fairly quickly. He continued to train boxers and even bought an interest in and managed a pro baseball team called the "Mission A's." He always loved boxing and baseball.

One of the happiest days of his life was when he took batting practice with the Yankees. The manager was a boxing fan, and when he found out Eddie had played baseball before becoming a boxer, he arranged it in exchange for Eddie sparring three rounds with him. The baseball manager told the story for years after.

"I was always a tough guy, and I couldn't resist laying my best shot on a contender. I knew he was pissed. His eyes got wide and he came forward. Eddie countered with a hook to the body. It hit me on the elbow. It drove my elbow into my ribs so hard that it cracked two of them. If I hadn't got my arm back, I'd probably be dead. The ribs could have splintered and punctured my lungs or heart. I knew then that I wasn't a fighter. I think he did better at batting practice."

Eddie only got one hit, but it was a doozy that went to deep center and almost went over the wall. Afterwards he decided he wanted to manage a team someday, and now he was. He recruited ballplayers like he recruited boxers -- sluggers over dancers.

San Francisco, 1942:

Red was having a drink in Murphy's, stressed about a lot of things. Maybe if he got drunk and had a good dinner he could feel better. He was sick of the fucking strike and the shit that went with it. He was sick of the war and the shit that went with it, too. The war was screwing up business. His personal life wasn't doing much better.

Titus Welliver III was seventy-two years old. He owned Welliver Aviation, which had produced airplanes since before the First World War. He'd inherited the company from his father, who had built it. He didn't run it into the ground, but he didn't really improve it either. Titus liked being a big shot. He always tried to move in high-society circles and have influence with the right people. But, like all "wanna-be's," he just missed. When America entered the war, he knew he'd hit the mother lode. He and his salesmen aggressively pursued government contracts and got one to build fighter planes.

The Steelworkers Union had organized his plants and secured a four-year contract in 1940. Now, in 1942 a lot of men were off fighting the war and women filled a lot of the factories jobs to help the war effort. The government even had a poster of "Rosie the Riveter," an attractive woman in coveralls flexing her bicep. It was meant to motivate and encourage women to help the war effort. Titus thought he could save money by paying the women half a man's wage.

The union complained that a contract was a contract. The agreement alluded to "labor" and "management." Nowhere did the contract state limitations on salaries according to the gender of the workers. Titus stonewalled, so the union convinced the women to go on strike and filed suit

243

in District Court. The judge in District Court agreed with the union that "labor" and "management" didn't specify gender. The women should be paid the same wages as a man made before the war started. The judge further ruled that Welliver Aviation could renegotiate in 1944 when the current contract expired, but until then had to abide by the agreement.

Titus was pissed. His lawyer tried to reason with him. "Titus, it'll take years to get a Supreme Court appeal to overturn the District Court."

"How can that be?" Titus asked.

The lawyer rolled his eyes and sighed. "First, you have to file an appeal in District Court. That will be denied."

"You're sure of this?" Welliver said.

"I'm sure," his lawyer replied. "Unless it's a total miscarriage of justice, which it wasn't, no District Court judge is gonna overturn another. That means you have to appeal to the State Supreme Court. Same thing, unless it's obvious you were railroaded, the appeal will be denied. Then you have to appeal to the Circuit Court, which handles all the cases on the West Coast. They're backed up. That will take years. By then the war will be over and you'll be out of business."

"What good are you lawyers anyway?" Titus grumbled.

"Look," the lawyer said, "if the Supreme Court heard your case tomorrow, you'd lose. A contract is a contract. The union hasn't broken that contract. You have. You're trying to find a loophole to pay the workers less. They've got you by the balls. The best thing you can do is ride it out and then try to really break their balls in 1944."

"We'll see about that," Titus said and left his lawyer's office.

Titus decided to take other action. They were women.

He would hire muscle to intimidate them. The union reps could say what they wanted, but they couldn't protect the workers, really. He went to see Tony Maretti to hire muscle. He was rebuked there as well.

"Mr. Welliver," Tony started. "We've known each other many years, or at least known of each other. You had a good business and your interests didn't conflict with mine, so we never had a problem, until now. You come to me and you ask me to intimidate and hurt a bunch of women filling in while the men are at war because you don't want to honor a contract that you signed a couple years ago with my godson. I must say 'no' to you, and I'll give you my reasons.

"Believe it or not, my whole life I've been the underdog. I have a weakness for supporting the underdog. You're trying to step on the underdog. But personal feelings aside, let's talk business. I see your reasoning of trying to pay the women less. If you could get away with it, great, but you can't. Further, you and I belong to the same golf club, yet never once have you asked me to join a foursome or play a round of golf with you. I understand. You didn't need my friendship and you were afraid to be in my debt. Fine, but now you come to me and ask me to do mayhem against innocent people, represented by a man I trust. That I cannot do."

Tony called all the other Dons on the West Coast and asked them to refuse Welliver as well. Everyone agreed except for Pistone in Los Angeles. Since Tony had retreated and become a "money man" some people underestimated him.

He'd kept the North Beach Enclave and kept recruiting soldiers to that reason. He was a businessman, not a martyr. Tony called Red Sullivan.

"I need a favor," Tony said when Red answered the phone.

"Okay, what kind of favor?" Red replied. "Give a nice kid a union job kind of favor or dump a body kind of favor?"

Tony laughed. "Neither. Titus Welliver came to me asking for muscle to break your strike. I refused."

"Thank you," Red said.

"Don't thank me yet until you hear the whole story," Tony said. "I asked every Don I knew to not help him. They all agreed except one. Pistone's still pissed about the shit that went down when I was in jail and Fresca tried to take over. He wants what Fresca promised him. He thinks we're not strong."

"What can I do?" Red asked.

"He's gonna send strikebreakers. I'd appreciate it if they got their heads busted."

"Done," Red replied without hesitation, knowing it would be a natural occurrence if the fools clashed with Blackie and his men.

"I'd appreciate it more if the cops did it," Tony replied.

"I can do that," Red said.

"I knew you could. I owe you one," Tony said and hung up.

Red called Tom Conway and gave him the heads-up. Blackie and his men would all wear "Mission A" baseball caps. Anyone else got their ass kicked. Blackie and his people wore the caps for three days. On the fourth day a bunch of goons arrived at the gate of Welliver Aviation where the strikers were. Blackie met one guy in the middle of the driveway.

"I don't want to kill you and you don't want to be dead," the goon said.

"I was gonna say the same thing," Blackie replied.

Blackie hit the thug in the nose with his left fist, which was enhanced by brass knuckles. The guy's face exploded and he went down. Blackie retreated behind the picket line and out of nowhere at least forty cops started kicking ass. Tom Conway received a commendation for being proactive and stopping crime before it happened.

It was beautiful for everyone, except Pistone who couldn't gripe to Tony or come after him in any way. Tony had given every Don on the West Coast fair warning. He'd said, "Don't get involved." Pistone hadn't listened. Further, it was cops who beat the holy hell out of and killed a few of Pistone's soldiers, not Maretti people or union people. If Pistone made a move, all the families on the West Coast would line up against him to avoid a war. Tony had kept his bargain, he was managing the money and he gave them the heads-up on a potential problem. Pistone was fucked,for the time being at least.

Timing is everything, and the little episode came just when Lieutenant Conway was taking the Captain's exam. Tom was promoted to Captain which delighted both the Steelworkers Union and the Maretti family.

"We got the fuckers now!" Tom had said to Red over a celebratory drink.

"Don't sell the badge so much that you can't buy it back," Red said.

"I'm ahead of you," Tom replied. "My first partner, McCluskey told me that about eighteen years ago. I never forgot it. But thanks for the reminder."

"Where's your brother?" Red asked.

"My sainted brother?" Tom replied.

"C'mon," Red replied, "he's a priest. Give him a break. He can't go out and get drunk or get laid or get in a fight like we can to blow off steam."

"That's his choice," Tom said. "I tried to help him."

"You tried to make him do what you would do. You're different people, you always have been," Red replied. "I knew that in second grade. I was getting my ass kicked. You guys both felt bad. He ran to get the teacher and you waded in like Joe Louis. Neither of you was wrong. You both did what you thought was right. Certainly I liked your approach better, but as far as I know, nobody ever died from a second grade schoolyard fight. The teacher stopped it and we got suspended. I never held that against Tim."

"I did," Tom replied.

"Speak of the devil," Red said.

"And the devil appears," Tim Conway replied jokingly.

Tim entered the bar and he shook hands with his brother.

"What are you doing here?" Tom asked.

"I came to congratulate you on your promotion," Tim replied.

Red stepped on Tom's foot and Tom replied, "Thank you. You didn't have to come. I know you're busy."

"Not too busy to see family and old friends," Tim said. "Let's do some shots in my brother's honor."

"You sure?" Red asked.

Tim laughed. "I have to stay celibate, not sober," he joked.

"All right," Tom said, loosening up. He patted his brother on the back. "Thanks for coming. That's nice."

After several shots, Tom started talking about Tim's prowess as an arm-wrestler. Tim took on all comers in the bar and beat most.

As Tim was leaving, he said loudly, "Gentlemen, I hope tonight's events can remain between us."

A parishioner of Tim's stood up and said, "Don't worry, Father, no one wants to admit that they got thrashed by a priest." The bar roared with laughter.

"He's really all right, underneath the bullshit," Tom said drunkenly.

"He's all right, period," Red replied. "The bullshit is in your mind. He doesn't make any more compromises than we do. Everyone puts priests on this higher level. You know him as a man, as your pain-in-the-ass brother. You rebuke him because he's not a textbook priest. You're definitely not a textbook cop, and he doesn't rebuke you."

"Yes, he does," Tom said.

Red laughed. "That's brother-to-brother shit. Playing devil's advocate, one-upmanship. If you two bull-headed bastards weren't related, you'd be best friends."

"Maybe," Tom replied, "but you still hold that title."

"We all have our crosses to bear," Red retorted.

"Fuck you," Tom said, laughing.

"Fuck you, too," Red replied.

They both walked away laughing.

Titus Welliver paid dearly for his mistake. The government threatened to pull the contract unless the strike ended and he caught up with demand. Besides having to pay back wages, he had to pay overtime to make the quotas to not lose the contract.

Red and Ellen Coyle had really hit it off. It wasn't on fire like his relationship with Kate, but he found himself uninterested in other women since he'd met her. She worked at a jewelry store on 24th Street and sometimes Red picked her up from work. They'd drive out to the beach and watch the sun set, or go to Dolores Park and eat tamales he'd bought on 24th Street. They went to expensive restaurants. Red even had a private room at one. Unbeknownst to Ellen, Red had okayed a loan from the union's pension fund to finance it. Paul Masson, the owner, always offered Red and Ellen the finest wines and most elegant desserts. Having been raised in an environment where everyone called her father "Champ" and wanted to be nice to him, Ellen didn't think it was unusual. When he proposed in Masson's, she agreed. However, it was the week after Thanksgiving 1941.

On December 7th the Japanese attacked Pearl Harbor and America entered the war.

Red and her father were concerned about how the war might affect business. The ports of the world would now be valuable. If the Japanese attacked San Francisco, what would happen? If Tom Franklin was killed, could Red and Blackie run the Dockworkers Union as well as the Steelworkers

Union? Would out-of-town mobsters try to step in? What would Maretti do? Would Eddie have to come out of retirement?

They postponed their wedding, however, nothing that bad came to pass. Except for women filling jobs while men were at war and a few shortages of gasoline and other things, life in the States didn't change that much.

Ellen's mother was being an unconscionable ball-breaker over the wedding. She wanted a big affair in her family's church. Red and Ellen wanted a small ceremony in Tom Conway's church because he was Red's childhood friend.

Never the twain shall meet. Finally, Red got so pissed that he told Ellen he didn't want to get married. She cursed her mother for ruining her life.

"I only wanted her to do it right," Mary said to Eddie, in a martyred tone.

Eddie exploded. "As opposed to how wrong we did it?

I was an orphan who became a prizefighter, who married the daughter of a madam! I'm sorry you didn't have a princess' wedding! You didn't complain that night, as I recall!

We've done right by each other and our kids. It ain't the ceremony, it's the relationship between the people. You ever gonna know that?" he growled.

"I know that, you son-of-a-bithch!" Mary yelled.

"You told me that you'd had women all over the world. I was sixteen and a virgin, and I'd never let a man even touch me before I met you. You come along, handsome, charming, man of the world. I'm working as a maid in a whorehouse in a shit town. A whorehouse my mother owned. What future did I have? You offered me a future. So I gave it up. All or nothing."

"Is that all I was and am, a meal ticket?" Eddie asked. "Nice of you to tell me now."

"You god damned son-of-a-bitch!" Mary yelled and began hitting him.

He didn't hit her back, but tried to keep her from hurting him. He finally got hold of her and restrained her.

"That's not how it is and you know it," Mary said, crying. "You're the only man that's ever touched me in any way. I love you and our children and I don't apologize for my life. That's one thing I learned from Doc. He told me one time, 'Mary, you can't please all the people all the time, you can't please all the people some of the time. You can't even please some of the people all of

249

the time. You can only please some of the people some of the time, and fuck all the rest. You chose who you please.'"

Eddie was a little surprised at Mary using the word "fuck," even when quoting Doc, who used it freely. *She must be really upset.*

"I'm not complaining that you and I didn't do it up right. We didn't have the chance. I wanted her to have the chance."

"For her or for you?" Eddie asked.

Mary started crying again. "Will you talk to her?" she asked.

"I'll do better than that," Eddie said. "I'll talk to him."

Eddie went over to Red's house. Red invited him and made him a drink, Jack Daniels on the rocks. Eddie had like the drink since Clawson's party and so had Red.

"Do you want to marry my daughter or not?" Eddie said. Before Red could respond, he added, "My other daughter is planning a wedding, too. And John's wife is pregnant again. At any given time, I have at least three crying women in my house. I can't take it. Do me a favor, marry my daughter or fuckin' shoot me. At this point I don't care which."

"I'll marry your daughter," Red said.

"Thank you. I didn't really want to be shot."

"You sure?" Red asked.

He and Eddie laughed themselves sick.

Reno, Nevada 1942:

Red was awake in his room at the Mapes Hotel-Casino. Ellen Coyle was naked, asleep in his arms. After Eddie's visit, he'd told her, "Look, I love you and I want to marry you. I'll do it any way your mother wants."

"No, you won't," she replied. "I know you, personally and by reputation. You've never given in once in your whole life. What did my father say to you?" she asked accusingly. Red looked surprised. "I knew it!" Ellen said. "I thought it, but I wasn't sure! Now I am. Damn her. She runs everything. She tells my sister who to date, what to wear, what to eat. She tries to tell me what to do, but

I'm not the good little girl my sister is."

"How do you know Eddie and I talked?" Red asked.

"Simple. That would be my mother's next move. My father is Hercules, Zeus and Superman all rolled into one. No one ever went up against Eddie Coyle and didn't regret it. She told my brother that Tommy Burns wouldn't return his and Doc's calls after he won the title. She thought he could intimidate you into doing the right thing. Did he?"

"I'm gonna say this now, and then we're never gonna talk about it again," Red said. "I respect your father.

I like him. He probably saved my life in 1930, but no man tells me to do what I don't want to do. I crossed the Maretti family and lived to tell about it. I wouldn't ever want to go up against your father, but if I had to,

I wouldn't plan on losing. I'm asking you to get married because I want to marry you. Period. There's no ulterior motives. I'm not that clever. You give your mother too much credit. Your dad is everything you say he is. A man like

251

that is not a lackey of women. He may love his wife and children and may spoil them, but when it comes down to brass tacks, he's still the boss."

"You want to get married?" Ellen said.

"Yes," Red replied.

"Then let's go to Reno," Ellen said.

"When?" Red asked.

"Tonight, right now. You can be 'honeymooning' with me by midnight."

"Okay," Red replied. "Let's go. But what if we can't get a marriage license?" he asked.

She gave him a burning kiss. "Then we'll get married after the honeymoon."

"Yes, we will," Red replied and kissed her again. "I'll get the car."

Ellen Coyle walked into the gym with purpose in her stride. It didn't bother her in the least to be in the presence of thirty or so sweaty, dangerous men. She'd grown up in the environment. Much to her mother's dismay, she didn't want to have fake tea parties and play with dolls, she wanted to hang with her dad. She'd exerted herself twice in the gym with different groups of boxers, but the legend stood.

When she was about seven, and Eddie was only a few years removed from being a contender, she ran in from school and interrupted Doc while he was working with a middleweight contender. Not knowing who she was, the boxer told her to shut up.

"No, you shut up, you big jerk!" Ellen sneered.

"And if I don't?" the boxer pressed.

"I'll have my dad kick your butt," Ellen said calmly.

"And who's your dad?" the boxer asked disdainfully.

"I am," Eddie said coldly, having heard the whole conversation, although Doc and Ellen didn't know he was in earshot. "You want to go a few rounds?" Eddie said icily.

"No, sir, Mr. Coyle," the boxer said, aghast at his predicament.

Eddie was a legend in his own time, at least among boxers and boxing writers. He was either getting fired or his ass kicked, or both. He tried to do damage control.

"I didn't know she was your daughter."

"My daughter or not, you get off on intimidating a child?"

"What's intimidate, Daddy?" Ellen asked.

"Scare," Eddie said, still staring down the young boxer, who was trying not to show fear. One could have heard a pin drop in the gym.

"He didn't scare me, Daddy. I told him you'd pound him if I wanted you to."

"I'd say that about covers it," Doc said.

The gym roared with laughter. Doc made a motion with his hand, and Eddie walked away after shooting the young boxer a murderous look.

Afterwards, she was always addressed as "Miss Coyle" by the boxers and shown the utmost respect for a few years, until a new crop came in.

When she was about seventeen, she came to see Eddie when a boxer stepped in front of her. "Where are you goin', pretty lady?" the fool said.

"Wherever I want," Ellen replied. "Get out of my way or you'll be sorry."

"Really," the guy said.

"I'm not gonna tell you again," Ellen said.

"And what are you gonna do if I don't move?" the fool said.

Ellen kicked him in the balls so hard it almost lifted him off the floor. He grabbed his genitals and howled in pain, then Ellen grabbed a stool from ringside and began to hit him with it. The boxer fell down and Ellen kicked him a few times.

"Told ya," was all she said and then walked back to Eddie's office.

Since then boxers addressed her as "Miss Coyle" and the fear in their voice was not only from Eddie's reputation, but hers as well. They got the message loud and clear -- fuck not with this bitch.

Ellen stormed into Eddie's office. Eddie was talking to Leroy "The Hammer" Washington, a welterweight contender.

"Could you give us a minute, Leroy?" Ellen said.

"Yes, ma'am, Miss Coyle," Leroy said, uneasy.

He didn't want to disrespect Ellen in front of her father, but also didn't want to disrespect Eddie by implying his daughter could interrupt a business meeting without consequences. Leroy was smart. He managed to save face in front of the other boxers.

"I still need to talk to you, Mr. Coyle, when you're done speaking to your daughter. It's really important, but

I know family comes first. Nice to see you, Miss Coyle," Leroy finished.

"I hope to see you *hammer* Jimmy Greene this month," Ellen said, realizing how this looked.

Leroy regained some of his swagger. "You better get there early or you might miss it," he said.

"Isn't that always the case?" Ellen said. "I'll be done in a few minutes."

"You have a nice day, Miss Coyle," Leroy said, strutting away like he was "cock of the walk."

The other boxers shook their heads. They weren't even going to go there. Leroy was wasting his time and energy.

Ellen closed the door to Eddie's office. "Where were you last night?" Eddie said. "I know you're over twenty-one, but it wouldn't hurt you to call."

"I got married," Ellen said proudly. Finally her parents couldn't tell her what to do.

"Oh, shit," was all Eddie said.

"I know you're a tough guy, Daddy, but thanks for that show of emotion," Ellen said sarcastically.

"Your mother's gonna have a fit," Eddie said.

"She's had fits before," Ellen replied.

"How are you gonna tell her?" Eddie asked.

"I'm not. You are," Ellen said. "Red and I are going to New York for a few days, see the Statue of Liberty, the Empire State Building, Ellis Island, maybe catch a game at Yankee Stadium. Look at it this way, Dad, now you only have to deal with Margaret's wedding. I did you a favor."

"No, you didn't," Eddie replied.

Ellen laughed. "You crack me up, Dad. You thumb your nose at the Mob and get away with it. Jack Dempsey says he doesn't want to spar you in an exhibition, because he's making a movie and doesn't want to look beat up.

This same man can't tell a hundred and ten-pound woman that his daughter got married."

"You tell her," Eddie said.

"I'm a married woman. I don't care what my mother thinks," Ellen said flippantly.

"I understand what you're saying," Eddie replied.

"I'll handle your mother."

"Thanks, Daddy," Ellen said and kissed him on the cheek.

San Francisco, 1943:

Red waited anxiously outside the delivery room. It was Thursday afternoon. He had a pocketful of dimes, and had called Blackie about five times. The last time, Blackie got on him.

"If you got struck by lightning or died in a car wreck, I'd have to run the union, at least on an interim basis, until the rank and file decided to hold an election to find your successor, which I'd probably win. I'd win because everyone knows you trust me, Eddie'd back me, Franklin would back me because he knows I know his history and he wouldn't want to fuck with some green pea who didn't live in the real world. Maretti would back me because of our friendship and my knowledge of how to do things. He wouldn't want any big changes. I'd have you job and god damnit, I'd do it pretty good. Maybe not as good as you, but the whole operation wouldn't fall to shit. That's worst-case scenario. That won't happen if you take a couple days off to be with your wife and new baby. You call me again and I'm gonna kick your ass."

Red laughed. "You'll try," he said.

"I will," Blackie replied.

"I know you will and I know you can run things. You've made your point," Red said. "You won't hear from me until Tuesday."

"I better not. Congratulations."

"Thank you, and fuck you," Red said. Blackie laughed.

"Mr. Sullivan?" the nurse said as Red hung up the phone.

"Yes?"

"It's a girl. The baby and the mother are doing just fine. You can go in in a few minutes. Congratulations."

"Thank you," Red replied. "What does she look like?"

"Like her mother," the nurse said. "But she has your eyes. I've never seen eyes that blue. That's how I knew to ask you."

Red looked around and saw other men were in the waiting room. "Thank you, that's nice of you to say," he replied.

"Good luck with that beautiful little girl, Mr. Sullivan."

"Thank you," Red said and the nurse walked away.

Another nurse came over. "Mr. Sullivan? You can go in now."

Red walked in and saw Ellen holding a blanket. He got closer and leaned over both of them.

"Isn't she beautiful?" Ellen said.

"She is, just like her mother," Red said, kissing Ellen on the forehead.

He saw wisps of blonde hair and the baby opened her eyes. The nurse was right, he'd never seen such blue. He stuck his finger out and the baby grasped it.

"She's got a grip already," Red said. "Hello, Katy," he cooed softly.

"What did you call her?" Ellen said.

"Her name is Kate," Red said, almost absentmindedly, like he was in a trance.

"I want to name her Mary Ellen, after my mother and me," Ellen said.

"Her name is Kate," Red said again, looking at the baby, not Ellen.

"That would have to be Katherine."

"Fine," Red said.

"Why do you like Katherine so much?" Ellen pressed.

Red stopped looking at the baby and looked annoyed.

"Do you really want to know?" he asked.

Ellen sulked for a minute, but when she saw that Red's expression didn't change and he wasn't going to say anything until she did, she relented. "I guess not," Ellen said.

"How about Mary Katherine, and we call her 'Kate?'" Red suggested.

"That would be okay," Ellen said.

"Thank you," Red said and kissed her on the lips.

He turned to leave and Ellen said, "Who was named Kate that's so important to you?"

"You said you didn't want to know," Red replied.

"You're right, I don't," Ellen said sullenly.

Red left to buy an expensive bouquet of flowers and a bunch of expensive cigars to give to his friends.

San Francisco, 1948:

The war had been over almost three years. GM, Ford and Chrysler were making cars again; television had been invented; and as Harry Truman had predicted, things were starting to roll.

Although the world was at peace, the winds of war were stirring in California. Joseph Pistone, the Don who ran the greater Los Angeles area and controlled one major studio and two unions that affected the movies as well as trucking and his most lucrative business, narcotics, was trying to expand. Movie stars and musicians all wanted drugs, as did people of lesser stature.

Some of the old "Moustache Petes" -- that's what the hard-line, older Sicilian bosses were called, who didn't want to traffic in drugs -- resisted and were crushed. Pistone knew with the money he earned from narcotics, he could buy more police and political protection. It was his dream to run all of California, and one day the West Coast. Only one man stood in his way -- Tony Maretti.

Pistone didn't like Maretti because Maretti hid behind legitimate business and political influence based on perception. In Pistone's eyes Maretti kowtowed too much to civilians and did favors when he didn't have to. Pistone decided to crush Maretti at all cost and then go forward as King of California. Like most of the fools who challenged him, Pistone had gravely underestimated Tony's power.

Tony had been "The Money Man" for ten years. A manager. He wasn't street-smart any more. Wrong again. The North Beach Enclave was a sleeping giant. Mario had run his regime well. Every man was a little too good and paid a little too much. An employee sent to jail knew he had only to keep

259

his mouth shut and his wife and children would be cared for. The living allowance they received was not miserly, getting what the man earned when free. The man knew if he didn't talk to law enforcement, a warm welcome would be his when he left prison. There would be a party and, depending on the man's rank, his crime that sent him to prison, and his sentence, he would be honored by the Don himself, or one of the sons dropping by to pay respect to such a stalwart, have a drink in his honor and leave a handsome cash bonus. Maretti soldiers were fiercely loyal.

Tony was a man of great vision. He had seen it ten years earlier, which was why he had tried to retire from the day-to-day ugliness of the business. All the great cities of America were being torn by underworld strife. Guerilla wars by the dozens had flared up, ambitious hoodlums were trying to carve themselves a bit of the empire. Tony saw that the newspapers and government agencies were using the killings to pass stricter and stricter laws, and to use harsher police methods. Tony foresaw that public indignation might even lead to suspension of democratic procedures, which could be fatal to him and his people.

His own empire, internally, was secure. He decided to bring peace to all the warring factions in the Bay Area and then the nation. He had no illusions of the danger of the mission.

There were two or three families too powerful to eliminate, but the rest -- the neighborhood Black Hand terrorists, the freelance shylocks, the neighborhood bookmakers operating with proper, that is paid protection of the legal authorities -- would have to go. He mounted a colonial war against them with all his resources. The pacification of the Bay Area took three years. Some bad luck came at first, but later worked out for the best.

Some mad-dog Irishman had decided to kill Tony, and one actually put a bullet in his chest. The assassin was immediately riddled with bullets, but the damage was done. The incident gave Tony, Jr. his chance.

With his father out of action, Tony, Jr. took command. He showed a genius for city warfare. He also showed a merciless, sadistic ruthlessness, the lack of which had been his father's only fault as conqueror. From 1945 to 1947, Tony, Jr. made a reputation as the most cunning and relentless executioner the underworld had yet known.

By 1947, peace and harmony reigned in San Francisco and the surrounding Bay Area, except for minor incidents or misunderstandings, which were, of course, sometimes fatal. Tony, Sr. had completely recovered ands was as hale and hearty as ever. He lived happily on Nob Hill until Pistone became ambitious.

The Maranello family of Los Angeles had long controlled the drug trade in Oakland. Sam Cerruti was a pimp. He had controlled prostitution in Oakland for fifteen years. He was happy to make his money off the trade of female flesh. In 1938, Dante Fresca had approached him, told him that Maretti was in jail and he could share in a big deal if he went along. Maranello and Pistone partnered up to take what Fresca promised them, even if Tony got out. Fresca promised they could run drugs and anything else they wanted through the docks in San Francisco and Oakland if they helped take Maretti down. Tony got out and Fresca was killed. Cerruti backed out and pledged his allegiance to the Maretti family. After Tony made the deal to be a "banker," the other families of the country were too supportive of him for Pistone and Maranello to make a move.

That was ten years earlier. With ruthless efficiency and patient planning, Pistone and Maranello had either bought out or killed all the "Moustache Petes" up and down the coast who wanted to do business the old way.

Maranello controlled the Teamsters in Los Angeles.

He sent people to the Bay Area to infiltrate the union there, then Cerruti was made an offer to join their side.

He refused, not wanting to be on the wrong side if a war started. He was killed and his territory absorbed by the Pistone/Maranello alliance. There was no complaints or retaliation, so they went to phase two of their plan.

In addition to his money management for the Mob, Tony Maretti still owned two construction companies, two real estate brokerage firms, a huge banking building downtownand a trucking company. Maranello had been hijacking Maretti trucks, and always seemed to be tipped off to the most lucrative loads. Tony knew someone on the inside was doing it. He needed to find out who, but he didn't want to use his own people fearing a leak. He asked Tom Franklin for a favor. Franklin sent Hank and Rabbit, his best men, to see Tony.

Franklin was more than willing to help because of the events of the last few days. Maretti had forgiven him for the misunderstanding in 1938 and they had done each other favors over the intervening years. He was worried that a big play was coming and he might need Tony's help protecting the union.

Two days before, two "business agents" from the Teamsters in Los Angeles had come into the Dockworkers

Local in Oakland and suggested they merge. Rafe Coyle was the president of the Local. He politely refused and they threatened him. Rafe had been a boxer in his teenage years and early twenties before going to work in the then-fledgling union. He beat the agents within an inch of their lives and threw them through the plate-glass window of the office. When they landed in the street, the driver of their car got out and pulled a gun. Rafe reached under his desk and pulled out his "negotiator" -- the cut-down pump shotgun that Doc O'Hearn used to carry and had given to Rafe weeks before he died. The three quick shotgun blasts to the car caused the guy with the pistol to run, abandoning both the car and his wounded buddies.

Tom heard it from street gossip and called Rafe, who verified the story and said, "I've already consulted my father and steps are being taken. Tom should be careful, too."

Eddie called Red. They agreed that the threat must have some merit and someone big had to be behind it. Red called Tony and a group of the North Beach Enclave's most ferocious, cunning and ruthless soldiers were dispatched to the San Francisco and Oakland docks to work and watch things.

The Steelworkers Union also had an incident. A group of Teamster drivers were delivering a load of steel to the site where the new baseball stadium was being built, when another "business agent" and some others showed up. They had declared a work stoppage and refused to allow the steel to be unloaded. The line boss of the steelworkers called Blackie, who came over. The business agent demanded to see Red.

"Mr. Sullivan's unavailable," Blackie replied. "Any beef you got, you can take it up with me."

"Can you merge your union with the Teamsters?" the thug asked.

"I can give you Mr. Sullivan's answer," Blackie replied calmly. "No."

"Then you won't be getting any materials until Mr. Sullivan comes to the table."

"I already told you, I have the power to speak for

Mr. Sullivan. Now stop delaying my men or I'll have to take action."

"You better take it," the lead thug said arrogantly.

He expected Blackie to hit him or pull a gun, but Blackie was smarter. He turned and went to the line boss' trailer. He knew the Teamsters had a contract that didn't expire until 1950. He also knew they had received good benefits and a big raise because of a no-strike clause in their contract, unless the employers broke the contract first.

These fuckers were Mob all the way, trying to force something for their boss, who obviously had a piece of a Teamster Locale, or maybe even the International.

A lesser man might have been intimidated. Blackie was one of those people who listened and learned from what was going on around him, even if the people around him didn't know it. He had over the years picked Doc's, Eddie's, and Red's brains. As Red's friend, he sometimes had lunch with Red and Tony Maretti. When Tony got some wine in him, he's start sermonizing about business and one of his sons would usually cut him off. Blackie listened, however.

Tony hadn't lived as long as he had and fought off as many challengers as he had by being stupid.

These thugs are daring me to call their bluff. Blackie thought about what Red or Tony Maretti would do. *The thug obviously wants violence, and therefore violence isn't the answer.* He got an inspiration. *The guy threatened a work stoppage. A wildcat strike in a big city like San Francisco would void the nationwide contract and cause undue problems for the Teamsters and the mob nationwide.*

Blackie used the line boss' phone and called the president of the Teamsters in San Francisco. He explained the situation.

"It'll be handled in fifteen minutes," was the San Francisco Teamster rep's answer before hanging up. Fifteen minutes later about fifty guys showed up, beat the shit out of the thugs and unloaded the trucks.

Tom Franklin was really worried afterwards because he knew some serious player was making a play for the unions in San Francisco and had made him a target.

He was having sandwiches with Hank and Rabbit in the park when they made their move. Like the others, in the same two-day period, it came at first as a veiled threat. Five wiseguys came over to their table.

"Mr. Franklin?" the apparent leader said.

"Yes?"

"Your colleague in Oakland was not very cooperative.

I hope you're a more reasonable man. It's in your best interest to merge with us."

Tom laughed. "I built this union. You want me to give it up for some out-of-town greaseball and piss off the Maretti family? Why don't you ask me to have myself re-circumcised. You'll have a better chance of success."

Hank and Rabbit laughed out loud.

"You two assholes think that's funny?" the leader sneered.

"I think that's damn funny," Hank said coldly.

"How about we change your sense of humor?"

Hank and Rabbit exchanged looks.

"I got it," Rabbit said casually.

"You sure?" Hank asked.

"Yeah," Rabbit replied and stood up.

The leader should have seen a red flag when Hank and Tom didn't move. Being a typical street thug, however, he didn't have enough sense to know he was in trouble. The five goons came forward. Rabbit casually picked up his bottle of root beer and took a swig. He then smashed it across the leader's face and cut the face of the one behind him with the broken part remaining in his hand. When the one to the leader's right threw a punch, Rabbit grabbed the man's wrist with his right hand, straightened the arm and then broke it at the elbow with a palm-heel strike of his left hand. The man fell to the ground screaming.

The other two came forward. Squatting like a Cossack dancer, Rabbit used his legs like pistons to kick their legs out from under them. They fell hard, landing on their backs. Rabbit got up and stomped on their balls, then spun around and kicked the one with the cut face in the jaw. He fell down on top of the other two. The leader was awake, bleeding from the scalp where Rabbit had hit him with the bottle.

"Don't make me have to use both guys," Tom said and walked away with Hank and Rabbit, who were laughing.

"Amateurs," Rabbit said to Hank's amusement.

Afterwards Hank and Rabbit went to Louie's to see Tony about helping with the situation.

"Gentlemen," Tony said. "I appreciate your help. The past couple days' events show us that we have a problem.

I know I have a mole in my organization. A little bird told me his name. I want you to go visit him and find out who he's really working for. If I have this information, I can solve everyone's problems without help. I just can't risk someone in my organization tipping the mole or his employers. I know how they're going to come after me now. Although they were rebuffed in their first attempt, they'll keep trying as long as they think I don't see it."

"And what is that, sir?" Hank asked.

"Do you know Red Sullivan and Eddie Coyle?" Maretti asked.

"I've never met them, but they're legends -- men of

Respect. My boss, Mr. Franklin, worked closely with them to build the union before it was split up. I know who they are," Hank said.

"If Mr. Franklin sent you, you must have all his confidence."

"I do," Hank said.

"Okay, I'm gonna speak frankly. My enemies think they can break me through the unions. If they shut down the docks until I let them run dope through there, if they shut down my construction businesses through work stoppages. They don't want to try all-out war, because the commission in

New York won't allow it. They're trying to backdoor me.

You gentlemen find out who it is and I'll be forever grateful, not only to your boss, but to you both personally. I've heard that you're both serious men, to be treated with respect. You have all my confidence," Tony finished.

"We won't let you down, sir," Hank replied.

"I'm counting on that. Have dinner on me," Tony said and then left.

Hank and Rabbit had all the food and desserts they wanted, then went home early to gear up for their mission.

A Teamster dispatcher named Kevin Noonan had been setting up Maretti trucks for the hijackings. A thirty-ish, plain-looking in the face, but built-like-a-brick-shithouse Jewish girl named Annabelle who worked in the dispatch office was one of Mario Maretti's playthings. Noonan didn't know it and, being a pussy-hound himself, had pursued her. He'd tried to impress her by telling her how much clout he had with the syndicate. Annabelle jokingly relayed the information to Mario one day after they'd had sex.

"I'm sleeping with you, and this little creep tries to impress me with who he knows in the Mob. Puhleeze."

Mario put two and two together and told his father that Noonan was probably the leak. Hank and Rabbit watched him discreetly for a couple days, and then decided when and where they'd move.

Noonan was having dinner in Bruno's, a bar and grill that had good food and live music on Friday and Saturday nights. He was dining with an obvious wiseguy. Hank parked the car in front of the place. It wasn't his car, but an old Chevy sedan with out-of-state plates that Mario Maretti had supplied. When they job was done they were supposed to dump the car in McClaren Park. If there were witnesses, the car couldn't be traced. Hank went to a pay phone and called the number Maretti had given him. Rocco Lampone answered.

"We're ready," Hank said. "Any last minute instructions?"

"We don't want 'im dead, but he better not get out of the hospital for a month."

"He's got a wiseguy I don't know with him."

"Fuck 'im. He's not one of our people," Rocco saidand hung up.

Noonan and his companion were hitting on two broads at the bar who weren't interested. Rabbit gave Hank a thumbs-up, then leaned against the car. Hank took up a position to the left of the bar door.

When the two men came out, Rabbit spoke. "Those broads sure brushed you two Casanovas off. Maybe they have good taste."

They looked at Rabbit with contempt. He was the perfect patsy for their rage. A tall, lanky and a country boy from the way he talked. They turned on him with glee.

The wiseguy was the bigger of the two and he charged Rabbit, throwing a wild overhand right. Rabbit slipped the punch and used the man's own momentum to send him crashing face-first into the side of the car. The guy turned around cursing and Rabbit destroyed his left knee with a perfectly placed sidekick. He howled in pain and began to fall, but before he could, Rabbit slammed him in the nose with a palm-heel strike of his left hand, which straightened him up and banged his back against the car. Rabbit finished by hitting the man on both sides of his head at the same time with open palms in a clapping motion, and then kicked him savagely in the groin. The man fell in a heap and was motionless. It had taken less than ten seconds.

Noonan tried to help his buddy, but was grabbed from behind and spun into the wall of the bar by Hank. Hank was on him quickly, raining endless volleys of blockbuster punches to the head and body. Noonan tried to fight at first, but soon gave up and began to beg for mercy.

"Take my wallet, take it!" he howled.

Hank twisted his arm until it cracked. Noonan howled in pain. "Jesus Christ, what do you want, man?"

"I want to know who you are working for," Hank said.

"They'll kill me if I tell."

Hank pulled his gun and stuck it in the man's face. "I'll kill you if you don't," Hank said calmly.

"Oh, shit," Noonan said. Hank cocked the hammer. "Maranello," Noonan said.

Hank hit Noonan in the jaw with the butt of his gun and he fell to the pavement. Everything had transpired in less than a minute and a half.

"Trouble," Rabbit said.

A Cadillac was coming up fast. Hank and Rabbit jumped in their car and took off. They saw four guys with guns get out of the Caddy. The rear window imploded as the goons shot at their car. Hank gunned it around the corner.

"You hit?" he asked Rabbit.

"No," Rabbit said. "I thought this guy was a piece of shit trucker who wants to be a big shot. Why in the hell would he have four bodyguards?"

"Good question," Hank replied as he saw the Cadillac gaining on them.

"Give me your piece," Rabbit said, pulling his own.

"Why?" Hank asked.

"If you can't outrun 'em, I may have to light them up."

Hank handed his gun over and shuddered as Rabbit started humming *Amazing Grace*.

They didn't know, nor could they have possibly known, was Noonan's dinner companion was Enzo Maranello, Don Vito Maranello's oldest son. He had come to offer Noonan more money and to guarantee his safety if he continued to help sabotage Maretti operations. The bodyguards were his, not

Noonan's. They were parked about half a block down the street as there was only one parking space in front of the bar. They were about to double-park, when the owner of the car already parked there came out and left.

The bodyguards weren't slow, it was just that the two men's beating only took a minute or two, and started so unexpectedly. Even if the guards had been watching the front of the bar intently, they wouldn't have rushed over just because Hank was standing by the door and Rabbit spoke to their boss. Rabbit could have been asking them if they'd seen his boss, or if they wanted girls, or just for a light for a cigarette. They might still have hesitated when their boss and Noonan made their move. It was only one guy, maybe two, if Hank was with Rabbit. Enzo had a tough-guy reputation that went beyond his name. He'd be pissed if his security team didn't let him whip the ass of some loudmouth on his own. By the time they realized there was a real problem, it was too late and the damage was done.

The old six-cylinder Chevy moved pretty good once it was up to speed, but it didn't accelerate very quickly. Hank was used to his Lincoln, with its big engine that moved like a scalded cat. The Cadillac was getting closer. Caddys had big engines too.

Hank turned onto a side street, sliding around the corner sideways. The heavier Cadillac couldn't slow down enough to make the turn. It skidded to a stop almost on the sidewalk. The driver had to back up and start after Hank. Hank zigged-zagged through the avenues. The lighter Chevy could corner better, but the Caddy had enough power to stay in sight. They were nearing the Great Highway.

"I have one more trick up my sleeve," Hank said. "If this doesn't work, we're fucked."

"No, they are," Rabbit said, cycling both guns. "We ain't never not made it yet."

There's always a first time, Hank thought.

As they hit the Great Highway, Hank slowed down to forty-five.

"Why the hell are you slowing down?" Rabbit asked.

"I know what I'm doing," Hank said.

The Cadillac came barreling up on them. Hank downshifted to second, pulled on the parking brake and wrenched the wheel to the left. The ass end of the Chevy swung around the length of its wheelbase in the middle of the road. Hank released the parking brake and tromped the throttle, sending up a rooster tail of tire smoke as the right rear tire became ablaze. He shifted gears and the car straightened. The Caddy's driver, seeing the Chevy spin in front of him, instinctively tried to avoid hitting the other car and wrenched his wheel to the right and slammed on the brakes. The Caddy spun wildly and flipped into the sand on the side of the road.

"Jesus H. Christ!" Rabbit exclaimed.

"No, John Henry Collins and plenty of practice on dirt roads with Grandpa's old Ford," Hank said proudly. "That's called a 'Moonshiner's turn.'"

"Whatever it was, it worked," Rabbit said, handing Hank his gun back.

As they were instructed, they dumped the car in McClaren Park. Mario had said that if they climbed the hill to the neighborhood above the park, there'd be a '33 Pontiac, also with out-of-state plates, with the keys in it waiting for them. The car, however, wouldn't start.

"I'll give you a push," Rabbit said, and pushed Hank down the hill.

Hank put it in first and popped the clutch. The engine roared to life. Just as Hank turned the headlights on, he crashed into a cop car that was parked at the bottom of the hill. The lights of the cop car came on and two cops got out with their guns drawn. Hank didn't resist arrest.

Rabbit ran as fast as he could the other way, and got a cab to Louie's where he met Rocco Lampone.

"We did the job for your boss. Maranello is his problem."

"Thank you," Rocco said.

"My friend got arrested for a traffic accident," Rabbit said.

"So?" Rocco asked.

"This accident followed a chase, where there may have been fatalities."

"I'm on it," Rocco said.

"You better be," Rabbit said. "If something happens to Hank...."

"I understand."

Rabbit left and Rocco shuddered. He'd worked in New Orleans. *One focused, foolish, bad-ass hillbilly is worth ten wiseguys.*

Hank sat in an interrogation room, getting more pissed off by the minute. He was especially pissed that they hadn't taken the handcuffs off. The cops who arrested him roughed him up a little when they found a gun, but then relaxed a bit when they saw his permit. They found out he worked for Tom Franklin. Hank had an official union card. He refused to say a word other than, "I have a permit for the gun."

Clark Shaughnessy came in. His face didn't look quite right and he was wiping his nose frequently. Shaughnessy pulled up a chair next to him.

"Well, if it ain't Jack Dempsey. We meet again," he said.

Hank sighed. "Look, you were off-duty and out of uniform and acting like an asshole. It was nothing personal."

"I understand," Shaughnessy said. Hank's face must have shown his surprise, because the cop smiled. "You fight in the war?"

"Yes," Hank replied.

"Me too. Killed a shitpot full of Japs on Tarawa.

Won two Purple Hearts. That why I got my job back after the war," Shaughnessy said proudly. "You?"

"Europe," Hank said. "I killed my share of Germans.

Won the Congressional Medal of Honor." Even though he knew he was risking an ass-kicking, he couldn't help one-upping the prick.

"We're the same, man," the cop said calmly. "We both fought in the war, and now we're both businessmen. Maybe we can do business."

"In what way?" Hank asked.

"You broke my jaw. The bones knitted badly and irritate a nerve in my sinus. Now my nose runs all the fuckin' time. Police medical insurance will only okay one surgery every six months, so I have to walk around lookin' like a glazed donut until April."

"You started it," Hank said. "I didn't know you were a cop. I thought you were just a big prick that needed a lesson. You were so cocksure you could beat me. I learned in the Army that there's always somebody better. If you want me to apologize, forget it. I'll just take the ass-kickin'."

"You're right, I started it," the cop said. "I'll forget the whole thing on one condition. You tell me what you were doing tonight, and who you were doing it for, and I'll forget about what I owe you."

"That easy?" Hank asked.

"That easy."

"I was drinking in the park. After I left the park I found this car with the keys in it, and decided I didn't want to walk home. I fucked up and ran into the cop car."

Shaughnessy laughed. "That's what your statement to the booking officer said. You signed your name to that bullshit?"

"I didn't sign it, I was handcuffed. But that's what I said," Hank replied.

"Last chance."

"Fuck you."

Shaughnessy hit him in the face, and Hank fell off the chair. The cop picked him up by his coat with his left hand and hit him in the face with his right. Shaughnessy wasn't in a hurry, he threw each punch with deliberation, and each one landed with a sickening thud or flesh splitting open. He sat Hank up in the chair again, and slapped his face until he had his attention.

"You gonna tell me something now, tough guy?" Shaughnessy sneered, leaning into Hank's face.

Hank grinned through his split lips. "Sure. I'll tell you something. Go fuck your mother," Hank said as he kicked Shaughnessy in the balls as hard as he could.

Shaughnessy doubled over. Hank stood up and kicked him in the knee. When he fell, Hank kicked him in the face a couple times before three more cops burst into the room and wailed on him with nightsticks.

He was in the chair again when he came around.

Shaughnessy was there, as were the three other cops. Shaughnessy's face was swollen and bloody.

"You gonna tell me something now, tough guy?" he said.

"You still here?" Hank said. "I thought I told you to go fuck your mother."

Shaughnessy knocked him off the chair again, and he was picked up by the other three.

"You want us to beat you to fucking death?" one of the three asked.

"You can't do that in this day and age," Hank replied. "At least not to anybody white. A friend saw me get arrested. I work for an important man. People will be looking for me. You fuckers kill me and you lose you jobs, other more important people lose their jobs, politicians get voted out, careers are ruined. I figured on getting the shit beat out of me when I got picked up. That's the nature of the business. Now kiss my ass."

One of the three raised his nightstick, when there was tapping on the room's window. Shaughnessy went outside.

Captain Tom Conway and Lieutenant John O'Reilly were waiting. O'Reilly had transferred from LAPD and was on Pistone's payroll. Tony Maretti himself had called Tom Conway and asked that toughest cop on the force question

Hank, with O'Reilly watching.

"How far do you want to go?" Conway asked.

"It has to look real," Tony said.

"Can this guy withstand that?" Tom asked.

"From what I've seen and heard, he's a Sicilian,"

Tony said. "He did me a favor."

"I understand," Conway said.

"That's enough," Conway said to Shaughnessy.

"Captain, I'll break him," Shaughnessy protested.

"No, you won't," Conway said. "If he's as tough as he acts, you could kill him and not get shit."

"Then what do we do? Dump his body in the bay?"

"Like the man said, not in this day and age. If he's not as tough as he's acting, you pricks beat him enough and he'll confess to killing Lincoln. That doesn't necessarily make it so. His boss and lawyer are downstairs trying to get him released. Officially he resisted arrest and wouldn't let us fingerprint him. That's why he got his ass kicked. Now get him ready to be released, and he better not look any worse than he does now."

"Captain...."

"Just do it!" Conway boomed. "Or you'll be on graveyard traffic duty for a fuckin' year! And your god damned cronies too!"

Shaughnessy left to do what he was told. Conway didn't like Shaughnessy. His fearsome rep was bogus. Shaughnessy was a coward. All the criminals he'd beat half to death were handcuffed or drunk. Three of Shaughnessy's eight shootings were questionable and that was only because, like the suspect said, those three were white. Conway didn't mind kicking someone's ass fair and square, or didn't care if a cop shot some hood who pulled a knife or gun on him. But planting a gun on some dumb-ass after shooting wrongly, or beating on some helpless drunk who talked shit was just sick and wrong. That was why Conway had allowed the guy to kick the shit out of Shaughnessy, although he paid for it. Any other cop and Conway would have interceded then and there.

"Satisfied?" he said to O'Reilly.

"Yeah. That's fine," O'Reilly said.

Hank was released to Tom Franklin and the Dockworkers Union's lawyer. He was told to take a few days off and Tom would call him with instructions. He figured out what happened from reading the newspaper and getting the street report from Rabbit. Kevin Noonan had two cracked ribs, a broken arm, a broken nose and various contusions and abrasions. Enzo Maranello had a broken kneecap, a broken nose, two ruptured eardrums, a concussion and a ruptured testicle. Maranello's four bodyguards were dead. According to the police, from what the cops could tell, they were chasing somebody and had an accident. Apparently, they had their guns in their hands, all single-action automatics, that were cocked and locked with the safety off. When the car flipped, the guns went off. In addition to the gunshot wounds, three of the four were thrown from the car. The coroner recovered all the bullets from the bodies and inside the car. There was no foul play, as least as far as gunplay was concerned. They had accidentally shot themselves.

Maretti already had a plan in place, but he played possum. Vito Maranello called him and said that Enzo was there investigating the strange goings-on at the request of the Teamsters International and he wanted Tony's help to find out who beat his son half to death.

After Hank's working over, Tony called him back.

"This man, he works for a ninety caliber type of pezzovante I know. The Feds can't even put his boss away, and they put me away. This guy, he's kind of a wild-ass. He broke this Sergeant Shaughnessy's jaw. He says he was drunk and joyriding when he crashed into the police car. The crash occurred near McClaren Park, miles away from the beach where Enzo's bodyguards bought it. Plus, he was driving a derelict stolen black '33 Pontiac. Witnesses said it was a blue '41 Chevy your men went after. I doubt this man knows anything, however, I had him worked over to be sure. Ask your man O'Reilly. He was there."

"I did," Maranello replied.

"Then we have no further business. I wish your son speedy recovery. Let me know if I can help you further," he said almost mockingly, feeling the man seethe through the telephone. Tony smiled.

Hank was fined $150.00 for reckless driving and for driving an unregistered vehicle. Since the registered owner could not be located, they couldn't get him for grand theft auto. He found an old car, took it for a ride, and ran into the police. Stupid, but not a felony and not worth the court's time. Both the District Attorney's charges of resisting arrest and Hank's lawyer's countercharges of police brutality were dismissed. The judge sentenced him to the fine and time served. He fared much better with the court of the street.

He was told to be at Buddy's, a nightclub owned by Tony, Jr., at seven o'clock. He was escorted inside by a guy in a suit, who knocked before opening the door. When he walked in, the room erupted in applause.

Tony, Sr. was there with both of his sons, as well as Rocco Lampone and Sonny Lauria. Tom Franklin and Rabbit were there also. A lot of other people were in the room, along with plenty of good-looking women in cocktail dresses. Besides the bar, there was a lavish buffet of Italian food set up. The band started playing, and everyone started eating and drinking and dancing.

Tony himself came over to Hank. "Let's have a drink," he said. They went over to the bar. "You did me a favor, and the police caught you. You told them nothing, and they have nothing. Reckless driving. Maybe someone won't let you drive a garbage truck, eh? You proved to me that you're a true Sicilian, in spirit if not lineage, a man of honor, worthy of respect. My gift to you," Tony said with an envelope of cash in his hand.

Hank had an inspiration. "That's not necessary. Your friendship is enough for me, Mr. Maretti," he said.

Tony was moved. "Finally, I meet a true man of honor. You have earned my friendship and loyalty. Now your enemies will become my enemies. Accept a gift from a friend," Tony said, offering the envelope again. Hank took it. "Enjoy the party and if you ever need a favor, let me know."

"I will, sir. Thank you," Hank said.

Tony went to talk to other people.

Mario came over and patted Hank on the back. "You came through for us. My father taught us never to forget a favor, or lose an opportunity to make a new friend."

"Thank you," Hank said.

"Listen, I'd like to hire this 'hammer' of yours -- Rabbit," Mario said. "Rocco's not scared of anything, and he scared Rocco. He's very devoted to you. How did you manage that?" Mario asked.

"I met him under battle conditions in the war,"

Hank replied. "We went through some bad shit together, so you just naturally get a bond. He's a Samurai."

"I know that type," Mario replied. "I have a few kamikazes like that who came back from the war."

"I doubt that you have any like Rabbit."

Mario nodded and spoke again. "A man like that can be a powerful weapon, if he likes and respects you. Since he doesn't fear death, he has only one fear -- that you may be the one to kill him. He is yours then. Is that how it is with you and Rabbit?" Mario asked.

"I am genuinely his friend. I really do like him,"

Hank replied. "But in a weird way, what you said could be a little true."

"I hope you never turn him on me," Mario said.

"I hope I never have to," Hank replied.

"Fair enough. Speak of the devil," Mario said.

"Do you know that redhead over there in the white dress?" Rabbit asked Mario.

Mario got a mischievous grin. "Excellent choice, my friend."

"I like redheads," Rabbit said.

Mario motioned at one of his men, who brought the woman over. "Marie, this is Rabbit, a good friend of mine. Make sure he has a good time tonight."

"He's a little shy," Hank put in.

"I just love the strong-silent type," Marie purred. "We'll get along just fine. Let's dance," she said, leading Rabbit to the dance floor.

"That's a lotta woman," Hank said approvingly.

"Think he can handle it?" Mario asked.

"He's an Airborne Ranger, they're very resourceful."

After patting Hank on the back, Mario laughed and walked away.

Tom Franklin came over. "I see you've made some new friends," he said.

"You can never have too many friends," Hank said.

"You getting a new job?" Tom asked.

"Not right now, but I have to keep my options open.

Too many people don't like you, and now you've pulled me into mob business."

"What the hell does that mean?" Tom asked, irritated.

"It means I'll work for you as long as it's profitable and not any more hazardous to my health than it has been.

I took that as an acceptable risk when I took the job, in order to make more in a week than most people make in a month. But if this comes out -- attacking the son of a boss, wasting his bodyguards -- we ain't ever gonna sell these tickets. We're goin' all the way, the whole ride. No one would ever believe I was doing the job at your behest. To Maranello and that fuckin' cop that hates me, I'm one of Maretti's people. Well, if that's the case, I may need some of Maretti's protection. My mom and dad and little brothers live here now. Maretti doesn't do families and crushes anyone who does. I just bought myself and my family a little life insurance," Hank finished.

"I thought I had your loyalty," Tom said.

"You bought my loyalty," Hank said. "Which means it was for sale in the first place. A man that sells his loyalty takes the best deal. And he's always looking for the bigger, better deal. We're all a bunch of god damned mercenaries. A mercenary's main loyalty is to himself.

Look out for number one. I'm not getting' killed or goin' to prison for you, because you wouldn't do it for me."

"Damn, Hank, you're a lot smarter than I thought,"

Tom said admiringly. "I once read, a man who hires someone who is smarter than he is, is actually the smarter of the two. I feel better already. I hear you loud and clear, and I'd be disappointed if you felt any other way. Just let me have a chance to counter-bid if someone makes you a better offer."

Hank shook his head and chuckled. "You son-of-a-bitch," he said. "You are one hell of a businessman. And I hate to admit it, but I'm one of the minority that likes you."

Tom laughed. "There's more of you than you think. Let's eat."

After some food and wine, Hank left to talk to Rabbit, who now had a gorgeous brunette at his table along with the redhead. The brunette got up and so did the redhead. They led Hank and Rabbit down a hall to some private rooms in the back. Hank took the brunette into one room and the redhead and Rabbit got another.

Tony Maretti had given Hank $5,000.00. Even though his was barely two years old, Hank decided to order a new Lincoln convertible. The new ones had a better interior and a more powerful engine, according to the salesman.

Hank drove the demonstrator they had and was convinced.

The salesman wanted him to buy the demonstrator, but Hank didn't like the color. It was green. In the Army, everything was green. He ordered a midnight blue one with a white interior and a white top. He gave the salesman a $1,000.00 deposit and said he'd trade his in when the new one came in. The salesman gave him a receipt for his deposit and a copy of the order. He said it would take six weeks to get an order from the factory and that he'd call as soon as the car arrived.

Mario Maretti called him and said that he and Rabbit should take a vacation. If Hank came by his office, he'd get two first-class plane tickets to

New York, and numbers to call there where they'd get the best hotels and have a great time.

"Why?" Hank asked.

Mario hesitated a moment, then said, "Oh, hell.

Enzo couldn't identify you. We got Noonan. He decided he'd like to keep breathing. He said he was knocked out immediately and didn't see anything. The cops don't suspect you, and neither does the Maranello family. But my father is a very cautious man. Some shit is going to happen, and if you're out of town, you're completely clear. He may want to use your services again discreetly in the future."

"Did you clear this with Tom?" Hank asked.

"I'm dealing with you," Mario said. "And if I ask or grant a favor in the future, it will be between me an you.

I don't need Tom Franklin as a go-between."

"Is your father retiring?" Hank asked.

Mario laughed. "I'm training to succeed my father in case anything happens to him or my brother. Like I said, my father is a very cautions man."

Hank was a cautious man too. If old man Maretti bought it, Mario may very well be in charge. Hank realized he needed to be his friend too. "I didn't mean any disrespect, Mario, I was just asking."

"None taken. I'll need my own allies, as well as my father's," Mario said and then hung up.

Tom Franklin didn't gripe. He thought he could use

Hank's newfound underworld celebrity to get more clout with the Marettis. He was very supportive of the little sabbatical, not that he had a choice. Tom was smart enough to realize, "If rape is inevitable, then lie back and enjoy it." He tried to act like he was doing them a favor, but it didn't go over. Even Rabbit knew they were acquiescing to a higher authority.

Hank and Rabbit went to New York and, as promised, had a great time. Mario's contacts got them Broadway show tickets, girls, executive suites in the hotels, ringside seats at fights, tickets to Yankee games -- anything they wanted. In New York, the center of the world news, one could get newspapers from almost any big city. Hank made sure to read the San Francisco and

Los Angeles papers every day. He found out what was happening by reading between the lines.

Vito Maranello was shot to death at the Hollywood home of his movie-star mistress. The actress was killed as well. It was in all the papers and cast bad reflections on the movie studios, especially the Maranello family. At the funeral, Enzo Maranello was killed, as were all the caporegimes of the Maranello family. No one expected a strike at a funeral. The cops, the attorney general of California, and the mob nationwide were shocked. It had never happened before. It was Tony, Jr.'s idea. He had sold it to the old man with the fact that it would actually save lives. If they didn't do it, the war would go on for years and both sides would lose many good people.

The Maranello holdings were incorporated into the Maretti empire. A tribute system was set up with all incumbents allowed to remain in their bookmaking, pimping, and policy number slots. As a bonus they were given a foothold in the movie business and the Los Angeles unions.

Pistone asked for peace, but Maretti put him off on one pretext or another, until a meeting was set for New Year's Eve, 1949. Joseph Pistone's own people led him to slaughter. The meeting was at an Italian restaurant in Hollywood. Maretti didn't show and the "waiters" gunned down Pistone. Again, it was all Tony, Jr.'s idea.

San Francisco, 1949:

Eddie Coyle was the Assistant Manager of the San Francisco Seals, who were later to become the Giants. He spent a lot of his time with the team. He still owned the boxing business, but his son John now ran it. Cash Williams was head trainer. A year before, at age thirty-seven, Cash had made one last, valiant run at the light-heavyweight title. He was ahead on all three cards after ten rounds, but he lost on cuts in the fourteenth. Eddie had been in his corner.

Eddie told Cash the same thing Doc had told him somany years before. "You've had your last great fight, son. It's time to move on."

"To what?" Cash said.

"I know Doc taught you to save and invest your money. You can't be hurtin'," Eddie said.

"I'm not moneywise, Eddie. But it gets in your blood.

I got to be around it," Cash said.

"You can. I'm running a baseball team, and don't have time for both boxing and baseball. John is the money man now, like Doc was. But we need a fight man. I can't think of a better one than you," Eddie finished.

Cash wiped his eyes. "You've been so good to me over the years, Eddie, I can't believe it. I don't know of any Negro head trainers in big gyms. Small ones in Cleveland, Harlem, yeah, but no big ones. I don't know what to say."

"Say 'yes,'" Eddie replied. "You bled in the ring just like I did. Your knowledge is as hard earned as mine. You've had four title shots. You were robbed of one, and gave the other three a helluva fight. Any boxer who won't listen to you is a fool."

Cash smiled. "I won't let you down, Mr. Coyle."

Eddie laughed. "You told me that when you were eighteen years old and you never have. I don't think you'll start now."

"You can bank on that," Cash said.

They shook hands and a new partnership was born.

Red was happy. Business was good. The mob war hadn't affected him or the Steelworkers union very much. Tom

Conway kept him informed of any real problems. His wife was pregnant with their second child. His daughter, Katy, was in first grade and was a real pistol. A beautiful little girl, she could still run faster, hit harder and belch louder than any boy in her class.

Red had a meeting with Blackie at a carnival. Blackie wanted to discuss something and Red told him it could wait until Monday as he was taking his daughter to the carnival. Blackie said he'd meet him there and Red agreed. They had eaten hot dogs and French fries, and were talking about business.

Katy started to gripe. "I'm bored! I just want to go on a few more rides," she whined.

"Daddy's talking business, honey. Just wait a few more minutes. We'll get some cotton candy."

"I don't have anything to do!" Katy griped.

Blackie pulled his brass knuckles out of his pocket. "Here, play with these, honey," he said.

Katy took them, slipped them on her small fists, and started banging on the table, telephone poles, and anything else in sight. Red and Blackie finished their discussion.

"C'mon, Katy, let's go," Red said. "Give Blackie back his tools."

"Can I take these to school on Monday?" Katy asked.

"No," Red said. "Why would you want to take something like that to school?"

"So I could pound Peter Topper."

Blackie laughed uproariously. "She's definitely your kid, Red."

"Why don't you like this Peter?" Red asked.

"He pushes me off the swing at recess," Katy said.

"I told the teacher and he said I was dead meat because

I told. I told him I was gonna pound him if he tried anything."

"That's the spirit, Katy, don't take no shit from no one," Blackie said.

"You're not helping!" Red yelled at Blackie, who was still guffawing over the kid's attitude. "It's not nice to fight in school, honey," Red said. "Try to get along with everybody, and tell the teacher if someone gets out of line."

"Okay, Daddy," Katy said happily. "But I'm still gonna pound Peter if he tries anything at recess."

"A chip off the old block," Blackie said, still laughing.

Red punched his arm. "Will you shut up?" he asked, exasperated.

Blackie only laughed harder, which caused Red to punch him in the arm harder. He was inconsolable now, sprouting some crackpot theory about genetics versus environment. Katy got her cotton candy and was happy. Blackie couldn't stop snickering, and finally Red had to laugh with him.

"Fuck you anyway," he said, still laughing.

Red was sitting in his easy chair watching Milton Berle.

"What do you want to name the baby if it's a boy?"

Ellen asked. She'd already decided on Karen if it was a girl to go with Katy, and Red didn't object.

"Dean," Red said.

"I like Graham," Ellen replied.

"Like in cracker?" Red said. "No way."

"Why not?" Ellen said, irritated.

"Dean is your buddy," Red said. "He doesn't mind if you throw up on him on a roller coaster ride. Graham is a fat kid that farts a lot. If you want that, name him after your brother. I remember Easter," Red said.

"He had gas," Ellen said defensively.

"If I ate a pound of ham, fifty eggs, and drank a quart of Jameson, I'd have gas too," Red retorted.

"That wasn't nice."

"You're tellin' me," Red said.

"You asshole," Ellen snapped, and Red laughed.

"How about Richard?" she said.

"Dick?" Red replied. "I guess I'd take that over Graham if I had to."

Ellen laughed involuntarily. "You are insufferable," she said. "I'm serious. How about Richard Dean Sullivan?"

"That's fine with me," Red replied. "But we call him Richard, or Rich, not Dick or Dickie."

Ellen laughed again. "I agree," she said. "I'm going to bed, I'm tired."

"I'll come when this is over," Red said.

Ellen kissed him and went to bed.

Hank got back from New York and was eagerly awaiting the arrival of his new car. His mother called him in a panic on Monday, the day after his father's forty-ninth birthday.

"Jack's dyin'," she said, excitedly.

"Isn't he like ten years old?" Hank asked.

"Yes, but a little boy down the street died of appendicitis. He says his stomach hurts, and he's been throwin' up all morning," his mother said, agitated.

"Look, Mom, I don't want to sound uncaring, but if you think he's really sick, then take him to the doctor," Hank said.

"I can't," his mother said.

"Why not?"

"Your dad usually takes the bus to work, and leaves me the car. It was raining this morning and he didn't want to walk to the bus stop in the rain. I told him to take the car, that I wasn't doing anything important anyway. You come over here and take your brother to the hospital," Elizabeth said in her "Don't you dare refuse me" mother voice.

"I'll be right over," Hank said, and hung up.

When Hank arrived, he walked through the kitchen and noticed the bottle of Jim Beam in the trash. He'd bought it for his dad, because he liked it, and Hank and his father had shared a few drinks to celebrate Dan's birthday. The bottle had been half full when Hank left the night before. He didn't think his dad had finished it, birthday or not. Unlike Grandpa Allen, Dan was not a big drinker, two or three, and he was done. Jack was puking in the toilet again. Hank went in the bathroom and closed the door.

"What's it taste like, little brother?" Hank asked.

"Corn. All I can taste is corn. I never want to eat corn again," Jack said.

Hank figured it out and laughed heartily. "That's why whiskey is called 'corn squeezing.' Mom is worried sick about you because of the kid that died of an appendicitis down the street," Hank said. "But his didn't come from a bottle." Jack looked at Hank, surprised. "You got the day off of school. Try to eat something and take some aspirin, it helps. I know a little bit about hangovers. I'll empty the trash and tell mom I think it's the flu."

"I owe you, Hank," Jack said, relieved that his crime wasn't going to the court of "mom and dad."

"You want to go to the Seals game on Saturday?" Hank asked.

"Sure, if I live," Jack moaned.

Hank laughed. "I'm gonna go out on a limb and buy tickets. I'll see you Saturday."

Hank told his mother that he examined Jack's belly the way he'd learned from a medic in the war. He did not have appendicitis and that he probably had the 24-hour flu that was going around. More than likely he'd be fine tomorrow. His mother was relieved and Hank left.

Hank took Jack to the ballgame on Saturday worried that the kid was starting down a bad road. Fifteen-year-old Bobby was busy playing baseball and chasing girls. Their father worked a lot, and his mother, although an intelligent woman, was from the country and didn't realize the pitfalls a boy could get into if allowed to run loose.

Hank remembered Jack bragging about fighting so much with a bigger kid in school that the P.E. coach finally made them get in the ring with boxing gloves and fight until neither one could hold their hands up. Hank saw that his own image was part of the problem.

Jack had fully recovered, and Hank bought him all the hot dogs, peanuts, popcorn and soda he wanted.

"Jack, I want you to quit fuckin' around in school and gettin' in fights, and smokin' and drinkin' and tryin' to be a tough guy," Hank said.

"Why wasn't I told that Dad died? Who put you in charge?" Jack said sarcastically.

Hank slapped his face. Jack looked at him, incredulous. "Obviously Mom and Dad haven't done that enough," Hank said.

"You hit me again and I'll...."

"You'll what?" Hank said, slapping him again. "As Grandpa always said, 'Don't let your bulldog mouth overload your canary ass.' And wipe that bad-ass look off your face, or I'll slap it off. Mom and Dad are nice, good-hearted country people. They don't know what happens in the city.

I do. You're a nice kid, Jack, and you should grow up to be a nice man. Get a job, get married, have some kids. Have a normal life. Don't be a tough guy."

"It worked for you," Jack said.

"I'm gonna talk straight to you, because I care about you and I love you. I changed your diapers for Christ's sake. Mom and Dad don't know what I do. They think I'm a union delegate. Yeah, I make a lot of money. But every day, there's a chance that I may be shot dead in the street. That's no way to live."

"I've heard your rep from my friends' older brothers," Jack said. "Nobody fucks with Hank Collins, or Rabbit, or Tom Franklin. I heard you killed a cop."

Hank sighed. "Street tales get taller every time they're told," Hank said. "This cop was off-duty and out of uniform and drunk, and he tried to hit me. I knocked the hell out of him. Rabbit knocked the hell out of a couple of his friends. We didn't know they were cops, we thought they were just usual Saturday night assholes. We didn't kill any cops. If we did, we'd be dead or in prison. Don't do what I do. Just because I was blessed with eyes that see what other people don't, and hands that move without being told, doesn't mean everybody can do it. I have the gift of fury. And I don't know why. Grandpa had it. It's not right or wrong, it's just there. Mom and Dad loved me. I wasn't beaten as a child, I have no excuse for this gift of fury. It's both a blessing and a curse. In the war and on the street sometimes it helped me. Other times it's hurt me.

I'm not saying this to hurt your feelings, or to say that I'm tougher than you, but you don't have what it takes tobe a gangster. You're too nice a guy.

And nice guys get killed. I don't want that and Mom and Dad don't want that."

"How damned tough were you when you were ten?" Jack asked.

"Not very," Hank said. "I was afraid of the dark until I was about six. Mom had to leave a candle in my room so I wouldn't cry. Could you kill somebody, Jack? Somebody who'd never done anything to you, that you didn't know?"

"Probably not," Jack replied.

"I did. Many times in the war," Hank said. "Yeah, we can say that Hitler was nuts and we were doing the right thing, which we were. I believed that then, and I believe that now. On the other hand, Mom always sent us to church and taught us to believe in the Bible. The Bible says, 'Thou shalt not kill.' It doesn't say thou can kill in wartime. Or thou can kill in defense of the common good. It says, 'Thou shalt not kill.' Am I doomed to hell? That remains to be seen. I don't apologize for my life. I made the choices I made. But I don't want you going down the wrong road trying to emulate me. It's easier to get along and be a citizen.

Be a citizen, Jack."

"Okay," Jack said. "You're right. I don't like to fight. I will if I have to, but I don't enjoy it. You've made your point. I'll straighten up."

"Thank you," Hank said.

"It's still cool that everyone thinks my brother is
King Kong."

Hank had a thought. "If anyone ever bothers you and
I'm not around, go to Jerry's on Sixteenth Street and ask for Rabbit. He'll take care of you."

"I didn't know Hank had a kid," a Pistone soldier said to another. "He looks just like him. I know that kid."

"What the fuck are you talking about?" the second one said.

"I see him at the Roxy Theater every Friday night."

"Why?"

"I play bingo there."

"You're a god damned fucking idiot," the second one said, making the kid up and down for future reference.

San Francisco, 1950:

Richard Dean Sullivan was born at 11:58 on July 3, 1950. He missed being a Fourth of July baby by two minutes. Red and Katy had gone home to get some things for Ellen at her behest. The phone rang and Red answered it.

"Bring me some makeup too," Ellen said.

"Katy!" Red yelled.

"What?"

"Get your mother's makeup. I know you know where it is."

"Let me talk to Katy," Ellen said.

Katy came in with most of Ellen's cosmetics in a bag.

"Talk to your mother," Red said.

"Hi, Mom," Katy said into the phone.

"What do you think we should name your brother?" Ellen said, playing with the girl, even though his name had already been decided.

"Blackie," Katy said without hesitation. Red cringed.

"Why would you think we should name your brother 'Blackie?'" Ellen asked, disgusted.

"Because he's handsome and he lets me play with his brass knuckles. And Daddy takes crap from him," Katy said innocently.

"Let me talk to your father!" Ellen yelled into the phone.

Katy held it away from her ear, and looked at Red like she was exasperated. "She's pissed," Katy said casually.

"Thanks, I needed that," Red said, probably with more sarcasm than he should have to a child about her mother, but he couldn't help it.

287

"Where do you take her?" Ellen yelled. "Union halls, boxing matches, the track?"

"That about covers it," Red said, not really being smart. Ellen really went off and finally he hung up.

He looked at Katy and she said, "It's your own fault. You told me to talk to her."

"I've told you not to talk that shit to your mother," he said sternly.

Seven-year-olds are literal. Katy fired back, defending herself innocently, but well. "You said not to tell her that we broke into Mr. Mayer's office. You said not to tell her that Grandpa got in a fight at the track. You never said I couldn't talk about Blackie. I like Blackie."

"Forget it. Let's go," Red said, picking up the stuff they had to haul to the hospital.

Eddie and Mary were there when he arrived, and Red was relieved. She wouldn't start a fight in front of her parents and by the time they left she'd be cooled off. It was funny, he'd face down any man, but he dreaded conflicts with women, especially ones he loved.

Tony Maretti, Sr. didn't make many mistakes when it came to business. He was semi-retired, enjoying going to ballgames, fights, the opera with his wife, Sicily every six months for two weeks, and spoiling and playing with his eight grandchildren. Four belonged to Franchesca and his son-in-law, two to Tony, Jr. and his wife, and two to Mario and his wife. The one mistake he made was letting mob tradition and his own values cloud his judgment, and his sons, although both had fearsome street reputations that they'd earned, would not go against his wishes.

Tony, Jr. may have been an uncaring wise-ass in his youth, but he had blossomed into a very smart, ruthless visionary who always looked ahead. He'd advised his father to kill Pistone's children as a warning to other families of the country and to avoid small vendettas of vengeance in later years, that may prove devastating because of circumstance. Tony, Sr. refused.

"We don't do women and children. Period," he said. "Pistone's oldest child is a woman. His other children are girls. There's no danger. It's over."

"It's not over," Tony, Jr. said. "I never thought I'd say this, but, Pop, you're acting like a 'Moustache Pete.' His underbosses will step up and try to carve their own niche. And don't dismiss a woman just because she's a woman. Look what they did for the war effort. Don't you think Franchesca would go after the men that killed you, if she didn't have brothers?"

"True men of respect would never allow that," Tony, Sr. said.

"Fair enough. But our sister has a husband who's involved in the family business, does she not?"

"She does," Tony, Sr. conceded.

"Do we not all agree that Carlo is influenced by Fran. If she told him he could be the new Don if he listened to her would he not listen."

"That's pretty far-fetched," Tony, Sr. said.

"Not as far as you think, Pop. We need to crush them while they're on the ropes."

"Mario, what do you think?" Tony, Sr. asked.

"I think my brother has a valid point. Better safe than sorry," Mario replied. It was the perfect answer. He supported his brother, but didn't argue with his father. Mario was always the better politician.

"We'll wait and see what happens," Tony, Sr. said.

Tony, Jr.'s genius for street warfare and his reluctance to defy his father was ultimately what got him killed. He was right. Pistone's son-in-law, Jimmy "The Gent" Solano, who was married to Pistone's oldest daughter stepped up. He gave the "Moustache Pete" speech to the Caporegimes of the bleeding Pistone/Maranello alliance. He said that the coup would be not in getting the old man, but Tony, Jr.

Tony, Jr. ran the street and was obviously the mastermind behind the Maretti family's most successful raids. Jimmy reasoned that if they accomplished it, Tony, Sr. might be so grief-stricken as to tell Mario to negotiate peace. But there would be no peace. They would crush the Marettis once and for all, and get what his father-in-law wanted -- may he rest in peace -- all of California.

Maria Pistone-Solano was a pit viper in an attractive woman's body. Her father used to joke that God did the world a favor by making her a girl, because if she was a man, her ferocity would know no bounds. She made a perfect grieving daughter speech that didn't offend the old hard-liners, but galvanized their support of Jimmy.

"If I was born a boy, this never would have happened. It never would have happened because I'd have been at my father's side advising him and helping him, no disrespect to his consigliere. My father was strong for his family, strong for his friends. If I could do that, I would. But

I am a woman and a mother. Women are nurturers, not killers. But Jimmy will do what I cannot, which is to lead this family back to greatness."

The caporegimes applauded. Jimmy "The Gent" was made head of the family. He set his and his wife's plan into action.

Jimmy "The Gent" had been a cop in the late 1930's before going to jail. He lived with his grandmother in an old two-story house. His mother had died when he was very young. His father was a cop, a twenty-year veteran who was killed during Prohibition when Jimmy was a teenager. His grandmother's Catholic values caused him to take revenge by becoming a cop and smiting the criminals who gunned down good men like his father.

The old lady lived upstairs and Jimmy basically had his own apartment downstairs. Since his father's insurance money paid for the house, and his pension provided for his grandmother, he paid no rent. The old lady cooked breakfast and dinner every night, so he had a lot of expendable income -- basically his whole check.

Gambling was his only vice. He went to after-hours clubs and soon became a preferred customer. He give the doorman $20.00 just for opening the door. He'd give the waitress a five-spot just for bringing him a drink. He was lucky at craps and 21, and usually left a winner. When he lost, he never made a beef or griped. Always a gentleman, hence his nickname. All the dealers and waitresses called him "Jimmy the Gent." The Pistone family underbosses made a note of it and he was always given first-class treatment.

That was where he met Maria. When they started dating, he had no idea who she was. He thought she was just a girl who hung around the club. She seemed kind of old-fashioned compared to other girls, but that was all right, he liked old-fashioned girls.

He was a good cop, a brave cop. He was one of the most feared officers on the L.A.P.D. and also one of the most honest. He once gave a ticket to a hotshot movie producer. The guy crumpled the ticket and threw it in Jimmy's face. Jimmy jerked him out of the car, arrested him and had his Cadillac impounded. He was transferred to Watts afterwards.

Partly because of his father's bigotry, he never liked Negroes and working in Watts made him like them even less. They were all on drugs or booze, and didn't work while they let their women work or peddle ass in the street. He had no use for any of the bastards, and color didn't have much to do with it.

He and his partner answered a call, a report of a deadly assault. A crowd was gathering outside a housing project. Jimmy pulled out his big flashlight and unsnapped the holster of his Smith and Wesson Model 10 .38 Special revolver.

A hysterical Negro woman said to him, "There's a man in there cutting a woman and a little boy."

Jimmy went down the hallway with his partner following behind. There was an open door on their left with light streaming out and he could hear moaning. He stepped inside and almost tripped over two bodies lying just inside the door. One was a naked Negro woman of about thirty and a little Negro boy who couldn't have been more than nine.

Both were semiconscious and moaning, bleeding from razor cuts on their faces and bodies.

In the living room, Jimmy saw the man responsible. He knew him. He was "Tyrone the Bone" a notorious pimp, dope pusher and strong-arm artist. His eyes were popping from the drugs he'd taken, and the bloody razor was quivering in his hand.

"You think you can take me in, motherfucka?" Tyrone sneered.

Jimmy decided at that moment that he wasn't going to take Tyrone in. The sight of the little boy all cut up sickened him. But a crowd of people and his partner were behind him.

"Drop the knife, you're under arrest!" he said forcefully.

Tyrone laughed and held his knife up. "Shit, man you got to use your gun to arrest me," he said.

Jimmy drew his pistol lightning fast and shot Tyrone in the right leg. He dropped to his knees and looked at Jimmy with a surprised look on his face.

"Christ, man, you shot me," Tyrone said, genuinely surprised.

"That's what you wanted. Now drop the knife," Jimmy replied, moving in to handcuff him.

Tyrone slashed at Jimmy with the blade, and Jimmy smacked him in the head with the butt of his gun. Tyrone dropped the knife and fell forward. He tried to get up, but was a little unsteady. It was obvious he was helpless. So Jimmy's second blow was inexcusable, as the police departmental hearing and his criminal trial later proved with the help of testimony of witnesses and his partner.

Jimmy holstered his gun and switched the flashlight from his left hand to his right. With his right hand he brought the flashlight down on Tyrone's head in such a powerful blow that it shattered the glass of the light, the enamel shield and the bulb popped out and flew across the room. The heavy aluminum tube of the flashlight bent, and only the batteries inside prevented it from doubling on itself.

One awed onlooker, who lived in the tenement, and testified later, said, "Man, that's a hard-headed nigger."

But Tyrone's head was not quite hard enough. The blow had fractured his skull. He died two hours later at the hospital. Jimmy was the only person surprised when he was brought up on departmental charges of using excessive force. He was suspended and criminal charges were brought against him. He was indicted for manslaughter, convicted and sentenced to one to ten years in prison. He was so filled with a baffled rage and hatred of modern society that he couldn't see straight.

They judged me as a criminal? They sent me to prison for killing an animal like that murdering pimp nigger! They apparently didn't give two shits about the woman and little boy that got carved up, and also died in the emergency room.

He didn't fear jail. He felt that having been a cop and the nature of the offense, he would be left alone. Several of his fellow officers said they would speak to friends.

Only his girlfriend realized that a man like Jimmy Solano had little chance of surviving a year in prison. One of his fellow inmates might kill him. If not, he was almost certain to kill one of them. Maria petitioned her father to help, who at first refused. "I'm pregnant" was all she had to say to bring her father's full might to bear.

The Pistone family knew about Jimmy. He was a legend as a legitimately tough cop. He had made a reputation as a man not to be taken lightly, a man who could inspire fear from his own person, regardless of uniform and sanctioned gun he wore. Joseph Pistone was always interested in such men. The fact that he'd been a cop didn't mean anything. Many young men started down a false path to their true destiny. Time and fortune, or misfortune, usually set them right.

Thus, James Edward Solano was told that the judge had reconsidered his case on the basis of new information provided by high police officials. His sentence was suspended and he was released. Jimmy was brought to Pistone's lavish estate directly from jail. He was no fool. He knew something was up. By now, he knew of his paramour's lineage.

He was led into Pistone's office by two men, who stayed.

"You get my daughter pregnant, yet you've never come to this house or asked for her hand like a man. Why is that?" Pistone raged.

Maria wasn't pregnant, but Jimmy was smart enough to know her father thinking so was the only thing keeping him alive.

"She didn't want you to know she was dating a cop," Jimmy said flatly. "I gave in to her wishes of keeping our relationship a secret. She didn't think you'd understand."

"And you couldn't come to me like a man and tell me your intentions?" Pistone retorted.

"Let's be honest, sir. You'd have been open-minded and allowed your daughter to date a cop, that's what you're saying? Come on, I'm a little thick, but I'm not retarded," Jimmy said.

"How about I have my men here take you outside and beat you until you beg for death?" Pistone asked.

"Those two?" Jimmy said skeptically. "That would be a mistake."
"Why?"

"Because your daughter would lose a father rather than gain a husband."

Pistone laughed. "What do you want to do, now that you're out of jail and cleared of false charges?" he asked.

"I want to work for you, sir," Jimmy said, knowing he could never be a cop again and not wanting to be either.

"Good, good," Pistone said.

Jimmy and Maria were married a week later.

He was watched closely at first, since he had been a policeman, and was tested carefully. His natural ferocity overcame whatever apprehensions he may have had about being on the other side of the fence, and in less than a year he had "made his bones." He could never turn back. Maria gave birth to their first child ten months after the wedding.

Her father was delighted that it was a boy, which further cemented his position. He was given a high salary and the take of a particularly rich south side "book." He was happy to be among men who appreciated a job well done.

Over the years, Maria had told him how to manipulate her father and the Caporegimes. He listened and prospered. To outsiders, she was the dutiful little wife, but she was definitely the power behind the man. She had even said to Jimmy, "I'm not gonna be denied an empire because I wasn't born with a dick." Thus Jimmy became the new head of the family.

Tony Maretti, Jr. hated being chauffeured. He liked to drive himself. He loved his Cadillac. Most wiseguys had black Caddys or Lincolns, but Tony's was Sky Blue with a specially dyed blue leather interior. He liked it because it was distinctive, and kind of a girly color, but no one would ever dare say that, not even behind his back, on the rare chance that it might get back to him. The Caddy gave him such a quiet peaceful ride. Its upholstery was so rich that he sometimes sat in the car for an hour when the weather was nice as it was more pleasant than sitting in the house. Taking a ride in the car always helped him think.

He was thinking about going against his father and crushing the Pistone/Maranello alliance, or what was left of it anyway. Mario would back him, and maybe his father would finally retire and let him do what he was born to do. He would lead the family to unprecedented heights, especially with the plan Mario and the old man were working on. He didn't take a bodyguard because he didn't want to try to think while having to make small talk with a trusted employee. He felt safe enough, though.

He followed his father's advice. Tony Sr. always carried his own piece and advised his sons to do the same. In Sicily, and in America, he'd seen it too many times. The bosses thought themselves like royalty. A king didn't carry a gun. Often his bodyguards were bought off and turned on him, or conveniently were around the corner, or in the can when a hit went down, and the boss was helpless against his enemy's hitters. Three times in his life, twice in Sicily and once here in America, Tony, Sr. had escaped death because he carried his own piece, and shot the would-be assassins himself.

Tony, Jr. carried a Walther P-38 9mm semiautomatic pistol that one of his men had brought back from the war.

He liked it because it held nine rounds and had very little recoil. He could shoot straight if he didn't have to shoot too far, which was fine, as statistics showed that most gunfights occurred at a range of ten feet or less. He knew if there was a hit on him it would be up close and personal.

There was a beef on a construction site of a housing development in Vallejo. He told Mario that he'd handle it.

A trusted line boss had called him. As he came off the bridge and headed toward Vallejo, a small town named after the Mexican General Vallejo, that was between Oakland and

Napa, he saw flashing red lights in his mirror. A California Highway Patrol car. He looked at the speedometer. He was going eighty. The car was so damned smooth he'd thought he was going fifty or sixty. He pulled over.

The cop came up to the window, which he had rolled down. "Sir, you were speeding coming across the bridge," the officer said, politely enough.

Tony decided to be nice. "I'm sorry, I didn't realize
I was going that fast," he replied.

"Can I see you driver's license and registration, sir?"

"Sure," Tony said, starting to get pissed, but determined to keep his temper in check. *I will be nice, take the ticket and have this fuck busted out of his job later.* He gave the guy his license and registration.

"Could you step out of the car, sir?" the cop asked.

Tony got mad. "What the fuck for? Give me the ticket and let me go on my way. What the hell's wrong with you? Give me that!" he said, grabbing his license and registration out of the cop's hand. "Do you know who
I am?" he yelled angrily.

"Yes," the cop said. He drew his gun and shot Tony, Jr. five times in the head and chest.

Another Highway Patrol car came on the scene about twenty minutes later and called it in.

San Francisco Homicide detective Dave Walton was pissed. S.F.P.D. had received a call from the Vallejo Police requesting assistance on a possible homicide. He started toward Vallejo when he got called on the radio and told he was to pick up Captain Conway before going to the scene. Conway ran a precinct. Walton knew him and respected him. Conway was basically a good cop, a fair cop, with his men and people his men arrested. On the street he was a legend. He'd been in six gunfights and won them all, never once being hit himself. Pimps, strong-arm men and even wiseguys stepped aside when he walked down the street.

But the fact remained -- Conway ran a precinct. He'd risen from patrolman to sergeant to lieutenant, and from lieutenant to captain over his twenty-six-year career, but he was not a homicide detective. Conway had never tried to make detective or go into Internal Affairs, he was content to climb the ladder the hard way.

Walton pressed the dispatcher, who put his boss on the line. He was told the call came straight from the chief, who got a call from the commissioner, who got a call from the Lieutenant Governor.

This stinks. It stinks worse than cat piss three days old. Shit rolls downhill. Walton wondered as he drove. *What congressman's son had wrapped his car around a tree or hit a pedestrian, or maybe strangled some Mexican whore in Vallejo? And what the hell does Conway have to do with it?*

He picked up Conway at the precinct and neither spoke until they came upon the scene.

"Oh, fuck," Conway said as he saw the light blue Cadillac. He was out of Walton's unmarked before it was completely stopped.

Conway looked in the car and under the car. He picked up shell casings off the ground. He looked at them and then demanded an evidence bag from one of the Vallejo cops. He put the casings in the bag and handed them to Walton. He called over the young Highway Patrolman who found the car.

"You found this?" Conway asked.

"Yes, sir."

"You didn't touch anything?"

"No, sir. I called it in and waited for the city police and the coroner. The city police called San Francisco and told me to wait here. I called my boss and he said to cooperate with SFPD."

"Good," Conway replied. "I need you to drive me back to the city, red light and siren, as fast as we can go."

"Yes, sir," the young trooper said.

"What the fuck is going on here?" Walton asked Conway.

"I'm going back to the city. It's your case, do your job," Tom replied, and started to walk away.

"Come back here, Conway," Walton sneered.

Tom Conway was way more powerful, and his reflexes were way faster than any forty-seven-year-old man's should be. He quickly grabbed Walton with his left arm like he was putting his arm around him, while squeezing the man's balls with his right hand. Walton's knees buckled, but Tom held him up, while still crushing his balls. Walton moaned in pain.

"Who in the fuck do you think you're talkin' to, boy?" Tom said menacingly. "I'm glad your daddy was a district attorney and I'm glad you made detective before you were thirty. And I know you're an idealist, just like your daddy was, who enforced prohibition fiercely. My best friend got killed on a liquor raid in 1933 that your self-righteous, self-promoting daddy set up with another wanna-be politician who was at that time a cop. The next fucking day Congress repeals Prohibition...the next fucking day. My friend died for the law of the land, that wasn't a law twenty-four hours after he died. He wasn't even buried yet. You listenin' to me, boy?" Conway said, squeezing the kid's nuts harder.

"Yes," Walton grunted, almost passed out from the pain.

"Good. Now I'll give you some advice -- don't be an idealist. Ideals and realities are sometimes very far apart. If you don't see that, someone will point it out to you, clearly. You don't want to die for ideals. Now go back to work, and the next time I hear you snarl, 'Conway,' there better be 'Captain' or 'Mr.' in front of it. Do this one by the book like a random highway killing," Tom said as he released him.

Walton stumbled back over to the crime scene, his eyes the size of silver dollars.

After returning to the city, Tom Conway made a report, but not to the police department. He had the CHP drop him at the precinct and then he took his cruiser to the Maretti compound on Nob Hill. He hugged Tony, Sr. when he came in. Tony started crying. Tom did too.

"I'm so sorry, Godfather," he said, and they held each other for a long moment.

"Don't cry, son," Tony said, wiping Tom's face.

It took Tom a minute or two to compose himself. It was not a rogue cop paying respect to a crime boss. It was a hungry twelve-year-old boy seeing the only adult male who was ever nice to him in his young life, distraught. The "Godfather" could not be brought down by anything, he was omnipotent. But as Tom looked at him, he was not powerful and omnipotent like Hercules or Atlas, he was a sad old man who was hurting. Tom shivered at the thought.

Mario came over and hugged him. He was crying too, at his father's pain and at seeing a man who was a teenager, a bad-ass, a king in the neighborhood when he was in kindergarten, crying. As Tony had comforted Tom, so Tom comforted Mario.

"It's okay. We need to talk. Why don't you get us a drink," Tom said.

Even though he had a fearsome street reputation and was now acting head of arguably the most powerful crime family in the United States, Mario obeyed Tom. He went to the bar and fixed his father a glass of anisette, an Italian liquor. For himself he made a glass of scotch and Tom a glass of bourbon. In families, the older kids were always dominant over the younger kids, even in adult life. Psychiatrists call it "The big kid/little kid syndrome." The Mafia's use of the word "family" was more than an anomaly, especially to people who came from broken homes. One belonged to something, one was accepted, faults and all. Age and experience meant something. Mario served the drinks.

"What happened?" Tony asked.

"It was a hit, I'm sure of it," Tom replied. "I've seen plenty of murder scenes in my time. Tony, Jr. was laying on the seat with five slugs in him. His driver's license and registration were lying on the floor. Why would he have his driver's license and registration out unless he was showing it to a cop?"

"You're saying a cop killed my brother?" Mario asked.

"No. A hit man impersonating a cop that wanted to send a message. The uniform is the only way they'd get close enough to Tony. He was expecting a ticket, or worst-case scenario, a trip to the station house. Tony's gun was unfired, still in his shoulder holster. If he thought he was in danger he'd have went for his gun. He didn't think he was in danger."

"How do you know it's an imposter and not a real cop?" Tony asked.

"Cops carry .38 Specials, or in some cases a .357 Magnum, which is what I carry. Tony was shot with a .45 ACP. I found shell casings under the car. That says they wanted you to know."

Tony nodded.

"How can you be sure of that?" Mario asked.

Tom spoke again. "Do you know much about guns?"

"Enough," Mario replied.

"What do you know about the difference between revolvers and semiautomatic pistols?" Tom asked.

"When you fire an automatic, the cases are ejected," Mario replied.

"Exactly. A pro would pick up the casings, so there would be no evidence. Unless you wanted someone to know what was done."

"God damn," Mario said.

"Yeah," Tom replied, and continued speaking. "A real cop wouldn't get involved in the rackets to the extent of committing murder. He might go so far as to look the other way over a drug-related killing or a numbers beef. But to actually pull the trigger himself, on the son of a boss? No one who can pass a Civil Service test is that ambitious or that stupid. If he was, why not pour liquor on him or plant a gun in the car? This so-called cop didn't know he was packing. Why didn't he leave a drop gun there and call it in. Wiseguy doesn't want a ticket and does something stupid. Cop kills him. End of story. With Tony's temper, that would be good enough even for you. But the killers didn't want to get away with it, they wanted to send a message. They wanted you to know."

"My son was right, why didn't I listen to him?" Tony said. "Kill them all," he said, putting his head in his hands.

"Wait a minute, Pop, that's not the answer," Mario said.

"You don't want to avenge your brother?" Tony asked, incredulous.

"I do. In my own time, in spades," Mario replied.

"But think about this. We're the bankers. Back in 1938 when you came up with this idea everyone invested big, except Pistone and Maranello because they were pissed over the Dante business. We tell the other families of the country that any family who helps the Pistone/Maranello alliance will suddenly have a lot of tax trouble and the IRS and the Justice Department breathing down their necks, as the Feds will have very, very sensitive information. No one will help. Without outside help, they can't defeat us. This is almost 1950, Pop. Not 1898 Sicily. A gun isn't always the answer."

The Marettis had a private funeral service with immediate family members only -- i.e. Tony, Jr.'s wife

and kids, Mario and his wife and kids, the old man and their mother, their sister and her husband and kids, and Tony, Sr.'s mother-in-law. They didn't want to take a chance that a hit would be tried at a public funeral. Jimmy "The Gent" then struck in an unexpected direction.

Two powerful officials in the Teamsters Union were killed, officials who were members of the Maretti family. They were replaced with officials from Detroit. The Maretti family shylocks were then barred from the waterfront piers, as were the Maretti family bookmakers. The Longshoremen's Union's locals had apparently gone over. Their biggest numbers banker in Oakland was brutally murdered. Some Teamster-controlled unions even threw wildcat strikes on Maretti construction sites.

Still Mario waited and didn't retaliate. He was quietly planning and cementing things that needed to be done, then he'd deal with all the family's enemies. Then an old friend gave him the answer to the puzzle of who was helping Jimmy Solano.

Red was visited by two guys from Detroit who said they were now in charge of the Teamsters Union out there and wanted to ask him a favor. They came in the office with Blackie.

"We wanted to speak to you in private."

"I trust this man with my life, to ask him to leave would be an insult."

They wanted the Steelworkers Union to throw a major strike at all the construction projects in the Bay Area.

"The strikes you've been throwing are wildcat are in violation of your contract," Red replied. "Why in the hell would I join a wildcat strike and break our contract?"

"Because Mr. Hoffa would be very grateful and so would Mr. Dallessandro."

Red laughed. "Jimmy Hoffa doesn't run things out here and neither does Don Dallessandro. Get out of my office."

"You're making a mistake," the apparent leader said.

"If I'm gonna take a Mafia Don in as a partner, it'll be one I've known all my life and trust, not some asshole that's three thousand miles away. Now get the hell out of here. I'm not gonna tell you again."

They didn't move, until Red pulled his .45 and Blackie showed his brass knuckles, then they left quickly.

Mario had his fiercest executioner and four other guys grab the Detroit men. They were beaten within an inch of their lives and put on a plane to Detroit.

Jimmy Hoffa received a telegram from Red Sullivan. It read: "Why should two Irishmen who came up the hard way get involved in a quarrel between Sicilians? If you wish me to consider you a friend, then I owe you a favor which I will pay on demand. Surely a man like yourself understand how profitable it is to have powerful friends who handle their own problems and stand ready to help you in some future time of trouble. If you don't want my friendship, fine, but then I must tell you, as I told your representatives, if I ally myself to a Sicilian it will be one I've called my friend for over thirty years, not some Finocchio who makes threats from afar."

The arrogance of the message was calculated. Hoffa's star was definitely on the rise and no one doubted that he would one day be the Teamsters national president.

But to have national power, Jimmy couldn't afford to have enemies in powerful locales in big cities like San Francisco. Further, Dallessandro's influence, however terrible and pervading it might be, didn't extend beyond

Detroit, Pontiac, Lansing and a few other Michigan cities. Dallessandro's public arrogance and the flaunting of his criminal wealth had cost him any and all political influence. The Marettis, on the other hand, had powerful friends in New York and many other cities.

It worked, at least on Red's end. He received a wire from Detroit. It read: "I agree with you completely.

If you're ever in Detroit, you can expect the red carpet treatment, and I'll expect the same when I visit San Francisco. James R. Hoffa."

Mario had to punish Dallessandro. Mario had been

Tony, Jr.'s consigliere, as well as running the North Beach Enclave. Mario didn't have one. As he told the caporegimes, "If I ever need counsel, who's a better consigliere than my father?"

No one could argue with that. Tony, Sr. was a brilliant tactician. He made a phone call, and said to Mario, "It's handled."

"What did you do, Pop?"

"I did you a favor," Tony said, and then explained to his son what would happen. Mario was impressed.

"The threat of turning people over to the IRS and the Feds was good as a silky threat," Tony said. "It sent the message that you were deadly serious, and that families nationwide were either with you or against you. You had a nuclear bomb, like we used on Japan. Even if the whole country lined up against us, you could flush everyone's money and enterprises out of spite. The organization as we know it would cease to exist. We make everyone too much money for them to risk that over a piece of shit like Pistone or Maranello, especially since Maranello broke the peace first. So no one helped them, except this idiot from Detroit. He must be punished for defying your order. But if you turn him over to the Feds, you'll be a rat. Other families will think you might turn them over. Then the whole country would come after us and we'd be toast."

"But we warned everyone, Pop, he didn't heed that warning," Mario said.

"I know," Tony said patiently. "But there's a difference between a veiled threat and the action you take. You tell a man you'll kill his family if he doesn't do what you want, chances are he'll give in. But if you actually killed his family, you'd be ostracized for committing an *infamnita*, breaking the code. You have blackmail evidence on a senator. You threaten him with it. But if you went public, your other powerful friends in politics would run for cover, because they think you'd do the same thing to them. They'd rather believe you killed the guy than blackmailed him. The same thing here," Tony continued. "I called Don Genoa in New York. He's sending his best man to Detroit."

"One man?" Mario asked.

"This man is Dino's Rabbit, only worse. Two days of this man in Detroit and the lesson will be taught nationwide, without the families losing faith in our money management operation. Trust me."

"Okay, Pop, I hope you're right," Mario said.

"I am. It'll be wonderful," Tony said.

Into Don Dallessandro's most lucrative bookmaking operation in Detroit walked a single gunman. With a 1927A1 Thompson submachine gun he killed everyone in the place, save for one guy. The gunman told the survivor, "Tell Dallessandro I'm here. Tell him he knows why."

The same day, the mysterious gunman also took out several more bookmaking operations, two whorehouses, a nightclub and a used-car lot owned by Dallessandro's nephew, leaving the same message at each locale.

The second day, he started on the operations of the other five families in Michigan. He hit their richest operations and killed everyone except one or two witnesses who all told the same story. "He said, 'Tell Dallessandro I'm here. Tell him he knows why.'"

By day three, the five families of Michigan had demanded that the commission in New York investigate.

They wanted to know what the fuck was Dallessandro doing to bring hellfire and damnation down on their heads.

The commission got a telegram from Tony, Sr. that read: "Gentlemen. I'm sorry this had to happen. My son warned everyone about getting involved in California affairs. Dallessandro didn't listen. Surely the other families in Michigan knew what he was doing, or maybe at least had wind of it. Per our agreement, they should have alerted us to this. I advised my son to observe the code of Omerta, and not carry out his original threat, as that might undermine your confidence in us.

"As we promised, your money is safely held. But my son and I are businessmen, not martyrs. Bankers or not, as the old cliché goes, we walk softly and carry a big stick. Dallessandro felt the big stick. If the families of Michigan want to retaliate, we can continue this. Or it can end right here. I ask for your assistance in everyone's best interests. I am semi-retired and don't want to be involved in the day-to-day business. Mario is more levelheaded than this brother, but he's still headstrong. He doesn't always listen to counsel. Regards, Anthony Maretti."

The commission moved swiftly. Dallessandro was killed and his territory divided among his underbosses and enemies.

Tony's message was clear -- I am still a sleeping lion. Fuck with the lion, and die.

He had also brilliantly re-exerted Mario's earlier threat by playing exasperated father. He acknowledged that Tony, Jr. was unreasonable and subtly said about his younger son, "I personally wouldn't do this, but I can't guarantee the kid won't."

Tony was laying the groundwork in case anyone tried to call their bluff. Worst-case scenario: if one family, or several, lined up against the Marettis as threatened, they would have a world of trouble from the IRS and the Justice Department. If it happened, Tony could plead his case before the commission. "We warned these families. They didn't listen. Everyone else is still secure."

The point of the message was well taken by the other families in the country. No one was going to risk their fortunes because Jimmy Solano had more balls than brains. The commission washed their hands of the problem. No national retaliation was forthcoming.

San Francisco, 1950:

Internal Affairs was cracking down big-time on corruption. To prove he wasn't on the take, Tom Conway had to order his men to hit Maretti family operations.

He ordered the hits on the less important ones, who would drop the Maretti name when questioned, but wouldn't really hurt anything, streetwise. It worked for a while. It became apparent, however, that if he didn't deliver a big fish, his job was on the line and possibly be brought up on charges.

He knew Tom Franklin was a big player, and although he'd heard rumors that he might be going outlaw, or pledging allegiance to someone else, at the present time he was under Maretti protection.

Fucking up his illegal operations will satisfy the brass, and I will explain it to Mario and the old man. In business, sacrifices have to be made.

In one big sweep, most of Franklin's loansharking, betting and whoring operations were shut down. Of course the public didn't know it because Franklin had good lawyers and hid his illegal wealth well. Since Maretti had obviously abandoned him, Tom Franklin decided to take matters into his own hands. He'd teach the cop a lesson. He wanted Rabbit to do it, but Rabbit absolutely refused.

"I won't hurt a police officer who's just doin' right by his job," Rabbit said.

"Don't you want to work for me anymore?" Tom asked.

"I never worked for you. I worked for Hank," Rabbit replied.

"Hank's out of town," Tom said.

305

"Then you'll have to wait until he gets back. And I may not help Hank, if that's what you're thinking. I take my own chances and pay my own dues. Sorry," Rabbit said and left.

Tom asked Hank to do the job.

"I'll kick his ass and warn him. But that's as far as I'll go," Hank said. "If he has backup and I get arrested, I'll keep my mouth shut, but that's it. I told you when I took the job I didn't want to kill anyone, especially a cop."

"Just send the message," Tom said.

"A death threat is more powerful than you think, especially to a family man. I hear he has five kids. That's as far as I'll go," Hank said.

"Fine. Do it quick," Tom said.

Father Tim Conway was walking toward his brother's house. He needed to see his sister-in-law about her youngest daughter's upcoming first communion. He wasn't wearing his collar because he'd just returned from a Catholic Youth League basketball game. He coached of one of the teams and felt good because his team had won an exciting, close game. On the sidelines one would think they were watching Red Auerbach, not a priest.

He saw a guy in a suit coming toward him. Tim still had his old street instincts, but in the neighborhood the chances of being mugged or strong-armed were pretty slim. Then the guy attacked him.

Hank sat in his car on Fairmont Street, waiting. It was a nice upscale family neighborhood, but not overly pretentious. Typical of where a rogue cop would live. He wouldn't want to have his kids go to school or live in the crappy neighborhood where he worked, but if he went really uptown, people would wonder how he could afford it.

Hank had a picture of the guy and his address. He was just about to give up and try again the next night when he saw the guy walking towards the house in street clothes.

He got out of the car and crossed the street. The guy nodded at him before Hank threw him into a parked car, and began hitting him. The guy tried to fight back.

Hank was actually disappointed. The guy had an awesome reputation, yet he couldn't fight worth a shit, although he was tough enough to keep trying.

Suddenly, Hank was forcibly turned around and a sledgehammer of a left smashed into his face. His knees buckled, but he didn't fall down. Hank countered with a howitzer left of his own, but the guy slipped it and smacked Hank flush on the jaw with a textbook straight right.

Hank reeled sideways, away from the car, and saw a red-haired guy a little smaller than him in his forties bouncing in textbook boxing stance. The guy came forward. He jabbed Hank's nose with his left, but Hank grabbed him and pulled him toward him, then roughly shoved the guy away, while laying a thunderbolt of a right square on the jaw.

Hank knew it was over. The guy fell down, but much to Hank's surprise, he got up and re-engaged. The guy obviously knew boxing, which was why Hank was having such a hard time. He'd hit quickly and with such force that it seemed like his fist was a portable typewriter that he'd swung three times around and then he'd dance away. Hank had never been hit that hard before. It unnerved him as he could usually laugh off anyone's punches and deliver more in return.

If I'm not careful, this guy is going to kick my ass. Fuck careful!

Hank waded in with both cannons roaring, taking three to land one, but doing some damage of his own with his heavy punches. They were both bleeding from the nose and mouth. The smaller, older man was starting to get a little winded, but showed no sign of quitting.

The guy Hank had attacked was up and trying to separate them. "Stop it, both of you!" he yelled.

"Tough motherfucker are you? Attacking a priest," the fighter said, with disgust in his voice.

"Priest?" Hank said, incredulous. "He's a piece of shit dirty cop."

"Ah," the first guy said. "You'd be looking for my brother."

"You're really a priest?" Hank asked.

"That I am," Tim said. "And my brother is at least half of what you think he is."

"I'm sorry, Father," Hank said. "Regardless of my current profession, I was raised in the Baptist church, and I'd never knowingly attack a man of the cloth of any denomination."

"I'm glad you retained some of your upbringing," the priest said.

"Never mind that!" the red-haired guy yelled. "Go in the house, Tim. Why are you trying to attack a police captain then?"

"And I should tell you my business why?" Hank asked.

The guy put up his fists and spoke in a serious tone of voice. "Because if you don't, you and I are goin' again, right here, right now."

Hank looked at the guy and realized he had never seen such force in one man, maybe not even Rabbit. Rabbit had ferocity and training, but for sheer force of will, the guy facing him was in a class by himself. So was Hank and he didn't want to back down, although he didn't particularly want to fight the bastard again.

Hank pulled his coat back, showing the Browning on his hip. The guy did the same, showing a Colt .45.

"I don't want to kill you," Hank said.

"And I don't want to kill you. What's that got to do with anything?" the guy asked. They looked at each other for a long moment and the guy spoke again. "If we're not gonna draw, then we might as will have a beer and talk this out."

Hank chuckled nervously. "Fair enough," he replied.

"I'd like to know who just kicked my ass though."

"Red Sullivan," the guy replied, extending his hand.

Hank shook it. "I'm Hank Collins."

"I've heard of you," they both said, almost in unison, and they laughed a little at the same time.

"Well, Red, you are one fightin' son-of-a-bitch," Hank said admiringly.

"So are you," Red replied. "Meet me at Murphy's. You know where it's at?"

"I do," Hank replied.

"I'll see you in ten minutes."

"Why were you going after Captain Conway, death wishes aside?" Red said.

"What do you mean?" Hank asked.

"You're lucky you got the wrong guy," Red replied. "Tom can fight almost as good as I can. But he's bigger than me and you both, and he has twenty-five years of copness behind him. He will win. He has the legal authority to win at all cost and he doesn't fuck around. He's a family man. He's not going to leave his wife a widow and his kids half-orphans because some asshole doesn't want to be arrested or won't drop a gun or knife. He'd have blown your brains out and not lost a minute's sleep. For who?"

"Jesus Christ," Hank said.

"I doubt you're working for him," Red quipped.

Hank had to laugh. "I work for Tom Franklin," Hank said.

"Oh, shit!" Red replied. "Why in the fuck would he send someone after Conway?"

"Conway closed down all our operations."

"I can't believe Mario allowed this," Red said, disgusted.

"Mario knows nothing about it," Hank said.

Red looked surprised. Hank relished the chance to one-up and impress the guy. "I've done freelance work for Mario before. I deal direct with him, no middlemen, for security reasons. Maretti family security reasons, which included a loyal police contract. Why would this happen?" Red asked, bewildered.

Hank hesitated.

"Hank, do you have family here?" Red asked. Hank didn't answer. "You do," Red said. "I can tell by the look on your face. Why would you risk them for some dumb-ass scheme that Tom Franklin came up with? I don't want to insult you, it's impressive that you can meet with Mario Maretti one-on-one at Louie's, or wherever else they tell you. Not many people can say that. But I can meet with Tony, Sr. in private, in his home. In his home where his wife sleeps and his grandchildren come to play with their toys. My word, and my word alone, kept Franklin from getting whacked in 1938, although he doesn't know that. It served my interests as well. I can't help you if I don't know what the problem is. Let me help you, Hank, and let me help Tom too, although he might not agree."

Hank thought hard. Red ordered another round while he did so. *Tom Franklin will not die or go to prison for Hank Collins. That is an irrefutable fact. Therefore Hank Collins should not die or go to prison for Tom Franklin.*

fckb.

Hank spoke, "Some guys from Detroit come out here, kick some ass, and say that they're taking over the Teamsters out here. At first we rebuffed them. Rabbit stomped on five of their hitters. You know Rabbit?" Hank asked.

"I've heard of him, through Mario, Rocco and Sonny," Red replied. "I wouldn't want to go against him unless I absolutely had to."

Hank nodded approvingly and spoke again, "They promise Tom that he'll be as big as Jimmy Hoffa, maybe bigger. Tom says he'll think about it. Then Conway hits us hard. Tom thinks the Marettis have abandoned him. If we don't have Maretti protection, we don't owe them any allegiance or their police contacts. Tom thought he could scare Conway into backing off. I'm his scariest guy, because Rabbit's unpredictable."

"Tom Franklin is never gonna be 'the man,'" Red said. "Not with the mob, because he's not Italian. Not with the press or the American public because he's an asshole.

I agree with his beliefs that politics, religion, etc. don't matter in labor disputes. But ideals and realities are sometimes far apart. If he'd declared himself a Christian and denied that he was a communist, he'd be the International President of the Longshoreman's Union right now, with power that Jimmy Hoffa only dreams about.

"But he's not only an asshole, he's arrogant. And an alien and an accused commie. An alien and an accused commie is never going to be a national anything. He's gone as far as he's going to go. He thought the Marettis disrespected him by letting Tom hit his operations? Tom made that decision in his office. I know that only because I know how Tom Conway thinks. IAD is on his ass. He's gonna lose his pension if he doesn't deliver a big-time bust that has the Maretti name on it. He delivers Franklin's operations, because Franklin's guys are so dumb they think the Maretti name can get them a walk. When the brass sees the scope of Franklin's operations they think they've hit the mother lode and get off Conway's ass. Conway explains it to Mario and the old man, who explain it to Tom, and there's no problem."

"In theory," Hank said.

"But Franklin can't wait, or think for one second, and makes a bunch of dumb moves that will not only get him killed, but other people as well. If I didn't know better, I'd swear he was French," Red said.

"Why French?" Hank asked, having been there.

"Because every Frenchmen I ever met was fucked up.

They fight with their feet, they fuck with their mouths and they think with their balls."

Hank laughed outloud.

"Where can I meet with you and Franklin without throwing up a red flag?" Red asked.

"Jerry's on Sixteenth street. Rabbit's uncle owns it, and I used to work there. Tom still drinks there."

"Tomorrow at lunchtime," Red said.

"Okay," Hank said.

Tom Conway was having a late-night snack and talking to his brother. Tim was concerned.

"This guy was coming to kill you," he said.

"No, he wasn't," Tom replied flatly, while taking another bite of his sandwich.

"How can you be so sure?" Tim asked.

"Because you're alive. Think, big brother," Tom said.

Tim was only eleven months older, though Tom was actually the bigger of the two. Tom always called Tim "big brother" when he wanted to irritate him, and it usually worked.

"He thought you were me. If he was supposed to kill me, he'd have blown your brains out. He just wanted to send me a message, kick my ass, threaten my family, whatever. It's not the first time some asshole has come after me."

The phone rang. Tom picked it up on the first ring because he didn't want it to wake his wife and kids.

"Conway," he said into the receiver. "Is it important? Okay, I'll be there. Yeah, for chrissakes, you can count on it. Let me give it to you in Quaker -- fucketh thou." Tom hung up and sat down and bit into his sandwich again.

"Who was that?" Tim asked.

"Red," Tom replied. "He wants me present at a lunchtime meeting tomorrow. Apparently something big is goin' down."

"Is it wise to be meeting with Red and other people with underworld connections right now?" Tim asked.

311

"You mean confidential informants?" Tom replied, correcting him. "The word on the street is gold is preventing and solving crimes. Brass won't have a problem with that. Besides, Red is my oldest, best friend. If he says he needs me, I'm there. And he's there for me. If I called him right now and said I needed a favor, you know what he say, 'A borrow my car kind of favor, or dump a body kind of favor?'"

Tim laughed.

"Go ahead, laugh, but either way, he'd do it. That's the power of friendship. All you know is the church, I don't expect you to understand."

"You're not the least bit worried about losing your job are you?" Tim said.

"No."

"Is Red gonna take care of you if you do?"

"Yes."

Tim threw up his hands and shook his head in disgust.

"Okay, I'm confessing to my brother the priest now. That means the Supreme Court can't even order you to tell what I said."

"I know. I've took your confessions."

"If by some amazing convergence of circumstance I was brought up on departmental and criminal charges of corruption, here's what I'd do. I'd be represented by a lawyer, an expensive lawyer. Not the police union rep who wants to protect the department's reputation. My lawyer dangles a deal to the department and the police union.

The D.A. is offering me immunity from prosecution if I give up other dirty cops and corrupt officials. Let me do my last three years on a desk, or retire early with full benefits because of medical reasons, and I won't tell the District Attorney about who's on the list of weekly payoffs that comes from the Marettis and other families. I won't tell about captains and lieutenants pulling the yellow sheet on assholes before they go to court."

"What's a yellow sheet?" Tim asked.

"A guy's criminal record is printed on a yellow piece of paper and updated every time he gets arrested," Tom replied and continued. "Guy has a long yellow sheet, he gets fucked -- maximum penalties, no matter what. If there's no yellow sheet, the judge thinks the guy's a first-time offender and may give him a light sentence, especially if the guy has a good lawyer. Yellow sheets have been pulled on stone-fucking killers and the judges knew it, but played along anyway. I won't say which judges are on mob payrolls, or that the corruption goes all the way to the chief's office. You bet your ass the department will deal, and deal quick. This is one battle they don't want fought in the press.

"Worst-case scenario, if I actually have to go to trial, my lawyer demands a mistrial on the basis that the judge hearing the case is on the list, even if he's not, and is making me a sacrificial lamb. If the judge won't grant a mistrial, my lawyer demands the judge recuse himself because he can't be impartial in judging the case. If that's denied, we go to trial. And we will win, or it will be dropped.

"Internal Affairs is just like a street shylock or loan shark. Ninety-nine percent of their victims don't fight back. The threat of a ruined career or lost pension is usually enough to make most guys rat out their own mother. They hate guys like me with balls, who dare them to do their worst. If I say, 'Fuck you, try to mess with me at trial,' it gets ugly for them. I'm innocent until proven guilty... beyond a reasonable doubt.

"If they lose, it makes it harder for them next time.

Maybe the next cop they decide to fuck over decided to fight back, because I won. Maybe a D.A. won't file corruption charges for them. He'll say, 'Remember what happened last time? I'm not going through that again to have egg on my face.' The department can't afford the bad press. IAD thinks they've got me by the balls, but in reality, I've got them. I would rat out the whole department all the way to the commissioner to get immunity and save my neck. People who know me will tell the prosecutors that. Cops have a code of silence just like the mob does. I adhere to that code to cover my ass and the department's, and my brother officers. If my brother officers and the department abandon me, then I'm not obligated to stay silent. The department and the District Attorney cannot afford the scandal this will bring. I win because I'm willing to go all the way. I will ruin fifty lives to save my own. The D.A., the Attorney General and the Governor are not willing to destroy fifty careers and put the police department of a major city into a shambles because one captain looked the other way over numbers and whores.

"It's all about what you are willing to do," Tom continued. "My first partner, McCluskey, taught me that. During Prohibition we had to raid bootleggers. One of them found out where McCluskey's kids went to school and threatened them. The next day, the bootlegger and his girlfriend are found in the bay with their heads blown off. No one ever threatened a cop's family after that. John told me the next day that he did it, and he said I could turn him in if I wanted to. He said he didn't care, because his family was safe. He was willing to do anything to keep his family safe, even if it meant going to prison and losing his job. He was willing to do what was necessary. Half of winning any fight is being willing to do what's necessary. Obviously I didn't turn him in. The brass is not willing to do what's necessary -- which is bring the whole department down with me. I'm clear."

"Do you have anything else to confess?" Tim said sarcastically.

"I'm a married man, what else would I have to confess?" Tom replied, just as sarcastically.

Tim shook his head. "If you really want to do a confession, I'm here for you," he said.

"Big brother, my soul is what I've already made of it," Tom replied. "You judge me for decisions I made with a gun barrel in my face. I'll make my peace with God when the time comes. I don't need my brother or anyone else as an intermediary."

"That I won't argue," Tim said. "God forgives whether or not you have counsel present. I'm not worried about your eternal soul, I'm worried about you, my brother."

"Why?" Tom asked.

"Because we're family," Tim replied. "I have five beautiful kids, I love them. They're yours, but I still love them. A beautiful woman cooks me dinner every Sunday. She's your wife, but I love her. I have the church, but because of you, I also have a real life. If you get killed, it's not just the end of you, it's the end of us. Before you had the police department and before I had the church, there was always us. I can't live my life without us."

Tom was moved. He stood up and went over and hugged his brother. "Thank you," he said. "That's one more reason why some skell is not gonna get the better of me. Or some snot-nosed Assistant District Attorney. I've asked myself many times, 'What if this is all there is?' What if Darwin was right and we are all animals? What if the decisions we make here don't echo in eternity? What if the decisions we make only impact the now? What should we do? We should protect ourselves and the ones we love. I'm doing that to the best of my ability. And church or not, I know you always have too," Tom finished.

"True enough," Tim replied. "How 'bout a drink for a thirsty padre before he goes home?"

"Help yourself," Tom said, chuckling.

Tim liked Jameson 1780 Irish whiskey, but couldn't afford it and wouldn't have it in the rectory if he could. However, he felt free to down a few whenever he visited Tom's house, which was often.

"You can have that bottle if you want," Tom said.

"I'll store it here," Tim replied.

"Why?"

"Because I'm not supplying the altar boys with Jameson. They steal enough wine as it is."

Tom laughed heartily.

The rear part of Jerry's Bar had been commandeered for a special meeting. In attendance were Hank Collins, Rabbit, Tom Conway, Tom Franklin, Red Sullivan, Blackie Wilson and Mario Maretti and his father. Klein's Deli had sent over sandwiches and, of course, the bar had plenty of beer, wine, whiskey or soda if anyone wanted it.

Tom Franklin was nervous. Everyone was pissed at him. He recalled a joke that a comedian from New York had told about his ownership of a club in Harlem and the lawsuit that ensued the New Year's Eve riot. "Fifty niggers fighting fifty white guys and everybody sues me." Tom knew he had to take his lumps or get whacked. He'd take it, but he didn't have to like it.

Tom Conway was first. "I'm at the precinct five days a week. I eat lunch at Mike's Coffee Shop every day. I go to the shooting range twice a week. I go to Murphy's Gym twice a week. I'm not a hard man to find. Yet you send a man to do me ugly at my house? Possibly in front of my wife and children? What's wrong with you? If your man had got me instead of my brother, he'd probably be dead. I'm not pissed that you sent someone to send me a message. People threaten me all the time, that's part of the job. I'm pissed that you put me in a compromising situation. What if your man and I really get into it, seriously? I am not gonna die in my own front yard. Where does that leave me? I want to smoke some fool in front of my house? That'll help me with IAD for sure. What's wrong with you?" Tom said for the second time. "If you had a problem you should have come to me with it, reasonably."

Mario Maretti spoke. "I know you thought you were abandoned by the family. Things are being negotiated now that are so sensitive that I can't meddle in local affairs. I don't fault you for being upset, but I wish you'd waited or acted more responsibly."

Tony, Sr. spoke. "I am semi-retired. That means I don't want to hear about every single day-to-day beef in every operation. On the other hand, I still want to know what's going on. If you thought you were being slighted, you should have come to me and asked for an explanation. My son is too polite. The rule is: you go against the family, you die.

I was going to tell you to go to hell. And believe me, when

I say that, that's where people go. But because of your position in the unions and the havoc your death would cause, killing you would be more expensive than negotiating with you. I'm a businessman and I always look at profits and losses. But don't push it. Sometimes I'm willing to take an acceptable loss."

Tom Franklin started to speak, but Tony cut him off. "Don't insult me or anyone else here. We all know the score. Let's not relive it or debate it. I'm sure everyone here has ideas. Let's hear them all."

Tom Franklin knew when to shut up.

Mario spoke again. "The Maretti family is moving into Nevada almost whole-heartedly. Legalizing gambling is the way of the future and we want to be on the ground floor.

Our friends that invest with us will do extremely well. There will be plenty of points to give out."

Hank spoke up. "I heard they're building ten hotel-casinos in Vegas and three in the Reno-Tahoe area. The market may be glutted, you may be too late with all that competition already there."

"The Maretti family is financing three of the hotels being built in Vegas," Mario said.

Hank and everyone else knew that meant the Marettis owned them and, as promised, there would be plenty of points to give out.

"I'm going to Reno next week, with my father," Mario said. "If the Longshoreman's Union and the Steelworkers Union want to invest in the Reno-Tahoe area, we would be glad to partner with them."

"I'll invest in exchange for interest and points," Red said.

"So will I," Tom Franklin said.

Tony, Sr. spoke again. "First, you'll tell Solano's people that you changed your mind and you want to continue running the Longshoreman's Union here in San Francisco."

"I never told Solano...," Tom started, but Tony cut him off.

"Don't insult my intelligence with bullshit. We're suddenly kicked off the docks, and Hank goes after Captain Conway? You thought you didn't need us anymore, that if your new friends took over, you'd be national with the Teamsters. Hoffa is gonna be their next national president. You're an accused commie."

Tom started to speak, but Tony dismissed his protest with a wave of his hand. "Don't protest. I don't care if you're a fuckin' communist, an atheist and a vegetarian as long as you don't cause me trouble. But in the current political climate you have to be a flag-waving Christian, or at least say you're one to get anywhere politically. You're never gonna be a national anything."

Hank stifled a laugh, remembering that Red Sullivan had told him the same thing.

"And you're causing me trouble. Now cut off negotiations with Solano completely."

"Yes, sir."

"I think some men from the North Beach are gonna need union jobs too," Mario said.

Franklin said, "Done."

Everyone nodded in agreement, knowing that Mario meant

Solano's moles wouldn't go quietly and some extra muscle might be needed.

"I could make sure there was extra police presence on the Embarcadero," Conway said.

"That's a good idea," Mario said. "Thanks.

"I want Hank to come with me and my father."

"Hank can come with me," Tom Franklin said.

"You're not coming," Mario replied. "You need to stay here and handle this Solano business. It would be uglier if you were out of town after breaking the news to them. They'd think you were scared and might pull something."

"Then I'll need Hank around," Tom said.

"It's not negotiable," Mario replied. "Rabbit, I want you to do some work for me while I'm gone."

Hey...," Franklin started to protest.

Mario said, "I'm not asking you, I'm asking him."

"I don't work for him," Rabbit said, pointing to Franklin. "I freelanced and helped Hank out, but I don't work for anybody. I'm a free man."

"Will you do some work for me, freelance?" Mario asked.

Blackie looked at Red, bewildered at the respect being shown the hillbilly. Red made a "don't ask" motion with his hand. He'd heard about Rabbit from Hank, and knew he had to be approached a certain way to get him to do anything. Mario was becoming every bit the artful negotiator his father was.

"I could do that," Rabbit said.

"Good. I want you to coordinate my men, like a military security operation around the docks," Mario said.

He continued for everyone's benefit. "Rabbit and my men can handle anything that happens, and if they can't, then we couldn't have stopped them anyway. Hank can give you details when he gets back. It's a preliminary, sort of 'If-I-could-would-you' type of meeting. Nothing's set in stone yet. I want a security man, but I don't even want our own people getting wind of this until it's a done deal. And any information about this meeting better not leak out."

"I should be going to the meeting. I don't like this at all," Franklin said.

Mario exploded. "I don't give a fuck what you like or don't like! Do you have any idea how close you were and are to being whacked. Do you think these fuckin' mercenaries are gonna protect you?"

"Are you threatening me?" Franklin asked.

Mario stood and knocked Franklin off his chair. At thirty-five, Mario was six feet tall, 180 pounds, lean and hard, his muscles forged from working construction in years past. Although his brother had the greater reputation, insiders always said Mario was the tougher of the two, both physically and mentally. When Franklin tried to get up, Mario kicked him in the ass, causing him to fall forward toward the bar.

What happened next was sickening. Tom tried to hang onto the brass railing on bottom of the bar. Mario tried to drag him away. His shirt ripped off in Mario's hands. Mario began beating and cursing him in a rage-choked vice. Tom Franklin, despite his size and strength, offered no resistance or cry for mercy or protest.

Hank and Rabbit dared not interfere. They thought Mario intended to kill him and had no interest in sharing his fate. Tom Conway and Red were stone-faced. Blackie was aghast. Tony Maretti shook his head in disgust.

What was sickening was Franklin's complete submission, but that probably saved his life. He didn't fight back despite the flurry of heavy blows being rained on him.

Finally, his chest heaving, Mario growled, "If I even think you're fuckin' with me, you're dead! Your family's dead! Your fuckin' house is burned to the ground! You fucking arrogant asshole!" The words released the tension in the room.

If Mario had intended to kill Franklin, he never would have uttered the threat. He uttered it in frustration because he could not carry it out. He knew his father was right, that killing Franklin would be bad for business, but the man's arrogance and obliviousness to the situation had just set him off. Mario had to kick his ass or implode from rage.

"What's the matter with you?" Tony asked as Mario sat down. "You dropped to his level. Never let your emotions show when negotiating business...never. What do you think these gentlemen think of you now?" Tony said, admonishing Mario as if he were nine years old.

"I think he made his point," Blackie said.

"So do I," Hank said.

"Me too," Rabbit said.

Tony looked at Red. "I think Franklin understands now," Red said.

"That's not the point," Tony replied.

"I got you, Pop," Mario said. "Sorry." Acting as if nothing unusual had happened, he then turned to Red and spoke. "It works like this, Red. The union makes the loan to help finance the hotel-casino. Instead of charging interest, you get points in the hotel. Business increases, the vig goes up. If the hotel goes belly up, which it won't, you write off the loans as losses. You can't lose. Have Blackie run the union while you come with us. Maybe bring Eddie with you, if he still has financial interest. Be at our place at eight a.m. sharp tomorrow. You too, Hank," Mario finished and got up to leave.

Tony, Sr. left with Mario, still telling him off about his outburst. A barmaid helped Tom Franklin to the bathroom to clean up.

"I'll see you when I get back from Reno," Hank told Tom and then left.

Rabbit went to his room in the back to prepared for a busy day tomorrow.

Reno, Nevada, 1950:

The drive from San Francisco to Reno was made in Hank Collins' new Lincoln. Tony Maretti rode in front with Hank, who drove, and Mario was in the back with Red and Eddie Coyle.

Since Mario had mentioned it, Red invited Eddie even though he was retired from union business. Eddie agreed, happy to have a couple days away from the baseball team and the opportunity to drink and gamble without his wife and grandkids. He was also considering investing personal money in the venture, and talked at length with Tony and Mario about how hosting professional boxing matches that could draw more gamblers to the casinos. Both boxing fans and good businessmen, the Marettis were interested.

"Whether you invest or not, I'll give you some points in one of the hotels if you'll work as a consultant. If for example Sugar Ray Robinson or Rocky Grazino or Jake LaMotta appeared on a fight card, that would certainly draw some high-rollers," Mario said. "Your contacts in the boxing world will be valuable. Also, maybe you could convince some of the Seal players to appear at the casinos during the World Series to sign autographs and speak to fans. All the casinos will have bars with games on TV or radio. We'll pay the players well for their trouble. Any help you could give us would be greatly appreciated. But if you're not interested, there's no problem."

"I'm interested," Eddie said. "I like a challenge. We'll see what happens."

"Fair enough," Mario relied and dropped the subject.

Edwin James Fitzpatrick was fifty-two years old. He'd worked for Meyer Lansky in New York and came out to Nevada when Bugsy Siegel and Moe Gronevelt had decided to build an empire in the desert at what used to be a stopover for GI's on the way to the West Coast. He ran the hotels and they flourished, but he was tired of working for others who didn't appreciate his genius. He knew he could do better and be swankier if he had the finances. In the Maretti family and their friends, he found willing investors. His club was small but nice and he did well with the motel he owned next door. But he had a vision. A vision that was sure to make him rich beyond his wildest dreams.

Fitzpatrick greeted everyone in one of his casino bars. A cocktail waitress in scanty nightclub costume came over.

"Drinks on the house for my friends," Fitzpatrick said.

"Yes, sir," the girl replied, smiling at Hank, who was the youngest and biggest of the group.

The waitress was a very beautiful girl, but Hank could see that she was all cold hustle, though she worked at it. She took their order and brought the drinks back, and served Hank last, leaning over him and putting her hand on his shoulder.

Hank gave her a five-spot and said, "Thank you, darlin'."

She parted her lips in a thank-you smile, her eyes went all smoky, her body tensed with the torso leaning back from the long legs in their fishnet stockings and high heels. A tension seemed to be building up in her body and her breasts seemed to grow fuller and strain against her low-cut blouse. Her whole body then gave a slight quiver. It gave the impression of a woman having an orgasm simply because Hank had smiled and said, "Thank you, darlin'."

It was very well done. It was done better than Hank had ever seen it done before, but by now he knew it was fake. And the odds were good that the ones who promised the most, delivered the least. She was probably a lousy lay.

"I'm glad you gentlemen could make it," Fitzpatrick said. "I have a lot to show you tomorrow. I have rooms for everyone reserved in the motor lodge."

"Which is so much classier than a motel," Eddie quipped. Everyone, including Fitzpatrick, laughed.

"Terminology is important my friends," Fitzpatrick said, addressing Eddie and everyone else as well. "Our rooms are not cheap, they're less expensive. Drinks for players are not free, they're complimentary. High rollers don't run up a tab, they have a line of credit. The terminology your employees use can inspire confidence in the consumer."

"Perception is everything," Mario said, quoting his father as Fitzpatrick nodded his approval, "more in this business than any other. I'm glad you understand that. I know you've had a long drive, let's talk business tomorrow."

A minor commotion started at a blackjack table when the waitress brought another round of drinks.

A big man in a white Stetson hat was arguing with the pit boss. On his lap, obviously not too happy, was a pretty cocktail waitress, dressed identically to the one serving the drinks to Hank's party. Hank could see the cowboy's left hand dug talon-like into her left breast.

"Who's that?" Hank asked the waitress as she set his drink down.

The waitress put her hands on Hank's shoulders and leaned down to whisper in his ear. "That's Big John Nelson. Has a ranch in Idaho with a government milk contract. Comes in twice a month and drops at least ten grand each time. But he's always trying to stick his hands up the girls' dresses. I'll tell you a secret. The way he throws hundred dollar chips at girls, I'd let him stick his hand up my ass."

"I may want to do that later," Hank said, and the girl grinned. "If that's the lay of the land...what's her problem?" Hank asked.

"Not everyone is as open-minded as me. If you don't like guys hitting on you, then you shouldn't take the job," the girl continued. "On the other hand, these bastards could keep their hands to themselves and show a tiny bit of respect."

"Excuse me," Hank said and walked toward the blackjack pit.

He grabbed Big Jim by his collar and flung him to the floor, while grabbing the girl by the arm and spinning her away. Big Jim was up quickly, his mouth on automatic. Hank shoved the waitress up against another blackjack table and began yelling at her. "You little whore! I knew you couldn't make that kind of money just serving drinks."

"Hey, partner...the little lady...."

"Happens to be my wife!" Hank growled. "You got a problem with a man arguing with his wife? Go home, you little slut. We'll talk later," Hank said to the girl, who by now had caught the drift and was looking at Hank in awe and admiration, but at the same time playing the poor little waif who married an overbearing lout.

"I didn't know she was married," Big Jim said. "It wasn't her fault, I was just foolin' around. Don't be mad at her, partner."

Hank acted as if his rage was ebbing. "You should keep your hands to yourself," he said.

"I will in the future," Big Jim said as he sat back down at the table. "Sorry 'bout that, George," he said to the pit boss.

"No problem, sir," George replied, waving at Fitzpatrick.

Hank came back to the table and Fitzpatrick put his arm around him. "What's your name?"

"Hank Collins."

"Well, Hank, that was masterful," Fitzpatrick said. "You taught him to keep his hands off the girls, but he's still gonna gamble here. I've been trying to figure out how to do that for a year. I've lost count of the waitresses that have quit because of guys like him. I could use a man like you to run my security teams. If you ever get tired of the city, you're welcome here."

"I'll keep that in mind, sir, thank you," Hank replied.

"Here's a story you'll like," Fitzpatrick said. "When I worked in Vegas, I had a guy we called Jumbo. He was about two hundred seventy pounds and not very fat. We had a regular who was okay until he got drunk, and then he'd get belligerent with dealers and customers alike. Jumbo escorts him out the back door. Two minutes later, he's in there again. Jumbo escorts him out the front door. Two minutes later, he's back again. Now Jumbo throws his ass out the side door. The guy stands up and asks, dead serious, 'Jesus, Jumbo, do you work at every club in town?'" Everyone laughed uproariously. "We'll talk business tomorrow. Get some rest, gentlemen."

"In the motor lodge," said Eddie.

Fitzpatrick grinned and shook his finger at Eddie, then walked off.

Everyone left to check into the motor lodge. Hank came back for one more drink and to give the waitress who'd flirted with him so brazenly his room number.

It was after midnight when the girl knocked on Hank's door.

"Come on in," Hank said.

The girl hesitated. "I don't really know how to say this," the girl started.

"I'll help you," Hank said. "How much?"

The girl began to act appalled, but Hank cut her off. "I'm a pro, honey, and I think you are. Save me the act that you give salesmen from Utah. How much?"

"Two hundred," the girl said.

"A hundred and twenty-five," Hank replied.

"I'm not staying the night."

"You're right, you're not," Hank replied.

The girl walked in and unceremoniously took her clothes off. Hank was impressed.

At four o'clock in the morning, when the girl left, Hank saw Mario Maretti in the hall of the motel.

"Was that expensive?" Mario asked.

"Not really, if you're talking value per dollar.

I got my money's worth," Hank said casually.

"I figured you did."

"We know why I'm up, why are you?" Hank asked.

"I can never sleep when I'm negotiating a big deal," Mario said.

"I couldn't sleep in the field early in the war," Hank replied. "Lieutenant Taylor helped me with that. He said, 'Son, when you go into battle, either you're gonna die or you're not. You're more likely to die if you're careless from lack of sleep. Always sleep and always eat. No matter the situation, if you're tired and hungry, you make the wrong decision.' That helped me get through the war."

"Thanks. You want a cup of coffee?" Mario said.

"Sure," Hank replied and they went to the casino's 24-hour coffee shop.

Breakfast was held at "Bill and Effie's" outside of town. Bill and Effie's was a truck stop/coffee ship on U.S. 40. Everyone ordered in the order that they were seated. Hank ordered ham and eggs with a side of biscuits and gravy.

"I'll have what he's having," Mario Maretti said to the waitress. Hank looked at Mario quizzically, and Mario said, "If we were in Italy and I ordered linguini with pesto sauce, you might do the same. I'm open to new culinary experiences."

"Biscuits and gravy is poor people's food," Hank said.

"So is Polenta and Cappelini Pomodoro, but you'd still like it. Poor people have the best recipes," Mario said.

"It was a poor Frenchman who came up with Boulibasse. All the fucking fish and shellfish he had in the kitchen."

Everyone laughed and sipped their coffee.

The waitress brought breakfast, and Mario Maretti spoke again, "What is it that you require, Mr. Fitzpatrick?"

"I want to build three hotel-casinos, one in Reno, one in Vegas and one in Tahoe. I need six million in cash, and I need protection from other, shall we say, competitors that may try to muscle in. I may also need political protection, not just in Nevada, but nationally," Fitzpatrick said.

"You're asking a lot," Mario said.

"I'll deliver a lot," Fitzpatrick replied. "Think of how you could clean up money in casinos. Prostitution is legal in Nevada. Not in Reno or Vegas, but in rural counties. The whole state is rural except for Reno or Vegas. Reno is in Washoe County where it's not allowed.

It's allowed in Storey County. I could walk to Storey County. You know what that means for conventions? Happy businessmen. But I want to go further. I want to have a coffee shop for families and truckers, a nice steak house for people to come to. I want to offer entertainment."

"What is my end, assuming we make a deal?" Mario asked.

"Twenty-five percent. The first year, your end should be six point eight million dollars. Then it would go up."

Mario looked at his father. Tony spoke, "What if I asked for fifty percent?"

"I'd say thanks, but no thanks," Fitzpatrick replied.

"What if I said you could name the next appointee to the Nevada Gaming Commission?"

Fitzpatrick shifted in his chair. "Hypothetically speaking, I'd be willing to give thirty percent of all three hotels."

"Would you argue thirty-five?"

"Not if I was assured of the gaming commission's appointee."

"So we receive thirty-five percent in exchange for finance and political protection, that's what you're saying?"

"If you consider six million and a guaranteed gaming commission appointee just financial and political protection, salud, Don Maretti," Fitzpatrick said, raising his coffee cup.

Tony looked at Red.

"I'd say the Steelworkers Union will invest," Red replied. "I want seven and a half percent interest in all three hotels and the right to organize the construction workers that are building them. Hank, do you think Tom will accept seven and a half percent for the Longshoreman's Union investment?"

"He might. He just might," Hank replied. "Plus the Maretti's thirty-five, that equals fifty percent."

"No go," Fitzpatrick said. "Thirty-five for the

Maretti family and seven each for the Steelworkers and Longshoreman's Unions. That equals forty-nine percent. That leaves me fifty-one percent and gives me control. If I wanted to be under somebody's thumb, I never would have quit working for Lansky. I have to have the final say on casino operations. That's a deal breaker."

The waitress brought more coffee. "Could I have some extra gravy?" Mario asked.

Hank laughed. "I'll make a hillbilly out of you yet," he said.

"I felt like a hillbilly when I was ordering that. But just for a minute," Mario retorted.

Hank stuck his tongue out and Mario gave him the "finger." Everyone laughed.

Eddie Coyle spoke up. "Mario and Tony have assured me that they'll take care of me out of their end. But I have some questions."

"And you would be?" Fitzpatrick asked.

"Eddie Coyle."

"Eddie 'The Animal' Coyle?" Fitzpatrick asked.

"The very same," Eddie replied. "You seem a little young to be one of my fans."

Fitzpatrick leaned over the table and shook Eddie's hand. "I've been a boxing fan all my life. I was sixteen when you destroyed the light-heavyweight champ, and when you got robbed on the Landon fight. Saved by the bell? Shit!" Fitzpatrick said. "I wish you'd have got a shot at Johnson."

"People say I couldn't have beat Johnson," Eddie said.

"People are full of shit. People said Dempsey couldn't take Willard. He destroyed him. People said Sugar Ray Robinson was unbeatable, yet LaMotta beat him twice. People said there was no way Graziano could take Tony Steele. They were wrong every time. What can I do for you, Mr. Coyle?"

"I can bring fighters like Rocky Graziano, Jake LaMotta, Carmen Basilio, and Sugar Ray Robinson to fight in Reno, Tahoe or Vegas. That will draw some highrollers.

I need assurances that these highrollers and the boxer's entourages will be treated with respect. By respect, I mean a suite in the big hotel, not a tiny room in the motor lodge. You treat these guys right, and they'll come and gamble even when a fight isn't in town."

Fitzpatrick spoke. "I can't guarantee everyone a suite. The regular rooms in the hotel-casino will be nicer than most people's apartments. The big players get a suite.

The medium ones get a regular room. The wanna-be's and moochbags stay in the motor lodge. That's the best I can do," Fitzpatrick finished.

"If I call you and say, 'This guy's not a moochbag, he deserves the red carpet,' you'll take my word for it?" Eddie asked.

"I will," Fitzpatrick replied.

Jimmy Solano was pissed. Sprawled on the couch of his lavish mansion outside L.A., he was as jealously drunk as any ordinary husband. His three younger children were with their grandmother. God only knew where his oldest son was, who was wilder than Jimmy at that age. It was four in the morning and he poured glass after glass of Jack Daniels and spun fantasies of murdering his trampy wife when she came home...if she came home.

At forty-two, even though she'd had four kids, Maria Pistone-Solano still looked like a movie star. Her raven hair had very little gray in it and went almost to her waist. She had green eyes and exquisite olive skin and her breasts were as firm as a twenty-year-olds'. And her ass, God, her ass was what sent most men over the edge. A friend of Jimmy's had said many years ago even before they were married, "Jimmy, you found the Holy Grail. A white girl with a nigger ass. Never let that go." Throughout their marriage, Maria had cheated on him impudently, but always played dutiful wife for her father. Now that her father was gone, she didn't even try to be discrete.

He heard her key in the lock. He kept drinking until she came into the room.

"Where in the fuck were you?" he snarled.

"Out getting laid," she said flippantly.

She had misjudged his level of drunkenness. He sprang from the couch, leaping over the coffee table and grabbed her by the throat. He looked into those green eyes and was helpless again.

But she made the mistake of smiling at him and taunting him. "What are you gonna do, Jimmy?" she asked.

He punched her in the stomach as hard as he could.

She fell down and he fell on top of her. He smelled her perfume as she gasped for breath. He punched her on the arms and on the thigh muscles of her awesome legs. He beat her as he'd beaten punks in the station house when he was a cop. A painful punishment would leave no lasting evidence of loosened teeth or a broken nose. But he wasn't hitting her hard enough. He couldn't. Her beauty was a natural shield.

She laughed at him. "You can't beat up a girl, and you can't screw. Come on, fuck me. You know you want to. Fuck me, Jimmy," she said tauntingly. "Two pumps and a squirt won't take that long," she sneered.

Jimmy punched her in the face. Really punched her. She spit out some blood and shook her head, and looked at him a little glassy-eyed. "When did your testicles drop?" she said.

Jimmy hit her in the face again. She didn't go out, and with a superhuman effort, spat in his face. He hit her a third time, but she was ready for it.

Glassy-eyed and slurring her words, she spat at him again. "You hit like a bitch, Jimmy. I swear I'll...."

Jimmy cut her off. "You'll what? Your father's dead. I'm head of the family. I own half the cops in this town. You're gonna learn tonight, you fuckin' bitch, who is really in charge."

She spit in his face again and he punched her again. She passed out.

Jimmy got up and went and poured another drink. *Bitch.* She was always holding over him how she'd got him out of jail and how she'd have her father kill him if he got out of line. *Well, her father is dead. Thank God.*

Twenty years of crawling was bottled up inside him, and he was letting it all out tonight. He hated the god damned Marettis, and he hated the Mafia's code of operation.

He remembered trying to fix the fight between Cash Williams and Johnny Walker. Walker had a glass jaw and only had a 25-0 record because of the tomato cans and fixes that had been put in front of him. Williams was a legitimate contender, undefeated in 28 fights with 19 knockouts, 12 in the first three rounds, plus Williams was owned by Eddie Coyle. Coyle was a big player in boxing on the West Coast and had never fixed a fight himself, or so his reputation said. Coyle told him to fuck off when Jimmy approached him with the deal. Jimmy used his father-in-law's name to get a meeting with Tony Maretti.

Maretti said he'd talk to Doc. "I won't even ask Eddie, because I already know the answer," Tony had said. "But if the price is right we may be able to negotiate with Doc. Doc's like a good-looking forty-five-year-old whore who can pass for thirty. Bitter and mean as a snake, but if you ask nicely enough and offer enough money, you get what you want."

Jimmy made bets and had backers make bets, totaling hundreds of thousands of dollars on Walker. The fight was a disaster.

Doc had told Cash, "It just ain't your night, son."

However, although told to take it easy, Cash didn't totally lay down. He followed Doc's instructions. He tried to make it look real, but Walker had a glass jaw and a glass head. A couple of jabs, a couple of belts to the head, and Walker was ready to fall down. Cash didn't know what to do. He knew the fix was in, so he knew not to win. He stopped punching. Walker came on, hitting Cash with everything but the kitchen sink, but Walker was a light puncher too. His fearsome record was arranged. Cash lay on the ropes with his arms at his sides and let Walker hit him unopposed. Finally the referee stopped the fight with Cash still on his feet and the crowd booing.

The boxing commission held both fighters' purses and investigated. Doc got a doctor to say that Cash got hit in the neck, which paralyzed his arms momentarily, which was why he didn't fight back. The fight was declared a no-contest. In a no-contest, all bets were off, except for a ten percent processing fee. No one really lost anything except for Jimmy, whose reputation was soiled almost beyond repair. He couldn't even fix a lousy non-title fight properly. He demanded his father-in-law take action and that backfired too. Joseph Pistone demanded reimbursement for the losses from the Maretti family.

He was refused.

Tony had said, "You asked me to fix the fight. I arranged with the fighter's manager for your guy to win, and for it to look legit. I didn't know the guy had so much glass in his jaw that he could be a chandelier. The next time you want to fix a fight, the winner has to be tough enough to take a few, to at least make it look real. You lost nothing on a no-contest but respect for your dumb-ass son-in-law. Be smart and leave it at that."

Joseph Pistone backed down. At the time it was good business sense. A full-scale war over a botched fixed fight was insane. Jimmy, however, never heard the end of it from his wife, how he'd embarrassed her father and the family. She taunted him constantly about what could have been.

"I could have married into the Marettis," she'd say. "We'd run the whole West Coast, maybe the country right now if I hadn't married you. Mario Maretti was hot for me."

"Mario was hot for anything in a dress and heels when he was young," Jimmy said. "But as much as I don't like him, he's a businessman. No skirt could influence him now. He'd be plotting how to take out your father and still keep the mother of his children, if any were his." She bristled at the barb. "You'd be worse off if you'd married into the Marettis," Jimmy said.

"I couldn't be worse off," she sneered.

But her lust for power kept her with Jimmy. She knew she couldn't run things on her own. Finally, after all these years, Jimmy decided he was very tired of her.

She was exciting in the beginning, and under the right circumstances, still was. But she was too high-maintenance and bitchy. He had a British sports car that he loved to drive when it ran, but it was so temperamental that he rarely drove it. Like the car, she was just too much hassle. He had come to a monumental decision.

He wasn't taking any more shit from her. The only reason he didn't kill her was because she was the mother of his children, and that was a minimal defense. If she tried to go to the cops, he'd have her killed.

He came to another decision. He was going to finish the Maretti family at all cost. No more Mr. Nice Guy, as the joke went. Jimmy was ready to do whatever was necessary to claim his place as King of California, and later, the whole West Coast. He felt better than he had since before he went to jail.

Hank Collins stood on the corner near his father's house. It appeared that the Reno meeting went well and that the deal was going to go through. Fitzpatrick made him another offer before he left and he said he'd think seriously about it. He was. The only real friend he had in the city was Rabbit, everyone else was just acquaintances. If he wanted to visit his family, it was only a four or five hour drive from Reno. The Nevada job intrigued him, and he'd finally be away from the big city. Nevada had a lot of open country like Missouri, although Missouri was green and Nevada was mostly desert and mountains.

It was Friday night and near dusk. Hank had come over to take his Mom and Dad and little brothers out to dinner. Jack had gone to the 4:30 show at the Roxy and had not come home yet. Hank stood by his car and waited for his little brother. He was starting to get a little pissed that the kid was late, especially after the talk they'd had a few weeks before.

Someone plowed into Hank and almost knocked him over. It was Jack.

"What's your hurry, little brother?" Hank asked.

"A man is chasing me," Jack said breathlessly.

"What man?" Hank asked warily.

"A big guy with a scar on his left cheek. He followed me from the theater."

Hank pulled his gun and held it discreetly at his side, which did not go unnoticed by Jack, but he didn't say anything. A scar-faced wiseguy in his thirties came around the corner. Hank stuck his gun in the guy's face.

"Hello, asshole," Hank said casually.

The guy started to reach inside his jacket, but Hank grabbed him by it and pulled him closer, while putting the barrel of his gun on the guy's forehead. "Blink your eyes, motherfucker, and you die in the dark," Hank sneered.

"Jack, go in the house, and tell Mom and Dad I had to do some business, and that I'll be back in twenty minutes."

"Hank...," the kid started.

Hank yelled at him. "Just do it! Now! No questions. Period!"

The kid ran toward the house. Hank forced the scar-faced man into the alley. He took his gun away and threw

it on the roof of the building they were standing by.

"You might as well kill me, 'cause if you don't, I'm gonna fuckin' kill you," the guy sneered.

Hank hit him in the jaw with the butt of his gun and kneed him in the balls. The guy fell down. Hank kicked him in the ribs as hard as he could several times. The guy tried to get up, getting into push-up position and Hank stomped on his right elbow, breaking his arm with a sickening crack. Hank leaned down and punched him in the face a few times until his face was a bloody mess. The guy was incoherent and glassy-eyed by now. Hank grabbed his hair, shook his head and slapped his face.

"Don't you pass out on me yet." When the guy's eyes cleared, Hank rammed the barrel of his gun through the guy's teeth and took the safety off. Through his pain, the guy still got animated.

Hank spoke, "After your little bullshit threat, I was gonna blow your brains out. But I decided I'd rather send a message to your boss.

"You come near my family again and I'll kill you, your girlfriend, your mother, your dog, your mailman, your second-grade teacher, and anyone who ever knew you. I'll kill your boss, his wife, his children, his grandmother, his maid, his fucking barber if I have to. I've killed more men in ten minutes than all you wiseguys have in your whole life. My family gets bothered again and everyone dies. Regardless of what the Marettis do. The Marettis cannot call me off no matter what. No god damned guinea can negotiate peace when my family's been fucked with. I always planned on goin' out in a blaze of glory. I been livin' on borrowed time for six years anyway. You tell Solano that," Hank said, gambling on who was behind it and knowing he was right from the guy's expression. "You fuckin' understand me?"

"I umerstam," the guy muttered around the barrel of Hank's gun, which was still in his mouth.

Hank punched him in the face one last time, holstered his gun and walked to the phone booth on the corner. He called Mario Maretti and told him what happened. He then took his family out to dinner. Neither he nor Jack mentioned the scar-faced man.

Hank was waiting to get his hair cut at the barbershop on 29th and Church Street. It was about three o'clock in the afternoon. He put down the two-month old magazine that he been reading and looked out the window. He saw a tall man in a long coat wearing a fedora hat standing in the schoolyard of the Catholic school across the street. Even though he had his back to Hank, the guy looked oddly familiar. He shouldn't be in a schoolyard.

Hank got up and walked across the street. As he did, the bell rang and a bunch of kids came charging out of classrooms. The man in the long coat grabbed a little blonde girl by the arm and started dragging her out of the schoolyard. He walked with a limp. She started biting him, kicking and screaming all the way. Hank confronted the man at the gate to the schoolyard. It was the scar-faced man he'd beaten half to death.

"I thought I warned you about this," Hank said, coldly.

"You said not to fuck with your family. Surely you're not related to her. I have help. You think you can take the four of us?" Scarface said smugly, pointing at a car parked at the curb that had its engine running and three other guys in it.

Hank punched him in the stomach and pulled his gun and pointed it at the driver of the car's head. The guy gunned the car and sped off. Hank pivoted and Scarface was again looking down the barrel of Hank's Browning.

A nun came over. "Problem, gentlemen?" she asked, recoiling when she saw Hank's gun.

Hank flashed his union ID quickly. "No problem, Sister," he said. "I'm a police officer. This man is a known child molester. He's under arrest."

"Katy, come with me," the nun said sternly.

"Sorry, Sister. I need to get a statement from Katy," Hank said, sounding very official. "I'd be obliged if you could call her parents and have them come down to the school though."

"I'd like to see those credentials again," the nun said.

"Call Captain Conway at the department and ask him about Detective Collins," Hank said.

"You know Tom?" Katy asked.

The nun looked at the little girl and back at Hank. "Sister, please, call her parents and Captain Conway. I've got it under control."

The nun went back into the school.

Scarface took off on a dead run, half-hopping because of his injured ankle. Hank thought about shooting him, but decided he didn't want to kill someone in front of a bunch of children and nuns.

"You know Tom?" Katy asked again.

"Yes, I do. He's a good cop," Hank said. "How do you know him?" he asked.

"He's my daddy's best friend."

"You're Red's kid?" Hank said, incredulously, while putting it together in his mind.

"You know my dad?"

"I do. He's a good man. I'll wait with you, Katy, until your parents get here," Hank said.

An ice cream truck came jingling down the street.

"Shit," Katy said.

Hank had to laugh. "What are you shitting about?" he said.

"I don't have any money on me and I want a Cho-Cho," she said.

"What's a Cho-Cho?"

"An ice cream with lots of chocolate in it."

"I'll buy you an ice cream, Katy," Hank said and flagged down the truck.

He bought a Cho-Cho and a strawberry freeze. Katy was a little hesitant when Hank tried to hand it to her. He admired her street smarts. "You saw me buy it. I'm not gonna hurt you. I'm just gonna sit here and eat ice cream with you until your mom and dad show up."

Katy figured since he knew her dad and Tom Conway, and had saved her from the scary guy, he was on the level. She took the ice cream and sat down next to him.

An Olds Rocket 88 came screaming up to the curb and Red Sullivan got out. He walked over toward the school and saw Hank with Katy.

"What the hell's going on?" Red asked.

"I'm eating ice cream with Officer Collins," Katy said.

"Officer Collins?" Red said quizzically, looking at Hank with an "all right, you better explain" look on his face.

"I need to talk to your dad for a minute, Katy.

You wait right there," Hank said.

Red nodded at Katy and followed Hank a few feet away where Katy couldn't hear their conversation.

"Some fuck was trying to drag her out of the schoolyard," Hank said. "The same guy was bothering my little brother last week. I warned him. Apparently he didn't listen. I'd be glad to take care of this for you," Hank said.

"Thank you. I know you would," Red said, "but my people will handle it. Katy, let's go," Red yelled. "Thank you again."

"No sweat," Hank said.

Emissaries were sent from L.A. to San Francisco to negotiate peace. Solano wanted a meeting with Mario and his father, and Red Sullivan and Tom Franklin. The rumor was the deal was so good for everyone that they couldn't refuse. Mario kept putting them off on one pretext or another. He was executing his plan to perfection. He knew the Pistone-Maranello alliance that was run by Jimmy Solano thought the Maretti family was weak and on the ropes. His brother's death had been a disaster. Tony, Jr. was a man to be feared, not to be taken lightly. His passing had forced Tony, Sr. to enter the fray once again and deprived Mario of a couple of years of valuable tutelage under his father and his brother. Also although Tony, Sr. was admired for sticking to his deal as the "money man," the fact that he had not avenged Tony Jr.'s murder had lost the family a great deal of respect. Even Mario's own people were worried. He scheduled a meeting with Rocco Lampone and Sonny Lauria.

They were annoyed with him because he had stopped recruiting for the North Beach Enclave, and had not reconstructed the Tony, Jr. regime. The Maretti family now had only two fighting divisions, with fewer personnel than before.

Mario began by telling them a little about his trip to Reno and the family's plans.

"I want you to go along with me for six more months without question. At that time, I will turn everything in the Bay Area over to you guys and you can form your own families. It goes without saying that we'd maintain our friendship. I won't insult you and your loyalty to my father by thinking otherwise for one second. But I must ask you to have faith. Things are being negotiated now that will solve all our problems, even the ones you think that are unsolvable."

"Godfather...," Rocco said.

Tony cut him off. "I'm retired. Mario is in charge of all family business. Either you're with him or against him. Make your choice now."

The chilly tone made Rocco shudder. He'd heard it many times before. He knew he did not want to be on the wrong side of whatever was going down.

"I'm sorry, Mario, old habits die hard. Of course,

I'm with you," Rocco said.

Sonny nodded in agreement.

After Rocco and Sonny left, Mario talked with his father.

"Pop, I want you to know what I'm doing is not purely out of vengeance for my brother. It's the right thing to do. Rocco and Sonny are right about Solano. The commission in News York isn't going to help, and he's not going to stop until we stop him."

"You've prepared for everything?" Tony asked.

"You have no part. I would refuse to let you veto it. If you tried that, I would go ahead anyway. You're not responsible."

Tony sighed. "That's why I retired. I haven't got the stomach for it any more. I guess I always knew you would be my true successor, not Tony, Jr., may he rest in peace. I want to stay retired as champion. Unlike Louis and other great fighters, I don't want to hang around for one fight too long. That's it then, I am officially out of it. Even old friends like Don Genoa or Red or Tom Conway will now deal with you. I'll tell them politely if you want me to."

"Thanks, Pop, if it comes to that I may ask you to say something," Mario said. "But it may not. I said I can handle it. I'll handle it."

"I know," Tony replied, appearing more melancholy than usual. He patted Mario on the shoulder and went and poured a drink.

Mario Maretti had taken precautions against every eventuality. His planning was faultless, his security impeccable. He was hoping to use the full six months to prepare, but fate threw a cruel twist against him. It was his father, the great Don of all Dons, who failed him.

Tony was watching the 49er's game against the Detroit Lions at Kezar Stadium when he got chest pains. A peanut vendor called security and they called an ambulance. He was rushed to the hospital.

Tom Conway got a call from the patrolman in his precinct who moonlighted as a security guard at games.

He got to watch the games and he got paid. Conway rushed to the hospital and told his right-hand man, Sergeant Brian Crane, to find Mario and bring him to the hospital under police escort. He even told Crane where Mario's mistress lived. Mario could get as mad as he wanted, but it was serious and needed serious action.

Tony was wheeled into the emergency room, and Tom was told to call the next of kin it was so bad.

Mario Maretti, Rocco Lampone, Sonny Lauria, Tom Conway, Red Sullivan, Tom Franklin, Hank Collins, Blackie Wilson and Rabbit convened for an emergency meeting at the Maretti compound on Nob Hill. The mood was somber, but businesslike, befitting the men in attendance.

Red cut right to the chase. "What are you gonna do, Mario, if your father dies?"

"The same thing I was going to do anyway. Bury the fuckers, only on an accelerated schedule," Mario replied.

"I hoped to have a little more time."

"Have you got all the political connections?" Tom Conway asked.

Mario shook his head regretfully. "Not all," he replied. "I needed about four more months. Dad and I were working on it. But I've got all the judges; we did that first, and some of the more important people in Congress. The big party boys here in California and in New York were no problem, because of our relationship to the Genoas. The Maretti family is a lot stronger than anybody thinks, and that's the way I want it."

"You know how they're gonna come at you?" Hank asked.

"Yes," Mario replied. "Solano figures Dad's a done deal. Even if he doesn't die, he's out of the family business forever. They don't know the planning that Dad and I did, or how wired I really am. In their eyes, if we lose the old man, we lose our political connections and half our strength. They figure I know that. They'll try to arrange a peace meeting where I'll be assassinated. Obviously I won't agree to the meeting. Jimmy Solano has got to shit or get off the pot. Either come after me or back off. I'm betting he'll come after me. He'll figure if he kills me, the rest of you will have to come under his thumb. I won't be going out much for a while. I want Rabbit for my personal bodyguard."

"That'll be expensive," Rabbit said.

"As long as I get what I pay for, I'm happy," Mario said. "Tom, I want my father's room guarded on principle.

If he dies of natural causes, they've lost something in the eyes of the street. This is gonna get ugly, gentlemen. We're gonna get bloody on this one."

"Shit," Hank said.

"Problem?" Mario asked.

"Yeah," Hank said. "I ain't ever gonna sell this ticket. I'm along for the whole ride, no matter what.

I don't like it, but I'm in."

"I appreciate that," Mario replied, ever the politician.

"Don't," Hank said. "Like I told the scar-faced motherfucker that threatened my little brother, 'I don't care what the Marettis do. They can't call me off or tell me what to do.' On the other hand, I want to be on the winning side. I want to come out of this alive and I don't want my family threatened. Anything I do, I do for my family and myself. If it helps you out in the process, fine. I want you to understand that up front."

"Fair enough. I'd rather have a guy like you for us, rather than against us. The best thing to do will be to watch Franklin's back." Mario said, as if Tom wasn't even present. "They'll figure if they kill him, maybe the Longshoreman's Union will roll over to their people.

You be careful too, Red."

"I always am."

"What should I do?" Blackie asked.

"Don't have contact with Red or be in the same place together unless it's absolutely necessary," Rabbit said. Everyone looked at him.

"From a military standpoint, you never put two strong leaders in a position where they can both be killed in one operation. This way, if they get one of you, the other one's still around to lead the troops. They get you both, and it'll fall under their thumb," Rabbit finished.

"Sound thinking. Good point," Red said.

Blackie agreed by nodding his head approvingly.

"It's gonna happen quick," Mario said. "Let's be alert for anything out of the ordinary. We've all worked too hard and long to build businesses to let someone just take them."

"I can give Red and Tom some additional security men,"

Rocco said.

"Not necessary," Red replied.

"You got 'em anyway," Rocco retorted. "The unions are important. If a Don can throw or avert a strike as he needs to, and get loans from the unions and get soldiers legitimate employment, he owns the world. We never owned you guys, but we always did business. Solano knows that even if he kills Mario, you guys won't play ball with him. He can't own construction without the unions, and he can't run contraband through the docks if the longshoremen don't cooperate. He may try to take the unions before taking the boss out."

Red got a call from someone claiming to represent the Teamsters International. They offered him a job as a head of a local in St. Louis, Missouri. The money was off the charts and they said he could write his own ticket, but it was a tough job and they needed a tough man. They'd heard what he'd done in San Francisco and were impressed. They knew he had a family, so they'd supply round-the-clock security for them. Red said he'd think about it.

The promise of security for his family threw up a red flag. *Why would I need that? If I am the new sheriff in town, people might come after me, but they wouldn't know about my family, they couldn't if I had just moved there. Unless somebody already knows.*

His friend Tim Conway's words came back to him.

Tim had told Red thirty years ago before he entered the seminary, before Tom became a cop and before Red had been a real player in the Maretti family.

"Your code of honor and your willingness to fight has earned you respect. But other people know the code and they'll use it against you. You learned to survive in the neighborhood, but the world stretches beyond the neighborhood. Every instinct that we learned in this neighborhood will only get us killed in the long run. Because we think we owe things that we don't owe. And we have this twisted definition of honor. Even though I feel the calling and I'm training to be a priest, if you or my brother said you killed someone, I wouldn't break confession for the law. They could pull my fingernails out and I wouldn't rat out you or Tom. But that doesn't make it right in any sense of the word. But I'd still do it."

Red thought about it...hard. *For argument's sake, let's say the offer was on the level, which I fear it isn't. St.*

Louis isn't a real entity by itself. It has always been basically an outpost of Chicago. If there is a real problem, why hasn't Chicago handled it? And why call me in San Francisco? There has to be hard-asses in Kansas City or New Orleans, or Memphis who could handle it.

Red decided to call in a favor. He called Jimmy Hoffa.

He had to go through a secretary, but once he gave his name, he was put through.

"Hoffa," the commanding voice said.

"I knew that," Red replied.

"Who is this?"

"Red Sullivan."

"What can I do for you, Red?" Jimmy said pleasantly enough.

"Give me some advice."

"I'm always willing to help a fellow union man."

"Can the shit, Hoffa, I'm in trouble and the FBI is not on the line."

There was silence for a moment, then Jimmy said,

"What the hell's goin' on that you need to call me?"

"I've been offered a job with the Teamsters in St. Louis. The offer is too good to believe," Red said. "What do you think about that?"

"I'm only telling you this because you saved me a bunch of grief a few years ago, even though you were kind of arrogant about it. Bottom line, I still owe you a favor. There's a problem in St. Louis, yes, but we're sending a guy up from Boston to handle it. He's a legend. No disrespect, but he doesn't need your help. You go to Missouri and you'll be killed. I think you should stay in San Francisco. Always fight on your own turf if you can. But you never heard it from me," Jimmy replied.

"Heard what?" Red said.

"Good answer. Keep the Irish end up," Jimmy said and hung up.

Red told the guy who'd made the offer that he was happy in San Francisco and that regardless of money, moving across the country would be a lateral move at best. Tom Franklin had gotten a similar offer and refused it.

Jimmy Solano was not pleased with the news. He'd hoped to buy the union bosses and send them to another city, then install his own people. That way he'd already have control in hand when he whacked Mario. He could see Franklin and Sullivan would be a problem.

"If they won't buy off, then let's kill the sons-of-bitches," Jimmy said to his caporegimes.

"That won't be easy," one of his underbosses said.

"If history has taught us anything," Jimmy replied, "it's taught us that you can kill anyone. A dumb-ass confederate sympathizer killed Lincoln. Somebody killed

Legs Diamond. Somebody killed Bugsy Siegel. You can kill anyone if you're determined enough."

Red Sullivan was walking toward the school to pick Katy up. It was such a nice day, he thought maybe they'd walk over to the park after leaving school.

Union business was going smoothly, so he could leave early once in a while to spend time with his daughter.

He saw two guys in suits trying to follow him discretely, but he made them. Their suits looked kind of cheap for wiseguys. He'd seen the Chevrolet sedan parked up the street from his house the past few days as well.

I'm surprised it isn't a Caddy, but maybe they are trying to be nondescript.

It pissed him off. He didn't want to kill someone in front of his daughter and a schoolyard full of children, but if they made a move toward him or Katy, he wasn't going to lose. He decided to confront them before he got to the school.

Red pretended to look intently at something in the toy store window at 29th and Noe. They wanted to act casual, so they had to walk past him. As they did so, Red spun around and slugged the one in front with a picture-perfect right cross, who reeled into his partner and they both fell down. As they jumped up, they were looking down the barrel of Red's .45.

"You assholes want something?" Red asked.

"Put the gun away, pal," the apparent leader said.

"You're not in a position to give orders," Red replied, still pointing his gun at them. "Who are you?" Red asked.

"I'm just gonna reach for my badge," the guy saidand Red nodded. The guy showed his FBI identification.

Red lowered his gun. "What the hell are you doing?" he asked.

"Protecting you," the FBI man said, sheepishly.

Red laughed. "From what?"

"We heard you might be in danger. We know you were told not to take the job in St. Louis."

"You have my phone tapped?" Red growled, bristling.

The guy Red slugged had regained his street swagger.

He spoke indignantly. "Look, hard-ass, we don't have to tell you shit."

Red slugged him in the face again, knocking him down, and pointed his gun at the other Fed again before he could pull his.

"You gonna tell me what's goin' on, or am I gonna keep whippin' up on your friend here?" Red asked.

"We had Hoffa's phone tapped," the second Fed replied. "Why would you call Jimmy for advice?"

"The job was with the Teamsters. He's 'the man' with the Teamsters. If you wanted advice on the Longshoreman's Union's potential business you'd call Tom Franklin, wouldn't you?" Red retorted. "I thought it was a lateral move at best anyway. Jimmy just confirmed my suspicions."

"Which were what?" the FBI man asked.

"That it was a powder keg I didn't want to touch," Red replied.

"What did Hoffa mean by owing you a favor?"

"I advised Jimmy to stay out of a problem here a couple years ago that could have been disastrous for him, both politically and personally. He was returning the favor.

It was professional courtesy."

"What was the problem?" the Fed asked.

"I said it was years ago. None of it matters now, to me or Jimmy. You're barking up the wrong tree," Red said.

"I have nothing further to say. I'm going to pick up my daughter."

"We're still gonna watch you for a few days."

"Fine, but park the car somewhere else. I'm tired of my daughter looking out the window and telling me every time one of you farts or lights a cigarette. If an eight-year-old can make you, do you think real hitters can't?"

"Okay," the Fed replied sheepishly, getting a little red in the face. "We're here to help."

"Thank you," Red replied, holstering his gun and started jogging toward the school as he heard the bell ring.

Red got a call from Tom Conway, who was at the hospital.

"Tony's just been given the last rites. He's not gonna last the night. I thought you'd want to know," Tom said.

"I'll be right there," Red replied.

"You think that's wise?" Tom asked. "Mario will understand if you don't come."

"That is a helluva thing for you to say to me," Red replied, genuinely pissed at his childhood friend. "Are you that much of a god damned politician now? I owe it to Tony to say goodbye to him, whether he's conscious or not. If I thought there was danger and didn't want to come,

I wouldn't worry about disrespecting somebody who was in diapers when I was ruling the neighborhood, and who was in junior high when I blew up one of his father's investments and lived to tell about it."

"I didn't mean it that way," Tom replied.

"Yes, you did," Red said. "You need to retire, Tom. Just staying alive and protecting that god damned badge and the shitty pension you're gonna get has clouded your judgement. You've abandoned everything we learned and did together."

Tom repeated Red's words. "That is a helluva thing for you to say to me."

There was silence for a moment. "Use the ER entrance, the main entrance is closed. You'll have to show ID to see Tony," Tom said.

"Tom, look...," Red started.

Tom cut him off. "I know, man, I know."

"Okay," Red said and they both hung up.

Hank Collins was on his way to the hospital to meet Rabbit. They were going to have dinner at Bruno's, Rabbit's favorite Italian restaurant. Even though he was a hillbilly, Rabbit loved Italian food. Olive oil and spice marinated steaks, salami, prociuitto and cheeses for appetizers, lasagna, cappellini pomodoro and linguini with clam sauce were his favorites.

Rabbit decided that the immediate threat was probably over. Old man Maretti was going to die before Solano could get to him, and then Mario would destroy Solano after the old man's funeral. Rabbit had saved a bunch of money, and he wanted Hank to open a restaurant and bar with him, so they could get out of this shit. He'd been running his uncle's place, so he knew the business. He was pumped.

Red Sullivan walked into the cardiac intensive care unit. He saw a cop, and for some reason the cop drew his attention. Red was lifelong friends with Tom Conway, and partly because of that, and partly because of his stature in the union, Red usually never gave cops a second glance, unless they had their lights on behind him in traffic. Unlike most people who got nervous when they see one, whether they've broken the law or not, Red just passed cops as if he was passing an old lady. They were none of his concern, but this one bothered him. The face didn't go with the uniform. The shoes were too new, the uniform was too pressed, the Sam Browne belt a little too stiff. Plus, the guy was uncomfortable. He was constantly adjusting his flashlight, his gun, his nightstick and his other gear. A rookie who had been on the street a week wouldn't fidget that much.

Red asked at the nurse's station, "Can I see Tony?"

The charge nurse said, "The doctor is in there, and you'll have to wait."

Hank Collins exited the elevator and came over to Red.

"How you doin'?" Hank asked.

"I'm doin'," Red replied.

"Me too," Hank said. "I'm supposed to meet Rabbit here."

Red nodded and then spoke, "I expect he's with Mario and Tony. The nurse said we couldn't go in just yet."

"You want a cup of coffee?" Hank asked. "It may be a while."

"Why not?" Red replied and followed Hank to the elevator, so they could go to the hospital cafeteria.

"This is so fucked up," Hank said.

"Like I don't know," Red replied.

They looked at each other for a moment, and both shrugged and rolled their eyes. There was nothing to say. Stating irrefutable facts or sniping at each other wasn't going to help, so they decided to have coffee together and not talk too much.

They were sipping coffee in silence in the cafeteria when out of the blue, Hank said, "I thought that cop looked out of place."

"Me too," Red replied.

They both looked at each other in horror.

"Oh, shit!" Red said and started toward the elevator. He knew Hank was with him without looking back. "You go left and I'll go right, Red said.

"Okay," Hank said as the elevator door opened.

Rabbit pulled his Lincoln up in front of the hospital from the rear parking lot. He'd always liked Hank's car and at Hank's urging, got rid of his Hudson and bought a new Lincoln himself. He thought about their conversation.

"Shit, Rabbit," Hank had said. "You make tons of money, and you live like a pauper in the back of your uncle's bar, you dress like a waiter, and you drive that piece of shit. You owe it to yourself to live a little."

"I like living at the bar," Rabbit replied. "I can protect my uncle's business, and I don't need much. I dress fine."

"You wear the same suit everyday," Hank replied.

"I do not," Rabbit replied.

He showed Hank his closet. Inside were fourteen black Sears and Roebuck suits, fourteen white shirts and fourteen black ties. Rabbit explained. He always had a week's worth of clean clothes while the others were at the dry cleaners. Regardless of the occasion, one couldn't go wrong with a black suit.

"But I do like your car. I'd get a tan one, with the wood on it though," Rabbit said.

"Trust me, don't get the wood," Hank had said.

So Rabbit bought a tan Lincoln, sans the wood-grain trim. He'd driven Mario to the hospital to see his father. Mario thought it was safer than taking his own Caddy or Rocco's limousine.

Jimmy Solano's best hitters were stationed outside the hospital, as well as their cop-impersonating comrade inside. Julio LaRocca, the one in charge, saw a red flag when Rabbit parked the car.

"Check that cracker," he said to his men.

"What?" his second-in-command asked.

"You don't know a bad-ass cowboy when you see one?" Julio asked. "The car shows he makes real money. The suit is cheap, but most cowboys aren't into clothes. The fact that he's here is a testament to his ability. He may not look it, but I'll bet that motherfucker is so fuckin' cool under fire, when he goes to sleep, sheep count him. Follow him, he'll lead us to pay dirt. But be alert."

"He's only one guy, Julio," the second-in-command said.

"It was only one guy that destroyed the Dallessandro family, or have you forgotten that?" Julio sneered.

His man bristled, but didn't say anything. They followed Rabbit to the elevator and got in at the last possible second. As LaRocca and three of his men got in, Rabbit tried to step out, but the doors closed.

"What's your hurry, pal?" Julio said.

"I left something in the car," Rabbit said casually.

"For a second there, I thought maybe you didn't want our company."

"That could be too," Rabbit said.

He slammed Julio in the Adam's apple with his left elbow. It gave with a hollow-sounding pop, and Julio made a gagging sound as he fell. He convulsed as he choked to death on his own blood and loosed his bowels at the moment of death.

The split-second after he'd hit Julio, he kicked the one beside Julio in the balls so savagely the man was lifted off the floor. The guy vomited and passed out.

The other two charged Rabbit and they crashed against the back wall of the elevator in a struggling clump. One of them tried to get a garrote around his neck, and almost did, but Rabbit's reflexes were so fast he got his left hand up. The other one started punching him in the stomach and the face. Rabbit slammed him in the nose with a palm-heel strike of his free right hand. The guy made a sighing sound and was dead before he hit the floor.

Professional killers use garrotes made of piano wire with diamond bits in them. As they strangle their victims, they also cut their throats as the wire tightens. If the victim manages to get a hand up, they can saw through his fingers and continue their work. It began to happen now. Rabbit slammed his right elbow back into the killer's midsection so hard that he dislocated it. In doing so, he broke three of the man's ribs, which splintered and punctured the man's right lung. He released his grip on the garrote and fell down. Screaming in pain, Rabbit straightened his arm.

The guy he'd kicked in the groin was trying to aim a .45 auto at him. His left hand was still trapped by the garrote around his neck, so ignoring the pain in his right arm, Rabbit drew his Browning and shot the man in the hand. The pistol flew out of his destroyed hand and blood bubbled out like champagne out of a bottle. The guy held his hand into his midsection in an attempt to stop the flow of blood. Rabbit kicked him in the jaw. He fell backward as blood spurted out of his hand.

Rabbit unwound the garrote from his neck and wrapped a handkerchief around his bleeding left hand. The guy he'd slammed in the chest was breathing blood out his mouth and nose, but was trying to aim a .38 revolver at him. Rabbit shot him in the head at point-blank range. The 9mm slug cored his skull and slapped brains against the wall of the elevator.

The wiseguy with the shot-off hand was trying to aim the .45 with his other hand. He got a shot off, hitting Rabbit in the leg, but Rabbit's return shot blew his head off. When the doors opened, with his suit and face covered in blood, Rabbit crawled out over the corpses and tried to stand.

Tom Conway was in plainclothes, but he had his Smith & Wesson Model 27 .357 Magnum revolver with a six-inch barrel on him. It was the most powerful handgun in the world to date. It blew past Old West cartridges like the .44-40 easily, and outperformed the legendary .38-44 cartridge by a mile. Legendary shootist Elmer Keith and some others were hot-loading the .44 Special to ungodly power, but were also blowing up guns and having trouble with accuracy and fierce recoil in trying to develop an ultimate handgun cartridge. The .357 Magnum was dead reliable in the big N-frame, and one didn't have to worry about the gun blowing up or special hand-loaded cartridges being duds. A .357 was a hand-held nuclear bomb. A man could kill a deer with it. A man could shoot clean through a deer with it. Most cops stuck with their .38's and had trouble qualifying every six months with those, but not Tom. He was a big man, 6'4" and 250 pounds, and not very much fat. He shot the hand cannon like it was a .22. In spite of the .357's massive recoil, he qualified expert every year.

The phone rang in Tony Maretti's room. Tony was comatose, near death. Mario answered it.

"I'll be right there," he said.

"You'll be right where?" Tom asked.

"Rocco and Sonny are at the nurses' station. They came to pay their last respects," Mario replied happily.

"Let me go see them," Tom said.

"And insult them?" Mario asked.

"They'll get over it," Tom replied. "Solano might still try a hit, just to prove his point."

"Bullshit," Mario said, and walked toward the nurse station.

Tom followed Mario and instantly knew they were fucked. He'd known Rocco and Sonny for years, and the men waiting were not them. Rocco and Sonny always stood tall and looked one in the eye. The guys were looking down with their hats pulled way down low.

"Mario, look out! Get back!" he yelled.

Mario looked at Tom, and then looked back at the two men standing by the nurses' station. Mario tried to move, but was not fast enough. Textbook killers -- shotgun and a backup. Mario took both barrels in the torso. He flew back and bounced off the wall. Tom dove through the glass partition at the nurses' station, landing on the floor in a shower of glass.

"Get down!" he yelled at the petrified nurse standing there.

He knew his face and arms were bleeding, but he had bigger problems. The backup man came over and tried to fire a Tommy gun. He just opened up on the general area. Tom fired his .357 back and the slugs sparked as they went through the hail of machine gun fire and hit the man squarely in the face. Tom stood and saw the shotgun-wielder stand also. He'd crouched below the desk to avoid the gunfight. The shotgunner reloaded, confident that he had plenty of time. Tom rammed the .357 through the remaining glass window at the nurses' station, put the barrel against the back of the man's head and pulled the trigger. The man's mind came through his mouth.

Tom didn't really want to treat all the nurses, doctors and people visiting family members to the sight of a man puking out his own brains, but he also didn't want a bunch of dead innocent bystanders.

"Police! Get back! Get back!" he yelled.

People retreated into patient rooms. He came out from behind the destroyed nurses' station and walked over and spoke to the uniform standing there. "Call for backup if you haven't already," Tom said, emptying the spent cases of his revolver and starting to reload.

The cop hit Tom in the face with his Billy club. Tom fell because it was unexpected, but he'd been hit with worse. The guy picked up the shotgun as the elevator door opened at the far end of the hall. A bloody man came out and said, "Officer." The cop shot him in the chest with the shotgun.

The cop turned to Tom and pointed the shotgun at his head. At that moment, like the Phoenix rising from the ashes, the man in the elevator stood up and leveled an automatic at the cop's back. Tom could see that it was Rabbit, covered in blood.

"Say goodbye, asshole," the "cop" said to Tom.

"Goodbye, asshole," Tom replied.

Rabbit opened fire. Ten 9mm slugs ripped the phony cop's midsection open and he fell face-down as the slide locked open on Rabbit's pistol. Rabbit staggered out of the elevator. The second elevator opened and Hank Collins and Red Sullivan came charging out, guns drawn. Red ran over to Tom, and Hank went towards Rabbit.

"Go see if Mario's dead," Tom said to Red, pointing to Tony's room.

The uniform screwed me. You never want to kill a friendly ally or a civilian by mistake. Rabbit was going to try to explain the bodies in the elevator to the cop when the cop shot him. He lay on the ground on top of the men he'd killed in the elevator. He was weak and hurting and his hands and feet were cold and going numb.

That was not a real cop. That was an assassin. The job isn't done. I have to finish the job, he thought to himself.

With a superhuman effort, he stood up and willed his tingling finger to squeeze the trigger. The gun was empty and his legs felt like rubber. He fell to his knees. He looked up and saw Sister Gabrielle. She was barefoot and wearing the dead peasant girl's clothes like he remembered. But she wasn't dirty, tired and beat up. She was radiant.

A great light shined behind her. She was standing in front of him. He could only see her feet and ankles.

"I'm sorry for my sins," he said, kissing her feet.

"Mr. Rabbit," she said in a soothing voice and he forced himself to look up at her. She extended her hand. "Your work here is done. Come with me."

He clasped her hand, smiled, relaxed and died.

Red and Mario Maretti walked out of the corridor.

"You wore your vest, smart man," Tom said.

Mario was holding the right side of his face as he unsteadily leaned on Red.

Tom pulled Mario's hand away from his face. "Oh, shit man! This is bad," Tom said.

"Take me home. I have a doctor who'll come to the house," Mario said.

Mario's right eye drooled from the socket, and half of his cheek was missing. "You're gonna need surgery," Tom said.

"I'll get surgery. Get me out of here," Mario growled.

"Take him and Hank out of here," Tom Conway said. "I'll handle this."

"You sure?" Red asked.

"I'm sure. You and Hank and Mario were never here. Gangsters tried to hit reputed mob boss Tony Maretti in his hospital room. A Maretti soldier and an off-duty police officer repelled the attack. The Maretti soldier and the other gangsters, including one impersonating a police officer, were killed. That's my story and I'm stickin' to it," Tom finished. "Go."

Red nodded. He and Tom shook hands, both squeezing hard. Brothers-in-arms, friends to the end. Red helped the unsteady Mario toward the stairs. Hank was on the floor with Rabbit, who was apparently dead. Red stopped to get Hank.

Hank saw Rabbit crawling and saw him kiss the ground, and reach upward before collapsing. He ran to him, but he was gone. Hank howled like a wounded coyote. He couldn't believe Rabbit was gone. He was startled when Red Sullivan slapped him hard enough to make his ears ring.

"Let's go," Red said forcefully.

"I have to take care of him," Hank said

"You can, after the police investigation. Think of your family, Hank. You can't be implicated in a mob war."

Hank thought about his mom and dad and brothers. The trial he'd have to go through would kill his parents.

He helped Mario down the stairs while Red went to get his car. They got into Red's Olds 88 outside a service entrance. Hank laid Mario on the back seat.

"Christ, it hurts," he said.

"Stay down," Hank said. "You're not gonna die."

"I'm too pissed to die," Mario said.

Red casually drove away from the hospital, passing cop cars with their sirens on.

After doctors on the family payroll were summoned to the Maretti compound on Nob Hill, Red drove Hank home.

They didn't dare go near the hospital, where Hank's car was parked.

"He not only saved Mario, he probably saved you and me," Hank said.

Red nodded. "Don't let his sacrifice be in vain. Get out of this shit, Hank," Red said.

"I might. I just might," Hank replied, and got out of the car.

The bodies of Rocco Lampone and Sonny Lauria were found in a car in the hospital parking lot. They'd both been shot in the head.

Tom Conway's story became the official version. Everyone wanted the case closed. Tony Maretti died the following day. With Tom Conway's and a doctor on the payroll's help, Tony was moved to the morgue under a John Doe. Mario wanted the mob and everyone else to think Tony was still alive. He'd give his father a proper burial after he'd handled his unfinished business.

He had three broken ribs from the shotgun blast, although the bulletproof vest had saved his life. Since shotgun shells spread out, part of the shot hit him in the face. The best surgeons in California had worked on him and his head was bandaged like a mummy. He could see out of his left eye and talk through his wired jaw, but it was painful.

He made his plans and gave his orders. He knew his father had done things that he found distasteful to be strong for his family and business, and he had to do the same. He didn't want his boys to go through what he and Tony, Jr. had gone through. He had ordered a terrible baptism of vengeance and he would not back down. He would go to war nationally if he had to. He was going to handle all family business in one swoop.

Jimmy Solano, his wife and children were murdered and their house burned to the ground. At first it was treated as an accident, but the coroner discovered that they were shot before the house was burned. The L.A. papers played it up big.

Solano's consigliere, his wife and children were killed in a similar fashion. Four of the five members of the commission in New York voted to take out the Marettis for the infamnita. Only Don Dino Genoa III voted for Mario. Within days, three of the members of the commission were arrested and indicted for tax fraud, securities fraud, income tax evasion and racketeering. The fourth member was murdered in his house on Long Island.

Two families in New Jersey figured the Genoas were helping the Marettis and made an attempt on Dino Genoa's life. Several key members of their families were arrested by the Justice Department and charged with racketeering and income tax evasion.

A meeting was called in New York, and then changed to San Francisco at the Huntington Hotel. Mario Maretti spoke to delegates of every family in the country and got a standing ovation. He wore dark glasses and a hat to hide his disfigured face, which was still healing from reconstructive surgery.

"How did things ever go so far?" he began. "An underboss got overly ambitious in 1938. And thirteen years later, people are dying and going to jail because of that man's decision. Dante Fresca always wanted to run the organization nationwide, and now he is, from the grave."

There was rumblings and whispers from the crowd.

"He promised the Pistone family things he couldn't deliver. Long after my father retired from the street and became a money manager for the organization, and drove it to profitability, respectable, untouchable by the government profitability, Pistone and his allies still wanted what Dante promised them. After the Dallessandro incident, they still went ahead.

"I want to know why Jimmy Solano, who was an American, who can't be traced to the old country, who wasn't a son, but a son-in-law, who defied the commission and tried to kill my father in a hospital bed after he'd been given the last rites, just to prove he could, is so god damned important to everyone. Several families have lost their fortunes because of Jimmy Solano's unbridled ambition and stupidity. I've been defending my interests without help from the Commission. Now we can reach a peace agreement or everyone's out of business because a dead man had more balls than brains. And there's people besides me that have the information. Killing me will only trigger the demise of the organization as we know it. I'm asking everyone to be reasonable, and let things go on as they were before this unfortunate business."

The proposal's arrogance was not lost on the men at the meeting. Mario sounded chillingly like his father and his proposal was as bold as anything Tony, Sr. had ever come up with. Basically, he was offering to give up nothing if things went on "as they were before this unfortunate incident." The Marettis had power over everyone in the country. Mario drops a name and someone would be out of business.

Don Bassini from New Orleans spoke up. At seventy-eight, he was still hale and hearty, and was still feared nationwide, but was also respected for being a skilled negotiator and a reasonable man.

"With a somewhat heavy heart, I have to take Mario's part," Bassini said. "Sorry, son, 'Don' Maretti will always be your father to me, may he rest in peace. And any respect I show you is for your father. Don't take it personal, I don't trust anyone under fifty."

Laughter pealed about the room.

"In this situation, the Maretti family reminds me of America, and the commission is the UN. The commission washed their hands of the problem. The commission said, 'Fuck you, handle your own problems.' Now the commission says, 'Even though we said, 'Fuck you, handle your own problem,' now we don't like the manner in which you handled it.'

"The commission can't have it both ways. You can't refuse to help with a problem and then gripe about its eventual resolution. I don't approve of his method. On the other hand, where was the commission's outrage when Pistone and Maranello, and later Jimmy Solano, were making move after move to take the Maretti's business, when they continued to be the bankers and hold up their end of the agreement made in 1938? Why can the Pistone family break the rules impudently, and when someone breaks the rules retaliating, it's an outrage?

"I have a guy on my payroll. Was a middleweight contender. Some schmuck slugs him in a bar. He beats the guy half to death. The D.A. and the guy's lawyer try to sue. The judge, who wasn't on the payroll, by the way, says to the guy and his lawyer, 'You started it. You can't take a swing at somebody and then press charges when they kick your ass. Jimmy Solano bought this. The people that tried to avenge Jimmy's ambition earned what they got. What was Mario to do? Hand over his business to Solano because he wanted it? Fall on his sword to avoid offending anyone?

I'd have done the same thing," the old man finished.

Everyone applauded.

"I'm a reasonable man," Mario said, "as my father was. I'm willing to do whatever's necessary to make peace."

Everyone applauded again.

Don Genassi of Kansas City spoke up. "I'm not going to debate what should or shouldn't have happened in street warfare. We all know it's ugly and we all know it's part of business. Murder is the only thing that keeps everyone in line. That's the nature of the beast. Let's be honest, anyone who gets whacked probably had it coming ten times over.

"On the other hand, I think the money management should be split. Divide the country into east and west.

That gives us some détente. A family in the west can't act with impunity, because they'll have to answer to a family in the East that they can't fuck over, or vice-versa. That way, no one person can fuck up the whole country."

Everyone applauded again.

Don Risotti from Philadelphia made another proposal. "Gentlemen, let's not jerk ourselves off, or file motion after motion as if we were lawyers. We all know the Marettis and the Genoas are the most powerful families in the country. The West invests with the Marettis and the East invest with the Genoas. It's simple, and the Marettis and the Genoas aren't going to fight over some hookers in the Bronx or some shylock on the San Francisco pier. The East backs the East, and the West backs the West, and there is the peace. If there is extenuating circumstances, it can go before the commission. In the past, the commission has been made up entirely of delegates from New York families.

The whole country needs representation."

The room applauded again.

An agreement was made. Mario gave up some power, but in reality, not much. The money management would be split. The Marettis would manage the country west of the Mississippi, and the Genoas would manage the east. The Commission would expand from five to eight members, so New York couldn't control by filibuster. Four from the East and four from the West. Mario would be given a seat on the Commission. Any major disputes had to be handled the old Sicilian way, without involving law enforcement agencies or lawyers. It was a good day.

Hank got a call from Rabbit's Uncle Jerry.

"I think you should come over here" was all Jerry said. Jerry had given Hank a job no questions asked when he was right off the bus from Missouri.

"Okay," Hank said and went to the bar.

"I found this in his room yesterday," Jerry said, trying to keep a straight face, but starting to cry. "That poor kid," Jerry said. "My damned brother was a drunk and a no-account and a wife-beater, then he found religion. He focused on 'Spare the rod and spoil the child.' Orris and his sister always had welts on their backsides, and they was sweet kids. When Orris got big enough, he stepped in front of his mother or sister and took on the old man. When he was sixteen he left Mississippi and went to Atlanta and got a job. He worked there for about five years. His sister used to write him all the time. She told him how active she was in the church and that she was in the choir, and that the old man wasn't beating on her since she went to church so much.

"Then she got pregnant at fourteen, and told Orris the preacher was the father. He came home and confronted the preacher. The preacher said his baby sister was a Jezebel and a whore and enticed him. He beat that preacher almost to death. He was supposed to go to prison for twenty years for attempted murder, but the preacher's wife came forward and said she knew he was having relations with teenage girls for years, and they'd left Kansas because of a similar scandal. She said she didn't want a good boy to go to jail for her husband's sins. The judge took pity on him. He had a choice -- go in the Army and learn some discipline or go to jail.

I think you know the rest. Poor kid. Everything he learned, he learned at the toe end of somebody's boot," Jerry finished.

"Not true. He knew I loved him like a brother," Hank replied.

"That he did. That letter says it all, and that's why I called you. I can't talk no more," Jerry said, turning away.

Hank read the letter and cried as he did. He knew Rabbit liked him, but even he was surprised. When someone likes you that much, you have to do the right thing.

The letter read:

"Uncle Jerry -- if you're reading this then I am most likely dead. I always planned on going out in a blaze of glory, and chances are that's happened. I've been living on borrowed time since 1942, so don't be sad. You were always good to me when I was a kid, and I appreciate your giving me a job after the war, and helping out my friend Hank when he came to the city. Tell Hank that he was the best friend I ever had and not to worry about me. I know it'll be a long time before I see him again, but that's okay. I should be out of Purgatory by the time Hank comes to heaven.

When I was wounded in France and thought I was dying,

I doubted my faith. Even though I'd been saved when I was thirteen, I thought I was going to hell for all the men I'd killed. My friend, Sister Gabrielle, told me not to fear death and not to fear hell. She said that God would take pity on me because I was defending the good people of the world from evil people like Adolf Hitler. She said sometimes fire had to be fought with fire, and that although I may have done evil things, perhaps I was the evil that opposed a greater evil so the good and the meek can inherit the earth. Perhaps my talent for warfare was God using me like the Sword of Gideon for his vengeance.

She told me that Catholics believe in Purgatory where people who aren't going directly to heaven, but don't deserve to go to hell do penance until they can be admitted to heaven. Knowing that I'll see Hank and Sister Gabrielle again will get me through whatever I have to endure in Purgatory.

Although it was wartime and we were all stretched to the breaking point, I was never happier than when I was with Hank and Gabrielle. We had devilled ham and told jokes in a beautiful meadow. I thought at the time I don't ever want to leave this meadow. If there's enough of me left to bury, I'd like to be buried in that meadow. I know Hank will take me back there if you ask him.

I've saved $50,000.00, which is in the floor safe under my bed. I want you to send for my sister and her kid, and the three of you open a really nice restaurant and bar. Sincerely, Orris John Simpson."

It took a few telegrams, but Hank was able to locate Marcel Dupré. Dupré stuck to his word of being there if Hank ever needed him. He was still a connected guy and helped Hank make arrangements. Hank took a ship to Paris and then hired a truck to drive him and Rabbit's body to the rural area outside Marseilles.

He couldn't believe how nice the countryside looked. He realized it had been seven years since he'd been here, but if one didn't know it, one would never believe a terrible war was fought here. He thought about his experiences there, and it made him both happy and sad. He couldn't shake the feeling of dread for some reason. He thought about his nun friend. He'd been so focused on just getting there that he'd forgotten to ask Marcel about her. He was anxious to see Sister Gabrielle.

When they parted, he'd said, "I'm never going to see you again, am I?"

"No, but I'll never forget you," was her reply.

He didn't even know what he'd say to her, but he wanted to see her, to hug her, to hold her, and maybe she could help him put Rabbit to rest, both literally and figuratively. Maybe she'd agree to tend his grave, since Hank wouldn't be able to do it.

When they reached the hilltop above the church, Hank started shaking. It was where it all began. He'd forced it out of his mind for all these years, but it came flooding back. The senseless slaughter of women and children, and his and Rabbit's revenge. He recalled at the time that he had been happy to be alive, but saddened over what they'd had to do. A nice country boy who was inducted into the Army and had lived in a nice little world in Lynchburg, Missouri.

Now the man he was viewed it differently. He was happy he and Rabbit had killed every Nazi son-of-a-bitch there.

He recalled the Kraut bastard pointing a Mauser rifle at him while he was furiously trying to reload and saying, "Time

to die, Yankee." He was too stressed to catch it then, but now, seven years later, he raucously enjoyed Rabbit's humor in the situation. As Rabbit's thrown knives pierced their throats and they drowned in their own blood, Rabbit had said, "We're not Yankees, you Nazi bastard," showing the Confederate pride that permeated the South to this day.

He started to laugh.

He was shaking and laughing, and the driver said in

English with a thick French accent, "Are you all right, *monsieur?*"

"No, I am definitely not all right," Hank replied.

"But don't worry about it. Just get me to the church."

He'd agreed to meet Marcel there and take Rabbit's body to the meadow on a horse-drawn wagon with a couple of hired gravediggers.

As they pulled up in front of the church, he saw Marcel Dupré standing there. He was a little heavier and had just a touch of gray in his thick black hair, but otherwise he was just as Hank remembered him. Tall, regal and always in command.

Hank got out of the truck and walked over to him.

"*Monsieur* Collins," Dupré said.

"Mister Dupré," Hank replied.

They shook hands and looked at each other. Dupré pulled him closer and hugged him. Dupré started to cry, and so did Hank. The gravediggers looked away.

"I was honored by your request, but saddened over the circumstances," Dupré said.

"Thank you, Marcel, I knew you'd help," Hank replied. "I halfway expected to see Sister Gabrielle."

"Come with me, my friend," Dupré said. Hank followed him.

Dupré stopped in the small graveyard behind the church. "I'm sorry, my friend," he said.

At first, Hank didn't understand, but then he looked at the grave they were standing in front of. It read: "Gabrielle Marie Cerdan. 1921-1951. Loving daughter and cherished aunt, and devoted servant of the church."

"How?" Hank asked.

"She caught a virus that was going around this winter and then got pneumonia. They were snowed in here for a while, and by the time they got the antibiotics here it was too late."

"When did this happen?" Hank asked.

"Last week," Dupré replied. "Wednesday."

Hank got one of those involuntary full-body shudders. Rabbit had been killed last Wednesday too.

"So sad, two good young people cut down in the prime of life," Dupré said.

"A damn shame. Let's get this over with," Hank said, trying to retain what little composure he had left.

"I have a proposal for you, *Monsieur* Collins. I hope you'll agree."

"I'm all ears," Hank replied.

"Sister Gabrielle's father owns the plot Gabrielle is buried in and the one next to it. I spoke to him about the situation. He said he would be honored to have Mr. Rabbit buried next to his daughter since she spoke so highly of both of you for years after the war. When she was delirious with fever shortly before death, she said, 'I have to go help Hank and Mr. Rabbit.' We said you guys were okay, but she said, 'No, I have to go,' and then she died."

Hank got another full-body shudder. He knelt down and hugged Gabrielle's grave. "Goodbye, Sister. I'll never forget you." Hank stood up. "Let's do it," Hank replied.

Dupré had one of the men start digging and the other start engraving the stone he had waiting. Hank and Dupré shivered a little in the cold spring air, but warmed up with some cognac Dupré had in his car.

Finally it was time. The priest from the church came out to perform the funeral rites in Latin. Hank approved the headstone. It read simply: "Orris John "Rabbit" Simpson. 1919-1951. Winner of the Congressional Medal of Honor.

A hero, a soldier, and most importantly, a friend."

Rabbit was in his military dress uniform. Instead of a Colt .45, the Browning that Dupré had given him that matched Hank's rode in the holster. The Congressional Medal of Honor with its faded red, white, and blue ribbon was around his neck. Hank put two cans of deviled ham on Rabbit's chest.

"Goodbye, brother." Hank said. "Say hello to the sister. And have lunch with her on me."

The casket was closed and lowered into the grave.

Hank hugged Dupré and said, "Thank you."

"You're welcome," Dupré replied.

Hank got back in the truck he'd hired and didn't say a word until he reached Paris. He was going to take Red Sullivan's advice. He was getting out of the shit.

He couldn't continue on in his current condition.

Red came into the kitchen Monday morning. He wished he didn't have to go to work. It was a beautiful spring day. He wanted to tell Katy not to go to school and take the family to the ballgame. It was opening day and the Seals were playing the Dodgers. Ever since he was a kid, he loved opening day. He decided he was going to catch more games this season than he had the last couple years. There'd been so much shit going on that baseball hadn't seemed that important.

Like today. He wasn't playing hooky and going to opening day because there was a beef at the new U.C. Hospital being built on Parnassus Street. The line boss of the steelworkers had called a work stoppage. He said the materials being supplied weren't up to code. The supplier naturally said they were, and the city and the construction company wanted to get the job done under deadline and below cost. Red did too, but not at the expense of public safety. God knows he didn't want the building to fall down next time there was a mild earthquake.

He'd urged both sides to be reasonable. The city and the construction company stonewalled, and the line boss called Blackie, who threatened a citywide walkout. The mayor and the city's finance manager asked Red to help avert a costly strike, and said they would go by his finding, if an independent building inspector from another city agreed with him. He was to meet the mayor, the finance manager, the independent consultant from Seattle, and the boss of the construction company (who had underbid the Maretti-controlled companies outrageously) at the job site to try to settle it without a strike or a court battle.

He glanced at the link sausages on the plate in the middle of the table as he continued tying his tie. He hadn't slept well and didn't feel like eating anything. Ellen was having her usual breakfast of black coffee and a cigarette while she read the obituaries. Red smiled. His father-in-law Eddie called them "The Irish Sport Sheet."

"Am I in there?" Red asked, as he dropped a kiss on baby Richard's head. Richard smiled and graciously offered his father the soggy zwieback cookie he was sucking on.

Red took a bite of the end that wasn't covered in slobber.

Richard giggled happily and Katy groaned, "Daaad! Ewww! Yuck!"

"Don't yell, Katy," Ellen said, and looked at Red. "You said something, but I didn't catch it over the 'ewww yuck.'"

"I asked you if I was in there," Red said pleasantly.

Ellen laughed. "No. Not today," she said jokingly. "Maybe tomorrow."

Katy was playing in a bowl of "Wheaties." Red suspected that she didn't really like them, but just had her mother buy them because they were the "Breakfast of Champions."

She was lifting spoonfuls of milk higher and higher over the bowl and watching it splash back down.

"Katy, stop making a mess and eat," Ellen said.

Katy started to plead her case, but Red gave her a stern look and said, "Just do what your mother says. Do you want me to take Katy to school?"

"Yes," Katy said.

At the same time Ellen said, "No. I'm taking Richard in the buggy and we're walking. I'm meeting my sister at the school and we're walking down Mission to the Majestic. What do you want for dinner?"

"I'll call you later," Red said, kissing Ellen on the cheek. "Behave yourself," he said to Katy, tousling her hair.

"You behave yourself," Katy said, grinning devilishly as Red winked at her and headed for the door.

When Red arrived at the job site he could see a heated argument ongoing between two guys in hardhats and several guys in suits. He recognized Blackie and the mayor. Everyone calmed down when he arrived.

He was introduced to the consultant from Seattle and the owner of the construction company, who was an Armenian and who probably didn't know he'd crossed the Marettis by stealing the job. The guy was smoking a big cigar and was so arrogant that Red wanted to slap him. Mario was being cool after the recent events and taking care of national issues, and was unconcerned about local shit at the moment.

Wait until the next major project is up for bid, you prick, Red thought to himself.

Everyone agreed the only way to resolve things were to go up and look at the situation. The small freight elevator only held a couple of men, so it was agreed that the mayor and the finance manager would go up in the elevator and everyone else would climb.

Red didn't feel like climbing, but he knew he had to do it to keep the respect of the working man. When they reached the sixth floor, he was sweating and a little out of breath. He took his jacket off and loosened his tie.

After twenty minutes of looking at materials and negotiating, it was agreed that the steelworkers were right -- the girders in question were inferior. Apparently the company had reconditioned iron girders from torn-down buildings rather than using all new ones.

The mayor and the finance manager told the consultant that they wanted his opinion in writing. They also told the Armenian to get better materials or lose the contract. His arrogance disappeared and his face became pale. He started to gripe about cost overruns.

The mayor said, "One more word and I'll call the newspapers about this and release why you were able to underbid everyone. You stick to the bid or you'll be out of business."

"Planning on smacking someone?" Blackie asked Red jokingly.

Red had been throwing jabs in the air, because his arm was tingling like he'd slept on it. "No, my arm's a little stiff," Red replied.

"You don't look too good, buddy." Blackie said.

"I don't feel too good. I think I'll take the rest of the day off," Red said.

"Good. I can take it from here," Blackie said. "Why don't you take the elevator down with the mayor?"

"Why don't you kiss my ass?" Red retorted.

"I'm serious."

"So am I."

"I was only trying to help, you look sick," Blackie said.

"I'll take that under advisement, doctor. I'll climb while all the men are watching, thank you."

Blackie shrugged and followed him down.

When Red reached the bottom, he waved to everyone and walked to his car. He was glad he'd left the windows down. He took a handkerchief out of his pocket and wiped his face and neck. He was really short of breath. Suddenly a crushing pain gripped his chest. He grabbed the steering wheel and groaned in agony.

The pain subsided and he decided to drive himself to the hospital. He started the car and put it in gear, when a second, larger thunderbolt hit him in the chest. He crashed into some scrap metal to the right. "Katy" was all he said as he fell over onto the seat.

Blackie ran to the car as it hit the pile of scrap metal. He opened the door and heard Red say, "Katy" as he fell over.

"Katy'll be fine, buddy. Come on, I'll drive you to the doctor." When Red didn't respond or get up, Blackie yelled to the foreman. "Call an ambulance! Now!"

The ambulance arrived in less than ten minutes. The paramedics pulled Red out and put him on a stretcher as they worked on him.

When the one in charge shook his head and put a blanket over Red's body, Blackie started screaming, "No! No!"

He punched the side windows out of Red's car. He was still crying when one of the medics started to bandage his bleeding hands.

Reno, Nevada. December 26, 1961:

Jack Collins felt good. He was blasting up U.S. 40 in his 1959 Pontiac Catalina. He loved that car. He'd bought it brand-new. It was jet-black and had the 425a Trophy engine. Three Rochester two-barrel carburetors sitting atop a 389-cubic inch engine. Since Semon E. "Bunkie" Knudsen took over Pontiac in 1956, they had definitely shed their stuffy image. "Win on Sunday, sell on Monday" was the motto. Smokey Yunick and Fireball Roberts were the scourge of NASCAR in their fire-breathing Pontiacs. It was the same on the street. All the 348-inch Impala or a 352-inch Fairlane was going to see of a 389 Catalina or Bonneville was its taillights. A Trophy-engined Pontiac was a lean, mean machine.

Jack squeezed his girlfriend's hand as they pulled into Reno. She smiled at him and squeezed back. He was happy.

She looked like Marilyn Monroe. But unlike a lot of good looking girls, she wasn't stuck up and full of herself. She was really down to earth. They'd come to Reno the day after Christmas to get married. They went to see his brother Hank.

He pulled into Hank's driveway. He saw a new Lincoln convertible in the driveway parked behind a '57 Fairlane. Hank always liked Lincolns. He parked the Pontiac behind the Lincoln. They walked up to the house together and rang the doorbell.

He could hear Hank yelling behind the door. The door opened and Hank kicked a scruffy-looking dog back into the house while saying, "What can I... oh, shit, it's my baby brother. Come on in," Hank said and stepped back.

Two little girls who were maybe two or three came running in in toy Indian headdresses and began dancing and whooping around Hank's legs. The dog began chasing the kids and barking. In one fluid motion Hank picked up the little girls and pointed them toward the kitchen while giving the dog another boot in the ass.

"Go see your mother," he said to the girls. "Belle!"

Go outside, or go eat the cat or something," he yelled at the dog, which crawled a few feet on its belly and then scampered into the kitchen behind the little girls.

A tall, voluptuous red-haired woman came out of the kitchen, her mouth on automatic. "Honestly, Hank, I don't know why you can't watch these kids for five minutes. And the dog...." She stopped abruptly in mid-sentence when she saw the visitors.

"This is my wife, Mary," Hank said. "Mary, my brother, Jack ,and his lady friend."

"Kate," Jack said. "This is my girlfriend Kate."

"Pleased to meet you, Kate," Hank said, shaking hands.

"What does a nice girl like you want with the likes of my brother?"

"Nobody likes him very much," Jack said before Kate could respond, and everyone laughed.

"You two quit it, right now," Mary said scoldingly to Hank and Jack both. "Pleased to meet you, honey. Sit down, both of you," Mary said.

"What brings you to Reno, little brother?" Hank asked.

"We came up to get married," Jack replied.

"You sure? After visiting here?"

Jack and Kate laughed. Mary said, "Oh, shut up. Congratulations."

"Yeah, congratulations to both of you. When did you
do the deed?" Hank asked.

"We haven't," Jack said. "That's why I came to see you, I need your help."

"What for?" Hank asked.

Kate spoke up. "My mother stole my purse and I don't have any ID."

"Are you eighteen?" Hank asked her.

"Yes."

"Okay," he said casually. "Mary, what judge owes me a favor?"

Mary sighed. "You don't need to call in a favor the day after Christmas. Let's go downtown and you say you're her father. Who's going to argue with you?"

"That's true," Hank replied.

"Do you have a white dress, honey?" Mary asked.

"Yes," Kate replied.

"Good. Let's get you ready."

Kate looked radiant in the dress she'd smuggled out of her house. She was also wearing some of Mary's pearls and a pair of Mary's high heels that matched her dress. Hank had put a suit on, and had deemed Jack's unsuitable for a wedding and demanded Jack wear one of his.

Six feet tall and strappingly handsome, Kate thought he looked like a cross between Elvis Presley and Jerry Lee Lewis. Mary left the girls with the next door neighbor, whose husband was a business crony of Hank's. The Pontiac was out of gas, so they took Hank's Lincoln downtown.

They walked up the steps to the courthouse and Hank stopped everyone.

"What's your father's name, honey?" he asked Kate.

"Martin Sullivan," Kate replied. "But everyone called him 'Red.'"

Hank froze. "You're Red Sullivan's daughter?" he said, incredulous.

"Yes," Kate said, wondering what the fuss was about.

"Is he still alive?" Hank asked.

"No, he'd dead," Kate said flatly. "You know my father?"

"I knew him," Hank said with pride in his voice. "He was one fightin' son-of-a-bitch."

Epilogue

Present Day

Eddie Coyle died of a brain hemorrhage in 1953 at the age of seventy-two.

Mary Nolan-Coyle lived until 1985. She never remarried. She was still hale and hearty at age ninety-one when she died, leaving behind numerous grandchildren and great-grandchildren.

Ellen Coyle Sullivan lived to be eighty-four, passing away in May 2002 after a long illness. She was visited often by her two children, six grandchildren and four great-grandchildren.

Tom Franklin worked with the labor movement for most of the rest of his life. As late as 1954, some people in law enforcement were trying to have him deported and charged as a communist. He successfully fought off the charges. The ILWU opposed the Vietnam War vocally under his leadership, and was one of the few unions to march with Martin Luther King, Jr. in 1963. He was elected to the Port Authority in 1970. He died in a San Francisco nursing home in 1990.

Hank Collins died of cancer in 1980 at the age of fifty-seven. He left behind a wife and two daughters.

Richard Dean Sullivan is a San Francisco police officer with over thirty years of service. He has numerous commendations for valor in the line of duty. He plans to retire this year. He has a wife, three children and one grandchild.

Jack and Kate Collins still live in Reno, Nevada.

Jack is still in the automotive business. They have three children and three grandchildren.

Shane Collins is a writer living in Reno, Nevada. He was a Golden Gloves boxer in the early '80's. The fire at the old "Cliff House" in San Francisco dismayed him because many irreplaceable photo images of his great-grandfather, Eddie "The Animal" Coyle were lost. He has a wife and two children.

Printed in the United States
95377LV00002B/193-219/A